PATERNOSTER THEOLOGICAL MONOGRAPHS

The Church as Moral Community

Christian Life in Karl Barth's Early Theology

Michael D. O'Neil

T0385273

First published 2013 by Paternoster

Paternoster is an imprint of Authentic Media
52 Presley Way, Crownhill, Milton Keynes, Bucks, MK8 0ES

www.authenticmedia.co.uk
Authentic Media is a division of Koorong UK, a company limited by guarantee

09 08 07 06 05 04 03   8 7 6 5 4 3 2 1

British Library Cataloguing in Publication Data
A catalogue record for this book is available from the British Library

ISBN 9781842277829

Typeset by M.D. O'Neil
Printed and bound in Great Britain
for Paternoster

Series Preface

In the West the churches may be declining, but theology—serious, academic (mostly doctoral level) and mainstream orthodox in evaluative commitment—shows no sign of withering on the vine. This series of Paternoster Theological Monographs extends the expertise of the Press especially to first-time authors whose work stands broadly within the parameters created by fidelity to Scripture and has satisfied the critical scrutiny of respected assessors in the academy.

Such theology may come in several distinct intellectual disciplines—historical, dogmatic, pastoral, apologetic, missional, aesthetic and no doubt others also. The series will be particularly hospitable to promising constructive theology within the evangelical frame, for it is of this that the church's need seems to be greatest.

Quality writing will be published across the confessions—Anabaptist, Episcopalian, Reformed, Arminian and Orthodox—across the ages—patristic, medieval, reformation, modern and counter-modern—and across the continents. The aim of the series is theology written in the twofold conviction that the church needs theology and theology needs the church—which in reality means theology done for the glory of God.

Series Editors

Trevor A. Hart, Head of School and Principal of St Mary's College, School of Divinity, University of St Andrews, Scotland, UK

Anthony N.S. Lane, Professor of Historical Theology and Director of Research, London School of Theology, UK

Anthony C. Thiselton, Emeritus Professor of Christian Theology, University of Nottingham; Research Professor in Christian Theology, University College Chester; and, Canon Theologian of Leicester Cathedral and Southwell Minster, UK

Kevin J. Vanhoozer, Research Professor of Systematic Theology, Trinity Evangelical Divinity School, Deerfield, Illinois, USA

For Monica

Contents

Acknowledgements

It is hard to believe that over ten years have elapsed since I first began this project. Having a mid-career opportunity to engage in this research was an enormous blessing, a healing and restorative journey for which I will ever be grateful. Completing such a project is never, of course, a solo endeavour, and I could not have done so without the substantial support and encouragement of a great many people.

First, I want to acknowledge Michael Parsons, formerly of Vose Seminary in Western Australia, and now editor for Paternoster. I first met Mike as my theology lecturer. He later supervised my dissertation for the Master's degree, and was principal supervisor for my doctoral studies from 2002-06. I am indebted to Mike for the contribution he has made to my life by his unflagging belief in me and in his interest in and enthusiasm for this project. His careful reading and gentle direction has vastly improved my work and opened doors of learning for which I am grateful. Similar thanks are also due to Alexander Jensen from Murdoch University in Perth, Western Australia. Alex was my doctoral supervisor from 2006-2008, and has also been constant in his support and encouragement, offering many helpful insights and penetrating questions.

Many other friends have given me tremendous support and cheered me on, especially Nancy Victorin-Vangerud, John Dunnill, Brian Harris, Hadyn Nelson, and many dear friends at Lesmurdie Baptist Church, Riverview Church and Vose Seminary. Scot and Kerry Puzey generously gave me a very comfortable place to work on their property in the final six months of my study which proved enormously helpful in getting some substantial work done. Ben Myers kindly lent me a book that I could not find anywhere else in Australia.

I also owe a special debt to Joseph Mangina, Christophe Chalamet, Chris Mostert and Peter Elliott, each of whom read a draft manuscript of this book and made gave me great feedback. Their insights and challenging questions have undoubtedly improved my work beyond what I could have hoped. Of course, any deficiencies in the work are entirely mine. It is, I have found, a great privilege to have other scholars take one's work seriously, and I have been greatly heartened.

When I began this study Clare, Jason and Aaron—our three children—were still adolescents. In the years that have passed, you have become wonderful adults who are the delight of our lives. And now, through you, we have a larger family! (And may the family grow larger yet!☺) Zac, Anna and Cassie: you have immeasurably enriched our lives with your love, friendship and laughter. Due to my study we did not always have either the time or money to do some of the things we would have loved to have done with you, yet you always expressed amazing support even when laughing at the titles of the books I was reading, and in your own inimitable ways reminding me not to take myself too seriously! Your mother and I are enormously proud of and grateful for each of you.

Finally, Monica, without you I could not have embarked on this project let alone have brought it to completion. Your unwavering love, encouragement and belief have sustained and spurred me. For thirty years we have been 'heirs together of the grace of life' and now in the grace of God a new phase of the journey opens before us and there is no one I would rather walk it with.

Soli Deo gloria

Michael O'Neil
February 2013

INTRODUCTION

To the very day of judgment we shall wait in vain for an Evangelical church which takes itself seriously unless we are prepared to attempt in all modesty to take the risk of being such a Church in our own situation and to the best of our ability....I am firmly convinced that, especially in the broad field of politics, we cannot reach the clarifications which are necessary today, and on which theology might have a word to say, as indeed it ought to have, without first reaching the comprehensive clarifications in and about theology which are our present concern. I believe that it is expected of the Church and its theology...that it should keep precisely to the rhythm of its own relevant concerns.[1]

These words, taken from the preface to the first part-volume of the *Church Dogmatics*, indicate that Karl Barth's motivation for writing the *Church Dogmatics* was driven, at least in part, by a concern for the very existence of the church as *church*. Barth was alarmed by the ready accommodation, indeed the captivity, of modern Protestantism to the political and cultural currents of the day. He was dismayed that so many of its preachers and adherents seemed to discover deep religious significance in their national and ethnic identity, and in their political *Führer*.[2] Already in August 1932, then, Barth was deeply concerned for the fate of the church in Germany. Less than two years later Barth found himself a leader of the fledgling Confessing Church, and had drafted the Theological Declaration of Barmen which included among its theses potent assertions of the utter freedom of the church to live in accordance with

---

[1] Karl Barth, *Church Dogmatics I/1: The Doctrine of the Word of God* (trans. G. W. Bromiley, 2nd ed. Edinburgh: T. & T. Clark, 1975), xv-xvi.

[2] Barth, *Church Dogmatics I/1*, xiv.

its own identity and integrity as it derives from Jesus Christ.[3]

Stanley Hauerwas has rightly observed that Barth thought that he was simply doing what he had to do. He also acknowledges that most theologians in Germany did not think that they had to oppose Hitler or that they had to write the Barmen Declaration. That Barth did both of these things cannot, insists Hauerwas, be incidental to any account of his theology.[4] Hauerwas recognises that Barth's opposition to Hitler was 'of a piece' with his denial of natural theology as well as the discovery of the christological centre in theology.[5] Contra Reinhold Niebuhr, who concluded from Barth's refusal to condemn communism in the 1950s, that his resistance to Nazism was dictated by personal experience of tyranny rather than by the frame or content of his theology,[6] Hauerwas indicates that it was precisely the frame of his theology that led Barth to take his stand in the 1930s.

In reality, Barth had been deeply concerned for the church in Germany for almost twenty years, and his stand with the Confessing Church was the fruit of a theological pilgrimage that had commenced much earlier. In this book I will argue that Karl Barth's early work demonstrates that an underlying concern of his theological activity was ethical—indeed ecclesial—and that he developed his theology with an explicit intention to shape and guide the way in which the church actually lived in the context within which he lived and worked. A careful reading of Barth's works is particularly relevant with regard to this topic, for as Joseph Mangina has noted, Barth has not developed a separate treatment of this topic, but allows it to unfold within the larger fabric of dogmatics. Mangina suggests that the absence of a separate account does not indicate Barth's lack of interest in these themes. Rather, because the practical enactment of the Christian life is *so* important to Barth he does not restrict treatment of it to a single place.[7]

In this book, therefore, I adopt an exegetical reading of Barth's early works that seeks to uncover and present the development, structure, content,

---

[3] For a discussion of the historical background and theological significance of the Barmen Synod and Declaration see Eberhard Busch, *Karl Barth: His Life from Letters and Autobiographical Texts* (trans. J. Bowden; Philadelphia: Fortress, 1976), 216-248; Eberhard Busch, *The Barmen Theses Then and Now* (trans. D. & J. Guder; Grand Rapids: Eerdmans, 2010); Timothy J. Gorringe, *Karl Barth: Against Hegemony* (Oxford: Oxford University Press, 1999), 117-133; Frank Jehle, *Ever Against the Stream: The Politics of Karl Barth, 1906-1968* (trans. R. & M. Burnett; Grand Rapids: Eerdmans, 2002), 46-56; Robin W. Lovin, *Christian Faith and Public Choices: The Social Ethics of Barth, Brunner and Bonhoeffer* (Philadelphia: Fortress, 1984), 101-125.

[4] Stanley Hauerwas, *With the Grain of the Universe: The Church's Witness and Natural Theology* (Grand Rapids: Brazos, 2001), 147.

[5] Hauerwas, *With the Grain*, 170.

[6] Reinhold Niebuhr, *Essays in Applied Christianity* (New York: Meridian, 1959), 184.

[7] Joseph L. Mangina, *Karl Barth on the Christian Life: The Practical Knowledge of God* (New York: Peter Lang, 2001), 4.

parameters, trajectories and logic of his thought in order to then explore this crucial topic. To this end I have intentionally included a great many citations from Barth himself, in order that his distinctive voice is heard as accurately as possible.[8] I also adopt a chronological reading of Barth's work from his initial break with his liberal heritage circa 1915 until the publication of the second edition of his commentary on Romans in 1922. I limit the study to this period for several reasons. First, these years were a time of incredible flux and development in Barth's theology, and a focus on this formative period of his career provides critical insight for understanding Barth's later development as well as formal continuities between his early and mature theology. In fact, although it is evident that his ethical thought developed throughout his career, it will be seen that major trajectories of Barth's development are present in germinal form even at this early stage.

Second, the period has natural boundaries as already noted: his break with liberalism, and his second commentary on Romans. A further boundary also applies: within a week of completing the second edition of his commentary Barth left his pastoral ministry at Safenwil to begin a life-long career as a theological professor in university settings. Thus, these years constitute the work of Barth-the-pastor wrestling with the great themes and implications of the gospel as he seeks faithfully to serve in pastoral ministry in the dark days of World War I and its immediate aftermath. In a very real sense, then, this is *pastoral* theology at its best.

Finally, although many substantial works in several languages have recently explored various aspects of Barth's early thought, much work remains to be done. It is hardly surprising that the bulk of Barth scholarship has devoted the majority of its attention to exposition and analysis of the *Church Dogmatics*. Even amongst those studies which are closely focussed on this period of Barth's career, none are similarly focussed on the particular aspect of his thought being investigated in this book, or follow the specific methodology being adopted here.[9] In this respect, the specific focus and methodology of this

---

[8] Please note that these citations (and those of other scholars and interpreters) are reproduced faithfully unless otherwise noted. Thus, gendered language in a citation may be understood as being original, as may any emphasis given unless accompanied by the note 'emphasis added'.

[9] Perhaps the study with the closest affinity to that undertaken here is David Clough, *Ethics in Crisis: Interpreting Barth's Ethics* (Aldershot: Ashgate, 2005), which presents a significant reading of Barth's ethics in the second edition of his Romans commentary and compares his treatment of particular themes found there with his treatment of the same themes in the *Church Dogmatics*. Clough's main concern, though, is not so much the content of Christian ethics, but Barth's development, and continuities in his ethical thought over the course of his career. Other treatments of Barth's ethics, such as those by Willis, Biggar and Spencer give the bulk of their attention to Barth's mature thought rather than to his early career—see Robert E. Willis, *The Ethics of Karl Barth* (Leiden: Brill, 1971), Nigel Biggar, *The Hastening That Waits: Karl Barth's Ethics*, Revised ed.

work provide a unique contribution to Barth studies.

Materials examined from this period include sermons, lectures, book reviews, personal correspondence and biblical commentaries, with particular care being taken to situate Barth in the historical context within which he was working. This method has the advantage of allowing Barth's development to become evident in this nascent period of his career. The material available for such a study has increased significantly in recent years with the publication of Barth's collected works, including the publication of various lectures and smaller pieces of writing, and importantly, some ten years of preaching manuscripts from the Safenwil years.[10] There is no doubt that close examination of these works will contribute much to our understanding of Barth in this period of his career. However, because an examination of all the available material was not feasible in this project—an examination of the sermons alone would justify several volumes—I have limited the works examined in this book to a selection from the materials offered by Barth himself for publication during this period. My presumption is that they represent that particular body of work which *he* chose to address, and which set forth the central theological positions he wished to communicate, to a broader audience.

When I began working through the various documents deriving from this period, I was unsure whether I would, in fact, find that Barth had a vision of the church as a moral community, of Christian and ecclesial existence, most particularly so when commencing examination of the second commentary on Romans. Thus the work progresses more as a hypothesis being tested than as an argument with a foregone conclusion.

This methodology arises from my persuasion that Barth's theology, if it is to be rightly interpreted, must be read in accordance with the particular, and at times, quite idiosyncratic convictions that he brought to his theological reflection. While it may appear that this assertion is self-evident, the history of Barth studies indicates that, in fact, Barth has often been misinterpreted and misunderstood precisely because of a failure to read him on his own terms. The first chapter attempts to justify this methodology by providing examples of several interpretations of Barth's ethics which fail to convince precisely because of problems arising at this methodological level. The first chapter also provides an orientation to Barth's treatment of ecclesial existence by examining criticisms that have arisen in recent discussions of his ecclesiology.

The second chapter begins by examining the reasons for Barth's break with

---

(Oxford: Clarendon, 1993), and Archibald James Spencer, *Clearing a Space for Human Action: Ethical Ontology in the Theology of Karl Barth* (New York: Peter Lang, 2003).

[10] Since 1971 over 47 volumes of the Collected Edition ('*Gesamtausgabe*') have been published, not including the *Church Dogmatics*, with other volumes still in preparation. For detail about the collection, see http://kbarth.org/collected-edition/ (the Karl Barth International Website).

the liberal theology of his training, as well as a discussion of his relationship with socialism in this period. These two sections of the chapter provide a contextual orientation to Barth's work in this period, while the following sections proceed to detailed examination of two lectures and a review, each developed between late 1915 and early 1917. Each of these works exhibits evidence of Barth's sheer thrill of theological discovery, as well as providing substantial verification of the present argument. In this brief period Barth is laying foundations which will support his work for the entirety of his career.

During this period also, Barth began writing his first commentary on Paul's epistle to the Romans (*Der Römerbrief*) which was published in December 1918, immediately after the end of World War I. It was this work which 'fell like a bomb on the playground of the theologians' bringing the Swiss country parson a degree of notoriety as well as an invitation to serve as professor of a newly funded chair in Reformed Theology at the University of Göttingen.[11] In this commentary Barth's new theology comes to expression for the first time in a full-bodied manner. The third chapter takes up examination of the major themes and contours of this work in order to expose and explore his understanding of the nature and life of the Christian community.

That Barth's theology was in a phase of rapid evolution and development in this period becomes evident in the fourth chapter where a further two articles, two lectures, and a series of sermons, all deriving from 1919-1920 are closely examined. During these years a discernible shift in Barth's thought occurred as a result of his continued theological reflection and interaction with others. The nature of this shift had to do with a change in the model in which he explicated his primary theological concerns rather than a shift in these concerns themselves. Nevertheless, a new and far more sober or even sombre note began to characterise his theology, with important implications for his vision of Christian and ecclesial existence. As was the case with the first edition of his commentary, so now these newer developments came to full-bodied expression in the second—and in some ways, quite remarkably different—edition of his commentary on Romans. Examination of this edition of the commentary is undertaken in the fifth chapter, together with an analysis of another lecture given in 1922, included here because of its chronological and material proximity to Barth's *Romans*.

The conclusion presents the findings of this study, which indicate that Barth's vision of Christian and ecclesial existence revolves around six primary ideas. That is, his ethics are an eschatological ethics of response to divine grace, which are necessarily ecclesial and thus a particular ethics, but which are also normative or universal in nature because they depict and bear witness to

---

[11] So wrote Roman Catholic observer Karl Adam in *Das Hochland*, June 1926, 276-277, cited in Joseph Mangina, *Karl Barth: Theologian of Christian Witness* (Louisville: Westminster John Knox, 2004), 3. Please note that I will generally refer to Barth's first edition of the commentary as *Romans I* and the second edition as *Romans II*.

the true nature of reality and the manner of life which corresponds to the being and activity of God. Further, Barth's ethics are *necessarily* an ecclesial ethics because of the manner in which he grounds Christian activity in the crucial and prevenient activity of the Holy Spirit.

Finally, my aim in beginning this work was to engage with Barth's theology in an attempt to understand him, and to be shaped by his life and thought. I had been introduced to Barth as an undergraduate student and had been gripped and inspired by the power of his theological vision and scholarship. I had done some initial work in Barth's ethics, and in his doctrines of election, scripture and revelation. I was ready for a more substantial engagement. As a pastor and theologian, I wanted to explore the shape and relevance of his ecclesiological vision, and as a teacher, to introduce others to this remarkable life and work. This book is the result of that study. Barth specialists will no doubt be familiar with much that they find here, though I hope the careful exposition of Barth's works will bring fresh insight into his theological development, the particular works examined, his ecclesiological vision, and his ethics.

I hope, too, that pastors and other church leaders might find a source of renewal for their own work and ministry as they join Barth-the-pastor in wrestling with the meaning and implications of the gospel for the life of Christian communities in a world created, loved and redeemed by God through Jesus Christ. Finally, I hope that readers new to Barth will find here an accessible introduction to major themes and aspects of his thought in such a way that they are encouraged to read Barth for themselves. Barth demands much of his readers and repays in kind. My own engagement with his theology has, over the years, proved an enriching, healing journey. My grasp of the gospel has been profoundly deepened, my life as a disciple of Jesus greatly enriched, and my ministry irrevocably changed and challenged. Most significantly, I have come to glimpse more clearly the wonder of the grace of God that shines in the face of Jesus Christ. I could wish nothing less for my readers.

> For we do not proclaim ourselves; we proclaim Jesus Christ as Lord and ourselves as your slaves for Jesus' sake. For it is the God who said, 'Let light shine out of darkness,' who has shone in our hearts to give the light of the knowledge of the glory of God in the face of Jesus Christ. But we have this treasure in clay jars, so that it may be made clear that this extraordinary power belongs to God and does not come from us (2 Corinthians 4:5-7, New Revised Standard Version).

CHAPTER 1

READING BARTH'S ETHICS

Close study of Barth's ethical writings is still in its infancy....[The] conventional treatment of Barth often revolved around an anxiety that the sheer abundance of Barth's depiction of the saving work of God in Christ tends to identify real action with divine action, and leave little room for lengthy exploration of human moral thought and activity....A great deal of work remains to be done. What is required more than anything else is detailed study of Barth's writings which, by close reading, tries to display the structure and logic of his concerns without moving prematurely into making judgments or pressing too early the usefulness (or lack of it) of Barth's work for contemporary moral theology....For Barth, ethical questions are not tacked on to dogmatics as something supplementary, a way of exploring the 'consequences' of doctrinal proposals or demonstrating their 'relevance.' Dogmatics, precisely because its theme is the encounter of God and humanity, is from the beginning moral theology. An inadequate grasp of this point often lies behind much misunderstanding, not only of Barth's ethics but of his dogmatics as a whole.[1]

On Approaching the Study of Barth's Ethics

In the beginning of his excellent treatment of Barth's ethics, Nigel Biggar notes that the English-speaking world has not been generous with the attention it has paid to the ethical thought of Karl Barth, and suggests that the cause of this neglect lies partly in the reputation that Barth acquired during the early period of his thinking, when the stress on divine judgement seemed entirely to devalue human activity and ethical reflection upon it.[2] I will argue to the contrary, that even in this period Barth wrote in order to provide resources for the Christian community for the ordering of their ethical existence. Nevertheless, responsibility for the reputation Barth gained, must at least in part, lie with himself and his strident use of language. For example, in the first edition of *Der Römerbrief* he bluntly asserts, 'from the point of view...we must take in Christ, there is no ethics. There is only the movement of God.'[3] In 1933, in face of the growing threat of National Socialism, Barth insisted that he would 'endeavour

---

[1] John Webster, *Barth's Moral Theology: Human Action in Barth's Thought* (Grand Rapids: Eerdmans, 1998), 1, 8.

[2] Nigel Biggar, *The Hastening That Waits: Karl Barth's Ethics*, Revised ed. (Oxford: Clarendon, 1993), 1.

[3] Karl Barth, *Der Römerbrief (Erste Fassung) 1919* (ed. Herrmann Schmidt; Zürich: Theologischer-Verlag, 1985), 524.

to carry on theology, and only theology, now as previously, and as though nothing had happened'. Indeed, he had 'ample reasons for being content to keep within the limits of [his] vocation as a theological professor,' and when pressed to speak 'to the situation' asked, 'would it not be better if one did *not* speak "to the situation,"' *but*, each one within the limits of his vocation, if he spoke *ad rem*?'[4] Later, as he developed his doctrine of the divine command, Barth could write that, 'Strange as it may seem, [the] general conception of ethics coincides exactly with the conception of sin.'[5] Still later, Barth's polemic is ferocious: 'What the serpent had in mind [in the temptation in the Garden of Eden] is the establishment of ethics!'[6]

Such rhetoric, however, should be understood as hyperbole, particularly in light of the substantial amount of material that Barth has written on ethical method and issues.[7] What is also clear is that Barth's motivation for the monumental *Church Dogmatics* was, at least in part, ethical, and lay in a desire for the renewal and the equipping of the church. At stake is not the correct delineation of particular doctrines, or the freedom of theology to continue on its esoteric way unhindered by the intellectual concerns of modernism or the practical concerns of human existence in the world. At stake, as we saw in the introduction, is the very existence of the church as *church*, that is, its distinctive existence and way of being in the world as witness to the kingdom of God. This motive has not always been noticed, however, and a number of searching criticisms and questions have been raised against Barth's ethics. For this reason I present a brief survey and critique of the kinds of ways in which Barth's ethics in general has been read, after which more extensive consideration will be given to some representative readings of his ecclesial ethics specifically.

Criticisms of Barth's Ethics

Reinhold Niebuhr, who like Barth was a towering figure of twentieth century theology, found Barth's work too transcendental to be ethically relevant. He claimed memorably that Barth's theology was

---

[4] Karl Barth, *Theological Existence Today: A Plea for Theological Freedom* (trans. R. B. Hoyle & C. Heath; London: Hodder & Stoughton, 1933), 9-10.

[5] Karl Barth, *Church Dogmatics II/2: The Doctrine of God* (ed. G. W. Bromiley & T. F. Torrance, trans. G. W. Bromiley; Edinburgh: T. & T. Clark, 1957), 518.

[6] Karl Barth, *Church Dogmatics IV/1: The Doctrine of Reconciliation* (ed. G. W. Bromiley & T. F. Torrance, trans. G. W. Bromiley; Edinburgh: T. & T. Clark, 1956), 448.

[7] Thomas Oden estimates that Barth devotes no less than 2,000 pages of the *Church Dogmatics* specifically to ethical issues, in addition to the many occasional essays which address ethical concerns. He wonders, therefore, 'if those who dismiss Barth's ethical thinking are actually aware of how extensively he has written in the area of ethics'— Thomas C. Oden, *The Promise of Barth: The Ethics of Freedom* (Philadelphia: J. B. Lippincott, 1969), 41-42.

too eschatological and too transcendent…for the 'nicely calculated less and more' which must go into political decisions.…I can only observe that if one reaches a very high altitude, in either an eschatological or a real airplane, all the distinctions which seem momentous on the 'earthly' level are dwarfed into insignificance.[8]

Niebuhr asserted that Barth's emphasis on the divine transcendence convicted humanity not of any particular breaches against human life and community, but more radically of being human and not divine.[9] His ethics were considered isolationist and sectarian, 'designed for the church of the catacombs,'[10] and as such had become 'irrelevant to all Christians in the Western world who believe in accepting common and collective responsibilities without illusion and without despair'.[11]

Niebuhr's primary mode of interaction with Barth was by way of brief *ad-hoc* essays written over three decades. A far more intensive engagement with Barth is found in the extensive and erudite treatment by Robert Willis who asserts that the *Church Dogmatics* can be interpreted 'as one long, sustained *ethical* treatise'.[12] He is particularly concerned, however, that Barth's theological method serves to marginalise, and indeed, vitiate human ethical identity, agency and continuity. Willis worries that the ontological convergence of God and humanity in Christ suggests or even entails an 'absorption' of humanity in that humanity becomes simply an extension of a mode of God's own being.[13] Further, Barth's actualistic construal of the divine command, says Willis, makes it unclear how Christian existence is restrained from collapsing into an unending series of individual responses or 'hearings' of the divine command.[14] Such a conception undercuts the possibility of an ethical *life*, and limits ethics to the realm of worship.[15] Willis asserts that 'as Barth sets things up…it is impossible that man could contribute *anything* to the ethical situation'.[16]

Helmut Thielicke is also scathing in his critique of Barth, concluding that

---

[8] Reinhold Niebuhr, *Essays in Applied Christianity* (New York: Meridian, 1959), 186.

[9] Reinhold Niebuhr, *Moral Man and Immoral Society: A Study in Ethics and Politics* (New York: Charles Scribner's Sons, 1960), 68-69. See also Reinhold Niebuhr, *The Nature and Destiny of Man: A Christian Interpretation Volume 1* (New York: Charles Scribner's Sons, 1941), 220.

[10] Niebuhr, *Essays in Applied Christianity*, 187.

[11] Cited in Robert E. Willis, *The Ethics of Karl Barth* (Leiden: Brill, 1971), 3. For a more recent exposition of Barth's ethics that has certain affinities with Niebuhr's position, see Robin W. Lovin, *Christian Faith and Public Choices: The Social Ethics of Barth, Brunner and Bonhoeffer* (Philadelphia: Fortress, 1984), 11-13, 40-42.

[12] Willis, *The Ethics of Karl Barth*, 4.

[13] Willis, *The Ethics of Karl Barth*, 147, cf. 236-240.

[14] Willis, *The Ethics of Karl Barth*, 201.

[15] Willis, *The Ethics of Karl Barth*, 271.

[16] Willis, *The Ethics of Karl Barth*, 183.

Barth introduces an abstract monism into theology, which generates a philosophical world-view and leads to the elimination of salvation history.[17] Barth's christological construction of the doctrine of election evacuates the incarnation of its character as event, and results in the dissolution of history and of eschatological expectation.[18] In this schema the reality of evil is denied, as is any tension that might characterise the history between God and humanity.[19] Thielicke contends that 'to establish the event of salvation on a primal perfect is thereby to deprive the event of historicity. Nothing remains but a play of waves over a timeless deep. Gone is the tension-packed commerce between God and the world....All that remains is a mere monologue of God with himself.'[20]

Noted American ethicist James Gustafson has questioned the viability of Barth's construal of the divine command, charging that his confidence that a particular divine command can be heard is overly-optimistic.[21] More significantly, Gustafson rejects as unwarranted Barth's refusal to acknowledge the created order as a source of moral norms. He is also critical of the interpersonal language used by Barth to structure the divine-human relation, and further, is unwilling to accept Barth's use of the concept of covenant as the organising principle of his theology.[22] Gustafson claims that these methodological moves by Barth have a certain anthropocentricity since they privilege the human as the centre of value in moral discourse and limit the sources, and thus the material content, of moral norms. Because

> the focus is on God's relation to man, who is then related to nature, and not on the
> ordering of the relationships in nature and man's place in it...our understandings
> of the interdependencies and orderings of the natural world are not legitimate

---

[17] Helmut Thielicke, *Theological Ethics Volume 1: Foundations* (Grand Rapids: Eerdmans, 1966), 100, 107.

[18] Thielicke, *Theological Ethics*, 112, 114.

[19] Thielicke, *Theological Ethics*, 113-114.

[20] Thielicke, *Theological Ethics*, 115.

[21] James M. Gustafson, *Ethics from a Theocentric Perspective Volume Two: Ethics and Theology* (Chicago: University of Chicago, 1984), 33. It is noteworthy that Gustafson's construal of the moral life as a 'process of discernment' bears a noteworthy resemblance to that posited by Barth—see James M. Gustafson, *Ethics from a Theocentric Perspective Volume One: Theology and Ethics* (Chicago: University of Chicago, 1981), 327-338 and Barth's essay entitled 'The Gift of Freedom' in Karl Barth, *The Humanity of God* (trans. J. Weiser & J. N. Thomas; Louisville: John Knox, 1960), 86-88. The difference between them, however, remains significant: in Barth's construal the action rendered by the moral agent is immediate obedience to God. In Gustafson's construal the action rendered is a self-determined good and right, offered to God by the human agent. In this case, Barth's criticism against ethics generally, that it is a human attempt at self-justification, might well apply to Gustafson specifically.

[22] Gustafson, *Ethics from a Theocentric Perspective II*, 29-30.

sources of ethical norms and values. We cannot ground patterns of obligation in those natural interdependencies.[23]

For Gustafson, therefore, Barth's ethics are too narrow in their scope, discounting too large a field of human existence as a source of moral reflection and norms.

Gustafson's position is echoed in the more recent work of William Schweiker who argues that theological ethics ought not to be defined solely by the notion of divine commands.[24] He further argues that Barth's understanding of responsibility (*Verantwortung*) in terms of an obedient answer (*Antwort*) to the command of God, while supported by the call-response structure of the moral life in the message of Jesus, fails at three crucial points.[25] First, it is practically inadequate because it is not sufficiently attentive to, or even aware of, the pluralistic nature of contemporary existence.[26] Next, as a moral theory it is reductionist because other important moral concepts such as virtue, and progress in the moral life, find no place in the call-response schema.[27] Finally, it is too narrow to address the complexity of life in a late-modern technological world.[28]

This brief survey indicates the kinds of criticisms raised against Barth's ethics. They are said to be too transcendental to be of practical use because they vitiate human volition and agency, they undermine any sense of moral deliberation, and provide no sense of continuity and growth for the Christian life. It is also suggested that they are occasionalist, insufficiently attentive to non-biblical sources for ethical reflection, and inappropriately anthropocentric. Finally, it is claimed they are a sectarian ethics, and as such insufficient to provide guidance for the kind of complexities faced by people in the pluralist context of modern life. Were the validity of these criticisms by Niebuhr, Thielicke, Gustafson and Schweiker demonstrated, Barth's ethics would have no future.

The Criticisms Reviewed

Of course, not all analyses of Barth's ethics have had a predominantly negative tone. Thomas Oden, for example, suggests that 'Barth holds special promise for us today precisely at the point at which he is most frequently dismissed, i.e., his ethics, his understanding of the Christian life, Christian

---

[23] Gustafson, *Ethics from a Theocentric Perspective II*, 36.

[24] William Schweiker, *Power, Value and Conviction: Theological Ethics in the Postmodern Age* (Cleveland, Ohio: Pilgrim, 1998), 158.

[25] William Schweiker, *Responsibility and Christian Ethics* (Cambridge: Cambridge University Press, 1995), 43, 98.

[26] Schweiker, *Responsibility and Christian Ethics*, 24.

[27] Schweiker, *Responsibility and Christian Ethics*, 44.

[28] Schweiker, *Responsibility and Christian Ethics*, 45.

freedom and ethical responsibility'.[29] So too New Testament theologian Richard Hays, while continuing to express reservations regarding the effect of Barth's hermeneutic on moral deliberation, nonetheless notes that

> [t]he Barmen Declaration stands as an emblem of the practical consequences of a community formed by a Barthian hermeneutic, witnessing prophetically in the name of Jesus Christ against all earthly pretensions to authority....[I]n a time when the church is enervated by lukewarm indifference and conformity to the surrounding culture, Barth's theology offers it a potent shot of courage.[30]

In recent years a surge of scholarship, much of it characterised by a prominent sense of re-evaluation, has borne a great deal of fruit in Barth studies. Particularly evident in this reappraisal is the conviction that in many cases, previous criticism of Barth has often been predicated on a misreading of his work. Although a full examination of the manner in which the authors cited above have read Barth is impossible here, it will be instructive to note aspects of their method which have skewed their interpretation of Barth, and which have therefore, led to inadequate conclusions regarding his work. In his *ad-hoc* engagement with Barth, for example, Reinhold Niebuhr appears to have read the entirety of Barth's theology and ethics through the single lens of his early eschatology, and thus failed to take note of the substantial developments in Barth's thought from the 1920s to the 1950s.

Similarly, Thielicke's discussion evidences a lack of chronological sensitivity. He argues, for example, that the ultimate basis for Barth's easing of the Lutheran antithesis of law and gospel is to be found in the principle of Christ's pre-existence as developed in his doctrine of election. 'This it is,' says Thielicke, 'that leads in the first place to the setting aside of the Law-Gospel dialectic.'[31] From a strictly historical perspective, Thielicke has misrepresented Barth's development in this instance. Barth's paper 'Gospel and Law' was prepared for an address to be delivered at Barmen in 1935, and was published later the same year. By Barth's own account the crucial stimulus for the christological formulation of his doctrine of election came in June 1936—well after the publication of 'Gospel and Law'.[32] Further, in his address Barth does not ground his doctrine in the eternal pre-existence of Christ, but in the

---

[29] Oden, *The Promise of Barth*, 109.

[30] Richard B. Hays, *The Moral Vision of the New Testament: Community, Cross, New Creation; A Contemporary Introduction to New Testament Ethics* (San Francisco: Harper Collins, 1996), 239, cf. 228-230.

[31] Thielicke, *Theological Ethics*, 110.

[32] Karl Barth, 'Foreword,' in *Predestination and Other Papers* (ed. P. Maury; London: SCM Press, 1960). See also the discussion in Bruce L. McCormack, *Karl Barth's Critically Realistic Dialectical Theology: Its Genesis and Development 1909-1936* (Oxford: Oxford University Press, 1995), 397-399.

historical reality of the incarnation.[33] It is precisely the historicity of the incarnation that leads Barth to posit the eternality of the election of Jesus Christ that there be no change in the divine essence because of the 'becoming' inherent in the incarnation. Barth does not argue from God's eternal being to his activity in time but from time to eternity, from revelation to ontology.[34] The concept of the eternal election of Jesus Christ is not mentioned in the earlier address for the simple reason that Barth is as yet unaware of it. Thielicke's lack of chronological sensitivity has led, therefore, to caricature Barth's position.[35]

The analyses of Barth by Lovin, Willis, Gustafson and Schweiker seem to share a common fault: each of them critique Barth from a presuppositional stance that he does not share.[36] Lovin's concern, for example, arises from his understanding of what ethics is, that is, a discipline of giving rational, public reasons for moral action which establish obligations that apply to persons generally.[37] He argues that Barth's insistence that the divine freedom be preserved serves to undermine the rational basis of ethics, and that consequently, Barth's position is 'impossible for a public ethics'.[38] By viewing ethics itself in terms that Barth categorically rejects, Lovin cannot help but misconstrue the nature of Barth's project.

Willis has a different concern. He seeks to guarantee the significance of human action through the establishment of an independent existence or status for humanity.[39] Yet it is precisely this focus on the independence of humanity

---

[33] Karl Barth, 'Gospel and Law,' in *God, Grace and Gospel* (ed. J. S. McNab; *Scottish Journal of Theology Occasional Papers* (Edinburgh: T. & T. Clark, 1959), 4-8.

[34] Barth, *Church Dogmatics II/2*, 150-152. See also Michael D. O'Neil, 'The Mission of the Spirit in the Election of God' (Unpublished Dissertation for the Master of Theology (Honours), Murdoch University, Western Australia, 2001), 9-10.

[35] A further example of Thielicke's chronological insensitivity is found on pages 106-108 where he cites isolated passages from works in the early 1920s to support his point, with the claim that the essential timelessness of Barth's theology has remained constant throughout the duration of his career. It is noteworthy that his citations, rendered without appropriate comment regarding the context from which they are taken, do not do justice to Barth's intended meaning in the passages.

[36] In what follows I shall provide only a brief indication of the problematic aspect of each theologian's reading of Barth. The purpose of this section is not extensive engagement with each of these theologians but the establishment of a specific methodological point, namely, that correct understanding of Barth's proposals can only be apprehended by a careful, indeed exegetical, reading of his work.

[37] Lovin, *Christian Faith and Public Choices*, 1-7.

[38] Lovin, *Christian Faith and Public Choices*, 42.

[39] Willis, *The Ethics of Karl Barth*, 36, 268, cf. 434. According to Paul Lehmann, 'the problem common to Christian and philosophical ethics and upon which their respective methodologies converge is the problem of the humanity of man....For philosophical ethics, "Man makes ethics"...and this is the secret and guarantee of his humanity. For Christian ethics, "God makes ethics", that is, God initiates and establishes the humanity of man....The difference between Christian and philosophical ethics is unbridgeable

that Barth opposed. Webster insists that one of Barth's primary theological objectives is to resist modern anthropological assumptions that 'being in Christ' is simply one particular form of existence grounded in something more humanly basic, and that human history and activity can be comprehended without direct reference to the history and activity of Jesus Christ.[40]

Also in contrast to Willis, Wolf Krötke shows that in Barth's view, creation itself and humanity as part of the whole exists, not independently of God, but precisely as the sphere called into existence by God as a space for the realisation of the covenant established between God and humanity in the eternal election of Jesus Christ.[41] According to Krötke, objections that Barth's ontology functions to eliminate the human, misunderstand God's election 'as an axiom of God's authoritarian lordship over the human' rather than as an act of grace by which humanity is established as a reality distinct from, and yet in relationship with God.[42] In this ontology humanity retains a form of independence, but it is a relative independence grounded not in the self as an autonomous subject, but in the grace given by God to one who is and always remains a dependent creature.

Krötke argues that Barth's is a practical anthropology which, while certainly applicable to all humanity, must be brought to particular expression 'in the Christian community and in the lives of individual Christians in the midst of society and in opposition to all the inhumanity that reigns there; it must be lived out in active service of a better human righteousness.'[43]

---

because the theological foundation of a Christian ethics is not merely expendable for philosophical ethics but must be denied' (Paul Lehmann, *Ethics in a Christian Context* (London: SCM Press, 1963), 274-276). Willis' attempt to secure an independent anthropology indicates that methodologically he is nearer to a philosophical rather than theological approach to the problem of humanity. This appears to be at the root of his critique of Barth. The same might be said of Niebuhr, Lovin, Gustafson and Schweiker.

[40] John Webster, 'Rescuing the Subject: Barth and Postmodern Anthropology,' in *Karl Barth: A Future for Postmodern Theology?*, (ed. G. Thompson & C. Mostert; Adelaide: Australian Theological Forum, 2000), 61. In his appreciative review of Willis' book, W. A. Whitehouse 'fears' that Willis moves 'off target' at this point: 'Willis is wholly seized of the truth that Barth's shortcomings, if such they be, are linked with his decision to take with thorough seriousness the Christological affirmations made in Col. 1:15-20, and to interpret them with reference to the Son of God in his history, to *Jesus*, in whom there is for all things human a preceding "humanity of God"...Willis suggests (p. 328) that "Barth never quite manages to turn sufficiently from his Christological commitment to undertake a genuine phenomenological analysis." *From* that commitment?'—W. A. Whitehouse, 'Review of *The Ethics of Karl Barth* by R. E. Willis,' *Scottish Journal of Theology* 29, no. 2 (1976): 177-182, (182).

[41] Wolf Krötke, 'The Humanity of the Human Person in Karl Barth's Anthropology,' in *The Cambridge Companion to Karl Barth* (ed. J. Webster; Cambridge: Cambridge University Press, 2000), 161, 167.

[42] Krötke, 'The Humanity of the Human Person,' 164.

[43] Krötke, 'The Humanity of the Human Person,' 174.

Krötke's incisive perception is grounded in recognition of the fundamentally relational structure of Barth's anthropology. While Willis provides a thorough overview of Barth's discussion of 'co-humanity' as the basic form of human existence, he fails to appreciate the ethical significance of Barth's formulation at this point, more concerned as he is with the agential structure of the individual subject.[44] Or, to state the matter differently, Willis understands humanity in terms of *esse* whereas for Barth, humanity is understood not in terms of *esse*, but *existere*.[45] In the end, therefore, Willis' interpretation of Barth's overall project is not convincing because he has failed to read Barth according to his own terms, and has therefore skewed interpretation of the manner in which Barth has developed his ethics.

The presuppositions underlying the works of Gustafson and Schweiker are similar, though not identical.[46] Both theologians endeavour to construct a rational and universal ethics in which human experience is accorded epistemological primacy, and in both cases they reject the kind of theological realism adopted by Barth in his understanding of ultimate reality. It is evident

---

[44] Willis, *The Ethics of Karl Barth*, 222-227, 236-240.

[45] For further discussion of these categories, see Daniel J. Price, *Karl Barth's Anthropology in Light of Modern Thought* (Grand Rapids: Eerdmans, 2002), especially pages 134-144. For Barth, to be (*esse*) *is* to exist (*existere*), and to exist is to live, to engage in relations, to act. Like Krötke, Price understands Barth's anthropology in relational terms, and argues that the trinitarian ground for Barth's anthropology creates an immediate ethical obligation. To be is to act, and to act rightly is to act in correspondence with the act of God toward us in the humanity of Jesus (144; cf. 157). Price further acknowledges that this ethic is universal: because Barth is describing the basic form of human nature its implications cannot be limited to the Christian community (154-155). Nonetheless, like Krötke he also acknowledges that the Christian community has a particular responsibility in light of the reality of the true humanity revealed in Jesus: 'the dynamic trinitarian anthropology that Barth develops in his *Dogmatics* should encourage the church to shift its perspectives regarding what it means to be fully human...that there is no authentic humanity apart from fellow humanity—to understand that the basis for Christian community is found right within the very nature of God himself....We are called to become for others what God has become for us: a cleansing, healing, life-giving presence' (307-308). See also Paul T. Nimmo, 'Barth and the Christian as Ethical Agent: An Ontological Study of the Shape of Christian Ethics' in *Commanding Grace: Studies in Karl Barth's Ethics* (ed. Daniel L. Migliore; Grand Rapids: Eerdmans, 2010), 216-238.

[46] Gustafson develops his ontology at length in the first volume of his project. Although the entire volume is significant, see especially Gustafson, *Ethics from a Theocentric Perspective I*, 82-99, 204-251. Schweiker's project is outlined in the two primary works cited above, namely, his *Responsibility and Christian Ethics* and *Power, Value and Conviction*. Differences between the two theologians include Gustafson's reliance on scientific empiricism in addition to human experience as epistemologically primary, and Schweiker's insistence that the ultimate power be construed in terms of personal agency in order to secure the ontic priority of value over power.

that these presuppositions do not only differ from those of Barth, but are, in fact, diametrically opposed to his position, and can finally only be addressed at the level of theological method. According to John Webster,

> [a]ll ethical reflection has implicit or explicit within it an anthropology and an ontology of history—a construal of the moral agent and of the field in which the moral agent acts. What is most striking about Barth's account (as well as what separates it from nearly all contemporary accounts) is its undeflected attention to one set of historical incidents as ontologically, noetically, and morally fundamental.[47]

In theological ethics generally, and Christian ethics particularly, this construal necessarily involves the concept of God and the divine-human relation. Clearly, this is of fundamental significance since one's praxis is decisively shaped by the theological or metaphysical system underpinning it.

Barth's rejection of any form of natural theology is grounded in his conviction that God has revealed himself decisively and definitively in Jesus Christ, and in so doing, has shown that he is *for* humanity. God—the sovereign, living and personal God portrayed in the narratives of Scripture—may be truly known, although, because he remains ineffable, not wholly apprehended. What Barth refers to as revelation, however, Gustafson considers reflection on human experiences in the face of the 'ultimate power and powers'.[48] Both Gustafson and Schweiker find it necessary to reject Barth's theological realism in order to overcome the particularism inherent in the Christian tradition's construal of God, and so secure a universal and normative ethics. The result is a truncated doctrine of God which utilises concepts drawn from biblical and Christian sources but which have been evacuated of their contextual referents.[49]

Gustafson and Schweiker have read Barth from the perspective of their own theological ontology, which in turn, was developed to serve an ethics that is in principle rational and universal. They have criticised and rejected Barth's ethics, therefore, because his ethics function to undermine the essential foundations of their own respective projects. It is evident that their theology functions for the sake of their ethics. I maintain that Barth's theology also functions in service of ethics, with the difference, however, that for Barth dogmatics and ethics cannot be separated, nor can the ordering of the two be

---

[47] John Webster, *Barth's Ethics of Reconciliation* (Cambridge: Cambridge University Press, 1995), 98.

[48] Gustafson, *Ethics from a Theocentric Perspective II*, 28.

[49] Gustafson explicitly states that he appropriates only those aspects of the tradition that he deems 'defensible' (see Gustafson, *Ethics from a Theocentric Perspective I*, 187). See also Paul Griffith's argument that an appeal to universal epistemic principle, when taken to be basic to theology, always results in a destructive, eviscerating and constraining effect on theology—Paul J. Griffiths, 'How Epistemology Matters to Theology,' *Journal of Religion* 79, no. 1 (1999): 7, 15.

reversed, for the ethics derive from and are determined by the theology. The ontology proposed by Barth is grounded, not anthropocentrically as is the case with Gustafson and Schweiker, but in a particular revelation. The ethics deriving from this, therefore, are perhaps better understood as particularist, finding expression amongst those to whom the revelation has been given and received.[50]

Just as my initial survey indicated the kinds of criticisms that have been raised by Niebuhr, Willis, Lovin, Thielicke, Gustafson and Schweiker regarding Barth's ethics, so this brief account of the *manner* in which these critics have read Barth has raised the question of the validity of their criticisms, based as they are on inadequate readings of his work. This suggests not that Barth is invulnerable to criticism, but rather that judgements pronounced on the viability of Barth's ethics are premature if they are not predicated upon readings that seek to interpret him in accordance with his own central concerns. It is my intention to provide a reading of Barth's early works that attends closely, as Webster has suggested, to the structure and logic of Barth's own concerns, in order to provide a more adequate account and critique of his ethics. Webster's call for a more careful reading of Barth's dogmatics raises the possibility that such a reading of Barth's work may overturn judgements of the kind previously surveyed. That this has, in fact, occurred in recent re-evaluations of Barth's work is unsurprising, as we shall observe in the next section.

Recent Re-evaluation of Barth's Ethics

The initial section of this chapter argued for the methodological necessity of a careful, exegetical reading of Barth by indicating the kinds of problems which may arise when this hermeneutical task is not given the attention it deserves. Happily, there has been a significant re-engagement with Barth's literary corpus since the mid-1980s, stimulated in no small part by the publication of his collected works, including a number of previously unpublished materials. This re-engagement has resulted in a new appreciation and deeper understanding of Barth's theology and ethics, and in some cases, a significant reappraisal of previously held convictions regarding his work. This section of the chapter examines the work of Nigel Biggar and John Webster, two scholars

---

[50] It is beyond the scope of this brief overview to engage the complex philosophical issues that impinge on this discussion. For an extended treatment of the epistemological matters and the varieties of critical realism involved, the plausibility of an ontology such as Barth's, and an argument for an ethics that is simultaneously particularist in form while universally normative in nature, see Michael D. O'Neil, 'Ethics and Epistemology: Ecclesial Existence in a Postmodern Era,' *Journal of Religious Ethics* 34, no. 1 (2006): 21-40. This essay includes a detailed examination of Schweiker's proposals.

employed in this re-engagement, particularly in the sphere of Barth's ethics, in order to illustrate how a more adequate reading of Barth not only addresses criticisms of Barth's ethics, but may also bear fruit in terms of my central thesis, namely, that Barth developed his theology with an eye towards shaping the life of the concrete Christian community.

Nigel Biggar

Nigel Biggar has written an account of Barth's ethics that gathers around three foci. First, he is concerned to provide an overview of the structure and development of Barth's ethical thought; second, he examines the sources or authorities which lie beneath Barth's account; and, finally, Biggar responds to specific criticisms that have been raised against Barth's ethics, particularly the accusations that Barth's construal of the divine command is occasionalist and irrational, and that his account of moral agency is reductionist.[51]

Biggar begins by showing that Barth's ethics seek to describe the context in which ethical decisions are taken, rather than attempt to describe the necessary content of those decisions, and that Barth's pre-eminent concern was to ground ethics in dogmatics and by so doing to preclude the possibility of human ethical autonomy.[52] He argues that this approach does not require the forfeit of ethical rationality, but also suggests two corrections or re-interpretations of Barth in the interests of ethical rationality.

First, Biggar argues that a form of limited casuistry be embraced, in which casuistry is viewed as a dialectical process in which rules provide moral guidance in familiar cases while being open to adaptation in the face of unfamiliar ones.[53] He suggests that Barth, in typically Protestant fashion, understood casuistry as the epitome of ethical rationalism. This, suggests Biggar, was a misunderstanding which failed to take account of the dialectical and open nature of traditional casuistry. He argues further that Barth's ethics are themselves systematic, rational, and even casuistic.[54] Nonetheless, Barth's suspicion of casuistry hindered his ability to provide a coherent account of the relationship between systematic moral deliberation and the hearing of the command of God.[55]

Second, Biggar suggests that the divine command be reconceived in terms of personal vocation.[56] Biggar worries that Barth's discussion of the 'exceptional

---

[51] Biggar, *The Hastening that Waits*, passim. See also Nigel Biggar, 'Barth's Trinitarian Ethic, in *The Cambridge Companion to Karl Barth* (ed. J. Webster; Cambridge: Cambridge University Press, 2000), 212-227.

[52] Biggar, *The Hastening that Waits*, 7-8.

[53] Biggar, *The Hastening that Waits*, 41.

[54] Biggar, *The Hastening that Waits*, 31-41.

[55] Biggar, *The Hastening that Waits*, 41.

[56] Biggar, *The Hastening that Waits*, 44.

case' of divine commanding subverts ethical rationality. According to Biggar, the problem is that systematic ethical reflection could be faced with a case that is simply unintelligible, with the result that the process of moral reason is not corrected but suspended.[57] By reconceiving the divine command as vocation Biggar seeks to retain Barth's emphasis on immediate obedience as the character of human ethical activity, but with the additional benefit of not forfeiting ethical rationality. Although particularly useful in cases of irreducible moral dilemma, this description of the divine command also helpfully emphasises the ultimate uniqueness of every moral decision.

Although Biggar's suggestion has merit, it requires a careful qualification, for in places his critique of Barth betrays an abiding rationalism. Biggar is quite forward in his assertion that Barth 'fails' to provide a coherent account of human freedom, and that his notion of human freedom is more apparent than real.[58] He argues further that

> if human reasoning about moral matters is to have any relative validity, God's command *must* be the expression of a divine will that is governed by the divine *Ratio* or Wisdom, and which is therefore intelligible in principle....This concept of God's command still permits it to contradict the moral assumptions and conclusions of human reason, but only in so far as their actual grasp of the divine *Ratio* is mistaken, and not because their attempt to grasp it is futile in principle....A command of God *must* be the expression of a divine will that is constant and therefore in principle intelligible to human moral reason.[59]

It is evident that Biggar still conceives of moral reason as in some sense able to function independently of God, and indeed, to be a higher court of appeal to which the divine command is subject. As we shall see, this position would prove unacceptable to Barth.[60] The required qualification of Biggar's position is to allow the kind of dialectical casuistry he suggests as a means of preparation for hearing the divine command, but with an explicit recognition that God in his sovereign freedom may indeed command that which is inexplicable to

---

[57] Biggar, *The Hastening that Waits*, 33.

[58] Biggar, *The Hastening that Waits*, 5-6.

[59] Biggar, *The Hastening that Waits*, 42, emphasis added.

[60] A more generous interpretation of Biggar is possible if one emphasises the '*but only in so far as their actual grasp of the divine Ratio is mistaken, and not because their attempt to grasp it is futile in principle*' in the above citation. In this case the human moral rationality is no longer independent of God but accepts Barth's theological ontology as the truth of our existence. It is precisely this kind of position taken in Matthew Rose, *Ethics with Barth: God, Metaphysics and Morals* (Barth Studies; Farnham: Ashgate, 2010), who understands Barth 'as endorsing a version of the Augustinian and Thomistic view that right living is in accord with created nature. To be good is to live in the truth about ourselves, to live in conformity with God's intentions for created order' (10). Where Barth is to be distinguished is in his insistence that 'created order' and 'nature' are theologically described and determined.

reason, as the biblical narrative clearly portrays.[61] In a more recent lecture Biggar has clarified his position:

> What I seek to tame is the notion that God's will is entirely unpredictable, that it cannot be articulated in terms of principles or rules, that it cannot be reflected upon and interpreted rationally, and that it expresses itself in such a way that leaves no room for the responsible exercise of creaturely discretion....My quarrel is rather with the notion that we learn what is *right* (as distinct from what is our vocation) by hearing an absolutely definite set of divine orders.[62]

Biggar also responds to concerns that Barth's account of human moral agency is deficient, neither showing how a person's character is formed by Christ, nor specifying that character in detail. He again utilises the concept of vocation to address these concerns, arguing that moral formation occurs as agents engage with the particular moral tasks their vocation presents to them. According to Biggar, present character can never be more than provisional, first, because it is always subject to renewal and development as the command confronts us afresh in every new circumstance, and second, because the full appropriation of our character will occur only eschatologically.[63]

Thus, while Biggar's engagement with Barth is not entirely satisfactory, his reading nevertheless indicates that Barth developed an ethic of Christian life, and he affirms Barth's conviction that the essence of this life consists in responding to the address of a reality beyond ourselves.[64] The value of his contribution lies in his insistence on the validity and primacy of the divine

---

[61] See, for example, Genesis 22:1–2; Numbers 20:8; Mark 6:37; numerous other references could also be supplied. Note, also, the discussion of Biggar's position in Webster, *Barth's Ethics of Reconciliation*, 226-227, and Trevor Hart, *Regarding Karl Barth: Essays Towards a Reading of his Theology* (Carlisle: Paternoster, 1999), 84-88. Hart's evaluation is especially pointed: '(T)he command of God, like revelation in general, is an act of God from first to last....Insofar as Biggar's attempt to rehabilitate the language of system misses or fails to account for this fact, it must be deemed misguided. The words are those of Biggar, but the voice has unmistakeable (and unfortunate) resonances with that of Brunner' (Hart, *Regarding Karl Barth*, 87-88).

[62] Nigel Biggar, 'Karl Barth's Ethics Revisited' in *Commanding Grace: Studies in Karl Barth's Ethics* (ed. Daniel L. Migliore; Grand Rapids: Eerdmans, 2010), 31, emphasis added. The lecture was given in June 2008. See also the response to his lecture: Eric Gregory, 'The Spirit and the Letter: Protestant Thomism and Nigel Biggar's "Karl Barth's Ethics Revisited"' in *Commanding Grace: Studies in Karl Barth's Ethics* (ed. Daniel L. Migliore; Grand Rapids: Eerdmans, 2010), 50-59. Gregory concludes that Biggar wants 'a more systematic, more eudaimonist, more exegetical, and more realist account of Christian moral reasoning that does not abandon fundamental Barthian convictions' (54). He continues to worry, however, that Biggar's approach 'tends toward an autonomous morality unqualified by evangelical proclamation' (56).

[63] Biggar, *The Hastening that Waits*, 136-138.

[64] Biggar, *The Hastening that Waits*, 144.

command, and that it is precisely through repeated obedience to the command that moral character is formed and moral life is lived.

John Webster

Another recent interpreter of Barth's ethics is John Webster, who takes with all seriousness Barth's proposal that dogmatics 'has the problem of ethics in view from the very first'.[65] With argument ranging over a number of volumes, Webster again and again asserts his primary thesis that the *Church Dogmatics* is a work of moral theology as well as systematic theology.[66] He seeks to show that Barth's construal of the freedom of divine action is inseparable from what he says of the active life of humanity in correspondence to God.[67] In addition to substantial accounts of the ethics in both the early and late periods of Barth's career, Webster has also provided resources for fruitful critical engagement with Barth by identifying the *Church Dogmatics* as a work of 'moral ontology' which he defines as an extensive account of the situation in which human agents act. According to Webster, Barth's ethics is devoted to describing the 'space' in which human agents have their existence, rather than to providing descriptions of normative character or analysis of the ethical quandaries that agents find themselves in.[68] I have already noted Webster's observation that for Barth, one set of historical incidents are 'ontologically, noetically and morally fundamental'.[69] He argues that the only reason 'an entire ontology of created being' may rest upon such a seemingly precarious foundation is that it has an absoluteness which is proper to God alone.[70] Although this principle is counter-intuitive to the idealist metaphysics and philosophical, moral and religious

---

[65] Webster, *Barth's Ethics of Reconciliation*, 1, citing Karl Barth, *Church Dogmatics III/4: The Doctrine of Creation* (ed. G. W. Bromiley & T. F. Torrance, trans. A. T. Mackay, et al; Edinburgh: T. & T. Clark, 1961), 3.

[66] Webster, *Barth's Ethics of Reconciliation*, 1. For other instances where Webster presses this primary thesis, see Webster, *Barth's Moral Theology passim*; John Webster, 'Introducing Barth,' in *The Cambridge Companion to Karl Barth* (ed. J. Webster; Cambridge: Cambridge University Press, 2000), 13-14; Webster, 'Rescuing the Subject,' 57-62

[67] Webster, *Barth's Ethics of Reconciliation*, 9.

[68] Webster, *Barth's Ethics of Reconciliation*, 1-2. Note the anticipation of the concept of 'moral ontology' in Oden, who rightly perceives that Barth is concerned more with describing the arena in which human moral activity occurs and is to be evaluated, than exploring specific moral dilemmas and issues. Thus, he notes that 'the strength of Barth's ethics is not in any sort of deliberative, calculative criteria for moral choice. If that is all that one is looking for under the heading of "ethics," then surely Barth will be a consistent disappointment....The real strength is in what might be called its "theologically interpreted radical contextuality"'—Oden, *The Promise of Barth*, 74-75.

[69] Webster, *Barth's Ethics of Reconciliation*, 98. See page 16 above.

[70] Webster, *Barth's Ethics of Reconciliation*, 86.

notions of subjectivity characteristic of modernity, it is only as interpreters are willing to follow Barth at this point, suggests Webster, that they will find his ethics satisfactory.[71]

Webster resolutely resists interpretations that would suggest that Barth's account serves to eradicate human agency, and insists that anthropology and ethics are ingredients within dogmatics, precisely because the theme of dogmatics concerns the ontic relation of God *and* humanity in Jesus Christ.[72] Thus, ethics does not comprise a separate theme from dogmatics, nor is it added in order to supply application or relevance to theology. From the very beginning, avers Webster, Barth's theme is God and humanity as agents in relation, constructed in such a way to call the presuppositions of modernity into question.[73] Neither divine nor human activity may be emphasised to the detriment of the other, but the carefully articulated distinction between and ordering of the two subjects must be rigorously adhered to.[74] Just as God is ontologically prior to humanity, so his action is prior to, and forms the ground of that of humanity.[75] Webster contends that Barth adopted the model of summons and response in his ethics precisely to rule out both abstract divine monergism and pure human autonomy.[76] Barth's adoption of invocation as the material concept of Christian existence is an effort to establish human moral existence in which 'dependence is not diminishment and resolute action is not self-assertion'.[77]

In light of recent work such as that by Biggar and Webster, it is evident that some earlier interpretations of Barth's ethics are flawed because he has not always been read in accordance with his own concerns.[78] George Hunsinger has

---

[71] Webster, *Barth's Ethics of Reconciliation*, 39; cf. Webster, 'Introducing Barth,' 11.

[72] Webster, 'Rescuing the Subject,' 62.

[73] Webster, *Barth's Ethics of Reconciliation*, 33, cf. 17-18.

[74] Webster, *Barth's Ethics of Reconciliation*, 107.

[75] Webster, *Barth's Ethics of Reconciliation*, 34.

[76] Webster, *Barth's Ethics of Reconciliation*, 57.

[77] Webster, *Barth's Ethics of Reconciliation*, 113-114.

[78] Other recent re-appraisals of Barth's ethics which build upon the work undertaken by Biggar and Webster include Archibald James Spencer, *Clearing a Space for Human Action: Ethical Ontology in the Theology of Karl Barth* (New York: Peter Lang, 2003), David Clough, *Ethics in Crisis: Interpreting Barth's Ethics*, Barth Studies (Aldershot: Ashgate, 2005), Paul T. Nimmo, *Being in Action: The Theological Shape of Barth's Ethical Vision* (Edinburgh: T. & T. Clark, 2007), Matthew Rose, *Ethics with Barth*, Gerald P. McKenny, *The Analogy of Grace: Karl Barth's Moral Theology* (Oxford: Oxford University Press, 2010), and David Haddorff, *Christian Ethics as Witness: Barth's Ethics for a World at Risk* (Eugene: Wipf and Stock, 2011). See also the collection of essays in Daniel L. Migliore, ed., *Commanding Grace: Studies in Karl Barth's Ethics* (Grand Rapids: Eerdmans, 2010). More general treatments of Barth's career which are also sensitive to his ethics include those by McCormack, *Karl Barth's*

suggested that although Barth is regularly acclaimed as a great theologian, he 'has achieved the dubious distinction of being habitually honoured but not much read'.[79] Doubtless, this is in part the result of the voluminous and difficult, at times frustrating, nature of his work. Too often, however, it is also the result of an over-dependence upon secondary sources, with only cursory examinations of Barth himself. It is then assumed that Barth is already understood, that his project is known, and that further extensive engagement with his work is not required.

A problem with such an approach is that caricatures abound. Berkouwer, recalling the early reception of Barth's theology, writes, 'we hastily contrived all sorts of handy characterisations of Barth'.[80] He proceeds to list a large and varied catalogue of interpretations of Barth's early work which demonstrates the kind of contrary readings of Barth that can and do arise if careful descriptive and analytical examination of his work is not carried out.[81] He similarly warns that criticism of Barth's theology and the objections to it can have importance only if they are based upon a legitimate and warranted analysis of his work.[82] He criticises one-sided approaches which fail to take the whole of Barth's writing into account, and argues that those who would criticise Barth have 'first of all the task of penetrating *deeply* into the elaborate explanations' in which Barth develops his theological concepts.[83] In like manner William Werpehowski has warned that our responsibility in reading Barth's ethics is first and always to try to make sense of the manner in which Barth used familiar words and concepts in new and idiosyncratic ways. He regards failure to perform this hermeneutic task as a particular cause of misinterpretation of his work.[84]

This present book, then, is an attempt to engage in the kind of study advocated by Webster at the outset of this chapter: a 'detailed study of Barth's writings which, by careful reading, tries to display the structure and logic of his concerns without moving prematurely into making judgments or pressing too

---

Dialectical Theology and Timothy J. Gorringe, *Karl Barth: Against Hegemony* (Oxford: Oxford University Press, 1999).

[79] George Hunsinger, *How to Read Karl Barth: The Shape of his Theology* (Oxford: Oxford University Press, 1991), 27.

[80] G. C. Berkouwer, *A Half Century of Theology: Movements and Motives* (trans. L. B. Smedes; Grand Rapids: Eerdmans, 1977), 41.

[81] Berkouwer, *A Half Century of Theology*, 41-46.

[82] G. C. Berkouwer, *The Triumph of Grace in the Theology of Karl Barth* (trans. H. R. Boer; Grand Rapids: Eerdmans, 1956), 384.

[83] Berkouwer, *The Triumph of Grace*, 387-388. Note that Barth, too, complained of reviewers who read only fragments of his work and proceeded to make judgements of the whole on that basis—see Karl Barth, *The Epistle to the Romans* (trans. E. C. Hoskyns; 6th ed. Oxford: Oxford University Press, 1933), viii.

[84] William Werpehowski, 'Command and History in the Ethics of Karl Barth,' *Journal of Religious Ethics* 9, no. 2 (1981): 303.

early the usefulness (or lack of it) of Barth's work for contemporary moral theology'.[85] Before engaging directly in this task, however, I will provide a brief survey of how various interpreters, specifically Stanley Hauerwas, Nicholas Healy, Reinhard Hütter and Joseph Mangina have understood Barth in terms of his vision for Christian and ecclesial existence.

Reading Barth's Ecclesial Ethics

It is noteworthy that several of Barth's interpreters examined above have recognised the ecclesial orientation of his ethics, although they have not necessarily appreciated or accepted his conclusions. Niebuhr, for example, considers Barth's ethics isolationist and sectarian, 'designed for the church of the catacombs'.[86] Lovin, too, notes that Barth understood the church as the particular community of those attentive to the Word of God, whose moral task consists in being the church and refusing to be anything else.[87] He argues that, for Barth, the church is the true object of the command of God and the true locus of obedience, and that through its obedience the church exhibits a pattern of responsible living within the new order God is creating in the midst of humanity.[88] Further, we noted that the responses of Krötke and Price to Barth's critics indicate that his theology must come to concrete expression in the life of the Christian community.[89]

Although these brief comments provide some indication that Barth develops his theology with an ecclesial motive, he has also been criticised for diminishing the place and role of the church in his theology. If this is the case, my argument that Barth has an ecclesial motive in the development of his theology would be difficult to sustain. Thus the sections that follow examine some of these criticisms in greater detail, beginning with the work of Stanley Hauerwas.

Stanley Hauerwas

One of the most prolific and widely discussed contemporary advocates for an ecclesial ethics has also engaged extensively with Barth's theology. Stanley Hauerwas, a prominent American voice in theological ethics, has, over the course of his career, engaged with Barth's theology and ethics on a number of related fronts. In the essay 'On Doctrine and Ethics' published in 1997,

---

[85] Webster, *Barth's Moral Theology*, 1.

[86] Niebuhr, *Essays in Applied Christianity*, 187.

[87] Lovin, *Christian Faith and Public Choices*, 12-13, 116, 122.

[88] Lovin, *Christian Faith and Public Choices*, 103, 40. Note that Lovin not only recognises the ecclesial orientation of Barth's ethic, but also its eschatological orientation as the church witnesses to the reality of the coming kingdom.

[89] See pages 14-15 above.

Hauerwas begins by citing Barth's claim that the general conception of ethics coincides exactly with the conception of sin.[90] Despite referring to Barth's claim as an exaggerated assertion, Hauerwas is nonetheless in broad agreement with Barth's intent, which constitutes a refusal to allow something called 'ethics' to exist prior to or independently of 'doctrine'.[91] Hauerwas, like Barth, is opposed to accounts of morality which endeavour to do ethics from the 'bottom up' because, in his view, they invariably confirm the modern presumption that God, if he is considered at all, is at best something added on to the moral life.[92]

Hauerwas argues that the quest for a universal ethics removed the subject of ethics from the realm of dogmatics because of the particularity of the latter. Ethics became a quest for rational foundations for morality in order to secure confidence that moral convictions were not arbitrary.[93] The rationalist presuppositions underlying this quest were imported into theological reflection particularly by Kant, and, under the influence of Schleiermacher, theological reflection became a civilisational project.[94] It is precisely here that Hauerwas approves Barth's method for Barth refuses to make the church a servant of such a project and thus a supplement for what is a prior conception of ethics.[95] Rather, theology, and thus theological ethics, is to serve the church in its distinctive calling to embody an alternative order in its corporate life, and so stand as a sign of God's redemptive purposes in the world.[96]

Hauerwas, therefore, concurs with Barth that ethics must be theologically established because theology, as reflection on the revelation of God in Christ, provides the ground for all we know and do.[97] He also perceives an ecclesial motive in Barth's theology and thus suggests that Barth's proposition that ethics is equivalent to sin is an implicit claim about the church's relation to the world that is not immediately apparent.[98] Hauerwas' project, then, includes an attempt to develop what he considers to be an implication of Barth's theology, namely, to render this relation explicit.

It would be premature, however, to conclude that Hauerwas finds in Barth a satisfactory ecclesial ethic. Over the course of his career Hauerwas has raised several pertinent criticisms of Barth's work. In 1975 Hauerwas gave sustained

---

[90] Stanley Hauerwas, 'On Doctrine and Ethics,' in *The Cambridge Companion to Christian Doctrine* (ed. C. Gunton; Cambridge: Cambridge University Press, 1997), 21.

[91] Hauerwas, 'On Doctrine and Ethics,' 22.

[92] Stanley Hauerwas, *Sanctify Them in the Truth: Holiness Exemplified* (Edinburgh: T. & T. Clark, 1998), 43.

[93] Hauerwas, 'On Doctrine and Ethics,' 29.

[94] Hauerwas, 'On Doctrine and Ethics,' 31.

[95] Hauerwas, 'On Doctrine and Ethics,' 33.

[96] Hauerwas, 'On Doctrine and Ethics,' 24. Hauerwas is citing Richard B. Hays, 'Ecclesiology and Ethics in 1 Corinthians,' *Ex Auditu*, no. 10 (1994): 33.

[97] Hauerwas, 'On Doctrine and Ethics,' 32.

[98] Hauerwas, 'On Doctrine and Ethics,' 24.

attention to Barth's ethics with a particular focus on the issue of character.[99] In this work he contends that by making decision the phenomenological centre of ethical behaviour and reflection, Barth's ethics are unable to provide a comprehensive account of the Christian life. He also suggests that in Barth the continuity of the human agent is marginalised, and that Barth's ethics tend to be occasionalist with a corresponding anthropology in which the human agent is passive and atomistic.[100] Christian life in Barth's theology is, therefore, a life that can only be constantly renewed in the ever new future of God's command, and that to follow Jesus one must therefore constantly take leave of all that they are.[101]

Hauerwas argues that Barth's use of the divine command predisposes his ethics towards an ethics of 'dialogue,' in which the Christian is simply caught within the dialogue between the accusing voice of the law and the accepting voice of the gospel.[102] His christology, however, requires him to conceive of existence as a journey in a way that qualifies his constant use of the language of command.[103] According to Hauerwas, this tension creates a space for an ethic of character in Barth's work which he does not develop. He argues that an ethics of character would help preserve the central insights of Barth's theology by providing a richer phenomenology of moral experience.[104] The real problem, says Hauerwas, is not that Barth has no place for character. Rather, it is that although Barth seems to imply the significance of character for Christian ethics, he has failed to integrate it into the main images he uses to explicate the nature of the Christian life. Hauerwas asserts that

> [t]he agonising thing about Barth's ethics, therefore, is not that he failed to appreciate the importance of the idea of character, but that he really does not integrate it into the main images he uses to explicate the nature of the Christian life. By describing the Christian life primarily in terms of command and decision, Barth cannot fully account for the kind of growth and deepening that he thinks is essential to the Christian's existence. In other words, Barth's exposition of the Christian life is not so much wrong for what he says, but for what he does not say. If Barth had used the idea of character he would have been able to explicate in a much fuller way the growth characteristic of God's sanctifying work.[105]

For Hauerwas, the journey metaphor is a superior means of depicting

---

[99] Stanley Hauerwas, *Character and the Christian Life: A Study in Theological Ethics*, 2nd ed. (San Antonio: Trinity University, 1985).
[100] Hauerwas, *Character and the Christian Life*, 1-8.
[101] Hauerwas, *Character and the Christian Life*, 173.
[102] Hauerwas, *Character and the Christian Life*, xxvii.
[103] Hauerwas, *Character and the Christian Life*, xxviii.
[104] Hauerwas, *Character and the Christian Life*, 178.
[105] Hauerwas, *Character and the Christian Life*, 176.

Christian life not only because its teleological conception of existence helps articulate a sense of growth and duration in the Christian life, but also because, once the centrality of character is acknowledged, provision is made for a thoroughgoing emphasis on the church as crucial for sustaining the Christian journey.[106]

In 1988 Hauerwas sharpened this criticism of Barth in an essay marking the centenary of Barth's birth.[107] In this work he develops his concern that Barth's ethics have a 'peculiar abstractness' that gives his account of the moral life an aura of unreality.[108] Hauerwas examines Barth's treatment of honour and finds 'extraordinary insights,' which, because they occur at a general or formal level, are nonetheless problematic. Hauerwas compares Barth's treatment with that of Trollope in his novel *Dr Wortle's School*, in which he characterises honour through the dilemma faced by the protagonist in his relations with the antagonists. Hauerwas suggests that Barth fails to provide an account of how honourable character emerges:

> Missing from Barth's account of honour is the kind of societal ethos, the concrete community, that is capable of producing a Wortle...What Barth fails to help us see is where such honesty comes and how it is sustained. And note that this is not a psychological or biographical question, but rather a question of how Christian ethics is done.[109]

The nub of Hauerwas' argument is clear: Christian ethics is necessarily an ecclesial ethics, because the kind of honour advocated by Barth requires, in Hauerwas' estimation, an account of the church.[110] Simply put, without a stronger theology of the church, Barth's theology and ethics suffer from abstraction, with the result that his formal accounts risk the kind of individualistic interpretation that his theological programme is meant to counter.[111]

Thus, in the earlier period of his career Hauerwas found Barth's ethics

---

[106] Hauerwas, *Character and the Christian Life*, xxxi.

[107] Stanley Hauerwas, 'On Honour: By Way of a Comparison of Barth and Trollope,' in *Reckoning With Barth: Essays in Commemoration of the Centenary of Karl Barth's Birth* (ed. N. Biggar; London: Mowbray, 1988), 145-169. The essay was actually presented as a lecture at the Oxford Conference in Commemoration of the Centenary of the Birth of Karl Barth held at Wycliffe Hall, Oxford 18-21 September, 1986.

[108] Hauerwas, 'On Honour,' 149. See also Stanley Hauerwas, 'On Learning Simplicity in an Ambiguous Age: A Response To Hunsinger,' in *Barth, Barmen and the Confessing Church Today: Katallagete, Symposium Series* (ed. J. Y. Holloway; Lewiston: Edwin Mellen, 1992), 133, 137.

[109] Hauerwas, 'On Honour,' 167-168. It is likely Hauerwas means to say, 'where such honesty comes *from*'.

[110] Hauerwas, 'On Honour,' 169.

[111] Hauerwas, 'On Honour,' 155, 169.

wanting for two reasons: first, the lack of focus on character rendered his ethics questionable because the continuity of human agency could not be adequately secured, and second, the formal nature of Barth's ethical description threatened to undermine his project because it rendered his ethics subject to individualistic interpretation.

In more recent years, however, Hauerwas has moderated his stance towards Barth. Discussion and critique of his own work by Werpehowski, Biggar, Webster and Mangina[112] has led Hauerwas to recognise that Barth's ethics are perhaps, not as flawed as he initially thought.[113] In 2001 Hauerwas delivered the prestigious Gifford Lectures in which Karl Barth emerges as the hero of his story of natural theology in the twentieth century.[114] His thesis in the lectures was typically provocative: Karl Barth is the great 'natural theologian' of the Gifford lecturers.[115] In the lectures Hauerwas sets Barth against other Gifford lecturers William James and Reinhold Niebuhr whom he assails mercilessly and critiques with devastating effect.

In keeping with the purpose of the Giffords, Hauerwas addresses the question of natural theology. He argues that natural theology, at least as it was conceived by the theological milieu in which Lord Gifford lived, actually represents an epistemological overcoming of theology for it seeks to secure the truth of Christian convictions in a manner that makes the content of those convictions secondary.[116] The problem arose when theology sought to secure the truthfulness of Christian convictions separate from and as a preamble for a comprehensive doctrine of God. In such a programme God is reduced to an abstract principle open and accessible to anyone 'without moral transformation or spiritual guidance' with the result that an unacceptable distance is opened

---

[112] See particularly Joseph L. Mangina, 'Bearing the Marks of Jesus: The Church in the Economy of Salvation in Barth and Hauerwas,' *Scottish Journal of Theology* 52, no. 3 (1999), Webster, *Barth's Ethics of Reconciliation*, 74, Werpehowski, 'Command and History,' and Biggar, *The Hastening that Waits*, 123-145. Because the concerns raised by Hauerwas in his earlier work have been adequately addressed in these works, it is not necessary to repeat their arguments here.

[113] Stanley Hauerwas, *With the Grain of the Universe: The Church's Witness and Natural Theology* (Grand Rapids: Brazos, 2001), 194.

[114] The Gifford Lectureship was established by Adam Lord Gifford (1820–1887), to 'promote and diffuse the study of natural theology in the widest sense of the term—in other words, the knowledge of God' (see *The Gifford Lectures* [Website] (John Templeton Foundation, [cited November 13, 2007]); available from http://www.giffordlectures.org/). Barth was invited to deliver the lectures in 1937-38. These lectures were later published as Karl Barth, *The Knowledge of God and the Service of God According to the Teaching of the Reformation* (trans. J. L. M. Haire & I. Henderson; London: Hodder and Stoughton, 1938).

[115] Hauerwas, *With the Grain*, 9.

[116] Hauerwas, *With the Grain*, 37.

between theological assertion and actual life.[117]

Hauerwas rejects this approach root and branch. It is here that he finds Barth so helpful an instructor, for the *Church Dogmatics* are nothing less than a massive theological metaphysics that attempts to overturn epistemology and to overcome metaphysics. Barth has a single concern, says Hauerwas, which is to show that our existence and that of all things are unintelligible if the God revealed in Jesus Christ is not God.[118] Hauerwas asserts that Barth in some sense intended the *Church Dogmatics* to be a training manual to enable Christians to view the world as it is and not as it appears.[119] Such training requires not only intellectual but also moral transformation.[120] He argues further that Barth himself understood that the vindication of such a theological program was to be found in the actual life required of Christians, which he characterised simply as *witness*.[121] In fact, early in his career Hauerwas recognised the importance of the category of witness in Barth's work, noting that the motif of *witness* functions in Barth's work as a summary of the overall direction and implications of his thought regarding Christian life.[122] Somewhat controversially he contends that any account of Barth's understanding of the possibility of our knowledge of God must end by attending to his understanding of the church's witness to God, as well as to his understanding of the moral life that the church makes possible.[123]

Hauerwas, though, worries whether Barth's ecclesiology is sufficient to sustain the witness that he thought was intrinsic to Christianity.[124] He finds Barth's affirmation that the world would be lost without Jesus Christ, but that it would not necessarily be lost without the church problematic,[125] and is thus concerned that Barth understates the role of the church in God's redemptive purpose. Barth cannot acknowledge that the church itself is constitutive of

---

[117] Hauerwas, *With the Grain*, 36.

[118] Hauerwas, *With the Grain*, 190-191. See also, page 39.

[119] Matthew Rose asserts the same thing in Rose, *Ethics with Barth*, 13.

[120] Hauerwas, *With the Grain*, 179, 183.

[121] Hauerwas, *With the Grain*, 39.

[122] Hauerwas, *Character and the Christian Life*, 140.

[123] Hauerwas, *With the Grain*, 192. William Stacy Johnson makes a similar point when he says that, 'even though Barth's own preferred vineyard was that of conceptual, doctrinal analysis, the broad trajectory of his thought suggests that ethics becomes the primary sphere in which his theology should be validated. We must think of all the many pages of doctrinal analysis that make up the *CD* as a prelude to ethics.' See William S. Johnson, *The Mystery of God: Karl Barth and the Postmodern Foundations of Theology* (Louisville: Westminster John Knox, 1997), 8.

[124] Hauerwas, *With the Grain*, 39.

[125] Hauerwas, *With the Grain*, 193. For Barth's comment that the world would not necessarily be lost without the church, see Karl Barth, *Church Dogmatics IV/3.2: The Doctrine of Reconciliation* (ed. G. W. Bromiley & T. F. Torrance, trans. G. W. Bromiley; Edinburgh: T. & T. Clark, 1962), 826.

gospel proclamation, and that through the Holy Spirit's activity Christians are made part of God's care of the world through the church.[126] What is needed, Hauerwas suggests, is a comprehensive ecclesiology under the aegis of a robust pneumatology, whereby the church, in and by the presence of the Holy Spirit, is to exemplify and display the truthfulness of the theological claims made in the gospel.[127] This cannot be reduced simply to an intellectual exercise, but must be shown forth in ethical life, an existence which portrays truthfully the reality of the world in which we live. For Hauerwas this means the adoption of practices which exhibit the content of Christian convictions and make 'habitable' the world exemplified by the church in its proclamation and life.[128]

In his final lectures on dogmatics, Barth addressed this issue and ruled out two extremes in the response of the church to the 'worldliness' of the world. The first extreme is that negative appraisal of the world in which the church adopts either an isolationalist, or else conversely, a crusading posture towards the world. The second extreme is the positive appraisal of the world on the basis of its reconciliation in Christ, in which the church assimilates itself to the secularity of the world. Instead, Christians are to maintain a middle course between the two extremes leaning this way or that as the situation requires.[129] Hauerwas, however, is critical of Barth's failure to

> specify the material conditions that would sustain his 'middle way.' Of course, Barth intentionally depicts the 'middle way' as unstable, but instability is as likely to lead to unfaithfulness as faithfulness. Barth's attempt to steer a 'middle course' between monasticism and the liberal embrace of the secular is but the other side of his overly cautious account of the role of the church in the economy of God's salvation. Because the church cannot trust in its calling to be God's witness, Barth seems far too willing to leave the world alone.[130]

In the end, Hauerwas wants to situate the Spirit-endued witness of the church in the place formerly occupied by a Giffordian natural theology.[131] He

---

[126] Hauerwas, *With the Grain*, 145.

[127] Hauerwas is not alone in his suggestion that Barth's ecclesiology needs at least to be supplemented by, if not relocated under a robust pneumatology. Yocum, *Ecclesial Mediation in Barth* (Barth Studies; Aldershot: Ashgate, 2004), xxi, calls for a strong sense of ecclesial mediation of divine grace grounded in a robust pneumatology, while Rosato laments Barth's refusal to acknowledge the sacraments as instruments of a new, salvific and eschatological act of the Holy Spirit—see Philip J. Rosato, *The Spirit as Lord: Karl Barth's Pneumatology* (Edinburgh: T. & T. Clark, 1981), 170.

[128] Hauerwas, *With the Grain*, 215.

[129] Karl Barth, *The Christian Life: Church Dogmatics IV/4 (Lecture Fragments)* (trans. G. W. Bromiley; Edinburgh: T. & T. Clark, 1981), 197-201.

[130] Hauerwas, *With the Grain*, 202.

[131] Hauerwas, *With the Grain*, 210. Note that Hauerwas affirms that the Spirit is not bound to the church so that the witness of the church necessarily incorporates that of the Spirit. The witness of the church may vary according to its situation, 'but if the Holy

argues that Barth's christological ordering of both pneumatology and ecclesiology serves to undermine his insistence that witness is the fundamental posture of the Christian life. Indeed, Hauerwas makes the astounding claim that 'real reality' can only be known in conjunction with the church, arguing that

> Christians betray themselves as well as their non-Christian brothers and sisters when in the interest of apologetics we say and act as if the cross of Christ is incidental to God's being. In fact, the God we worship and the world God created cannot be truthfully known without the cross, which is why the knowledge of God and ecclesiology—or the politics called church—are interdependent.[132]

Clearly, this argument advances beyond the bounds within which Barth himself worked. Nonetheless, Hauerwas' concerns raise fundamental questions especially with regard to the adequacy of Barth's theology and ethics. He has argued that Barth's understanding of the possibility of our knowledge of God must end by attending to his understanding of the church's witness to God, as well as to his understanding of the moral life that the church makes possible. He has further argued, however, that Barth's refusal to allow any point of contact for the gospel functions to compromise his account of the church and the Christian life. Barth fails to elucidate the material conditions necessary to sustain the kind of witness he deems necessary for faithful obedience to God.

It may be that Hauerwas has overstated his case. Biggar, for example, notes that Barth affirms the importance of the Christian community as the place where Christians may expect to hear God's command and as the school in which they are trained to discern his voice. He continues, however, with a warning that, for Barth, the community is no more absolute than the individual, and unless the training received in the church culminates in personal acts of response, it will all have been in vain, for character is ultimately formed, not by the training Christians receive in the Church but by their active response to God.[133] Biggar also rightly reminds us that at times the divine command reaches us and moral character is formed *in spite of* the prevailing ecclesial culture.[134] Nevertheless it remains the case that while human response to the divine command is thoroughly personal, it is never a solo effort. Rather, the command is mediated to us, and our response is enabled and supported, through the 'community of character' of which we are part.[135]

Barth does, then, to some extent at least, 'specify the material conditions to sustain his "middle way"', while still insisting that specific obedience to the

---

Spirit does not witness to the Father and Son through the witness of Christians, then Christians have no arguments to make. Christian argument rests on witness, and both argument and witness are the work of the Spirit.'

[132] Hauerwas, *With the Grain*, 16-17.

[133] Biggar, *The Hastening that Waits*, 145.

[134] Biggar, *The Hastening that Waits*, 145.

[135] See also Hart, *Regarding Karl Barth*, 98-99.

divine command is the final criterion of faithfulness. Barth's reason for prioritising the divine command was to avoid the possibility of treating either the human agent or the church independently of God, as though ethical life could be grounded anthropologically, and thus proceed as it were, under its own steam. This is in accord with his methodological principle that since Christian life has no independent existence it ought not to become an independent object of thought.[136]

Biggar also notes an important methodological distinction between Barth and Hauerwas' use of Scripture. For Barth, the primary contribution of the Bible is its revelation of the encompassing reality within which we are set, which is nothing other than the living God who has eternally elected humanity in Jesus Christ. For Hauerwas, the narrative of Israel and Jesus *is* the story of God's self-revelation in history, and as such is the constitutive narrative of the church into which we are called and according to which we, too, are to live. The narrative, therefore, functions normatively to form the identity of the Christian community and thereby provide the rationale for its morality. Thus, for Barth, the Bible 'leads to an ethics at whose heart stand acts of prayer and worship' while for Hauerwas, 'the Bible's contribution to Christian ethics turns out to be the provision of a theological vision of reality that legitimizes a distinctively Christian ethic in which acts of prayer and worship feature only incidentally'.[137]

David Fergusson also questions whether the category of narrative in Hauerwas' ethics functions to blur the relation between Christ and the disciple.[138] For Fergusson, the true nature of discipleship cannot be grasped simply in terms of a moral emulation of Jesus, because discipleship involves a recognition of the priority of Jesus, and our dependence upon his life and work *extra nos*.[139] Hauerwas' criticism that Barth fails to specify the material conditions of sustaining his middle way appears to overlook the degree to which Barth envisaged an informed community gathered around Scripture in an attitude of worship and prayer as the place where the divine command is heard. That this was the case even in the early period of his career will become evident.

Fergusson also suggests that Hauerwas has over-determined his doctrine of the church, and that his work evidences 'a slide from christology into ecclesiology'.[140] Fergusson argues that Hauerwas' emphasis on Jesus as the exemplar and initiator of the new social order of the kingdom tends to mute

---

[136] Biggar, *The Hastening that Waits*, 140.

[137] Biggar, *The Hastening that Waits*, 117-118.

[138] See the discussion in David Fergusson, *Community, Liberalism and Christian Ethics* (Cambridge: Cambridge University Press, 1998), 54-57.

[139] Fergusson, *Community, Liberalism and Christian Ethics*, 72.

[140] Fergusson, *Community, Liberalism and Christian Ethics*, 72.

traditional language of incarnation and atonement.[141] He argues that because he has failed to adequately treat dogmatic issues such as how the work of Christ is complete in the resurrection and ascension, and how he is present in the church through the Spirit, Hauerwas blurs the distinction between Christ and the church so that the church, as the linear continuation of that which Christ began, functions more as an extension of the incarnation than as existing to bear witness and to live faithfully in light of his unique and unrepeatable work.[142]

Fergusson's suggestion that Hauerwas has over-determined his ecclesiology at the expense of christology is not universally held. Indeed, this raises perhaps the central issue of contention in contemporary discussion of Barth's ecclesiology. Hauerwas' criticisms of Barth might be rephrased in the form of a question: does the outpouring of the Holy Spirit at Pentecost which issued in the creation of the church represent a distinct mission of the triune God in the economy of salvation? Hauerwas accepts the conclusion suggested by Mangina that his criticisms of Barth would be better stated as a *pneumatological* worry regarding the role of the church in the economy of salvation.[143] Mangina, in contrast to Fergusson, asserts that Barth's christocentrism serves to 'short-circuit' the work of the Spirit so that he appears only as a predicate of Christ's reconciling work rather than as having an agency of his own. He asks whether the church is 'merely a human echo or analogy of Christ's completed work, as in Barth? Or is it also somehow the herald of new activity in which God is engaged between now and the eschaton?'[144]

Likewise, Robert Jenson suggests that

> the final reason for the whole web of Spirit-avoidance in the *Kirchliche Dogmatik* is avoidance of the *church*. For if the Pentecostal creation of a structured continuing community were identified as the 'objectivity' of the gospel's truth *pro nobis*, then this community itself, in its structured temporal and spatial extension, would be seen as the *Bedingung der Möglichkeit* (the condition of the possibility) of faith.[145]

Jenson goes on to remark that Barth's 'practiced binitarianism' may in fact be his final resistance against the Roman Catholic insistence that the church be

---

[141] Fergusson, *Community, Liberalism and Christian Ethics*, 68. For an analysis and an assessment of the sometimes selective manner in which Hauerwas uses Scripture see Hays, *The Moral Vision of the New Testament*, 253-264, and especially, 260.

[142] Fergusson, *Community, Liberalism and Christian Ethics*, 69-71.

[143] Mangina, 'Bearing the Marks of Jesus,' 282. For Hauerwas' acceptance of Mangina's proposal see Hauerwas, *With the Grain*, 194-195.

[144] Mangina, 'Bearing the Marks of Jesus,' 282. See also Joseph L. Mangina, *Karl Barth on the Christian Life: The Practical Knowledge of God* (New York: Peter Lang, 2001), 87, n 13.

[145] Robert W. Jenson, 'You Wonder Where the Spirit Went,' *Pro Ecclesia* II, no. 3 (1993): 302-303.

considered an active *mediatrix* of faith.[146] So, too, Rosato complains that Barth's pneumatology is so constrained by his christology that the entire notion that the Spirit is the generous outpouring of the love of the Father and the Son into the world is lost.[147]

The matters raised in this section by Hauerwas (and Mangina, Jenson and Rosato) pose a serious question: to what degree is it possible to state that the motive underlying Barth's theology is fundamentally ecclesial, if Barth fails to provide adequate dogmatic 'space' for the reality of the church and the extension of Christian life and character in and across time? This question has been sharpened recently by a number of theologians participating in a movement that has been labelled 'the new ecclesiology,' who argue for the instantiation of the economy of salvation in practices which are constitutive of the church, and who thus also criticise Barth for diminishing or even eradicating the church as a historical reality.

The 'New Ecclesiology'

Nicholas Healy, for example, argues that Barth, in concert with almost all twentieth century ecclesiology, can be faulted methodologically for developing a conceptual model which seeks to identify the theoretical and essential nature of the church at the expense of its historical and concrete identity.[148] In addition, Barth's actualism produces a bifurcation between the visible and empirical church, so that the so-called 'real church' occurs only as the Holy Spirit acts upon the human church in the moment. Only in the event of divine action is the human and sinful church actually the Body of Christ.[149] Healy considers that such bifurcation between the theological and human aspects of the church to be irreconcilable with Scripture. In fact he suggests that to think of an 'invisible-yet-real' Israel or the church as distinct from its socio-cultural identity is not only odd but quite unbiblical, and that neither the Old nor the New Testament makes a division between the empirical church and its essential reality.[150]

Healy proposes, therefore, an 'ecclesiology from below,' a narrative ecclesiology that begins with the concrete, human history that is constitutive of the church.[151] For Healy, ecclesiology is a practical discipline, oriented towards

---

[146] Jenson, 'You Wonder Where,' 303.

[147] Rosato, *The Spirit as Lord: Karl Barth's Pneumatology*, 138.

[148] Nicholas M. Healy, 'The Logic of Karl Barth's Ecclesiology: Analysis, Assessment and Proposed Modifications,' *Modern Theology* 10, no. 3 (1994): 253. See also Nicholas M. Healy, *Church, World and the Christian Life: Practical-Prophetic Ecclesiology* (Cambridge: Cambridge University Press, 2000), 3, 26-29.

[149] Healy, 'The Logic of Karl Barth's Ecclesiology,' 258-259.

[150] Healy, 'The Logic of Karl Barth's Ecclesiology,' 264.

[151] Healy, 'The Logic of Karl Barth's Ecclesiology,' 266. Healy argues that Christianity is a way of life which takes concrete form in a web of social practices, and which has as

the concrete church. He suggests that theoretical ecclesiologies such as Barth's which seek to discern the 'essence' of the church, function to remove focus from the historical identity of the church and provide idealistic definitions which deny its earthly and sinful reality, and which also hinder its ability to form authentic lives of discipleship which embody the truth of the gospel.[152]

According to Healy, Barth avoids the error of a one-sided sociological description of the church's identity by presenting a one-sided doctrinal description.[153] This way of construing the church undermines Barth's theological agenda, because with the loss of the socio-cultural particularity of the church comes the risk that Christianity becomes a more or less dispensable part of an individual's private worldview, an outcome clearly antithetical to Barth's overall intention.[154]

Similarly, Reinhard Hütter is convinced that Barth has developed an abstract ecclesiology. He argues that Barth adopts the Word of God as a critical ecclesiological principle ('genuine Protestantism') in order to steer a middle path between Neo-Protestantism on the one hand and Roman Catholicism on the other. Because the Word of God both addresses and stands over against the church, it defines the normative nature of what constitutes the church as church. Hütter regards Barth's theological principle as superior to those of both Neo-Protestantism and Roman Catholicism, yet it comes at a high price, namely the loss of the church's concreteness. Because 'genuine Protestantism' serves as a critical theological concept to be employed over against all real existing churches it cannot really exist in an ecclesially embodied form.[155] Thus, Hütter characterises Barth's critical ecclesiology as 'transcendental,' and as a recipe for a theology without any tangible ecclesial roots.[156] Like Healy, he is also concerned that Barth's actualistic construal of the church results in a loss of concreteness. Because the witness of the community is entirely dependent for its fulfilment on the activity of the Holy Spirit, the church itself has no signifying or communicative potency whatsoever.[157]

Thus, both Healy and Hütter suggest that Barth marginalises the embodied character of the human community. It is arguable, however, that Healy has erred by identifying the narrative of human history as constitutive of the church. Although his insistence that the concrete realities of the church in

---

its goal the embodiment of ultimate truthfulness and goodness. Nonetheless, because the church itself participates in the radical sinfulness that afflicts all humankind, it performs its calling only very poorly—see Healy, *Church, World and the Christian Life*, 4-5, 9-11, 15.

[152] Healy, *Church, World and the Christian Life*, 3, 14-15, 21.

[153] Healy, 'The Logic of Karl Barth's Ecclesiology,' 263.

[154] Healy, 'The Logic of Karl Barth's Ecclesiology,' 265.

[155] Reinhard Hütter, 'Karl Barth's Dialectical Catholicity: *Sic et Non*,' *Modern Theology* 16, no. 2 (2000): 142-143, 147.

[156] Hütter, 'Karl Barth's Dialectical Catholicity,' 144, 148

[157] Hütter, 'Karl Barth's Dialectical Catholicity,' 146.

history become part of theological reflection on the church is surely correct, his approach in this earlier essay at least, seems to remove the church from the broader scriptural narrative in which it finds its distinctly theological identity, that is, the church as a distinct mission of the triune God in the Holy Spirit.[158]

Hütter's argument is more substantial. First, like Healy, Hütter also argues that the church is a way of life, a distinct set of practices interwoven with normative beliefs, concretely and distinctly embodied.[159] He asserts that as the work of the Holy Spirit the church is also characterized by duration, concreteness, and visibility, and as such '*is identical* with distinct practices or activities, institutions, offices and teachings. In this way the work of the Spirit acquires its own, eschatological extension "in time."'[160] Hütter argues that it is precisely through these practices that God's saving economy instantiates itself and the Holy Spirit enacts his regenerating and sanctifying work.[161]

According to Hütter, it is this identification between the work of the Spirit and the practices of the church that Barth has failed to recognise. Rather, Barth, working with a 'disembodied pneumatology and critical ecclesiology' not only misrepresents the concrete ecclesiology of the Reformation, but effectively bifurcates the church by positing a radical disjunction between the work of the

---

[158] In more recent work Healy modifies his own criticisms, and interacts extensively with Hütter and Hauerwas, suggesting that they both fail because their ecclesiology is not sufficiently grounded in an account of the triune God as the starting point for ecclesiological reflection. He now sets ecclesiology within a more developed doctrine of the economic trinity in a way that does not bind the action of the Holy Spirit to the church's practices, or identify church and kingdom. See Nicholas M. Healy, 'Practices and the New Ecclesiology: Misplaced Concreteness?,' *International Journal of Systematic Theology* 5, no. 3 (2003): 302, and Nicholas M. Healy, 'Karl Barth's Ecclesiology Reconsidered,' *Scottish Journal of Theology* 57, no. 3 (2004), 287-299.

[159] Hütter, 'Karl Barth's Dialectical Catholicity,' 149.

[160] Cited in Joseph L. Mangina, 'After Dogma: Reinhard Hütter's Challenge to Contemporary Theology: A Review Essay,' *International Journal of Systematic Theology* 2, no. 3 (2000): 338, Mangina's emphasis. The citation comes from Reinhard Hütter, *Suffering Divine Things: Theology as Church Practice* (trans. Doug Stott; Grand Rapids: Eerdmans, 1999), 119.

[161] Hütter, 'Karl Barth's Dialectical Catholicity,' 149-150. Hütter elicits support for this position from Luther, arguing that Luther names specific practices that he considers are constitutive of the church, including proclamation of God's Word and its reception in faith; baptism; communion; the 'office of the keys'; prayer, worship and teaching; and the way of the cross. For Hütter, Luther's account has several advantages over that of Barth. Because the Holy Spirit has a distinct salvific economy in which the church's constitutive practices are central, the church is a distinct people that can be localised and identified. In addition, says Hütter, Luther's account of the church's marks as constitutive practices and his understanding of the Holy Spirit doing his work precisely in and through them, allows him to begin ecclesiologically with the concrete, yet without becoming a sectarian.

Holy Spirit and the actual practices of the Christian community.[162] Hütter insists that theology think of the Spirit and the church in a way that avoids transcendental moves by giving proper emphasis to both the Spirit's embodiment in distinct practices and thereby to the church's concreteness, and also the church's brokenness.[163]

Hütter's emphasis on the link between the Holy Spirit and the practices of the church is also prominent in the thought of Joseph Mangina, who, as we have seen, shares concerns regarding Barth's christocentric development of ecclesiology. Because the victory of God's kingdom that effects salvation has already been enacted in the life and death of Jesus Christ, it seems, says Mangina, that public history is irrelevant to the actual salvation of creatures, and that Barth has left little for the Holy Spirit to accomplish.[164] Mangina finds in Barth's ecclesiology a peculiar gap between his theological description of the church and its ordinary empirical practices in history.[165] Because Barth's understanding of the church is actualistic, it is not clear how the church 'as a configuration of human practices' makes much difference to its task of witnessing to the lordship of Christ.[166] It further means that the term 'church' is stripped of its ordinary, denotative reference, with a resulting loss of the perceptible community existing across time, the subject of its own actions. Mangina acknowledges Barth's concern regarding triumphalism but insists that the best check on triumphalism in the church is the discerning and forceful application of the doctrine of justification in its church-critical use.[167]

Further, in Barth's theology the nexus between gospel and church is said to be construed in a 'weak' sense, so that the community in God's hands is no more than a sign or instrument of his grace.[168] Mangina, however, wants to assert not just that the church has a function of proclamation, but is itself a part of the very gospel it proclaims. On this view, the church is actively involved in the communication of saving grace, set in 'cooperation' with the triune God over against the individual believer, so that faith in Jesus Christ not only involves acceptance of the church's message but acceptance of the church itself as the binding medium in which faith takes shape.[169] Mangina states the matter in sacramental terms: 'On the strong view of mediation, the church is the *signum* of God's action, as the Protestant view readily acknowledges; but it is *signum* in such a way that it also participates in the *res*. As with any

---

[162] Hütter, 'Karl Barth's Dialectical Catholicity,' 148, 151.

[163] Hütter, 'Karl Barth's Dialectical Catholicity,' 151.

[164] Mangina, 'Bearing the Marks of Jesus,' 300.

[165] Mangina, 'Bearing the Marks of Jesus,' 270.

[166] Mangina, 'Bearing the Marks of Jesus,' 278.

[167] Mangina, 'Bearing the Marks of Jesus,' 271, 281, 303.

[168] Mangina, 'Bearing the Marks of Jesus,' 293.

[169] Mangina, 'Bearing the Marks of Jesus,' 292-295.

sacramental reality, the church conveys the very thing that it signifies.'[170] Thus, for Mangina, the reclamation of the visible people of God as a *theological* category is a way of rescuing the church from its sociological captivity.[171]

It would be incorrect to suppose, however, that Mangina faults Barth for a failure to develop a theology of the Christian life. Indeed, in his book *Karl Barth on the Christian Life*, Mangina argues precisely the opposite, that throughout his career Barth's theology includes significant insight and exposition on various aspects of the Christian life. His contention, like that of Hauerwas, is more nuanced. Specifically, although Barth can speak of the Christian life as having a distinct character, it remains unclear in his theology just how this character comes to expression in everyday life.[172] Mangina, therefore, contends for an acknowledgement of the Spirit as the subject of a distinct salvific economy, working through the practices and structures of the Christian community.[173] Such a theology will be one of discipleship, attentive to the specific means by which persons are drawn into the life of the triune God.[174] He argues that the church's practices do not exist as ends in themselves, but as the means through which the Spirit forms believers so that they 'bear the marks of Jesus'.[175] In this theology of discipleship the Christian community is the necessary matrix in which believers acquire the habits, skills and requisite formation over time that allow them to locate their lives in God in accordance with the provisions of salvation.[176]

Mangina is aware that Barth would certainly be suspicious of an emphasis on habits and virtues in individual ethics, and of talk about the practices that build up and sustain the community. Nonetheless, he endeavours to show both that Barth's construal of human agency does not exclude elaboration along these lines,[177] and also that framing ethics in concretely ecclesial terms actually helps to underscore the grounding of ethics in christology.[178] The fundamental problem arises from Barth's refusal to grant the church 'possession' of revelation or of any form of mediatorial function with regard to grace.

Mangina considers Barth's fear of a self-satisfied and complacent church justified, but that his proposed therapy was unnecessarily drastic. Rather than exclude the concept of 'sacrament' he prefers to develop a sacramentality

---

[170] Mangina, 'Bearing the Marks of Jesus,' 294.
[171] Mangina, 'Bearing the Marks of Jesus,' 280.
[172] Mangina, *The Christian Life*, 188, 184.
[173] Mangina, 'Bearing the Marks of Jesus,' 301.
[174] Mangina, 'Bearing the Marks of Jesus,' 304-305. See also James J. Buckley & David S. Yeago, eds., *Knowing the Triune God: The Work of the Spirit in the Practices of the Church* (Grand Rapids: Eerdmans, 2001).
[175] Mangina, 'Bearing the Marks of Jesus,' 271.
[176] Mangina, 'Bearing the Marks of Jesus,' 297.
[177] Mangina, *The Christian Life*, 192.
[178] Joseph L. Mangina, 'The Stranger as Sacrament: Karl Barth and the Ethics of Ecclesial Practice,' *International Journal of Systematic Theology* 1, no. 3 (1999): 325.

oriented around the gospel story and the call to discipleship. Far from giving the church free rein to pursue its own course, these actions bind the community in memory and hope to the story of the crucified Saviour.[179] Arguing that the church is constituted by the Spirit's work in and through Word and sacrament, Mangina suggests that 'the turn to ecclesial practice as a locus for ethics need not mean a loss of the christological centre, but a situating of christology in a wider trinitarian context'.[180]

It is evident in each of the critiques by Healy, Hütter and Mangina, that Barth's ordering of ecclesiology and pneumatology to christology is viewed as inadequate for the establishment of a viable sense of ecclesial and Christian existence. Also problematic for each of these theologians is the way in which Barth's actualism impacts his ecclesiology by forcing a distinction between the so-called 'real' church, and its historical appearance. These two factors remove the possibility of the church acting as a mediator of divine grace, or in Jenson's phrase, as 'an active *mediatrix* of faith'.[181] This, of course, was precisely Barth's intent. But, is this criticism warranted? Do these dogmatic moves undertaken by Barth actually serve to render the formation of moral community technically impossible?

Pneumatology (and further treatment of ecclesiology?) was, of course, precisely that aspect of Barth's work which were to occupy him in the unfinished volume of the *Church Dogmatics*. In a sense it is unfair to register a full complaint against Barth for what he did not live to complete. Certainly there are many instances where Barth indeed employs idioms which suggest a non-agential understanding of the Spirit. Hunsinger is almost certainly correct, however, in his astute observation that

> Barth's chosen idiom is appropriate to the doctrine of reconciliation, where he understands the accomplishment of reconciliation in a thoroughly christocentric way. One would expect the other, more agential idiom (which recurs throughout the *Dogmatics*) to have re-emerged prominently in the doctrine of redemption.[182]

Even Hunsinger, though, questions the adequacy of Barth's account. In a brief essay, Hunsinger provides a succinct overview of the thoroughly christocentric nature of Barth's ecclesiology. In the essay he notes that Barth prefers to speak about a correspondence between Christ and the church more often than about their coinherence: 'as the church bears witness to Christ, he will typically say, Christ also bears witness to himself'. This language, however, tends to emphasize the distinction between Christ and the church at the expense of their unity. Hunsinger would prefer to speak in terms of

---

[179] Mangina, 'The Stranger as Sacrament,' 339.

[180] Mangina, 'The Stranger as Sacrament,' 339.

[181] Jenson, 'You Wonder Where,' 303.

[182] George Hunsinger, *Disruptive Grace: Studies in the Theology of Karl Barth* (Grand Rapids: Eerdmans, 2000), 161.

coinherence:

> If we say, as Barth of course will also sometimes say, that Christ bears witness to
> himself *in* and *through* his community, or more strongly, that Christ takes form *in*
> and *through* his community, then the emphasis shifts to seeing the community as a
> vessel of coinherence, participation and mediation. In Barth this emphasis is not
> sustained. This is precisely an emphasis that ecumenical ecclesiology needs to
> sustain, however, if it is to reconcile the idea of the church as witness with that of
> the church as sacrament.[183]

Hunsinger, then, like Mangina, wants to view the church in terms of
mediation, although with a more obvious christocentric emphasis. Hunsinger
follows Barth more closely with an insistence that neither the divine life, nor
grace, nor the gift of the Holy Spirit reaches us apart from the self-mediation of
Christ, for Christ is himself the *res* inclusive of all other relevant
designations.[184] Nonetheless, he offers a possible correction of Barth's theology
predicated on an analogy with Jesus Christ as the one true Word of God.
Hunsinger appeals to Barth's doctrine of the threefold form of the Word of
God, and suggests that there is no compelling reason why Jesus Christ could
not be the one true sacrament Barth insists upon while yet allowing also for
secondary and dependent sacramental forms.[185] In this construal, baptism and
eucharist, as 'visible words,' would correspond to the Word of God in the form
of proclamation. When considering which form of sacrament might correspond
to Holy Scripture, Hunsinger suggests that the church as sacrament would seem
the obvious candidate.[186]

Hunsinger argues further that witness and mediation are not, as Barth
suggested, mutually exclusive concepts, but are in fact mutually
complementary representing respectively the 'upward' and the 'downward'
vectors of the divine-human relation. The secondary forms of Word and
sacrament witness to the primary form *and* provide the instrument by means of
which the grace of the primary form is mediated and imparted to faith.[187] Of
course, the secondary forms of Word and sacrament have no capacity in
themselves to witness to and mediate the grace of the primary form, but do so
only by virtue of grace alone.

These moves by Hunsinger suggest that Barth's theology may be amenable
to a more robust and concrete ecclesiology and theology of discipleship without
compromising his christocentric commitment. Place is also reserved for the

---

[183] George Hunsinger, *The Church as Witness* (Center for Barth Studies, 2001 [cited
December 21 2001]); available from <http//www.ptsem.edu/grow/barth>.
[184] George Hunsinger, 'Baptism and the Soteriology of Forgiveness,' *International
Journal of Systematic Theology* 2, no. 3 (2000): 265.
[185] Hunsinger, 'Baptism,' 255.
[186] Hunsinger, 'Baptism,' 255.
[187] Hunsinger, 'Baptism,' 258.

Holy Spirit whose work it is to mediate 'the *koinonia*-relation (mutual indwelling) between Christ and the sacramental element, who brings this visible Word to faith and faith to this visible Word, and who mediates the union and communion with Christ that thereby ensues'.[188]

Finally, Hunsinger's proposal allows the development of a sacramental ecclesiology in which the church and its ministry are granted a significant mediatorial role within the divine economy while also avoiding two concerns recently raised by Healy. While he is appreciative of the renewed emphasis on practices, Healy is concerned that the 'new ecclesiologies' threaten to restrict the freedom of the Holy Spirit by tying his activity too closely to the practices of the church, and to confuse sanctification with performance of the practices themselves rather than with concrete obedience to Christ. In a remarkable echo of Biggar's critique of Hauerwas, Healy insists that 'the Spirit not only works within the church's traditions and practices, but also apart from them and even, at times, over against them' and that finally, 'it is our obedience to Christ that trumps all other virtues, practices, precepts and principles'.[189]

Conclusion

This chapter set out to accomplish two objectives. First, it sought to demonstrate that study of Barth's ethics must be predicated on a reading of his work that takes seriously his own concerns, commitments and methodology. Failure to attend to this basic exegetical task will result in a misunderstanding of his rhetoric, and misrepresentation of his conclusions. Second, this chapter sought to indicate the kinds of responses Barth's work with respect to ecclesiology and Christian life has engendered. Serious questions regarding the adequacy of Barth's ecclesial vision have been raised by competent, sympathetic interpreters of his work. The primary questions concern the manner in which Barth subsumes pneumatology and ecclesiology under the aegis of christology, and the implications of his actualistic doctrine of revelation, both of which, charge his critics, result in an abstract ecclesiology. As a result of his thoroughgoing commitment to preserve the sovereign freedom of divine grace, Barth has, so his critics allege, failed to provide a viable account of the church and Christian life. In his account the reality of the church as a distinct work of the Holy Spirit in the temporal realm is marginalised, with the corresponding loss of a concrete description and duration of Christian life and discipleship.

Clearly, and not unreasonably, the critiques of Barth surveyed above have focussed predominantly on his theology as set forth in the *Church Dogmatics*. Nonetheless, I have pointed out that Barth's motivation for writing the *Dogmatics* was driven, at least in part, by a concern for the very existence of

---

[188] Hunsinger, 'Baptism,' 263.

[189] Healy, 'Practices and the New Ecclesiology,' 295, 299, 306.

the church as *church*. I have also suggested that this primary motive underlay the development and structure of Barth's theology from the earliest days of his career after breaking with the liberal tradition. In the next chapter I take up this suggestion in earnest by focussing on the reasons for Barth's dispute with his heritage, his relationship with socialism vis-à-vis the church, and by undertaking an examination of his initial theological explorations after he began the reorientation of his theology.

CHAPTER 2

IN SEARCH OF A NEW WORLD

> How we cleared things away! And we did almost nothing but clear away! Everything which even remotely smacked of mysticism and morality, of pietism and romanticism, or even of idealism, was suspected and sharply interdicted or bracketed with reservations which sounded actually prohibitive![1]

T. F. Torrance labels the period following 1915 as one of great importance, ferment and discovery for Karl Barth.[2] In this initial period of his career, Barth is not so much constructing a new theology as he is disentangling and reorienting his theology from that theology which had dominated European Protestantism since at least the time of Schleiermacher, and investigating the lines upon which a new theology might be developed. Driven by his need to preach each week to his parishioners in Safenwil, and by what he perceived to be the failure both of liberalism and socialism, Barth's intensive biblical and theological studies eventually issued in a renewed awareness of divine sovereignty over against all human existence and activity.

This chapter explores Barth's theological development in the period immediately following the outbreak of World War I up to early 1917. The first section provides an overview of Barth's dispute with his liberal heritage and argues that it was the *ethical* failure of his theological mentors that sent him in search of a new theology. The second section examines Barth's relationship with Religious Socialism during this period, together with his somewhat ambivalent relationship with the church. This section shows that the reason for this ambivalence was the political indifference which was generally characteristic of the church, and that Barth found in socialism a prophetic challenge to the church, which demanded that the praxis of the church be reformulated to include a social and ethical dimension. These first two sections provide a brief orientation to the historical context in which Barth's new theology was taking shape, and strongly suggest the prominence of ethical factors in his development. Following this orientation to the early Barth, three of his works are examined in detail, namely his two lectures on 'The Righteousness of God' and 'The Strange New World in the Bible,' as well as a short book review entitled 'Auf das Reich Gottes warten' ('Waiting for the

---

[1] Karl Barth, *The Humanity of God* (trans. J. Weiser & J. N. Thomas; Louisville: John Knox, 1960), 43.

[2] Thomas F. Torrance, *Karl Barth: An Introduction to His Early Theology 1910-1931* (Edinburgh: T. & T. Clark, 1962), 16.

Kingdom of God'). These works clearly show that not only is the view that Barth did not give place for a valid ethics or ecclesiology in this period incorrect, but also that the major themes of his mature thought in these areas were already present in germinal form.

Karl Barth's Dispute with Liberalism

On the Eve of War

Bruce McCormack suggests that Barth's turning point came sometime after April 1915, and that during the course of the following summer, evidence emerged that Barth had now adopted a new *Ansatz*—a new starting-point for theological reflection.[3] In distinction to the theology he had been trained in, Barth began to conceive of God standing over against the 'godless' world as a reality complete in himself, radically calling all human existence and endeavour into question. This turning point, however, was not without ample preparation in preceding years, most particularly his encounter with the misery of the working classes which occurred after his first appointment as a minister to Geneva in 1909, and especially, his appointment to the Safenwil pastorate in 1911. McCormack notes that 'if Barth's disappointments over the ethical failure of his theological teachers was the impetus which sent him in search of a *new theology*, his search for a *new world* had been set in motion much earlier'.[4]

Already prior to the outbreak of the first world war Barth had become estranged from the ethos and liberal world of his theological instructors.[5] Reflecting on his own beginnings from the vantage of later years, Barth recalls that

> [a]lthough in Geneva I had still lived completely and utterly in the religious atmosphere which I brought with me from Marburg...when I moved to the industrial village of Safenwil, my interest in theology as such had to step back noticeably into second place....Because of the situation I found in my community,

---

[3] Bruce L. McCormack, *Karl Barth's Critically Realistic Dialectical Theology: Its Genesis and Development 1909-1936* (Oxford: Oxford University Press, 1995), 123-124. I am indebted to McCormack's magisterial account for much of what follows.

[4] McCormack, *Karl Barth's Dialectical Theology*, 79.

[5] Christophe Chalamet has argued that it is inaccurate to portray Barth as a thorough-going liberal, even in the period prior to World War I. As a student of Herrmann, Barth had learned well the methodological necessity of a dialectical theology if theology was to provide a faithful account of its subject matter. Chalamet presents several lines of evidence to demonstrate that even prior to World War I, Barth criticised and articulated perspectives from both the right and the left of the theological spectrum. See Christophe Chalamet, *Dialectical Theologians: Wilhelm Herrmann, Karl Barth and Rudolph Bultmann* (Zürich: Theologischer Verlag Zürich, 2005), 65, 70, 72, 74, 79-80.

I became passionately involved with socialism and especially with the trade union movement.[6]

During the Safenwil years Barth gave no fewer than forty-three addresses on socialist themes, and in his early period there also drew the ire of members of his congregation on account of his 'socialist sermons'.[7] His socialism, however, was clearly not Marxist, but rather emphasised the necessity of first creating new men and women in order then to create a new and just order. The new world would be the product of a new ethos.[8]

In a lecture delivered six months after his arrival in Safenwil, Karl Barth sought to show that Christian faith and a commitment to socialism were not incompatible.[9] In the lecture, where Barth first uses the expression 'the new world,'[10] he insists that the kingdom 'is not *of* this world, but of God. It is *in* this world, however, for *in* this world God's will is to be done.'[11] In a sermon given to his church Barth remonstrates:

> It is not only 'we,' that is to say, our souls, our inner and personal life which must become light. Rather, the world must become light. We must not separate the two from one another. Unbelief is hidden in this separation.…Where do you get the right to set yourself apart in this way, as if God's actions were directed to you alone?…We must acquire for ourselves that holy sense of solidarity which bears

---

[6] See Barth's 'Concluding Unscientific Postscript on Schleiermacher,' in Karl Barth, *The Theology of Schleiermacher: Lectures at Göttingen Winter Semester of 1923/24* (trans. G. W. Bromiley; Edinburgh: T. & T. Clark, 1982), 263. Also relevant here is Busch's account of Barth's time in Geneva (see Eberhard Busch, *Karl Barth: His Life from Letters and Autobiographical Texts* (trans. J. Bowden; Philadelphia: Fortress, 1976), 52-59). Busch notes that Barth spent a great deal of time in pastoral visitation and relief work amongst the poor. Nonetheless, Busch also shows that Barth's preaching at this time was thoroughly in accordance with the theology of Marburg, and especially Herrmann. See also McCormack, *Karl Barth's Dialectical Theology*, 80.

[7] McCormack, *Karl Barth's Dialectical Theology*, 86 n.23, 92.

[8] McCormack, *Karl Barth's Dialectical Theology*, 89. McCormack does concede, however, that although Barth differed from the Marxists in terms of tactics, 'with regard to the goal, Barth was very close to the Marxists indeed'. In a radio programme recorded shortly before his death Barth insisted that he 'was never a doctrinaire socialist' and that his interest in socialism 'was very limited and for the most part practical'. See Karl Barth, *Final Testimonies* (trans. G. W. Bromiley; Grand Rapids: Eerdmans, 1977), 39.

[9] Karl Barth, 'Jesus Christ and the Movement for Social Justice,' in G. Hunsinger, ed., *Karl Barth and Radical Politics* (Philadelphia: Westminster, 1976). The lecture was delivered on December 17, 1911.

[10] Barth, 'Jesus Christ and the Movement for Social Justice,' 28.

[11] Barth, 'Jesus Christ and the Movement for Social Justice,' 27.

the suffering of the world in its heart, not in order to sigh and shake our heads over it, but rather to take it in hand so that it will be otherwise.[12]

A departure from the interiority and individualism that characterised his earlier sermons at Geneva can already be seen in this sermon and his earlier lecture on 'Jesus Christ and the Movement for Social Justice'.[13] In these addresses Barth, in a conscious repudiation of Harnack's view of the kingdom, insists that the internal change effected by the presence of the kingdom of God in the human soul must seek expression in external relations.[14]

Other divergences from the theology of his instructors can also be detected in these years. In an examination of Barth's sermons of 1913 McCormack highlights various themes which are often thought to have only arisen during the so-called 'dialectical phase' of his theology, but which also demonstrate that Barth had already drifted considerably from the theology of his Marburg days. He includes Barth's emphasis on the judgement and wrath of God, his criticism of religion, and the 'wholly otherness' of God.[15] Nonetheless, these various divergences and repudiations do not indicate Barth's break with liberal theology. Rather, they constitute an insider's critique of liberalism. Methodologically, Barth was still heavily indebted to Herrmann.[16]

Ethics in Crisis

It was the outbreak of World War I, and particularly the religious justification for it, which led finally to Barth's turn from the theology of his liberal forebears. In a letter to his lifelong friend and confidant Eduard Thurneysen, Barth's dismay is almost palpable:

---

[12] Cited in McCormack, *Karl Barth's Dialectical Theology*, 96. The sermon was given on February 23, 1913.

[13] For examples of the content of Barth's addresses from his Geneva period see Busch, *Karl Barth*, 53-54.

[14] McCormack, *Karl Barth's Dialectical Theology*, 89-91. Again, Barth himself notes, 'The concept of "God's kingdom" was portrayed in various ways...but certainly no longer in the form familiar to us from Ritschl and his followers' (Barth, *The Theology of Schleiermacher*, 263). For more on Harnack's view, see the discussion that follows in the next section.

[15] McCormack, *Karl Barth's Dialectical Theology*, 92-104. See also Barth's famous 'On the Sinking of the Titanic' (April 21, 1912) in *The Word in this World: Two Sermons by Karl Barth* (ed. Kurt I. Johanson; Vancouver: Regent College Publishing, 2007), 29-42.

[16] McCormack, *Karl Barth's Dialectical Theology*, 91. McCormack cites Barth's understanding of revelation, christology, anthropology and soteriology as thoroughly Herrmannian and Ritschlian at this point in time (103-104). See also Joseph L. Mangina, *Karl Barth on the Christian Life: The Practical Knowledge of God* (New York: Peter Lang, 2001), 24, and Chalamet, *Dialectical Theologians*, 73-79.

The unconditional truths of the gospel are simply suspended for the time being and in the meantime a German war-theology is put to work....Here is sufficient proof that the 'truths' were nothing more than a surface varnish and not an inmost possession of this *Christian Welt* Christianity. It is truly sad! Marburg and German civilization have lost something in my eyes by this breakdown, and indeed forever.[17]

This sense of pathos continued with Barth throughout his life. Four decades later he reflects:

At this point some of us were appalled after we, along with everyone else, had drained the different chalices of this theology to the last drop. We then concluded (from approximately the middle of the second decade of our century on) that we could not side with it any longer. Why?...Was it—*this has played a decisive role for me personally*—precisely the failure of the ethics of the modern theology of the time, with the outbreak of the First World War, which caused us to grow puzzled also about its exegesis, its treatment of history, and its dogmatics?[18]

One day in early August 1914 stands out in my personal memory as a black day. Ninety-three German intellectuals impressed public opinion by their proclamation in support of the war policy of Wilhelm II and his counsellors....I suddenly realized that I could not any longer follow either their ethics and dogmatics or their understanding of the Bible and of history. For me at least, 19th-century theology no longer held any future.[19]

These oft-cited recollections show the degree to which in his own mind Barth's dispute with liberalism was finally occasioned because of *both* the ethical *and* the theological failure of his teachers; indeed, it was their *ethical* failure which revealed their theological weakness. For Barth, his teachers had been hopelessly compromised by what he regarded as their failure in the face of

---

[17] John D. Smart, ed., *Revolutionary Theology in the Making: Barth-Thurneysen Correspondence, 1914-1925* (London: Epworth, 1964), 26. The letter is dated September 4, 1914. *Christian World* was a German theological magazine edited by Martin Rade who chose Barth as assistant editor in the year following the completion of his studies (1908-09 academic year).

[18] Karl Barth, 'The Humanity of God,' in *The Humanity of God* (Louisville: John Knox Press, 1956), 40, emphasis added. The statement was made in a lecture given September 25, 1956.

[19] Karl Barth, 'Evangelical Theology in the Nineteenth Century,' in *The Humanity of God* (Louisville: John Knox Press, 1960), 14. From a lecture given January 8, 1957. See also Barth, *The Theology of Schleiermacher*, 263-264: 'An entire world of theological exegesis, ethics, dogmatics, and preaching, which up to that point I had accepted as basically credible, was thereby shaken to the foundations, and with it everything which flowed at that time from the pens of the German theologians.' Note that the public declaration of the German intellectuals occurred on October 3, 1914, and not early August, as Barth recalls (McCormack, *Karl Barth's Dialectical Theology*, 112).

the crisis and the ideology of war. Their ethical failure indicated that their exegetical and dogmatic presuppositions could not be in order.[20] If Barth's later reflections are reliable, it indicates that the unity which he later developed in his thought between dogmatics and ethics was already at work in this early period. Gollwitzer suggests as much:

> The 'unity of dogmatics and ethics' is nothing but the theological program for the knowledge practiced in Safenwil: God is concerned about the kingdom of God; the kingdom of God is the true socialism; therefore, the socialist movement is a 'reflection' of God's kingdom....This he had not heard from Wilhelm Herrmann; this was the deepest break with Marburg. The break with Marburg occurred not only because there Wilhelm II's war was acclaimed and the treaty with the Armenian-murdering Turks defended, but even more because there the separation between dogmatics and ethics was ratified.[21]

Only one of Barth's former teachers had not signed the terrible manifesto: the 'honourable Martin Rade'.[22] Yet even Rade argued that God was the only possible ground and author of the heartfelt unity experienced by the German people during the first days of the war. He further argued that Barth, as a Swiss neutral, would have difficulty understanding the German people precisely because of his lack of 'the experience of war'.[23] When Barth noted Herrmann's signature on the document affirming Wilhelm II he wrote in dismay:

> Especially with you, Herr Professor...we learned to acknowledge 'experience' as the constitutive principle of knowing and doing in the domain of religion....Now, however, in answer to our doubts, an 'experience' which is completely new to us is held out to us by German Christians, an allegedly religious war 'experience;' i.e. the fact that German Christians 'experience' their war as a holy war is supposed to bring us to silence, if not demand reverence from us. Where do you stand in relation to this argument and to the war theology which lies behind it?[24]

---

[20] Busch, *Karl Barth*, 81.

[21] H. Gollwitzer, 'Kingdom of God and Socialism in the Theology of Karl Barth,' in *Karl Barth and Radical Politics* (ed. G. Hunsinger; Philadelphia: Westminster, 1976), 85. Gollwitzer affirms Barth's later explication of the unity of Gospel and Law as but 'a theologically clarified resumption of the unity perceived in Safenwil between kingdom of God and socialism' (86).

[22] Busch, *Karl Barth*, 81.

[23] Rade to Barth September (Oct?) 5, 1914, cited in McCormack, *Karl Barth's Dialectical Theology*, 113.

[24] Barth to Herrmann November 4, 1914, cited in McCormack, *Karl Barth's Dialectical Theology*, 113. Chalamet's note that 'Herrmann's radical distinction between God and the world was sometimes put into brackets when it came to the theme of religious experience' is particularly apt in this instance. See Chalamet, *Dialectical Theologians*, 92.

Barth understood the war not as holy, but as wholly unholy, as the culmination of decades of armaments and fear, of immense ambition and jealousy and pride. 'All of these things,' he proclaimed, 'are completely alien to the innermost being of God. And if they nevertheless take place, then there is only one explanation for it: the innermost being of God is also completely alien to humankind.'[25]

It is at this point, as Barth begins to question that which previously had been unquestioned—the role of religious experience in humanity's knowledge of God—that his decisive shift commences. Initially, as his letter to Herrmann shows, he was concerned with what he perceived to be the blatant manipulation of the concept of religious experience. If religious experience could be used as a foundation for the German *Kriegstheologie* (war theology) it was no longer reliable as an adequate ground and starting point for theology.[26] Over the next several months Barth's reflections led him to the point where he could no longer align himself with the theology he had received. On June 19, 1915 Barth wrote a letter to Rade in which the first evidence of his new theological starting point is discerned. Barth claimed that in Jesus a new world had broken into this one, calling into question everything human. The ethical response of Germany's theological elite had precipitated for Barth a crisis of ethics. All at once, the central question of ethics—*What should we do?*—had become exceedingly problematic.[27]

This all-too-brief account of Barth's dispute with theological liberalism is crucial, not only for this present work, but also if Barth's theology as a whole is to be properly understood, particularly in view of the many criticisms of Barth that suggest that his theology, not only in this period but throughout his life, was constructed in such a way as to exclude the realm of the ethical. From the very beginning Barth's theology is ethical, and conversely, his ethics are theological. As Barth continued his reflections it became apparent to him that 'the entire theology which had unmasked itself in that manifesto, and everything which followed after it (even in the *Christliche Welt*), was grounded, determined, and influenced decisively by him [i.e. Schleiermacher]'.[28] There could be no question of following that way and that theology any longer.[29]

---

[25] Barth, Sermon, September 6, 1914, cited in McCormack, *Karl Barth's Dialectical Theology*, 115.

[26] McCormack, *Karl Barth's Dialectical Theology*, 113.

[27] McCormack, *Karl Barth's Dialectical Theology*, 124.

[28] Barth, *The Theology of Schleiermacher*, 264.

[29] It is necessary to note that Barth's dispute with the liberal theology of his mentors is not to be understood in an absolute sense of complete discontinuity with what had gone before, but in the relative sense that he could no longer accept a fundamental equation between revelation and human religious experience. The relative sense, which allows for both continuity and discontinuity between the theology of the pre-WWI and post-war Barth, is the way in which I use the language of Barth's 'break' with liberal theology.

The Young Socialist Pastor

Barth's political affinities and his relationship to socialism have stimulated enormous scholarly interest, especially since the publication of Marquardt's controversial *Theologie und Sozialismus* in 1972.[30] In the previous section I noted in passing that Barth had given a lecture in December 1911 on 'Jesus and the Movement for Social Justice,' and that his so-called 'socialist sermons' had created a level of controversy in his pastorate. In this section I will examine Barth's relationship to socialism during this turbulent period because of the important light it sheds on his developing ecclesial and ethical commitment and thought.

A Matter of Praxis

In late 1915 Barth delivered a lecture entitled 'Religion and Socialism' in which the transition in his thinking becomes apparent.[31] His major concern in this lecture was the kingdom of God by which he meant simply that 'God is living, that God rules and will rule.'[32] Barth insists that although God's lordship is already established, it has yet to be universally acknowledged. Nonetheless, 'everything made, artificial, untrue must give way to that which is original'.[33] Basic motifs of Barth's later theology are present in the lecture, including his theological criticism of religion, and his celebrated phrase 'The world is the

---

Also note Chalamet's contention that the expression 'reorientation' is a more appropriate term than 'break' to describe Barth's relation with theological liberalism after the outbreak of the war, and his corollary assertion that 'there was no "break".' McCormack, as we have seen, is quite prepared to speak of this movement in Barth's life in terms of a 'break.' See Chalamet, *Dialectical Theologians*, 89-90, and McCormack, *Karl Barth's Dialectical Theology*, 123-125.

[30] Friedrich-Wilhelm Marquardt, *Theologie und Sozialismus: Das Beispiel Karl Barths* (München: Chr. Kaiser Verlag, 1972). The literature here is substantial. For further understanding and commentary on the debate that arose around Marquardt's thesis, see particularly, George Hunsinger, ed., *Karl Barth and Radical Politics* (Philadelphia: Westminster, 1976). Jüngel's response to Marquardt's thesis is found in Eberhard Jüngel, *Karl Barth: A Theological Legacy* (trans. G. E. Paul; Philadelphia: Westminster, 1986), 14, 32, 82-104. Also valuable is Gerhard Sauter, 'Shifts in Karl Barth's Thought: The Current Debate between Right- and Left-Wing Barthians,' in *Eschatological Rationality: Theological Issues in Focus* (Grand Rapids: Baker, 1996), 111-135. See additionally McCormack's important discussion of the impact of political factors on Barth's theological development in McCormack, *Karl Barth's Dialectical Theology*, 78-125, 184-203.

[31] The lecture was delivered in Baden on December 7, 1915 at a socialist gathering. I am indebted to McCormack, *Karl Barth's Dialectical Theology*, 131-132, and especially to Jüngel, *Karl Barth*, 89-97, for the following discussion of this speech.

[32] Cited in McCormack, *Karl Barth's Dialectical Theology*, 131.

[33] Cited in McCormack, *Karl Barth's Dialectical Theology*, 131.

world. But God is God.'[34] The kingdom itself may not be identified with either religion or socialism, but these may signify it. Both are reflections or symptoms of the kingdom in the world, among many other such reflections in the realms of nature and history.[35] Barth is careful to subordinate both religion and socialism to the kingdom of God because both are thoroughly human in their nature, and are therefore subject to human frailty and aberration, and as such, are also at best, ambiguous reflections of the kingdom.[36] This distinction between the kingdom of God and socialism constitutes a revision of the position expressed in December 1911 when Barth was able to affirm that

> Jesus *is* the movement for social justice, and the movement for social justice *is* Jesus in the present....I really believe that the social justice movement...is not only the greatest and most urgent word of God to the present, but also in particular a quite direct continuation of the spiritual power which, as I said, entered into history and life with Jesus.[37]

It is precisely the continuity between God and humanity implied in this assertion that Barth now wishes to oppose.[38] The reasons for Barth's change of perspective lie close to hand. Not only did the support of his theological teachers for the war policies of Wilhelm II convince him of the inadequacy of their theology and ethics, but he was also disappointed, indeed 'completely flabbergasted' with the capitulation of the socialist movement in the face of the ideology of war: 'From *Sie Müssen* we had more or less definitely expected that socialism would prove to be a kind of hammer of God, yet all along the national war fronts we saw it swinging into line.'[39]

Neither the failure of socialism, however, nor the impossibility of its identification with the kingdom of God, rendered it irrelevant to the progress of God's kingdom. Rather, socialism remained a sign that God was still very

---

[34] Jüngel, *Karl Barth*, 31. Note that McCormack's research, already mentioned, shows that Jüngel's claim that this constitutes the first appearance of Barth's theological criticism of religion is, in fact, incorrect. McCormack does assert, however, that criticism of religion became a *central* feature of Barth's concerns at this time. See McCormack, *Karl Barth's Dialectical Theology*, 131.

[35] Jüngel, *Karl Barth*, 90.

[36] Jüngel, *Karl Barth*, 90.

[37] Barth, 'Jesus Christ and the Movement for Social Justice,' 19-20.

[38] Barth's thought in 1911 maintained a Herrmannian orbit as the citation indicates. At that time Barth was not rejecting the fundamental presuppositions of Herrmann's theology, as much as applying them to the public arena of history as a kind of 'social existentialism' (see Mangina, *The Christian Life*, 24). Now, in 1915, Barth has broken, as we have seen, with those fundamental presuppositions.

[39] Cited in Busch, *Karl Barth*, 82. *Sie Müssen* had been published in 1903 by Zürich pastor Herrmann Kutter. McCormack describes the book as the spark which birthed the Swiss Religious Socialist movement. See McCormack, *Karl Barth's Dialectical Theology*, 83.

much at work in the world; indeed, more so here than in the field of religion.[40] According to Jüngel, Barth's ethical concern at this juncture is evident. While according equal status to both religion and socialism as reflections of God's kingdom, he nevertheless assigns a certain preference to socialism. The great fault of religion is its political indifference, its failure to strive toward the kind of earth-shaking praxis in which human work corresponds to God's work. Because socialism strives for this, at least in principle, it corresponds more closely to the kingdom and thus is preferred to religion. The fact that socialism was often hostile toward Christianity did not bother Barth: he considers it safer and better to stand with God alongside the godless rather than to stand against them without God.[41]

Jüngel notes that in this lecture Barth is seeking a 'worldly praxis,' indeed an 'earth-shaking' praxis. It is not sufficient to simply enter into discourse about God as religion is wont to do. Discourse about God must be accompanied by an engagement in the worldly affairs of the common life if it is to be a genuine sign of the work and the rule of God's kingdom.

Barth's criticism is directed against forms of Christianity which conduct themselves in isolation to the realities of social existence. It is likely that Barth has both liberal and conservative forms of Christianity in view with these criticisms. With regard to the former, Barth plainly rejects Harnack's insistence that the gospel is above all questions of mundane development, concerned not with material things but with the souls of humanity. Commenting on Jesus' words, 'My kingdom is not of this world', Harnack insists that 'it is no earthly kingdom that the Gospel establishes. These words…forbid all direct and formal interference of religion in worldly affairs.'[42] With regard to the latter, Barth also rejects the kind of religion envisaged purely as a private or inward matter, and concerned with individualised experience, salvation and blessedness.[43]

---

[40] Busch, *Karl Barth*, 88.

[41] Jüngel, *Karl Barth*, 92-93.

[42] Adolph von Harnack, *What is Christianity?* (trans. T. B. Saunders; New York: Harper & Brothers, 1957), 115-116. Harnack is addressing precisely socialist action on behalf of gaining 'rights' for the working classes. He does not forbid such action, and even encourages it, but only with a caveat: 'but do not let us expect the Gospel to afford us any direct help' (116). It is also possible that Barth has the radical inwardness advocated by Herrmann in his sights. Mangina states that 'the radical turn inward encouraged by Herrmann looked like a retreat from the public world'. See Mangina, *The Christian Life*, 20.

[43] See Eberhard Busch, *Karl Barth and the Pietists: The Young Karl Barth's Critique of Pietism and Its Response* (trans. Daniel W. Bloesch; Downers Grove: Inter-Varsity Press, 2004), 26-30 for an important discussion of Barth's relation to Pietism in this period. Busch also makes the valuable observation that Barth found significant material similarities between the experiential theology of the conservative Pietists and of the liberal Herrmann. Busch indicates that Barth's criticism of 'religion' in this period is directed primarily against 'religious individualism', and as such was not limited only to

For Barth, praxis is human work which corresponds in some measure to God's work. In his lecture Barth speaks of religion and socialism as symptoms and indications (*Anzeichen*) of the kingdom. Neither, as we have seen, may claim identity with the kingdom, but rather both function as witnesses to the kingdom. To the extent, therefore, that religion—whether liberal or conservative—fails in its responsibility to bear witness to God's activity in the world its witness is compromised.

It would appear, then, that in this lecture Barth marginalises the church. He looks for the work of God outside and beyond religion, and thus, by way of metonymy, outside and beyond the church. Again, however, this is not to suggest that the failure of the church renders it irrelevant to the progress of God's kingdom, or that for Barth, its marginalisation is absolute. Indeed, Barth commences the lecture with a joyful avowal: 'I am glad to be a pastor.' Barth's sense of joy is derived from the 'great cause' he served, a cause which also allowed him to become a socialist, precisely because he saw that the kingdom of God was reflected in the world apart from religion.[44]

It seems likely, however, that Barth's marginalising of the church was a deliberate rhetorical ploy employed in view of the audience he was addressing. In a letter to Thurneysen dated December 7, 1914, Barth writes that

> [o]ur difficulty in addressing the Social Democrats became clear to me once more: either one strengthens them in their party loyalty by providing a religious foundation and all manner of Christian aims for their political ethos—or one tries to lead them out beyond themselves and thereby, as I had the impression yesterday, one lays upon them a burden which is too heavy for many of them to bear. In spite of everything, the latter is the right thing to do if one is going to give such lectures at all. Indeed I hold it to be certainly the right one if the question is asked.[45]

It is clear in this statement that Barth's intent in providing lectures for socialists was to lead them beyond the pale of materialistic socialism into a

---

the conservative forms of Christianity. For an account of religious individualism in Herrmann see Hendrikus Berkhof, *Two Hundred Years of Theology: Report of a Personal Journey* (trans. J. Vriend; Grand Rapids: Eerdmans, 1989), 143-150, and Mangina, *The Christian Life*, 15-20. In addition, Busch provides an indication of Barth's understanding of 'religion' in this period by referring to a sermon delivered to his Safenwil congregation on October 9, 1917. In this sermon Barth categorises religion as merely a 'private matter', the salvation of the 'individual soul' and as personal experience. It is mere 'inwardness' and 'attitude', 'an emotional condition'. People remain in religion 'as in a thick tank turret' because it is, in some sense at least, 'comfortable'. Busch concludes: 'In Barth's view, what makes a smashing of the tank turret necessary is the simple fact that religion is out of touch with reality and passes life by' (28-29).
[44] Jüngel, *Karl Barth*, 89.
[45] Smart, *Revolutionary Theology*, 27.

broader reality in which their praxis was linked with the movement of God in history. Jüngel cites an unpublished sketch dated August 12, 1915, in which Barth argues that if socialism is to have a future, it must recognise the category of 'spirit' and recover its essence, which is the quest for justice for all people. Further, says Barth, it must not draw its strength from the struggle for political and economic power, but from an entirely different source.[46] In this paper Barth, unfortunately, does not specify what this source is. Nonetheless, the attitude reflected in the letter cited above indicates that he is thinking of the way of 'Jesus and his disciples'. Thus, although Barth appears to marginalise the church in this lecture, it is likely that he seeks to lead his socialist listeners into a relation of faith in God without the loss their distinctive praxis.

Nonetheless, a certain tension is apparent in Barth's ecclesial thought at this point. On the one hand, Barth views religion in terms of Schleiermacher's *Gefühl*, as bound to the human world, as a human response to God in the realm of piety rather than concrete praxis in service of the coming kingdom.[47] It is precisely this privatised form of piety which led the church to its inferior form of praxis. On the other hand, this is not the way things should be, and Barth reacts against this form of piety and praxis. It is not that the concept of religion (and thus church) is inherently wrong, but that the form of praxis is inadequate. Barth is convinced that faithfulness to God must include that kind of 'earth-shaking praxis' that corresponds to God's own work. Thus, in a letter to Thurneysen he gives his reason for joining the Social Democratic Party:

> Just because I set such emphasis Sunday by Sunday upon the last things, it was no longer possible for me personally to remain suspended in the clouds above the present evil world but rather it had to be demonstrated here and now that *faith in the Greatest does not exclude but rather includes within it work and suffering in the realm of the imperfect*…And I myself hope now to avoid becoming unfaithful to our 'essential' orientation as might very well have happened to me had I taken this step two years ago.[48]

This statement indicates that Barth's political engagements issued from his conviction that faithfulness to God and correspondence to the movement of God in history demanded such engagement. Precisely because of his pastoral role Barth felt constrained to model for his parishioners the unity of faith and

---

[46] Jüngel, *Karl Barth*, 88-89. The sketch, *Die innere Zukunft der Sozialdemokratie*, is held at the Karl Barth-Archive, Basel.

[47] In his lecture on 'Religion and Socialism' Barth outlines his view of religion: '"Religion" is a very weak and ambiguous word. *Religion* is pious feeling [*Gefühl*] in individual men and women, together with the particular morality and the particular worship which proceeds from it'—cited in McCormack, *Karl Barth's Dialectical Theology*, 131.

[48] Smart, *Revolutionary Theology*, 28, emphasis added. The letter is dated February 5, 1915.

praxis. The statement also indicates the primacy of theology over politics in Barth's thought—a disputed point in contemporary Barth studies.[49] Jüngel, for example, insists that 'for Barth, the political is surely a predicate of theology, but theology is never a predicate of the political'.[50] Gorringe, however, protests that Jüngel inverts this formula too easily: 'It is true to say that Barth's theology was never a predicate of his politics, but also true that politics is never simply a predicate of his theology. Either extreme misses the dialectical unity of theory and praxis at the heart of Barth's whole theology.'[51]

That this dialectical unity of theory and praxis was a feature of Barth's theology since his break with liberalism is affirmed by Thurneysen. In his introduction to a collection of early correspondence between himself and Barth, Thurneysen insists that from the beginning Barth's theology was directed towards the life of humanity understood

> in distinction from and in antithesis to all merely pietistic devotional thinking, not just the inner life but the inner life as the interior of an outer life, in short, man in the wholeness of his existence, man as he exists ever in a certain given time and world....Understood in this way, Karl Barth's word from the beginning was a 'political word'.[52]

Into the Church

Before bringing discussion of Barth's relationship to socialism to a close it will be instructive briefly to examine Barth's relationship with two primary leaders of Swiss Religious Socialism in this period: Herrmann Kutter and

---

[49] In 1972 Friedrich-Wilhelm Marquardt, to employ Timothy Gorringe's playful idiom, 'dropped a bomb in the playground of Barth scholarship with his claim that Barth was a lifelong socialist, and that socialist praxis was the interpretive key to Barth's theological output'. See Timothy J. Gorringe, *Karl Barth: Against Hegemony* (Oxford: Oxford University Press, 1999), 5. In Marquardt's own words, 'The real origin of Barth's theology was his theological existence in Safenwil. As such, that existence was socialist praxis.' Marquardt also locates the genesis of Barth's ecclesiology in his socialist involvement: 'This was where Barth's ecclesiology had its origin. In the thought and life of this "more than Leninist" anarchist party-comrade, who at the same time was the pastor from Safenwil, the Christian community became the agent of revolution.' See Friedrich-Wilhelm Marquardt, 'Socialism in the Theology of Karl Barth,' in *Karl Barth and Radical Politics* (ed. G. Hunsinger; Philadelphia: Westminster, 1976), 58, 56, and also page 72. While this book is not intended as an answer to Marquardt, it will become evident that the position taken here is contrary to that propounded there.

[50] Jüngel, *Karl Barth*, 104, cf. 114, 141.

[51] Gorringe, *Against Hegemony*, 9. George Hunsinger shifts the accent of the debate a little by preferring to say 'Socialism was a predicate of the *gospel*.' See Hunsinger, *Karl Barth and Radical Politics*, 11, emphasis added.

[52] Eduard Thurneysen, 'Introduction,' in *Revolutionary Theology in the Making: Barth-Thurneysen Correspondence, 1914-1925* (ed. J. D. Smart; London: Epworth, 1964), 14.

Leonhard Ragaz.[53] Although both theologians had had a formative influence on Barth since his earliest student years, and represented two options or directions that the Swiss Religious Socialist might take, Barth found it necessary in this period to move beyond them. Of the two leaders Ragaz was the more militant, a committed political activist and a passionate critic of religion. In his estimation, Christ did not want 'a religion, but rather a kingdom, a new creation, a new world'.[54] In contrast, Kutter was a more reflective personality, inclined to think in more explicitly theological or philosophical categories, more disposed towards spiritual formation, and to work primarily with pastors and 'circles of friendship' within the churches, while 'waiting' for the kingdom of God. During this period Barth began to wrestle with the relation between the church and socialism in an attempt to find a mediating position which affirmed and transcended the positions of both men. In a letter to Thurneysen he wrote, 'Isn't it better to strive for the point where Kutter's "no" and Ragaz's "yes," Kutter's radical tranquillity and Ragaz's energetic tackling of problems…come together? I believe in the possibility of such a position, even if I cannot describe it at the moment.'[55] According to Busch, however, Barth's struggle at this time led him to the very 'fringe of the church,' where at times he found the pastoral role 'extremely questionable'.[56]

In an important letter to Thurneysen in September 1915, however, Barth outlines several differences between the two socialists which he had heard in a lecture by Zürich pastor and socialist leader Hans Bader. While especially appreciative of Ragaz' concern to 'put principles into practice', Barth feels 'forced' to express a preference for Kutter's position. Especially significant is Bader's conclusion to the discussion, with which Barth appears to agree: 'Conclusion: the religious-socialist "concern" (*Sache*) is finished, the taking of God in earnest is at its beginning.'[57] Barth continues the letter by expressing a desire to implement a plan suggested by Bader: that local pastors meet fortnightly to spend a morning in Bible reading together.[58]

The significance of this correspondence is twofold. First, the supplanting of Religious Socialism by God as *die Sache* (object, subject matter) of thought indicates that there could no longer be any identification or equality between

---

[53] It is beyond my purpose here to provide a full historical discussion of the complex relationship and issues which characterised Barth's relationship to socialism. Interested readers are directed particularly to Busch, McCormack and Gorringe.

[54] Cited in Gorringe, *Against Hegemony*, 33. Note the similarity to language used by Barth.

[55] Cited in Busch, *Karl Barth*, 86.

[56] Busch, *Karl Barth*, 86.

[57] 'Schluß: Die religiössoziale "Sache" ist aus, das Ernstmachen mit Gott fängt an.' See Eduard Thurneysen, 'Die Anfänge' in *Antwort: Karl Barth zum Siebzigsten Geburtstag am 10. Mai 1956* (ed. E. Wolf, C. von Kirschbaum & R. Frey; Zürich: Evangelischer Verlag AG, 1956), 842.

[58] Smart, *Revolutionary Theology*, 30-32. The letter is dated September 8, 1915.

these two realities. Second, the correspondence shows Barth beginning to decide in favour of the church in his struggle to define the relationship between church and socialism. This provides further evidence for my suggestion that Barth's marginalising of the church in 'Religion and Socialism' is a rhetorical rather than substantive move.

In 1932 Barth would reflect on these times and his eventual 'falling out' with Ragaz:

> If we grant that there is truth in it, that the modern world, and perhaps Socialism in particular, has something decisive to say to the church...*the only result of the encounter must be that the Church, recognizing God's voice in this alien voice from without, lets itself be called to itself thereby,* lets itself be reminded of the burden of its particular ministry with all its promise....Of Ragaz one may say...that *he has never wrestled carefully or profoundly enough with the attempt to take seriously the Church's encounter with Socialism along these lines.* [59]

Barth himself began to wrestle along these lines as early as 1911. In his lecture on 'Jesus Christ and the Movement for Social Justice' Barth plainly declared that social democracy *calls to* and *preaches to* the church:

> Regarding the goal, social democracy is one with Jesus. It has taken up the conviction that social misery *ought not to be* with a vigor which has not been seen since the time of Jesus. It calls us back from the hypocritical and slothful veneration of the Spirit and from that useless Christianity which intends to come only 'in heaven'. It tells us that we should really believe what we pray every day: 'Thy Kingdom come!' With its 'materialism' it preaches to us a word which stems not from Jesus himself, yet certainly from his Spirit. The word goes like this: '*The end of the way of God is the affirmation of the body.*'[60]

Although Barth evidently experienced a sometimes quite profound degree of ambivalence with regard to the church between 1911 and 1915, it seems likely that by this time he was becoming more settled on the notion that socialism functioned as a prophetic voice calling the church to the integrity of its own being and mission.[61] By the end of 1916 Ragaz and Barth had all but ceased any interaction. Barth remembers that 'Ragaz and I roared past one another like two express trains: he went out of the church, I went in.'[62] This significant statement, together with Barth's comments in 1932, indicate the importance of

---

[59] See Karl Barth, *Church Dogmatics I/1: The Doctrine of the Word of God* (trans. G. W. Bromiley; 2nd ed. Edinburgh: T. & T. Clark, 1975), 74, emphasis added.

[60] Barth, 'Jesus Christ and the Movement for Social Justice,' 28-29.

[61] Mark Lindsay also notes that Barth regarded socialism as a prophetic challenge to the church. See Mark R. Lindsay, *Covenanted Solidarity: The Theological Basis of Karl Barth's Opposition to Nazi Antisemitism and the Holocaust* (New York: Peter Lang, 2001), 87-88.

[62] Cited in Busch, *Karl Barth*, 92.

the church as a motive in his theological development. Thus, as the reality of *God* continued to break in upon Barth, it appears that a corresponding awareness of the special role of the church also developed, even though it remained a thoroughly human and imperfect witness to the reality of God and his kingdom, especially, it seems, in the weakness of its praxis.

In sum: it is clear that in his engagements with socialism and in his lecture 'Religion and Socialism,' Barth wanted to affirm the distinctive praxis of socialism as a form of praxis which accurately reflected the coming kingdom of God. He sought further, to bring the socialists to a conscious awareness of the connections between their political commitments and activities, and the movement of God's kingdom in the world. Barth's criticism that the church was politically indifferent, that it lacked the kind of precise, earth-shaking praxis in which human work corresponds to God's work, served not to dismiss the relevance of the church but to suggest that the praxis of the church itself needed to be reformulated to include this social and ethical dimension. Henceforth, this would be of a piece with Barth's theological project.

'The Righteousness of God'

Barth never published 'Religion and Socialism'. The first publication reflecting his break with the prevailing theology was a lecture given just one month later entitled 'The Righteousness of God'. In 1924 Barth chose this address to stand at the head of his first collection of early essays and addresses, in spite of the qualifications he then made regarding it.[63] This suggests, perhaps, the programmatic nature of this paper in his development.

The Voice of Conscience and the Hearing of Faith

Barth's lecture progresses in three distinct movements. In the first, Barth asserts that the cry of human longing is answered by the trumpet blast of conscience. This longing arises from the oppression and suffering experienced in the world at the hands of a perverted and evil human will. In the blare of conscience the person is confronted by a will which is wholly other and which announces 'the deepest, innermost, surest fact of life: God is righteous. Our

---

[63] Originally addressed to the Town Church of Aarau in January 1916, 'Die Gerechtigkeit Gottes' was published in *Neue Wege*, X, No. 47, 1916, and subsequently incorporated into a volume of collected essays, *Das Wort Gottes und die Theologie* ['The Word of God and Theology'] published in 1924. The volume appeared in English translation as Karl Barth, *The Word of God and the Word of Man* (trans. D. Horton; New York: Harper & Brothers, 1956). I use Horton's translation in this book, although English readers are now directed to the recently published new translation, Karl Barth, *The Word of God and Theology* (trans. Amy Marga; London: T. & T. Clark, 2011). See Barth's prefatory remarks on page 7 for the qualifications he made.

only question is what attitude toward the fact we ought to take.'[64] The righteousness of God is the will of God, a will which

> is above this warped and weakened will of yours and mine, above this absurd and senseless will of the world, another which is straight and pure, and which, when it once prevails, must have other, wholly other, issues than these we see today. Out of this will, when it is recognised, another life must grow. Out of this will, when it emerges, a new world will arise. Our home is where this will prevails.[65]

It is immediately apparent that Barth's lecture is not simply a meditation on an abstract notion of the divine will as opposed to the human will, but is oriented to the form of life which arises out of each of the 'wills'.[66] Whereas the absurd and senseless will of the world results in oppression and suffering, God's will heard and recognised will result in 'another life,' and the arising of 'a new world'. For this to occur, declares Barth, 'we must let conscience speak for....[I]t remains forever the place, the only place between heaven and earth, in which God's righteousness is manifest.'[67]

Yet this is exactly what humanity fails to do. The theme of the second movement of Barth's lecture is that although we are aroused by conscience, we fail to heed its message, we fail to allow conscience to 'speak to the end'.[68] Rather, we make haste to establish our own righteousness in order to soothe and bring to silence the blare of conscience which confronts us and interrupts our whole existence. For Barth, this is

> the most fundamental error of mankind....We arrogate to ourselves, unquestioningly, the right to take up the tumultuous question, What shall we *do?* as if that were in any case the first and most pressing problem....And before we know it, the trumpet blast of conscience has lost its disturbing tone....The righteousness of God itself has slowly changed from being the surest of facts into

---

[64] Karl Barth, 'The Righteousness of God,' in *The Word of God and the Word of Man* (New York: Harper & Brothers, 1956), 9.

[65] Barth, 'The Righteousness of God,' 13.

[66] McCormack characterises the lecture as a 'meditation on two wills' and, although he recognizes its ethical implications, is primarily interested in the specifically *theological* aspects of Barth's development. See McCormack, *Karl Barth's Dialectical Theology*, 132. Archibald Spencer, following McCormack, also characterises the lecture as a 'rumination on two wills', and, in accordance with his own concerns, discusses the *formal* issues of human moral agency as Barth portrays them. See Archibald James Spencer, *Clearing a Space for Human Action: Ethical Ontology in the Theology of Karl Barth* (New York: Peter Lang, 2003), 91-98. While acknowledging the valuable contribution of both these scholars, my reading seeks to elucidate the *material* aspects of Barth's ethical vision as presented here.

[67] Barth, 'The Righteousness of God,' 10.

[68] Barth, 'The Righteousness of God,' 14.

being the highest among various high ideals, and is now at all events our very own affair.[69]

Barth's protest here is clearly against the reductionist ethical idealism of contemporary liberalism which posited God as the source of a humanly-derived moral imperative. Spencer rightly suggests that if we miss this aspect of Barth's argument we miss the thrust of his whole ethical-theological enterprise.[70] In their haste to establish their own righteousness humans arrogate to themselves what is essentially, a divine task. God alone is righteous, and he alone can make humanity righteous.

Humanity seeks to establish its own righteousness through a variety of vehicles: morality, state and culture, and above all, religion. The fault of these vehicles, however, is that they are bound to the world of the human will and human righteousness, and thus are actually and ultimately oppression and unrighteousness. Barth asks, 'Is it not remarkable that the greatest atrocities of life—I think of the capitalistic order and of the war—can justify themselves on purely moral principles?'[71] That humans would attempt to establish their own righteousness is indicative of their pride, and equally, of their despair in the face of the voice of conscience.

In the third movement of the lecture, Barth labels the human realities of morality, culture and religion 'towers of Babel' and the 'God' to whom these towers are built, an 'idol' of our own making. 'It becomes evident that we are looking for a righteousness without God, that we are looking, in truth, for a god without God and against God....It is clear that such a god is not God.'[72] Barth insists that we only encounter the true and living God when we are brought to silence and listen to conscience. Such listening requires the lowliness of faith in the place of pride and despair, a faith characterised by humility and joyful hope. In the quietness of faith we let God speak within—'And then God works in us. Then begins in us, as from a seed, but an unfailing seed, the new basic something which overcomes unrighteousness....[T]here is born a new spirit out of which grows a new world, the world of the righteousness of God.'[73] For Barth, this 'inner way, the way of simple faith, is the way of Christ....[T]his childlike and inadequate solution is the beginning of the vast plan of God.'[74]

In a marvellous rhetorical twist Barth sets his 'childlike and inadequate solution' over against the entirety of the Protestant ethical-idealist tradition deriving from Kant. The 'beginning of the vast plan of God' is not discovered in a rationally grounded moral imperative, but in the simplicity and humility of

---

[69] Barth, 'The Righteousness of God,' 14-16.

[70] Spencer, *Clearing a Space*, 95.

[71] Barth, 'The Righteousness of God,' 18.

[72] Barth, 'The Righteousness of God,' 22.

[73] Barth, 'The Righteousness of God,' 25-26.

[74] Barth, 'The Righteousness of God,' 26-27.

the hearing of faith. Barth resolutely insists that true righteousness does not begin with human action or doing, but with hearing.[75] It would be erroneous, however, to understand Barth's rhetoric as reducing the human agent to an essential passivity. Certainly Barth's construal portrays the emergence of the new world of God's righteousness in terms which prioritise the divine action. Divine priority does not annihilate human agency, however, but rather indicates that human agency is derivative, that human work and activity can be righteous only as it follows the divine.

For Barth, therefore, the first ethical duty is to listen to that which conscience speaks:

> When we let conscience speak to the end, it tells us not only that there is something else, a righteousness above unrighteousness, but also—and more important—that this something else for which we long and which we need is God....We make a veritable uproar with our morality and culture and religion. But we may presently be brought to silence, and with that will begin our true redemption.[76]

Barth is also quite clear that listening entails surrender, a recognition of God's right and his rightness over against us and our wrongness, and a recognition that our wrongness is not simply something requiring adjustment or repair, but something far more radical:

> Here one must give himself up in order to give himself over to God that God's will may be done. To do his will, however, means to begin with him anew. His will is not a corrected continuation of our own. It approaches ours as a Wholly Other. There is nothing for our will except a basic re-creation. Not a reformation but a re-creation and re-growth.[77]

Lights of God in the Darkness

The quietness of faith referred to by Barth does not imply a quietist ethic. Indeed, Christian existence is neither quietist nor activist, but responsive: 'We ought to apply ourselves with all our strength to expect more from God, to let grow within us that which he will in fact cause to grow, to accept what indeed

---

[75] Thus, Gorringe's comment that the 'lecture begins with a solid Kantian appeal to the conscience' is incorrect. See Gorringe, *Against Hegemony*, 36. Although Barth utilises the language of conscience, and will indeed adjust this use of language in later works, even here his conception of conscience is not Kantian. See also Spencer, *Clearing a Space*, 96. In a similar manner Berkhof, who locates Barth's break from Marburg liberalism with the first edition of the *Römerbrief*, underestimates the extent to which this lecture represents an opposing position to Herrmann's view of conscience. See Berkhof, *Two Hundred Years*, 182-189.

[76] Barth, 'The Righteousness of God,' 23-24.

[77] Barth, 'The Righteousness of God,' 24.

he constantly offers us, watching and praying that we may respond to his originative touch.'[78] In the one who will listen, God is constantly at work, ever anew, ever offering and originating new things. Christian existence is existence oriented to the new world of the righteousness of God even now at work and breaking into the old world. The new world is nothing other than the work of God in and through the people who entrust their all to God in faith, and who wait on him in prayerfulness and joyful hope.[79]

Although Barth sets the church alongside morality and culture as belonging and bound to this world, his construal of the church is not entirely negative. As a human endeavour in pursuit of a good conscience, religion and church are an illusion, an exercise in self-deception, which can never *in and of themselves* bring forth the kingdom of God. Thus Barth assails the church for all its various attempts at righteousness and efforts towards relevance:

> What is the use of all the preaching, baptizing, confirming, bell-ringing, and organ-playing, of all the religious moods and modes, the counsels of 'applied religion'...the efforts to enliven church singing, the unspeakably tame and stupid monthly church papers, and whatever else may belong to the equipment of modern ecclesiasticism? *Will something different eventuate from all this* in our relation to the righteousness of God?...Are we not rather hoping by our very activity to conceal in the most subtle way the fact that the critical event that ought to happen has not yet done so and probably never will?[80]

The difference for which Barth longs is, of course, neither an increase in religiosity, nor yet cleverly devised programmes by which the relevance of Christianity is set forth, but rather the birthing of a new world through the Spirit. It must be seen, however, that Barth's criticism is not directed against the church per se, but against the kind of theological persuasion represented by Harnack, against the form of Christianity, whether liberal or conservative, which conducts itself in isolation from the realities of social existence:

> There seem to be no surer means of rescuing us from the alarm cry of conscience than religion and Christianity. Religion gives us the chance, beside and above the

---

[78] Barth, 'The Righteousness of God,' 25.

[79] Barth did not limit God's work to the people of faith, however. In a letter to Thurneysen dated October 5, 1915, Barth asks, 'Are there not also "breakthroughs" on a broad front, under certain circumstances borne by the masses? For instance, think of abstinence!....[W]e cannot and we dare not resist, making deadening prescriptions, when the new spirit, stammering and stumbling in its broken way, is about to burst through somewhere at a single point. We shall evaluate such breakthroughs as relatively as each deserves; we shall not be willing on any account to cultivate them, but when they take place without our doing, we shall not say anything fundamentally against them, but rather we shall be able only to rejoice in them as small realizations of the kingdom of God' (Smart, ed., *Revolutionary Theology*, 33-34).

[80] Barth, 'The Righteousness of God,' 20, emphasis added.

vexations of business, politics, and private and social life, to celebrate solemn hours of devotion—to take flight to Christianity as to an eternally green island in the gray sea of the everyday. There comes over us a wonderful sense of safety and security from the unrighteousness whose might we everywhere feel. It is a wonderful illusion, if we can comfort ourselves with it, that in our Europe—in the midst of capitalism, prostitution, the housing problem, alcoholism, tax evasion and militarism—the church's preaching, the church's morality, and the 'religious life' go their uninterrupted way....A wonderful illusion, but an illusion, a self-deception![81]

It is seen here that Barth rejects in the most vigorous terms any form of Christianity which would isolate itself from the wider social context in which it is found. Privatised religion is escapist and self-indulgent in its orientation, and actually suppresses the righteousness of God which confronts humanity in the conscience. The true church, and therefore, true Christianity, is that which arises when the voice of conscience is allowed to speak, where God then 'plants' a new seed within the human person, and so occurs a new spirit and a new beginning, out of which is to grow a new world. This new world, however, is not that of the eschaton, but grows

in the midst of the old world of war and money and death....Lights of God rise in the darkness, and powers of God become real in weakness. Real love, real sincerity, real progress become possible; morality and culture, state and nation, *even religion and the church now become possible—now for the first time!* One is taken with the vision of an immortality or even of a future life here on earth in which the righteous will of God breaks forth, prevails, and is done as it is in heaven.[82]

This lecture, then, which Barth placed at the head of this early collection of addresses, clearly indicates the ecclesio-ethical orientation of his thought in this period. In it Barth betrays a clear concern for social issues. He speaks of 'the fiendishness of business competition and the world war...antagonism between classes and moral depravity within them, economic tyranny above and the slave spirit below'.[83] He decries the 'capitalism, prostitution, the housing problem, alcoholism, tax evasion and militarism' which are rampant in Europe, and scorns the so-called cultural 'God' who 'is not even righteous. He cannot prevent his worshippers, all the distinguished European and American apostles of civilization, welfare, and progress, all zealous citizens and pious Christians, from falling upon one another with fire and sword to the amazement and derision of the poor heathen in India and Africa.'[84]

In contrast, the character of the new world envisaged by Barth, and therefore

---

[81] Barth, 'The Righteousness of God,' 19-20.
[82] Barth, 'The Righteousness of God,' 25-26, emphasis added.
[83] Barth, 'The Righteousness of God,' 12.
[84] Barth, 'The Righteousness of God,' 19-20, 22.

also the content of Christian existence, is that of the will of God—'purity, goodness, truth, and brotherhood....[A] will with character, a will blessed and holy.'[85] That Barth so readily juxtaposes tragic realities of human existence with the will of God is suggestive that the church will be a *moral* community which stands in as stark contrast to 'war and money and death' as light does to darkness.[86] Barth envisages this community as a community of prayer and faith, joyfully and watchfully gathered and listening to the voice of conscience, and waiting for the 'originative touch' of God to which it might respond. His ecclesio-ethical vision is, therefore, neither *activist* (in the sense that the community is self-determining in its ethical activity and posture in the world), nor *quietist* (in the sense that the community is wholly passive as it awaits the divine establishment of the righteous Kingdom), but rather *responsive*. In this lecture Barth addresses the church, calling it to begin with God anew, to listen to the voice of conscience to the end, and implicitly, to order its existence in accordance with the righteous will of God as it is made known in the voice of conscience. In this construal the community—as a *moral* community—is active and energetic, but its activity is subordinate to and follows the prior activity of God. Barth's hope is that the church will in reality experience a new beginning, the breaking forth of the new world in its midst.

'Action in Waiting'

The Influence of Blumhardt

In September 1916 Barth published an article entitled 'Auf das Reich Gottes warten,'[87] a review of a book of devotions recently published by Christoph Blumhardt. It had originally been intended for inclusion in Ragaz' *Neue Wege*, but the latter had rejected it because of its 'quietist' emphasis.[88] Although only a short work, the review provides interesting and significant insight into Barth's early development generally, including his vision of ecclesial and Christian existence. In addition to being a short work, the review consists largely of citations (almost 60%) drawn from Blumhardt's devotional. An important methodological point arises here. Barth's unambiguous affirmation of Blumhardt's message in this article indicates his broad concurrence with the latter's vision of Christian and ecclesial existence. I assume, therefore, that Barth's selection of passages from Blumhardt's book reflect issues which Barth himself found interesting and penetrating.

---

[85] Barth, 'The Righteousness of God,' 24.

[86] Barth, 'The Righteousness of God,' 25.

[87] In *Der Freie Schweizer Arbeiter*, 15th and 22nd September, 1916. The translation used here is from Karl Barth, 'Action in Waiting for the Kingdom of God,' in *Action in Waiting*, (ed. Society of Brothers; Rifton, NY: Plough, 1969).

[88] Busch, *Karl Barth*, 92.

The importance of the Blumhardts' influence on Barth should not be underestimated.[89] Indeed, Timothy Gorringe has gone so far as to suggest that Christoph Blumhardt was Barth's single most important theological teacher despite the fact that he was not a theologian![90] Throughout his career Barth continued to refer to the Blumhardts, including an important discussion of their influence in his final lectures on dogmatics where he declares that his theological understanding of the Kingdom of God 'could not have been stated and developed as it has without the impulse they gave and their influence through other mediations and modifications'.[91]

Although Barth had visited Christoph Blumhardt on several occasions during his student years, he was at that time dismissive of him on account of his

---

[89] Barth was influenced not only by Christoph Blumhardt but also by his father, Johann Christoph Blumhardt. For a brief overview of their lives and ministries see Roger Newell, 'Blumhardt, Johann Christoph (1805-80) and Christoph Friedrich (1842-1919),' in *The Dictionary of Historical Theology* (ed. T. A. Hart; Grand Rapids: Eerdmans, 2000), 76-77. For a more extensive account of the Blumhardts, including a collection of nineteen sermons from Christoph Blumhardt, see R. Lejeune, *Christoph Blumhardt and His Message* (trans. H. Ehrlich & N. Maas; Rifton, NY: Plough, 1963). The decisive account of the Blumhardts' influence on Barth is the recently published Christian T. Collins Winn, *'Jesus is Victor!' The Significance of the Blumhardts for the Theology of Karl Barth*, Princeton Theological Monograph Series (Eugene, OR: Pickwick Publications, 2009). For Barth's own account of their lives, thought and significance, see Karl Barth, *Protestant Theology in the Nineteenth Century: Its Background & History* (trans. B. Cozens; 2nd ed. London: SCM Press, 2001), 629-639, and also Karl Barth, 'Past and Future: Friedrich Naumann and Christoph Blumhardt,' in *The Beginnings of Dialectic Theology* (ed. James M. Robinson; Richmond: John Knox Press, 1968).

[90] Timothy J. Gorringe, 'Eschatology and Political Radicalism: The Example of Karl Barth and Jürgen Moltmann,' in *God Will Be All in All: The Eschatology of Jürgen Moltmann* (ed. Richard Bauckham; Edinburgh: T. & T. Clark, 1999), 93. Gorringe also says of their influence: 'they lived the affirmation "God is God" which was at the heart of Barth's early theology, and they did so in the midst of society without ever giving politics priority over faith' (see Gorringe, *Against Hegemony*, 34). James Smart agrees: 'The Blumhardts in Bad Boll had recaptured in actual life the eschatological dimension of the New Testament faith'—James D. Smart, *The Divided Mind of Modern Theology: Karl Barth and Rudolph Bultmann, 1908-1933* (Philadelphia: Westminster, 1967), 61.

[91] Karl Barth, *The Christian Life: Church Dogmatics IV/4 (Lecture Fragments)* (trans. G. W. Bromiley; Edinburgh: T. & T. Clark, 1981), 257. In addition to Barth's discussion in his *Protestant Theology*, see also Karl Barth, *Church Dogmatics II/1: The Doctrine of God* (ed. G. W. Bromiley & T. F. Torrance, trans. W. B. Johnston, T. H. L. Parker, H. Knight & J. L. M. Haire; Edinburgh: T. & T. Clark, 1957), 633-634; Barth, *Church Dogmatics II/1*, 633-634; Karl Barth, *Church Dogmatics IV/3.1: The Doctrine of Reconciliation* (ed. G. W. Bromiley & T. F. Torrance, trans. G. W. Bromiley; Edinburgh: T. & T. Clark, 1961), 168-171, and Karl Barth, *The Epistle to the Romans* (trans. E. C. Hoskyns; 6th ed. Oxford: Oxford University Press, 1933), 312.

pietist reputation.[92] In April 1915, however, Barth and Thurneysen spent five days visiting Blumhardt, during which it seems likely that Barth began making the intellectual connections which led to his decisive break with liberalism.[93] Upon his return from Bad Boll Barth read Zündel's biography of the elder Blumhardt and found himself stirred by what he read.[94] What Barth discovered in Bad Boll not only shaped his immediate theological reflections, but remained with him, at least in part, for the entirety of his life.

Barth's review of Blumhardt's *Hausandachten* (*Family Devotions*) is perhaps better understood as an introduction. He provides not so much an analysis, or even a summary, of its contents and ideas, as a selection of passages gathered around what he regards as Blumhardt's major themes. In fact, his initial description of the book is almost damning:

> Blumhardt puts forward no guiding principles. He produces no historical and psychological deductions. He neither reasons nor discusses; he talks neither politics nor philosophy. There is no probing into problems, or drawing conclusions, or building systems. He remains silent in the face of our urgent questions....[H]e passes by the dogmatic and the liberal, the 'religious-ethical' and *us socialist theologians*. He refutes nobody, and nobody needs to feel refuted by him, but he does not concur with anybody else's views either. He pins down neither himself nor anyone else with precise formulas. He has written a very inconsistent, indifferent book.[95]

In spite of all this, however, Barth calls it an 'important and beautiful book' and says of it, 'for me it is the most direct and penetrating Word from God into the need of the world that the war years have produced so far'.[96] Barth found in Blumhardt one who could do what most others could not: 'represent God's cause in the world yet not wage war on the world, love the world and yet be completely faithful to God'.[97]

For Barth, one outstanding thing about the book was the fact that Blumhardt

---

[92] Busch, *Karl Barth and the Pietists*, 31. Busch dates Barth's first visit to Blumhardt as December 27, 1907.

[93] See Busch, *Karl Barth*, 85, and also McCormack, *Karl Barth's Dialectical Theology*, 123. Both authors suggest that this visit to Blumhardt in Bad Boll was a decisive point in Barth's development.

[94] Busch, *Karl Barth*, 85. See also Barth's letter to Thurneysen, dated June 14, 1915 (in Smart, ed., *Revolutionary Theology*, 30). Note that Barth wrote the letter to Rade in which the first indication of his break with the theology of Marburg is discerned only days after this letter to Thurneysen—June 19th (see page 49 above).

[95] Barth, 'Action in Waiting,' 20-21, emphasis added.

[96] Barth, 'Action in Waiting,' 19. Note the similarity of Barth's language here to that used in 1911: 'I really believe that the social justice movement...is not only the greatest and most urgent word of God to the present...' See Barth, 'Jesus Christ and the Movement for Social Justice,' 20. Barth's shift of emphasis is evident.

[97] Barth, 'Action in Waiting,' 22.

did *not* address himself to the situation confronting Germany and Europe at that time. The reason for his silence was not that he had nothing to say to the situation, but that it is not important enough for him to say it—other things were more important! According to Barth, 'he evidently expects the answer on different ground, and he is actively preparing that ground'.[98] What Blumhardt does do, and what Barth finds so powerful, is that 'he lets us experience the echo which the Bible texts of the Moravian Brothers aroused within him from day to day. He does not want to say anything brilliant, let off any fireworks, or strike any blow: he simply tells us the divine truth in the world as it meets him.'[99] In a telling passage which indicates powerfully his growing disenchantment with socialism, Barth confesses that one reason for his appreciation of Blumhardt's book 'is the conviction that our cause, our hope, is at the moment served better with prayers than with treatises. Our dialectics have come to a dead end, and if we want to become healthy and strong, we have to *start from the beginning* and become like children.'[100]

What, then, is this beginning? A close reading of this article shows that Barth identifies several key features of Blumhardt's message, the first and most important of which is Blumhardt's insistence to 'always begin right away with God's presence, might and purpose: he starts out from God'.[101] For Blumhardt, the whole of existence occurs within the great circle of divine sovereignty. This sovereignty is not understood as raw power, however, because God is gracious, 'always the life-bringing, wonderful God who touches us also so that we have hope for our own life'.[102] The same divine glory which orders the movement of the cosmos is also palpably near. Second, Blumhardt's thought occurs within a thoroughly eschatological context. God's sovereignty is moving the world and history towards the goal of his purpose, which is the kingdom of God on earth.[103] What presently hinders this movement is the human will which resists God's will, and which is itself influenced by forces hostile to both God and humanity.[104] Nevertheless, God has promised a restoration of justice and peace and will bring it to pass; ultimately, all resistance will be overcome. The consummation of this promise, however, is something that can only be achieved by God, although, as we shall see, humans may work *with* God, helping the coming of the Kingdom.

The third feature Barth identifies as the key to all. He states that 'here lies the key to everything—with *Jesus* the good actually began already, the good to which mankind and nature alike are called, which towers right into our own

---

[98] Barth, 'Action in Waiting,' 21.

[99] Barth, 'Action in Waiting,' 21.

[100] Barth, 'Action in Waiting,' 22, emphasis added.

[101] Barth, 'Action in Waiting,' 23-24.

[102] Barth, 'Action in Waiting,' 25-26. Note that the citation is Blumhardt's.

[103] Barth, 'Action in Waiting,' 29.

[104] Barth, 'Action in Waiting,' 30.

time also and goes forward toward a revelation and a consummation'. In words which could apply to his own project in later years, Barth continues, 'Blumhardt takes his bearings untiringly from this point again and again, using it as his point of departure in ever new ways.'[105] For Blumhardt, the coming of Jesus introduced a change into history, a movement of his presence and reign which will not cease until all is fulfilled.[106]

Barth introduces the fourth feature by asking how this is to become reality. Blumhardt's answer is that 'the consummation is being prepared in a *double movement in heaven and on earth*,' although the 'actual decision lies not in the visible but in the invisible world'.[107] The actual fulfilment of the divine purpose can belong only to God. His people, however, may pray, and in praying participate in the new creation. According to Barth, with Blumhardt's emphasis on prayer 'we are face to face with the innermost of his thought…*this living waiting on God for the world*…constitutes the nerve center of this book'.[108] The intercessory nature of this 'waiting' leads directly to the fifth and final feature highlighted by Barth in this introduction, which concerns the concept of God's 'little flock'.[109] Because of the specific relevance of this feature for my argument I will devote a little more space to outlining aspects of Blumhardt's thought regarding this matter.

The Living Church

At the outset it is essential to recognise that for Blumhardt, the 'little flock,' the chosen people of God, is not a reference to the institutional church, or even to the revivalist fellowships and sects, but rather refers to those few who 'wait' for the Lord Jesus. For Blumhardt, the kingdom of God functions to relativise the church and all the 'traditional ways of Christianity'. 'The year of the churches is past!' he used to say.[110] His own relation to the churches was characterised by tension, both on account of the extraordinary nature of his experiences, and especially by his commitment to the social movement, which

---

[105] Barth, 'Action in Waiting,' 32.

[106] In a sermon delivered in this period, Blumhardt declares, 'In Jesus a new reality appears, a reality which is opposed to that of world history. Something new is to begin alongside the old. The old reality does not suddenly disappear; it continues alongside. Yet in Jesus we have a new reality. A new history begins, a new working of God….This new history is to become revealed in each individual person…it must become evident….This is no dogma; it is not just a new word….It is the living person of Jesus Christ, in whom dawns a new history of mankind.' The sermon was delivered just prior to the outbreak of the War on March 29, 1914. See Lejeune, *Christoph Blumhardt*, 230-231.

[107] Barth, 'Action in Waiting,' 34.

[108] Barth, 'Action in Waiting,' 34, emphasis added.

[109] Barth, 'Action in Waiting,' 37.

[110] Lejeune, *Christoph Blumhardt*, 51-52.

he regarded as a sign of the kingdom, and a prophetic voice in the world and to the church.[111] When, in 1899, Blumhardt gave public support to the Democratic Socialists, he was banished by large numbers of former supporters and required by the Royal Consistory to renounce the rank and title of pastor of the Church of Württemberg.[112] Blumhardt, then, expected little from the organised church. Neither church nor social democracy would be responsible for establishing the kingdom of God because both shared 'the doubtful nature inherent in all human undertakings and movements.'[113]

In place of the institutional church Blumhardt longed for the arising of a *living church*, a 'community (*Gemeinde*) upon earth, a society of men in which peace and joy will reign…a community of men, a society in which people strengthen each other' toward the goal of God's kingdom on earth.[114] For Blumhardt, the kingdom of God must be foreshadowed in a human society. It is as this community lives in accordance with its belief that the kingdom of God is truly present in the world, albeit only in a proleptic sense:[115]

> God always wants to have a place, a community, which belongs to Him really and truly, so that God's being can dwell there. God *needs* such a place from where He can work for the rest of the world. There *must* be a place on the earth from where the sun of God's kingdom shines forth.[116]

How is such a community to arise? In a sermon on Matthew 16:13-19 Blumhardt grounds the existence of the living community in the event of revelation, specifically the recognition of Jesus as *Christ*, as divine representative, and thus, in the fullness of his humanity, as true humanity. As the light of the living God dawns in the life of a person they are bound to Jesus

---

[111] Lejeune, *Christoph Blumhardt*, 59-61, 65.

[112] Lejeune, *Christoph Blumhardt*, 69.

[113] Lejeune, *Christoph Blumhardt*, 76.

[114] Christoph Blumhardt, 'Joy in the Lord,' in *Action in Waiting* (ed. Society of Brothers; Rifton, NY: Plough, 1969), 54. It is interesting here to note Barth's discussion in his 1948 Amsterdam address regarding the use of *Gemeinde* (understood as *congregatio*) as an alternative for 'church.' Barth uses the term to designate, not the existence or condition of the community, but the church as a 'living congregation' in the *event* of its gathering to wait upon and hear the Word addressed to it. See Barth's address 'The Church: The Living Congregation of the Living Lord Jesus Christ' in Karl Barth, *God Here and Now* (trans. Paul M. van Buren; 2003 *Classics* ed. London: Routledge, 1964), 81-83, and also Karl Barth, *Church Dogmatics IV/1: The Doctrine of Reconciliation* (ed. G. W. Bromiley & T. F. Torrance, trans. G. W. Bromiley; Edinburgh: T. & T. Clark, 1956), 651-652.

[115] Blumhardt, 'Joy in the Lord,' 55, cf. 62.

[116] Lejeune, *Christoph Blumhardt*, 81, emphasis added. Cf. Lejeune, *Christoph Blumhardt*, 165: 'Do not think that God's cause can just fall from heaven. There *has* to be a living church' (emphasis added).

Christ, and so the church of God arises.[117]

The character of the *Gemeinde* is the character of the kingdom of God, which comes not in destructive or punitive judgement as though God's intent is the damnation of the world and humanity, but in the 'unutterable compassion' of God's triumphant grace revealed in the saving events of the gospel.[118] As Jesus entered into solidarity with the most wretched, so too those bound to him will hunger, not only for personal grace but for justice and equity in all human affairs.[119] Blumhardt insists that Jesus is not to be worshipped 'all by himself in his elevation' but in the conspicuous company he himself adopted:

> Jesus sets his hopes on the poor, on the outcasts, on those who are rejected by kings and emperors....Do we want to follow Jesus on this way? Then we must accept him in this company. Then the call comes to us to set to work wholeheartedly, for *here* is Jesus....Here must be your whole heart; here you must do the deeds of faith; for it is from here that the power comes which will overthrow the world.[120]

Blumhardt's eschatological orientation to the kingdom of God establishes perhaps the most distinctive aspect of his ecclesial vision: the freedom and independence of the Christian community. Because the community is wholly oriented towards God and his action it is freed from all lesser worldly allegiances. Being bound to the lordship of Christ means it is no longer chained to the world. This is not to result, however, in pietistic sectarianism. Blumhardt rejects all forms of privatised piety:

> Neither in heaven nor on earth is it possible just to settle down comfortably in something through grace and do nothing and care for nobody else. If I am saved by grace, then I am a worker through grace. If I am justified by grace, then through grace I am a worker for justice. If through grace I am placed within the truth, then through grace I am a servant of truth. If through grace I have been placed within peace, then through grace I am a servant of peace for all men.[121]

So too Blumhardt resists the temptation towards monasticism. The community represents the kingdom of God in the world, and cannot cut itself off from it, adopting a posture which is fundamentally aloof to the wider affairs of the common life.[122] Rather 'the church of Jesus Christ is to be the light of creation, of the existing world....Jesus is truly Lord over the whole creation, and God's kingdom penetrates all that is created. His church is to have the

---

[117] Lejeune, *Christoph Blumhardt*, 162. The sermon ('The Church of Jesus Christ') was delivered June 29, 1897.

[118] Lejeune, *Christoph Blumhardt*, 161. Cf. Torrance, *Karl Barth: An Introduction*, 36.

[119] Lejeune, *Christoph Blumhardt*, 151.

[120] Lejeune, *Christoph Blumhardt*, 192, 190.

[121] Blumhardt, 'Joy in the Lord,' 66.

[122] Lejeune, *Christoph Blumhardt*, 163.

width and breadth of Jesus, of God, of all creation.'[123] So too it must also become a community of virtue, 'of sterling quality in every aspect, not only communal but also truthful....In the society of Jesus Christ it is a matter of virtues, God's virtues, not human ones. Not customs, not people's views, not what a nation happens to believe is right.'[124]

Prophetic Existence

It is evident from this overview how similar Barth's thought in this period is to that of Blumhardt. We have already noted in the previous sections of this chapter a number of aspects in Barth's ecclesial vision which echo emphases found in Blumhardt. Barth, like Blumhardt, views socialism as a sign of the kingdom of God, but looks to God for the ultimate establishing of the kingdom. He is critical of the church as a religious institution and seeks its renewal and re-establishing on a new basis in God. For both men a praxis that conforms to the kingdom of God revealed in Christ is a crucial element of the church's true being. However, the most pertinent aspects of Barth's treatment of Blumhardt, are Barth's reference to the Bible, which I have already mentioned, his sense that in Blumhardt the kingdom develops 'organically,' and his emphasis on 'waiting,' which echoes and extends his call in the previous sermon to 'let conscience speak to the end'. Barth was impressed by the 'organic' manner in which Blumhardt conceives of truth. Blumhardt allows no dualisms to exist in his message, either between God and the world, good and evil, or divine action and human action. In this context he says of Blumhardt that 'he sees God creating light out of darkness, one taking shape out of the other and growing in the peace of God'.[125]

We have also noted Barth's comment that '*this living waiting on God for the world*...constitutes the nerve center' of Blumhardt's book.[126] It is this 'waiting and hastening' (*warten und eilen*) which Barth wants to commend to his readers: '...pleading unceasingly and unwaveringly before God and to God "Thy Kingdom come!" and waiting and hastening with men toward this coming. *Is that not the highest and most promising thing a man can do at this moment?*'[127]

It is evident, of course, that for both Barth and Blumhardt this waiting signifies not inactivity, but is, rather, 'in its essence, revolutionary'.[128] First, and

---

[123] Lejeune, *Christoph Blumhardt*, 163.

[124] Blumhardt, 'Joy in the Lord,' 63.

[125] Barth, 'Action in Waiting,' 23.

[126] Barth, 'Action in Waiting,' 34.

[127] Barth, 'Action in Waiting,' 23, emphasis added. It is precisely this claim, and its corollary that the present moment is 'served better with prayers than with treatises' (22) which Ragaz rejected as quietist.

[128] Barth, 'Action in Waiting,' 40.

most significantly for Barth, waiting means invocation—calling on God.[129] The reason we call upon God is simply that the establishing of the kingdom is pre-eminently *his* concern. To cry out to God is to seek the divine establishing of his kingdom in the entire world. Prayer that cries for the action of God, however, finds itself caught up in a divine movement which instigates responsive human action. Prayer, then, is neither the cessation, nor the end of, human action, but its beginning and proper foundation. Thus Barth says, 'When we "hasten and wait" toward God like this, the consummation is prepared, coming from God himself. For Blumhardt, divine and human action are closely interlocked; again not in a mechanical but in an organic sense.'[130] Waiting for the kingdom of God, then, 'means just the opposite of sitting comfortably and going along with the old order of things'.[131]

Second, waiting is revolutionary because it functions to liberate a person from the powers of this world, from the trust in its strength and from the fear of its forces. In this freedom one is able to recognise God's will, to take up his task, to do his work, to fight his battle, to take his sacrifice upon himself.[132] Although this notion of the freedom and independence of the church will find its sharpest expression as a critical tool during the Barmen period, Barth is already moving in this direction.[133] Barth's emphasis on waiting in this article functions in a similar manner to the emphasis on conscience in 'The Righteousness of God.' Both concepts serve to direct the Christian community to God as the primary focus of its activity, so that all other activity in which it engages may be a faithful expression of its own integrity and identity. In this way the church is freed from its debilitating enculturation to become a genuinely prophetic voice of an alternative way and an alternative world. This is what lies behind Barth's approval of Blumhardt's seeming 'irrelevance,' and his refusal to address the current situation or grant it primary importance.[134]

Barth believes that the people of God are to 'represent' God and his goodness in this world, sowing justice, and crying out against sin and death, opposing self-will, greed and all evil.[135] The people of God 'gather round Christ not for their own blessedness *but for the redemption of the world*, comparable to the servant of God in Deutero-Isaiah. They are to represent God's cause in a

---

[129] Barth, 'Action in Waiting,' 34.

[130] Barth, 'Action in Waiting,' 42.

[131] Barth, 'Action in Waiting,' 40.

[132] Lejeune, *Christoph Blumhardt*, 78.

[133] See James Y. Holloway, ed., *Barth, Barmen and the Confessing Church Today*, vol. 28, *Symposium Series* (Lewiston, NY: Edwin Mellen, 1992), 5-8 for a copy of the Barmen declaration.

[134] Barth, 'Action in Waiting,' 20-22.

[135] Barth, 'Action in Waiting,' 27, 36, 44. For further evidence that Barth thought the church ought to maintain a 'prophetic' stance towards the world deriving from life in accordance with 'the norms of the world of the gospel,' see his letter to Thurneysen dated October 5, 1915 in Smart, *Revolutionary Theology*, 33-35.

special way and in doing this they are encompassed by God's love in a special way too.'[136] Importantly, this shows that for Barth, Christian life, far from being an idealistic or amorphous entity, has a definite shape and tendency. He utilises the image of the Isaianic Servant to indicate the 'special way' in which the church is to 'represent God's cause'. The church's existence is not for itself, but it is *in* the world *for* the world. The posture of the church toward the world is that of the Servant. It is clear, of course, that redemption and blessing are not bestowed by the church, but rather, these gifts come *through* the church. Barth's citation of Blumhardt perhaps indicates the role he sees the church occupying in the economy of salvation:

> There needs to be a people of faith on which God can lean, so to speak, and to whom He can give the victory. When God can say, 'These people are my children,' then comes the blessing, and the blessing comes all around to those who have contact with the people whom God has in mind. It all depends on this one thing alone, that the people whom God has chosen can remain quite firm.[137]

Finally, it is arguable that Barth sees Blumhardt himself as an exemplar of Christian life. The active waiting which is 'the highest and most promising thing a man can do at this moment' is a 'living waiting on God *for the world*'.[138] And this last phrase is significant, of course. Christian life is seen as an intercessory existence. Barth speaks of Blumhardt as a 'priestly person,' one who is able to 'suffer with the world' while speaking frankly to it about its need and redemption; able to 'carry the world up to God and bring God into the world,' to be an 'advocate for men before God and a messenger of God bringing peace to men'.[139]

Not only does Blumhardt exhibit the intercessory nature of Christian existence, he is also an example of the nature of Christian life as a kind of pilgrim existence. Shortly after the death of Blumhardt in 1919, Barth wrote another article which in some ways functioned as a eulogy for Blumhardt. In it he writes:

> Blumhardt's secret was his endless movement between hurrying and waiting, between lively participation in the fullness of what is and astonished inner waiting for that which seeks to be through the power from on high....The unique element, and I say it quite deliberately, the prophetic, in Blumhardt's message and mission consists in the way in which the hurrying and the waiting, the worldly and the divine, the present and the coming, again and again met, were united, supplemented one another, sought and found one another. It is no wonder that this man made a strange, forbidding, baffling impression on so many. He was of

---

[136] Barth, 'Action in Waiting,' 37, emphasis added.
[137] Barth, 'Action in Waiting,' 38.
[138] Barth, 'Action in Waiting,' 23, 34.
[139] Barth, 'Action in Waiting,' 22.

necessity a stranger among all those who were willing and able to feel at home in present-day society, church and world.[140]

In a sense, Christian and ecclesial existence is a prophetic existence, the experience of being caught between two worlds. One is in the world yet not able to feel entirely at home within it because of the impinging reality of the new world to come. Yet it is neither a static nor a predictable existence. It is an 'endless movement' between a series of poles, a dialectical existence which embodies the dialectical eschatological reality in which we find ourselves. Those who live in accordance with this reality will always, Barth suggests, find themselves in the minority, necessarily strange and baffling to those around them.

In Blumhardt's bold proclamation of Jesus Christ as universal Saviour, in his refusal to accommodate himself to the dictates of the prevailing culture (including religious culture) and its priorities and concerns, in his solidarity with the struggling masses and his political championing of their cause as a theological necessity, and, lastly, in his unwavering hope in the ultimate victory and fullness of the kingdom of God, Barth saw an expression of the Christian life—not as an expression to be slavishly imitated, but as an example of the organic development of God's kingdom in one who would 'wait.'

In sum, *Auf das Reich Gottes warten* indicates clearly that, in this period at least, Barth had a definite vision of Christian and ecclesial existence. His emphasis on waiting and prayer was not a capitulation to a pietistic quietism, but an attempt to establish the being and activity of the church on an entirely new foundation. By radically orienting the life of the church to its one Lord, Barth sought to enable it to live faithfully and prophetically in accordance with its own integrity and identity as *God's* people. Thus the (living) church is envisioned as a prayerful community of hope and liberty, actively reflecting the compassion and virtue of the inbreaking kingdom in its communal life. It is neither institutionalised, pietistic nor monastic, but rather thoroughly engaged in works of witness and solidarity with the world at large, and especially with the oppressed and suffering. The church is against the world in that it refuses to capitulate to the alien lordship of worldly demands and priorities, but it is against the world in order that it might be more thoroughly and more deeply *for* the world. The posture of its existence in the midst of the world is one of intercession and servanthood, and the timbre of its proclamation is not ultimately judgement and rejection, but acceptance, solidarity and affirmation.

---

[140] Barth, 'Past and Future,' 44-45.

Finding the *New World*

Encountered by the Reality of God

At several points in the foregoing sections we have noted in passing Barth's relation to the Bible: in his weekly responsibility to preach the biblical text to his parishioners, his positive response to the suggestion made by Zürich pastor Hans Bader that local pastors meet regularly for a morning of Bible reading, and in the impact Blumhardt's scriptural devotions made upon him. In early June 1916 Barth and Thurneysen had several days holiday together during which they determined 'to go back to academic theology to clarify the situation'[141] and to find a '*wholly other* theological foundation' for their preaching, instruction and pastoral care.[142] After rejecting both Schleiermacher and Kutter, and canvassing Kant and Hegel, the pair found themselves 'compelled to do something much more obvious. We tried to learn our theological ABC all over again, beginning by reading and interpreting the writing of the Old and New Testaments, more thoughtfully than before. And lo and behold, they began to speak to us.'[143]

It is evident from his letters that Barth did not cease his engagement with academic theology and philosophy. On June 26, 1916 Barth writes with some enthusiasm of his renewed systematic engagement with Kant, and exhorts Thurneysen, 'you must open fire at another point!'[144] This initial enthusiasm is short-lived, however, and within a month it is directed to an alternative object:

> Discovery of a gold mine: J. T. Beck!! As a biblical expositor he simply towers far above the rest of the company....I came on the track of him through my work on Romans...a copy book with 'comments' is coming into being in which I summarise everything in my own language. Also I give some attention to the different dismal Kantian tables, although with less joy and profit and more from a feeling of duty.[145]

Barth's study of Romans with the aid of 'a stack of commentaries' apparently commenced the morning after his early-June conversation with

---

[141] Bernd Jaspert, ed., *Karl Barth~Rudolph Bultmann Letters 1922-1966* (Grand Rapids: Eerdmans, 1981), 154-155.

[142] Barth, *The Theology of Schleiermacher*, 264. Barth recalls that it was Thurneysen who first used the phrase 'wholly other'.

[143] Barth, *The Theology of Schleiermacher*, 264.

[144] Smart, ed., *Revolutionary Theology*, 37-38.

[145] Smart, ed., *Revolutionary Theology*, 38. The letter is dated July 27, 1916. For comment on Beck's influence on Barth in this period see Busch, *Karl Barth and the Pietists*, 30-35. See also Barth's later treatment of Beck in Barth, *Protestant Theology*, 602-610.

Thurneysen.[146] Initially Barth made good progress with Romans so that by the end of October he had studied through to the end of chapter three, although by September the following year he was still working on chapter five of the epistle.[147] Nonetheless, it was the simple (and 'more thoughtful') reading of the Scriptures, and more particularly, the discovery that 'lo and behold, they began to speak to us,' which was ultimately responsible for Barth's theological 'conversion'. In his outstanding study of Barth's hermeneutics in the *Römerbrief* period, Richard Burnett claims that

> Barth did not come to an understanding of theology's true subject matter as a result of abstract thinking or as a consequence of any philosophical inquiry. He did not arrive at it by means of Idealism nor was it the product of anything he learned from neo-Kantianism. It came from reading the Bible. As important as Herrmann, neo-Kantianism, and other influences were in providing Barth critical tools to articulate the *Sachlichkeit* (objectivity) of the biblical *Sache* (subject matter), none of these were ultimately decisive. What was decisive was Barth's discovery that God, that revelation, was the subject matter of the Bible.[148]

Barth provided his first public account of this decisive discovery in a sermon delivered on February 6, 1917 at a study week in Thurneysen's Leutwil parish.[149] Originally Thurneysen, who organised the study week, had asked Emil Brunner to deliver a message on the topic 'The New World in the Bible,' but Brunner declined the topic on grounds that the theme did not appeal to him. Subsequently Barth agreed to deliver the topic for his friend.[150]

Like the lecture, 'The Righteousness of God,' this lecture also progresses in three movements, and addresses the question 'What stands in the Bible?' Barth

---

[146] Jaspert, ed., *Barth~Bultmann*, 155.

[147] Smart, ed., *Revolutionary Theology*, 38, 42. McCormack provides several reasons for the slowing of Barth's progress. See McCormack, *Karl Barth's Dialectical Theology*, 135-138. Busch also indicates that ill health slowed Barth's progress. See Busch, *Karl Barth*, 101.

[148] Richard E. Burnett, *Karl Barth's Theological Exegesis: The Hermeneutical Principles of the Römerbrief Period* (Tübingen: Mohr Siebeck, 2001), 73-74. Note that Barth would later recall that it was 'the very strong influence of Christoph Blumhardt...[which] first led me back simply to more concrete biblical exegesis'. See Jaspert, ed., *Barth~Bultmann*, 157-158.

[149] The date given (from Busch, *Karl Barth*, 101) is also contrary to that given with the English translation, which is simply, 'Autumn 1916'. See also Barth, *The Word of God and Theology*, 15 n.1.

[150] See John W. Hart, *Karl Barth Vs. Emil Brunner: The Formation and Dissolution of a Theological Alliance, 1916-1936* (New York: Peter Lang, 2001), 14. The sermon is found in Barth, *The Word of God*, 28-50. The English translation by Horton is unfortunately titled 'The *Strange* New World within the Bible'. Neither the title nor the text of Barth's sermon contains the word 'strange' (*fremd, seltsam*, etc). This error is corrected in the new translation: see Barth, *The Word of God and Theology*, 15-29.

begins by surveying the biblical narrative from the call of Abraham to the final cry of John the Divine, and concludes with an answer to his homiletical question: within the Bible is a new world, the world of God.[151] This introductory section, however, is far more than the fine homiletical rhetoric required to introduce the topic. Rather, it also reveals and restates a set of Barth's presuppositions which are emerging in this period, and which were to have fundamental significance for the entire shape and direction of his theology, including his vision of Christian and ecclesial existence.

One such presupposition—often overlooked precisely because it is so apparent—is Barth's discovery that the whole Bible bears a unified witness.[152] More important than this view about the Bible itself, however, is the question regarding what, or more correctly, *who* the Bible bears witness to. Barth's answer to this question is that the Bible bears witness to *God*. The identification of God as the theme or the content (*der Inhalt*) of the Bible constitutes a significant aspect of Barth's theological development.[153] In his examination of the early Barth's view of Scripture, Burnett finds that as a young liberal, Barth believed that the Bible had primarily to do with religion, piety, and the pious thoughts and experiences of those who had been filled, more or less, with what he called 'Christian certainty'.[154]

Barth's new identification, then, reflects already a decisive shift from an anthropocentric theology. Later in the lecture Barth insists that 'it is not the right human thoughts about God which form the content of the Bible, but the right divine thoughts about men....The *word of God* is within the Bible.'[155] In a somewhat autobiographical statement Barth continues with what is his first public criticism of Schleiermacher:

> Our grandfathers, after all, were right when they struggled so desperately in behalf of the truth that there is revelation in the Bible and not religion only, and when they would not allow facts to be turned upside down for them even by so pious and intelligent a man as Schleiermacher.[156]

---

[151] Karl Barth, 'The Strange New World within the Bible,' in *The Word of God and the Word of Man* (New York: Harper and Brothers, 1956), 33.

[152] Burnett, *Karl Barth's Theological Exegesis*, 77. Burnett notes that Barth speaks over fifty times in this sermon about the Bible as if it were a whole, as if it bore a unified witness, as if, to borrow his image, all its voices were singing the same song. Burnett claims that this view is simply not seen in Barth before his break with liberalism in 1915. He further elucidates the hermeneutical implications of this view in pages 78-84.

[153] Barth, 'Strange New World,' 46.

[154] Burnett, *Karl Barth's Theological Exegesis*, 66.

[155] Barth, 'Strange New World,' 43, emphasis added.

[156] Barth, 'Strange New World,' 44. Both Barth's grandfathers were ministers who were generally opposed to Schleiermacher's theology. See Barth, *The Theology of Schleiermacher*, 263, and also Burnett, *Karl Barth's Theological Exegesis*, 68-69.

Equally as important as his rejection of the presupposition that the Bible is about humanity rather than God, is Barth's thoroughgoing theological realism. In speaking of the new world in the Bible Barth does not intend to construct an imaginary world, nor does he speak in idealist terms as though the new world were merely a new perspective or worldview. For Barth, as we shall see, the new world is nothing other than the reality of the living God breaking forth into this world which he has created and redeemed.

Barth begins the second section of his lecture by asking once more, 'What is there within the Bible?'[157] This time Barth surveys three answers commonly given in Neo-Protestantism: history, morality and religion. In a move, however, which displays his distance from the anthropocentric theology of his teachers, Barth employs a palpable sense of theological realism to subvert a liberal-anthropological reading of Scripture.[158] In the case of history, for example, the Bible is problematic, because the necessary nexus of historical causation continually breaks down. In its place, Barth says

> [t]he decisive cause is *God*....When God enters, history for the while ceases to be, and there is nothing more to ask; for something wholly different and new begins—a history with its own distinct grounds, possibilities, and hypotheses....A new world projects itself into our old ordinary world.[159]

Such is the case also with morality, for the prime consideration of the Bible according to Barth,

> is not the doings of man but the doings of God—not the various ways which we may take if we are men of good will, but the power out of which good will must first be created...not industry, honesty and helpfulness as we may practice them in our old ordinary world, but the establishment and growth of a new world, the world in which God and *his* morality reign.[160]

Finally, Barth also dispenses with religion, for as we have already seen, 'the Bible tells us not how we should talk with God but what he says to us; not how we find the way to him, but how he has sought and found the way to us'.[161]

There are two particularly noticeable aspects of Barth's treatment of these topics in this section of the lecture. First, as is evident in the citations above, Barth views the new world as the result of God's action. His entry into history

---

[157] Barth, 'Strange New World,' 34.

[158] Hart probably overstates the matter when he says that 'this lecture shows that Barth has completed his theological breakthrough' (Hart, *Karl Barth Vs. Emil Brunner*, 14). Barth's own recollection indicates that he was still in the process of coming out of the eggshells of the theology of his teachers up until and including the writing of *Der Römerbrief* (see Busch, *Karl Barth*, 99).

[159] Barth, 'Strange New World,' 37.

[160] Barth, 'Strange New World,' 39.

[161] Barth, 'Strange New World,' 43.

and his activity in the affairs of specific human beings transpires in a 'new history,' the 'establishment and growth of a new world,' in the midst of the old and continuing world. This metaphysic will become a primary aspect of Barth's ontology as he develops it in the first edition of his Romans commentary.

Also particularly noticeable is the way Barth closes the discussion of each topic with an exhortation or challenge, something more akin to a sermon than a lecture.[162] Further, these exhortations point towards a final challenge at the end of the lecture. Despite the oddity of their inclusion in a *lecture*, it is nonetheless profitable to note the content of these challenges.[163] In each case Barth confronts his hearers with a call to decision, a call to recognise the reality of *God*, and so respond to his sovereignty by allowing themselves to be led into this new world:

> It is certain that the Bible, if we read it carefully, makes straight for the point where one must decide to accept or to reject the sovereignty of God. This is the new world within the Bible. We are offered the magnificent, productive, hopeful life of a grain of seed, a new beginning, out of which all things shall be made new. One cannot learn or imitate this life of the divine seed in the new world. One can only let it live, grow, and ripen within him. One can only believe—can only hold the ground whither he has been led. Or not believe. There is no third way.[164]

In each challenge Barth refers to the recognition of God's sovereignty and the corresponding obedience which issues from this recognition as *faith*. By setting the challenge to the contemporary hearer within the overarching framework of the biblical narrative, Barth is clearly intimating that the faithful obedience of the former is an echo and a further instance of the faithfulness and obedience demonstrated by Abraham, Moses, Gideon, Samuel and so forth. People of faith, as Barth understands them, are neither passive nor restrained, but *dare* to entrust their destiny to the sovereignty of God as one would entrust oneself to a mighty river and be carried along by it. Such faith is the child of the 'spirit in the Bible' which will lead us to 'grow beyond ourselves towards

---

[162] Barth, 'Strange New World,' 37, 41 and 44-45.

[163] In an earlier version of this chapter I referred to Barth's two lectures ('The Righteousness of God' and 'The Strange New World' as 'sermons' addressed to particular congregations. In response Christophe Chalamet gently insisted—correctly—that the addresses were *lectures* rather than sermons. Nonetheless, the rhetorical style of both addresses, and the structure, particularly of this lecture, are sermonic in form, and appropriate to the congregations to whom they were delivered. Interestingly, Dr Hans-Anton Drewes, former archivist of the Karl Barth Archive in Basel, notes that when Barth sent his lecture 'The Righteousness of God' to Ragaz for publication in *Neue Wege*, Ragaz remarked that the lecture 'had all the fundamental characteristics of a sermon' (see Barth, *The Word of God and Theology*, 3). This feature of the addresses suggests Barth's intent to *call* the church—in these cases, specific churches—to become a moral community.

[164] Barth, 'Strange New World,' 41.

the highest answer'.[165] Joseph Mangina, too, draws attention to the self-involving nature of Barth's rhetoric in this lecture. He suggests that for Barth,

> [w]hat the Bible does is to set us into the midst of a new world in which human beings are caught up and find themselves out of control. The various biblical personalities [that Barth cites] should be considered not as models, but as figurative representations of the reader's own situation *coram deo*....To pick up the Bible, to enter the world to which it bears witness is to have one's life called into question.[166]

The 'Worldliness' of the Triune God

In the first two sections of this lecture, then, we have seen that Barth speaks of 'God' as the theme and content of the Bible, and of the 'new world' which he is bringing into being. Barth speaks variously of the new world as God's sovereignty, glory and incomprehensible love.[167] The new world is the 'world of God,' the 'coming world' and the 'world of the Father' which 'projects itself into our old ordinary world'.[168] The new world is offered to us as a grain of seed which we are to let 'grow and ripen within us according to the laws of the great life process set forth in the Bible'.[169] In the final section of his lecture Barth now seeks to clarify his understanding of God, and in so doing also clarifies somewhat the means by which the new world emerges in human society.

Having argued that the content of the Bible is 'God,' Barth now asks, 'what is the content of the contents?'[170] Who is this God who encounters us in and through the Scriptures? The manner in which Barth answers this question is highly significant. Instead of stating the matter directly, Barth exploits 'a series of ready answers, serious and well-founded answers taken from the Bible itself'[171] in order to launch an assault against privatised, interior and wholly eschatological understandings of God's identity and purpose in salvation. While it is true that the Bible teaches that those turning to God will inherit a kingdom of blessedness in the next life, and may experience even in this world inner comfort and peace, Barth asks

> [i]s *that* all of God and his new world, of the meaning of the Bible, of the content of the contents?...that here and there specimens of men like you and me might be

---

165 Barth, 'Strange New World,' 34.
166 Mangina, *The Christian Life*, 28.
167 Barth, 'Strange New World,' 45.
168 Barth, 'Strange New World,' 33, 37, 40.
169 Barth, 'Strange New World,' 41, 45.
170 Barth, 'Strange New World,' 46.
171 Barth, 'Strange New World,' 46.

'converted,' find inner 'peace,' and by a redeeming death go someday to 'heaven.' Is *that* all…Is not God—greater than that?[172]

When Barth turns to answer the question 'Who is God?' he utilises the trinitarian formula to provide a positive statement of the divine identity. Nevertheless he develops his statement in such a way as to repudiate dualistic and privatised forms of Christian thought and existence. Thus,

[w]ho is God? The heavenly Father! But the heavenly Father even upon *earth*, and upon earth really the *heavenly* Father. He will not allow life to be split into a 'here' and 'beyond'…He purposes naught but the establishment of a new *world*.[173]

In a similar manner, God is the Son, not merely as 'mediator for my soul,' but as the redeemer and mediator of the whole world. The events narrated in Scripture about him are the 'glorious beginning of a new *world*'.[174] Finally, God also is 'the Spirit in his believers'.[175] By means of a hymn-citation Barth affirms that it is the Spirit by whom 'we own the Son' and which 'through quiet hearts forever flows'. But once more he is unwilling to allow this to be the limit or extent of the divine activity. Thus he affirms that

God is also that spirit (that is to say, that love and good will) which will and must break forth from quiet hearts into the world outside, that it may be manifest, visible, comprehensible: behold the tabernacle of God is with men! The Holy Spirit makes a new heaven and a new earth, and, therefore, new men, new families, new relationships, new politics.…The Holy Spirit establishes the righteousness of heaven in the midst of the unrighteousness of earth and will not stop nor stay until all that is dead has been brought to life and a new *world* has come into being. This is within the Bible. It is within the Bible for us. For it we were baptized. Oh, that we dared in faith to take what grace can offer us![176]

In this brief and potent conclusion Barth makes clear that the purpose of the Father is nothing less than the establishment of a new *world*. As such, the coming of Jesus must be understood as nothing less than the commencement of the new *world*, while the activity of the Spirit is nothing less than the making visible of the new *world* purposed by the Father and inaugurated in the Son, precisely through his regenerating activity in the old world.

Barth's emphasis on the 'worldliness' of the triune God in this section reiterates his contention against forms of dualistic Christianity which would separate faith from life, the inner from the outer, the heavenly from the earthly,

---

[172] Barth, 'Strange New World,' 47.
[173] Barth, 'Strange New World,' 48-49.
[174] Barth, 'Strange New World,' 49.
[175] Barth, 'Strange New World,' 49.
[176] Barth, 'Strange New World,' 49-50.

and the future from the present. God's love is directed toward the *world*, not the soul or even the church—his purpose is all-encompassing. Indeed, in face of the devastating realities of life in this world, God does not bless us 'with the power of the church but with the power of life and resurrection'.[177] Barth, therefore, will brook no theology, ideology or spirituality which would deny, despise or forsake the world.

This is not to say, however, that Barth has no place for the church, or that he is dismissive of Christian and ecclesial existence. As was the case in his lecture on the righteousness of God, so here. Barth assails the church and religion, not that they might be abolished, but that they might be renewed and re-established on new grounds. What he rejects is a church grounded in its own life and power. All religions, even the 'most perfect,' are no more than 'a delusion and a snare' without the reality of God.[178] For Barth, the coming into being of the new world belongs entirely to God—it is he who establishes it and causes it to grow.

But it is equally clear that Christian existence is an essential aspect of this development. 'For [this] we were baptized,' says Barth. The Christian community is the harbinger of the new world, not as responsible for its emergence, but in the sense that it announces and indicates the approach of the new world in and through its being and life. Through the Spirit's activity in its midst, it makes visible and comprehensible the new world in the midst of the old. The 'new men, new families, new relationships, new politics' which are indicative of the new world are to be found and seen here first of all.

Once again, then, a close examination of Barth's work reveals that he had a definite vision of Christian and ecclesial existence at this point in his career. In this lecture Barth's criticism of the church is attenuated although it is still present. In and of themselves, the church, religion and Christianity are incapable of producing a true relation to God, a genuine service of God, or the emergence of the new world. Nonetheless, if the church and Christians will dare to seek *God* in the Bible, if they will 'listen, watch and wait,' they will find themselves encountered by him, and granted a new beginning in the Holy Spirit which has the capacity to renew their entire existence. The Holy Spirit does not simply renew their inner life, but intends that the very righteousness of heaven is made visible and manifest amongst them in the midst of the continuing unrighteousness of this world. The primary aspect of Christian existence displayed in this lecture is faith, which is described as the daring which entrusts itself wholeheartedly to God in recognition of his sovereignty, and which is demonstrated in faithful obedience to the divine call and command.

---

[177] Barth, 'Strange New World,' 49.
[178] Barth, 'Strange New World,' 44.

The Nature of Barth's Ecclesial Ethics

In this chapter I have argued that from the earliest days of his pastorate, Karl Barth's theology was ethical in its orientation. Additionally, I have sought to show that this theological-ethical orientation in Barth's work had an ecclesial dimension which was an essential aspect of his work. Barth's break with liberalism occurred because of his conviction that the war and nationalism of his era were foreign to the being of God, and thus incompatible with authentic Christian existence. He joined the Social Democratic Party precisely because it 'had to be demonstrated' to his congregation that 'faith in the Greatest does not exclude but rather includes within it work and suffering in the realm of the imperfect'.[179]

Barth found in socialism a form of praxis which he believed was superior to that generally found in the church of his day. Socialist praxis, at least in its better moments, modelled the kind of thorough engagement with the realities of worldly life demanded by the kingdom of God. Nonetheless, commitment to socialist praxis was not, for Barth, an '-ism,' a philosophical commitment which stood in relative independence alongside or prior to his theological and ecclesial commitments. Barth understood socialism as a prophetic call to the church to live in accordance with its own integrity. His critique of the church vis-à-vis socialism was a critique of the church made from *within* the church, and *for the sake of* the church. This ecclesial motive in Barth's deliberations during this period becomes especially evident in his relationship with Ragaz. Confronted by the choice represented by Kutter and Ragaz, Barth rejected the Ragazian option, and in his own words, the two 'roared past one another like two express trains: he went out of the church, I went in'.[180]

Thus, in contrast to Marquardt's claim that Barth's theology and ecclesiology were the predicate of his politics,[181] it is here seen that Barth's ethics were theological, just as his theology was also ethical in its orientation. This orientation, which was already evident in Barth's initial break from his Marburg heritage, was dramatically sharpened as a result of Blumhardt's influence from whom Barth learnt the fundamental insight that '*God* is God' and 'God is *God*.'[182] From Blumhardt Barth also learnt to 'wait,' a proclivity which became the basic posture of an ethics which he would retain for the entirety of his career. Barth used the various insights gained from Blumhardt to establish the being and activity of the church on a new foundation. Being bound to one Lord, the church is loosed from all lesser lords and allegiances, and is thus freed for its own decisive being and activity as a kind of prophetic community in the midst of the broader society, and especially in solidarity with the weaker and poorer members of that society.

---

[179] Smart, ed., *Revolutionary Theology*, 28.

[180] Cited in Busch, *Karl Barth*, 92.

[181] See notes 30 and 49 above.

[182] Hart, *Karl Barth Vs. Emil Brunner*, 10.

Blumhardt's influence was also noticeable in the two lectures ('sermons'?) examined in this chapter on the righteousness of God and the new world in the Bible, in which the contours of Barth's ecclesio-moral vision begins to emerge. We have seen that Barth envisages a virtuous community of faith and prayer, waiting on and listening attentively to the voices of conscience and Scripture. He calls the communities addressed to an existence in contrast to the greed, injustice, isolation, immorality and violence of the world, yet also in solidarity with the world, as they testify through their life and proclamation to the new world already breaking into human society. The virtues mentioned by Barth in these lectures include especially hope, faith which issues in faithful obedience, purity, goodness and brotherhood. These might be supplemented by those in his article on Blumhardt which include liberty and compassion.

Particularly evident in these works is Barth's hope that the church would experience the new world of the kingdom of God breaking forth and growing vigorously in the world. The means by which this will occur remains under-developed in these works, but it is evident that the primary agency of this growth is the Holy Spirit. In 'The Righteousness of God' Barth provides an indication of how this will occur when he says, 'And then God works *in* us. Then begins *in* us, as from a seed, but an unfailing seed, the new basic something which overcomes unrighteousness.... [T]here is born *a new spirit* out of which grows a new world, the world of the righteousness of God.'[183] Although in this lecture Barth mentions the 'spirit' rather abstractly and only in passing, that he considers the new world to be the product of *the Holy Spirit's* activity is clear in the 'The New World.'[184] Further, although Barth has not yet developed the trinitarian underpinning of his theology, its essential orientation is here present, albeit in nascent form. The fact, however, that the Spirit is not limited to working solely within the realm of the church, and is ever pressing the church into a living solidarity with the world, shows that this ecclesial ethic is not to be construed in a sectarian sense.

A criticism that might be made against Barth's moral vision in these lectures is that raised by Hauerwas many years later: that Barth is too abstract, that he does not provide any concrete guidance which will enable his hearers to take practical steps towards the fulfilling of his grand vision.[185] Interestingly, this very criticism was put to Barth personally, seventy years prior to Hauerwas'

---

[183] Barth, 'Strange New World,' 25-26, emphasis added.

[184] Cf. note 79 (page 62) above, for a similarly abstract reference to 'the new spirit, stammering and stumbling in its broken way.'

[185] Stanley Hauerwas, 'On Honour: By Way of a Comparison of Barth and Trollope,' in *Reckoning With Barth: Essays in Commemoration of the Centenary of Karl Barth's Birth* (ed. N. Biggar; London: Mowbray, 1988), 149. See also Stanley Hauerwas, 'On Learning Simplicity in an Ambiguous Age: A Response To Hunsinger,' in *Barth, Barmen and the Confessing Church Today: Katallagete Symposium Series* (ed. J. Y. Holloway; Lewiston: Edwin Mellen, 1992), 133, 137.

article. In May 1916 Barth's 'The Righteousness of God' was discussed at a Swiss Religious Socialism Conference in Brugg. Following the conference, one of the attendees, Emil Brunner, corresponded with Barth and suggested that the faith-response Barth calls for is not clear. Brunner was concerned that Barth's description of Christian response as *faith* was too passive a description. Brunner wants some way to direct his energy and will to a different goal, and in this sense, to *do* something.[186] In a second letter, Brunner again complains, 'I soon find that all I have in my hands is an empty word with four letters [that is, "G-o-t-t"]…an abstract thought, with which I can neither understand nor master my life.'[187]

It must be admitted that in this respect Barth leaves much to the initiative of his hearers. But it is incorrect to say that Barth provides no guidance whatsoever for his hearers. Three observations from Barth's lecture on 'The New World' may be made which may diminish the force of this criticism. First, the various challenges issued by Barth in the course of his lecture, and culminating at its conclusion with an invitation to 'Come, for all things are now ready…' are challenges to embark on a journey which can only be legitimately described as a daring venture of faith, modelled on the examples of the characters in the biblical narrative highlighted in the beginning of the lecture. Barth clearly implies that his hearers are to echo the faithfulness of these characters in their own time and place.

In addition, Barth's characterisation of the New Testament church as 'a little crowd of folk who listen, watch and wait,'[188] also serves to remind his hearers of their responsibility. They too are to wait that they too might be encountered by the living God. It is noteworthy that even at this early stage in his career Barth adopts the call-response schema to depict ethical faithfulness. Christian existence for Barth is constituted by obedient response to the divine call and command, which comes as the believer 'waits.'

Second, it must be remembered that the entire conceptual framework within which Barth constructs his argument is the idea that the new world is *in the Bible*. Not only is the Bible a witness to the sovereignty of God, and a record of the great events by which the new world was established, it is also the vehicle by which we are presently encountered by God. Barth says, 'there is a spirit in the Bible that…begins to press us on…it presses us on to the primary fact whether we will or no….[T]he Bible unfolds to us as we are met, guided, drawn on, and made to grow by the grace of God.'[189] When we read the Bible 'rightly,' 'honestly' and 'carefully'[190]—by which Barth no doubt means in terms of theological realism, and with a view to the sovereignty of God—we

---

[186] See Hart, *Karl Barth Vs. Emil Brunner*, 12. The letter is dated June 9, 1916.

[187] Cited in Hart, *Karl Barth Vs. Emil Brunner* The letter is dated July 3, 1916.

[188] Barth, 'Strange New World,' 31.

[189] Barth, 'Strange New World,' 34.

[190] Barth, 'Strange New World,' 34, 41 and 44.

are confronted by the Word of God itself which summons us to a decision of faith, and which is itself the 'living grain of seed out of which a right relation to God, a service of God "in spirit and in truth," necessarily *must* issue'.[191]

These observations lead us to consider that Barth anticipated that as they carefully read their Bibles, his congregation would be grasped by the God who makes himself known through Scripture, and be led out 'beyond themselves' as they, like the patriarchs before them, obeyed the command which came to them, so becoming partakers of the new world. Although this may well seem a naïve and unrealistic expectation, it must be recognised as expressive of Barth's own experience with regard to Scripture—'lo, it began to speak to us!'

Third, the criticism that Barth's vision was too abstract may also be assuaged by recalling the earlier observation that he utilised the suggestive persona of the Isaianic Servant to represent the distinctive manner in which the community is to have its being in the world. Although he does not develop the implications of this motif, its use indicates the shape or contour of his vision of Christian and ecclesial existence. This image captures the faithful and obedient devotion, the intercessory and in-spirited character, the thirst for justice, and the redemptive and suffering identification with the oppressed—all of which were characteristic of Blumhardt, and which are also to characterise the church's identity and mission. These observations, then, while not diminishing the fact that Barth demanded much of his hearers, do indicate that in his view Christian life, far from being an idealistic or amorphous entity, had a definite shape and tendency.

Conclusion

The major elements of Barth's vision outlined in the works examined in this chapter include, of course, the sovereign priority of God and his unimpeachable righteousness over against all human activity and unrighteousness, the eschatological orientation of Christian life under the purview of the Holy Spirit as the immanent power of the coming kingdom, and the shape of Christian and ecclesial existence as waiting and hastening in the obedience of faith, and as brotherhood and solidarity with the oppressed. These themes are also found, and indeed, find their climax in this form in the first of Barth's major works, the first edition of his commentary on Paul's epistle to the Romans in 1919. To an examination of this work we now turn.

---

[191] Barth, 'Strange New World,' 44-45, emphasis added.

CHAPTER 3

LIFE IN THE THIRD DIMENSION:
DER RÖMERBRIEF (1919)

Your last special letter was worth a great deal to me. It cannot be otherwise than
that our ship *nolens volens* (whether we will it or not) approaches the doctrine of
the church as though it were a new continent; I, too, see it no differently and
actually it must be so, for we cruised about in the waters of the third article of the
creed since the beginning; there, one might say, lie our home port and ancient
coaling station, for the 'Holy Spirit' was perhaps somehow our starting point;
only we cannot remain spiritualists with Kutter and Ragaz and perhaps also the
younger Blumhardt but have to push on further to the point from which the Holy
Spirit comes: to the church as the bearer with its doctrine and Scriptures.[1]

Barth's first commentary on Paul's epistle to the Romans[2] has not received the
scholarly attention that has been given to his other works for several reasons.
First, it has been neglected in the English-speaking world simply because it has
not yet been translated. In addition, prominent interpreters of Barth's
theological development focussed primarily on the second edition as the
epitome of Barth's early work, and accordingly gave little or no attention to the
first edition.[3]

---

[1] Letter from Thurneysen to Barth dated March 26, 1925, in John D. Smart, ed.,
Revolutionary Theology in the Making: Barth-Thurneysen Correspondence, 1914-1925
(London: Epworth, 1964), 217-218.

[2] Karl Barth, *Der Römerbrief (Erste Fassung) 1919* (ed. Herrmann Schmidt; Zürich:
Theologischer-Verlag, 1985). Hereafter cited as *Romans I*. Please note that the
translations are my own, although I have used the following works as a guide: Bruce L.
McCormack, *Karl Barth's Critically Realistic Dialectical Theology: Its Genesis and
Development 1909-1936* (Oxford: Oxford University Press, 1995), David P. Henry, *The
Early Development of the Hermeneutic of Karl Barth as Evidenced by His
Appropriation of Romans 5:12-21* (Macon, Ga: Mercer University Press, 1985),
Eberhard Busch, *Karl Barth: His Life from Letters and Autobiographical Texts* (trans. J.
Bowden; Philadelphia: Fortress, 1976), and Eberhard Busch, *Karl Barth and the
Pietists: The Young Karl Barth's Critique of Pietism and Its Response* (trans. Daniel W.
Bloesch; Downers Grove: Inter-Varsity Press, 2004).

[3] See, for example, the scant treatment given to *Romans I* by Hans Urs von Balthasar,
The Theology of Karl Barth (trans. Edward T. Oakes; San Francisco: Ignatius, 1992),
and Thomas F. Torrance, *Karl Barth: An Introduction to His Early Theology 1910-1931*

However, by far the primary reason for this lack of attention, including the probable grounds for the first two reasons derives from Barth himself. In his preface to the second edition Barth claimed that the original has been so completely rewritten that whatever its merits and failings, the first edition could now 'disappear from the scene'.[4] In light of these comments it is not surprising, perhaps, that the first edition has been marginalised in scholarly discussion of Barth's theology. McCormack has recently argued, however, that Barth overstated the difference between the two editions in order to focus public attention solely on the revised version.[5] Be that as it may, examination of *Romans I* is nonetheless a profitable venture if Barth's theological development and the connections between the earlier and later periods of his work are to be accurately understood. The aim of this chapter in accordance with my aim and methodology overall, therefore, is to provide an examination of this work, with particular concern to observe Barth's construal of Christian existence.[6]

The outline of the chapter is straightforward. First, two introductory sections on the composition, purpose and theological framework of *Romans I* provide an orientation to the primary contours of Barth's thought in this work, and thus also, a foundation for understanding his vision of Christian and ecclesial existence. The next section investigates whether the manner in which Barth develops his theological ontology with its strong emphasis on the universal objectivity of the fall in Adam and redemption in Christ, functions to evacuate the concept of human agency of any genuine meaning. This section argues that Barth does, in fact, provide an account of human agency, but that this agency, while genuine, remains ever contingent on the prior and encompassing divine agency on which it is dependent. The fourth section of the chapter examines Barth's critique of religion and ethics, both of which share the common fault of being human attempts at the establishment of self-righteousness. This begs the question, of course, of whether any genuine religion or morality is actually possible, especially in light of Barth's blunt assertion that 'according to the ultimate standpoint we must take in Christ, there are no ethics. There is only the

---

(Edinburgh: T. & T. Clark, 1962). In his examination of Barth's ethics Willis contends that study of Barth's theological development must consist primarily 'in a delineation of the central thrusts' of the second edition—Robert E. Willis, *The Ethics of Karl Barth* (Leiden: Brill, 1971), 21-22. Similarly, Colm O'Grady omits discussion of the first edition entirely in his treatment of Barth's ecclesiology. See Colm O'Grady, *The Church in the Theology of Karl Barth* (London: Geoffrey Chapman, 1968).

[4] Karl Barth, *The Epistle to the Romans* (trans. E. C. Hoskyns; 6th ed. Oxford: Oxford University Press, 1933), 2. Hereafter cited as *Romans II*.

[5] McCormack, *Karl Barth's Dialectical Theology*, 180-182.

[6] For the following discussion, I am indebted especially to McCormack, *Karl Barth's Dialectical Theology*, 135-183, Henry, *The Early Development*, Timothy J. Gorringe, *Karl Barth: Against Hegemony* (Oxford: Oxford University Press, 1999), 37-48, and Busch, *Karl Barth and the Pietists*, 26-68.

activity of God.'[7] It will be seen, however, that Barth has a quite particular notion of ethics in mind when he makes this assertion, and that he is, in fact, clearing the ground of competing claims in order to commence construction of his own form of ecclesial ethics. This is the focus of the final two sections which seek to elucidate the specific nature and shape of Christian and ecclesial existence as envisaged by Barth at this time.

The Composition and Purpose of *Romans I*

On January 1, 1916 Barth wrote a letter to Thurneysen in which he says, 'Today I looked into Ritschl's history of pietism and scented in it something of the air that Wernle breathes. When the time comes to strike the great blow against the theologians, these ideas, too, will have to be considered and digested very thoroughly.'[8] Later that year, shortly after commencing his studies in Paul's epistle to the Romans, he writes again that 'the decisive strokes for which we now prepare cannot come for another ten years'.[9] Little did he know, however, that the little 'copy-book with comments' in which he was recording the fruit of his exegetical endeavours would itself become a significant blow against the prevailing theology.

Barth, as we saw in the previous chapter, began his investigations in Romans as a result of a conviction that he had to find an entirely new foundation for theological and pastoral activity. In addition, he wanted 'to snatch it from [his] opponents' as he explained to Ragaz in November 1916.[10] The commentary was written, of course, against the tumultuous backdrop of wartime Europe and the social dislocation that arose as a result of the war, as well as the Bolshevik Revolution of 1917. The war ended as Barth was reviewing the final proofs of the book, but social conflict continued with the failed Sparticist revolt in Germany and the *Landesstreik* in Switzerland.[11] Yet for all that, Barth notes that the book was written 'with a joyful sense of discovery'.[12] In his study he found himself confronted by 'something from afar, from Asia Minor or Corinth, something very ancient, early oriental, indefinably sunny, wild, original, that somehow is hidden behind these sentences'.[13]

---

[7] Barth, *Romans I*, 524.

[8] Smart, ed., *Revolutionary Theology*, 36.

[9] Barth, letter to Thurneysen dated July 27, 1916, in Smart, *Revolutionary Theology*, 38.

[10] Busch, *Karl Barth*, 98.

[11] For a brief account of the political unrest in Germany from October 1918 through March 1919, see Lynn Abrams, *Bismarck and the German Empire, 1871-1918* (London: Routledge, 1995), 64-66, and for an account of the Swiss *Landesstreik* ['national strike'], see McCormack, *Karl Barth's Dialectical Theology*, 185-187.

[12] Barth, *Romans I*, 4.

[13] Barth, letter to Thurneysen dated September 27, 1916, in Smart, *Revolutionary Theology*, 43.

Barth also complained that modern commentaries on Paul missed perhaps as much as ninety-nine percent of the real content of Paul's letter.[14] Hart refers to Barth's commentary, therefore, as 'a frontal attack on the contemporary state of New Testament studies', while Smart suggests that it was 'an experiment in a new form of exegesis which was to have far-reaching hermeneutical significance'.[15] In his careful examination of the exegetical sources Barth utilised in the preparation of his commentary Henry concludes that although Barth made careful and judicious use of historical-critical commentaries and studies, he nevertheless maintained a fundamentally different presupposition which dramatically affected the structure and tone of his work. Henry notes that the major contrast between Barth and the historical-critical scholars was that the latter only want to know Paul from a 'purely historical view' leaving possible applications of Paul's thought for modern audiences to the reader, whereas Barth wants to know Paul as someone whose thought bears contemporary relevance, and through whom God continues to speak to people in all ages.[16]

Barth, in other words, wants to penetrate beyond a merely historical interest in Paul and his thought, in order to hear afresh the very Word of God that Paul heard in the concrete political realities of his day.[17] Barth did not write to produce a new historical-critical account of Romans. His purpose rather, was to try to discover how the message of Romans could be preached in the Church.[18] Barth said as much in his 1922 lecture 'The Need and Promise of Christian Preaching.' Here Barth recalls that the impetus to his study in Romans was the weekly struggle to relate Bible and life in his ministry of preaching.[19] He notes that 'naturally and evidently there are many subjects mentioned in the book— New Testament theology, dogmatics, ethics, and philosophy—but you will best understand it when you hear through it all, the minister's question: What is preaching?'[20]

The origin of this work in Barth's pastoral ministry helps account for the

---

[14] Barth, letter to Thurneysen dated September 27, 1916, in Smart, *Revolutionary Theology*, 43.

[15] See John W. Hart, *Karl Barth Vs. Emil Brunner: The Formation and Dissolution of a Theological Alliance, 1916-1936* (New York: Peter Lang, 2001), 15, and James D. Smart, *The Divided Mind of Modern Theology: Karl Barth and Rudolph Bultmann, 1908-1933* (Philadelphia: Westminster, 1967), 81-82. For a comprehensive study of Barth's hermeneutical principles at this time, see Richard E. Burnett, *Karl Barth's Theological Exegesis: The Hermeneutical Principles of the Römerbrief Period* (Tübingen: Mohr Siebeck, 2001).

[16] Henry, *The Early Development*, 92-93.

[17] Gorringe, *Against Hegemony*, 48.

[18] Henry, *The Early Development*, 93, see also 121-124.

[19] Karl Barth, *The Word of God and the Word of Man* (trans. D. Horton; New York: Harper & Brothers, 1956), 100.

[20] Barth, *The Word of God*, 102-103.

homiletical tone of the commentary. Barth's explosive language pours forth with the bold conviction of a preacher seeking, struggling to bring forth the message of the gospel that the Word of God might be heard once more, even in so dark, desperate and dangerous days as those in which he lived. Further, and more significantly, this homiletical form indicates that Barth is not simply aiming at the establishment of an esoteric worldview, or the vanquishing of an abstract or contrary academic perspective. Rather his work is expressly intended to help shape the existence and life of the church in concrete ways. He sought to preach to his congregation in such a way that they were enabled to relate 'Bible and life'. Similarly, Henry suggests that the aim of *Romans I* was to invite readers to 'active participation with Paul in the world of God'.[21] In both his preaching and writing ministries, Barth was working in accordance with an ecclesio-ethical motive.

This is not to say, of course, that Barth did not write polemically or in order to delineate a theological worldview, but to say that his polemics and theological worldview function in service of a practical end. The nature of this end might be partially discerned by examining the targets of his criticisms. McCormack identifies four major groups targeted by Barth in the commentary. These are a) Liberalism-Pietism; b) Idealistic epistemology and ethics; c) the 'Positives' (what McCormack names churchly Christianity or 'religion'); and d) Religious Socialism. According to McCormack,

> [i]f there is a common thread which joins these four (in the details, quite different) movements it is the element of individualism. Barth's new theology represented an assault on a central feature of late nineteenth-century bourgeois culture: the understanding of the human individual as the creative subject of culture and history....Barth was at the same time attacking a religion which had assimilated itself to the needs of idealistically construed cultural development; a religion which prided itself on being the animating principle for that development. He was attacking a religion which provided bourgeois culture with perhaps its most crucial ideological support.[22]

McCormack makes clear the inherently ethical and ecclesial orientation of Barth's theology as expressed in *Romans I*. For Barth, as we shall see, such individualism is the very essence of the fall, and thus the complicity of religion (the church) in support of such individualism was tantamount to apostasy, an abandonment of its true calling and essence. Rather than assimilation to the idolatrous character of the prevailing culture, the church is to be ordered in accordance with its own distinctive character and charter. Clearly, then, Barth was not engaged in theology for theology's sake, but had a definite ethical and ecclesial orientation and purpose in his work.

---

[21] Henry, *The Early Development*, 122.
[22] McCormack, *Karl Barth's Dialectical Theology*, 140-141.

The Theological Framework of *Romans I*

The Two-Dimensional World

In the difficult and dangerous days of November 1918 Barth laments as he refers to

> these extraordinary times....*What* is there to say? One stands astonished, does he not, and can only state how the face of the world changes visibly: on *this* side of things. But the *other* side: the meaning and content, the actual trend of it all, the movements in the spiritual realm that now take place, the doors of God that now open or close....Who is there now with a comprehensive view who is able to see to the very roots of world events in order to speak and act from that standpoint?...If only we had been converted to the Bible *earlier* so that we would now have solid ground under our feet! One broods alternately over the newspaper and the New Testament and actually sees fearfully little of the organic connection between the two worlds concerning which one should now be able to give a clear and powerful witness.[23]

It is precisely the relation between these two worlds, between 'this side of things' and 'the other side' which Barth was struggling to bring to light in *Romans I*. Indeed, Henry has suggested that Barth's commentary facilitates the meeting of these two worlds, the world of the bible and particularly of Paul, and that of the turn-of-the-century Europe in which Barth lived.[24]

The manner in which Barth brought these two worlds into relation was through the development of a particular conception of world history cast in an eschatological framework. Barth, influenced by the works of Beck and Schweitzer,[25] believed he had found this understanding of world history in Paul himself, particularly Romans 5:12-21. Many of Barth's contemporaries agreed that Romans 5:12-21 involves what could be called a philosophy of world history. Barth, too, accepts this view, although he disagrees with them concerning the importance of this philosophy of world history with regard to the actual message of Romans. Whereas many of Barth's contemporaries regarded Paul's worldview as a relic of his age, Barth interpreted it in terms of theological realism.[26] Furthermore, Barth's interpretation was unique in that he also introduced the inclusion of the other-side (*jenseitig*) dimension of reality as an essential part of the understanding of these verses.[27]

---

[23] Barth, letter to Thurneysen dated November 11, 1918, in Smart, *Revolutionary Theology*, 45.

[24] Henry, *The Early Development*, 113.

[25] Henry, *The Early Development*, 64-71. See also Busch, *Karl Barth and the Pietists*, 30-35.

[26] Henry, *The Early Development*, 67.

[27] Henry, *The Early Development*, 94.

Barth's contribution at this point is highly significant. Underlying world history and world events is another history and other events, a cosmic history, a history which occurs in God, or better, in the *jenseitig* dimension of reality, and which punctuates earthly history and becomes visible there. It is this notion which is behind Barth's expressed longing for a 'comprehensive view' which is 'able to see to the very roots of world events in order to speak and act from that standpoint'.[28] McCormack rightly suggests that *Romans I* is best understood as an attempt to engage in a thoroughgoing criticism of obvious or surface reality in order to create an open space for 'real reality'—the kingdom of God—to emerge.[29]

In *Romans I*, therefore, Barth writes that

> [t]here is...not only a truth which is beyond this world (*jenseitige Wahrheit*), but also events beyond this world (*jenseitige Ereignisse*); a world history in heaven, an inner movement in God. What we call 'history' and 'events' are only a confused reflection of turns occurring there (*jenseitiger Wendungen*). One such turn of the times (*jenseitige Wende der Zeiten*) is marked in our 'history' by the *cross of Christ*. God's faithfulness breaks through the inescapable necessity of his wrath hanging over humanity, creating righteousness on earth which he can crown with eternal life. [30]

Here Barth posits a dynamic relation between the two worlds, albeit, a dynamism which travels in a singular direction: from *Jenseits* (the other side) to *Diesseits* (this side). In speaking of the action of God, Barth uses the imagery of a 'breakthrough' to indicate the character of this dynamic relation: God's

---

[28] Note that in his letter to Thurneysen Barth does not use precisely the *Jenseits-Diesseits* terminology found in *Romans I*. Here Barth says, 'on *this* side ('auf *dieser* Seite') of things. But the *other* side ('Aber die *andere* Seite').' Although the terminology differs, the conceptuality is the same.

[29] McCormack, *Karl Barth's Dialectical Theology*, 140. In an examination of Barth's early rhetoric, Stephen Webb suggests that Barth's style could be labelled as 'Expressionist' and associated with the cultural movement known by that name. Webb does not claim any direct influence of expressionism on Barth, but rather that they both maintain a similar 'relationship to a culture in crisis'. Although expressionism 'was in no sense disconnected from reality...it wanted to distort, extend and even fragment and shatter the surface of reality in order to uncover something even more real hidden beneath the surface....Complacency could only be battled by exaggeration, and this gave the expressionists their prophetic edge.' See Stephen H. Webb, *Re-Figuring Theology: The Rhetoric of Karl Barth* (New York: State University of New York, 1991), 10, 12. It should be noted that Webb's discussion is focussed entirely on the second edition of Romans, although the features noted apply also to the first edition. That Barth himself was aware of this emphasis in the expressionist movement in art is evident in his 1919 Tambach lecture. See Barth, *The Word of God*, 292. See also my own discussion of this lecture in chapter four below.

[30] Barth, *Romans I*, 161.

faithfulness, his decision of redemption in the face of human sinfulness, has broken through from his side to our side and become visible on our side in the cross of Christ.[31] Barth uses this same imagery a few pages later:

> With the breakthrough: Immanuel! God with us! (Matt. 1:23) which has taken place in now-time, in the messianic present, in the decisive turn of the aeons *in heaven*, a life process is also inaugurated *on earth*, on the historical-psychological side of our existence. We are no longer the same. We have been placed into the process which reaches from the beyond (*vom Jenseits*) into the present (*ins Diesseits*).[32]

Again Barth declares that the relation between the two worlds proceeds from *Jenseits* to *Diesseits*, and so indicates the ontological priority that inheres in *Jenseits*. Events and history on earth are determined by and subject to events and decisions which occur in the *jenseitig* dimension of reality. The two dimensions, then, are not to be considered in terms of a dualistic or static confrontation, but in terms of a movement proceeding from the one side to the other.

Barth employs this worldview to situate the entirety of God's saving activity in a cosmic context. The great events by which human existence and history have been determined, that is, the Fall and the redemption accomplished in Christ, are both *jenseitig* events, determinations which had their origin in the *jenseitig* or *geistig* (spiritual) dimension and are reflected on this side, in the world of space and time. In addition, not only does movement occur between the two worlds as described, but world-history itself is set within a broader eschatological movement in which Adam gives way to Christ, Fall to restoration, and the realities of earthly history to the kingdom of God.[33] Thus, not only have we 'been placed into [a] process which reaches from the beyond into the present' but the same process presses inexorably forward toward the goal which God has ordained for his entire creation.

Humanity under Sin

It is important to recognise that not only the incarnation and death of Christ, but also the Fall itself was a *jenseitig* event. When Barth speaks of the Fall, he is not referring to an earthly-historical event revolving around Adam alone:

---

[31] This is a prominent metaphor in *Romans I*, with *durchbrechen* or *Durchbruch* being used many times by Barth to describe such things as the breakthrough of God's power (91, 146), or his righteousness (148), or grace (195, 234), as well as breakthrough into freedom (242) and so on.

[32] Barth, *Romans I*, 167.

[33] Henry, *The Early Development*, 126.

The breakthrough (*Durchbruch*) of sin and death occurred just as the breakthrough of righteousness and life, one time for the *first* time....The 'historical Adam' as such is as insignificant, as unimportant, as the 'historical Jesus' as such! Adam's fall and Christ's death are important on account of the universal, comprehensive, other-side turnings in heaven...which in both instances have taken place *behind* the solitary historical event....It is not a matter of an individual and, as it were, the first in a series, but rather of the absolute disposition of a whole....It is a matter of a *presupposition* of all happening, which indeed in *one* point of history breaks through (*durchbricht*) and becomes visible for the first time.[34]

The decision to sin, therefore, is a supra-temporal decision made by *humanity* as such, a *jenseitig* decision, on the *geistig* as opposed to the *seelisch* ('soulish,' emotional or psychological) side of humanity, but one with inevitable consequences of sin and death on this side.[35] The nature of human sin was the desire of humanity for autonomy over against God, by which they fell 'out of immediacy of being with God'.[36] For Barth, this is the 'one sin': it was too little for humanity to simply be God's.[37] Humanity seizes the honour and thanks due to God for itself, thinking of and giving to itself what it should think of and give to God.[38] Nor was the decision to sin a matter of fate or destiny. Rather, it was a decision freely chosen by humanity, and which became the source of all incidents after the manner of Adam's trespass.[39]

Prior to the Fall humanity existed in a relation of immediacy with God, not only in harmony with him but also as a participant in his creative power. It is this participation which rendered the Fall so devastating. Barth attributes a creative power to the human will in its immediacy with God that affects the whole cosmos. So long as humanity remained in this union of immediacy with God, everything in creation also remained in harmony with God. The human decision for autonomy from God, however, also brought about separation from God for the creation.[40] Although humanity has fallen out of a relation of immediacy with God it has not 'become detached' from its Origin (*Ursprung*), but rather bears unconscious memory of him in all of life. In the suppression of this memory humanity commits an unnatural deed and thus becomes not only unfaithful to God, but also to itself.[41]

---

[34] Barth, *Romans I*, 182.

[35] Henry, *The Early Development*, 148, 130.

[36] Barth, *Romans I*, 177. '*Aus der Unmittelbarkeit des Seins mit Gott.*' Note that in contrast to Schleiermacher and the liberal tradition, Barth views the relation of immediacy as one of being rather than feeling. See Terry L. Cross, *Dialectic in Karl Barth's Doctrine of God* (New York: Peter Lang, 2001), 66.

[37] Barth, *Romans I*, 177-178.

[38] Barth, *Romans I*, 27.

[39] Barth, *Romans I*, 183.

[40] Henry, *The Early Development*, 149.

[41] Barth, *Romans I*, 28.

Falling out of a relation of immediacy with God, humanity came under the terrible lordship of death, which Barth (citing Beck) refers to as a 'perverted, downward, centrifugal, disintegrating movement'.[42] Death, as an alien power, drives everything away from its centre in God, and from everything else.[43] Barth, again following Beck, also refers to death as a 'power of disorganisation' (*Desorganisationskraft*) which 'deranges, makes sick, undermines and disintegrates the organisms in their vitality (*Lebenskräften*), functions, and ultimately in their existence'.[44]

The Victory of Life

God, however, in spite of human wilfulness and unfaithfulness, has not allowed this profound and devastating alienation to continue to exercise lordship over humanity. In accordance with Paul's typology in Romans 5, Barth gathers human and world history around the two archetypal figures of Adam and Christ. The incarnation, death and resurrection of Christ are a counter-movement inaugurated by God in opposition to the disintegrating movement of sin and death. These events in the *diesseitig* dimension constitute the breaking through of the decisive decision and turn already accomplished on the other side. And just as the initial *jenseitig* turn in Adam was cosmic and universal in its scope and effects in the realm of space and time, so too the *jenseitig* turn in Christ is cosmic and universal in its scope and effects, although these effects are set within the encompassing framework of eschatology, as we see in the passage cited earlier:

> With the breakthrough: Immanuel! God with us! (Matt. 1:23) which has taken place in now-time, in the messianic present, in the decisive turn of the aeons *in heaven*, a life process is also inaugurated *on earth*, on the historical-psychological side of our existence. We are no longer the same. We have been placed into the process which reaches from the beyond into the present.[45]

In addition to the two-dimensional view of reality evident in this passage, are indications of two further significant aspects of Barth's theology in this commentary. First, says Barth, 'we are no longer the same.' Barth's soteriology here, as throughout the entirety of his career, is understood firstly in objective terms. The divine-human relation has been fundamentally altered as a result of the obedience of Christ, through which he has 'fulfilled the true destiny of human life'.[46] In his obedience Christ regained the relation of immediacy that God had always purposed with and for humanity, thereby restoring human

---

[42] Barth, *Romans I*, 176.
[43] Henry, *The Early Development*, 128.
[44] Barth, *Romans I*, 176, cf. 180.
[45] Barth, *Romans I*, 167.
[46] Gorringe, *Against Hegemony*, 39.

essence to its 'proper' (*gerechte*) condition.[47]

Christ's obedience is ultimately demonstrated in his death where his will—a free and wholly human will—is at one with God's will.[48] This death constitutes a reversal of the death that has reigned over humanity because it was the death of one obedient to and in immediacy with God.[49] In his death is revealed the struggle, and in his resurrection is revealed the consummated victory of divine power over the powers of sin and death.[50] Barth boasts, therefore, of 'world-redemption on the basis of world-reconciliation'.[51] As a result of his death which has altered the disposition of the whole of life in its relation to the Origin, there is no one who cannot and may not be righteous and live. 'In the One,' says Barth, 'all are righteous, and in the One all are drawn into the victory of life.'[52]

Although this 'victory of life' is an accomplished reality in heaven, it remains 'in process' on this side of reality. This is the second significant feature of Barth's theology indicated in the citation above, where Barth says that 'a life process is also inaugurated *on earth*, on the historical-psychological side of our existence'. This life-process commenced with the coming of Christ. He himself is the divine seed of the new world, the 'germ-cell of life' planted once more in both nature and history, the beginning of the new creation in which death will be no more.[53] According to Barth, God has now cut the knots of the hopelessly entangled situation into which humanity has fallen, inaugurating a messianic, divine-earthly history in which humanity has been turned again to God.[54] Through his death 'he introduces something new into the history of the world. In finishing his life in this way, he fundamentally overcomes the old'.[55]

Barth's use of 'process' language functions to complement, and to some extent, ameliorate the language of 'breakthrough'. The latter indicates that the relation of the two dimensions of reality is conceived only as a series of 'moments' which poses the problem of the continuity of divine activity on this side of things. In addition to 'process' Barth also uses other metaphors of continuity such as 'movement', 'development' and above all, the terminology learnt from Blumhardt and Beck: 'organic' and 'organism'.[56]

Barth uses the concept of the organic in two primary ways. First, he uses it

---

[47] Barth, *Romans 1*, 22. Henry notes that by using *gerecht* here, Barth draws a link between the 'proper' human condition and the righteousness (*Gerechtigkeit*) of God. See Henry, *The Early Development*, 14.

[48] Barth, *Romans 1*, 197-198.

[49] Barth, *Romans 1*, 225.

[50] Barth, *Romans 1*, 98.

[51] Barth, *Romans 1*, 200.

[52] Barth, *Romans 1*, 198.

[53] Barth, *Romans 1*, 24, 302.

[54] Barth, *Romans 1*, 20.

[55] Barth, *Romans 1*, 225.

[56] Gorringe, *Against Hegemony*, 40.

to stress the idea that the kingdom of God is an *organism*, that is, a unity, or a totality, something complete in itself. Not only is the kingdom of God a unity, it *unifies*; not only is it an entity complete in itself, it embraces all reality within itself and brings it into fundamental relation. Barth, therefore, uses the concept of the organism to proclaim the universality and all-inclusive nature of the kingdom of God against all religious and secular forms of individualism, isolation and fragmentation that characterise life under the hegemony of sin and death,[57] which is, as we have already seen, the 'power of disorganisation'.[58]

Second, he uses the concept of the organic as a description of the way in which the kingdom grows: 'The coming world does not come mechanically but organically', says Barth,[59] by which he means that the growth of the kingdom takes place quietly, gently and steadily by the power of the life process inaugurated in Christ and at work in the world.[60] Barth uses this concept to insist that the kingdom of God is not the result of our own activity and effort, or built upon any existing realities, but is solely the work of God in and among us. Further, this remains a *hidden* development which leaves traces in worldly history but is never simply identical with visible progress or growth.[61]

This latter point highlights an important distinction between the use of the concept in Barth and Beck. According to McCormack,

> [i]n Barth's hands…the category takes on a significance which had scarcely been envisioned by Beck. What Beck intended with the phrase 'organic growth' was 'a new unique nature principle,' a cosmic and naturalistically conceived Christ-principle which transforms the world from within. Against such naturalism, Barth insisted that the history of God was a hidden 'absolutely not-given' history (*Romans I*, 136). The history of God is always grounded in the moment-by-moment, present action of God and never passes over into a 'nature principle'.[62]

The continuity of the development of the kingdom in history, then, remains grounded in God, and the teleology of the 'history in God' in the *jenseitig* dimension of reality.[63] The work of God cannot be explained simply in terms of events, causes and processes occurring on the surface of history: the movement of the kingdom occurs *within* history, but it is not *of* history. Barth's construal of reality in this manner allowed him to situate the reality and activity of God within history while placing it beyond the reach of historical investigation, and the constructivist epistemology of historicism.[64] By insisting that the growth of

---

[57] McCormack, *Karl Barth's Dialectical Theology*, 153-154.

[58] Barth, *Romans I*, 176.

[59] Barth, *Romans I*, 21.

[60] Busch, *Karl Barth and the Pietists*, 33, 52.

[61] McCormack, *Karl Barth's Dialectical Theology*, 154.

[62] McCormack, *Karl Barth's Dialectical Theology*, 153.

[63] McCormack, *Karl Barth's Dialectical Theology*, 155.

[64] McCormack, *Karl Barth's Dialectical Theology*, 146-147.

the kingdom is everywhere and always the result of divine action Barth was also able to set faith beyond the reach of psychological investigation.[65] As we shall see in the following sections, these are fundamental moves made by Barth which not only enabled him to undermine the basic tenets of the historicism, psychologism and pietism which prevailed in contemporary theology, but which also enabled him to develop and delineate a particular vision of Christian and ecclesial existence.

Origins of Barth's Theological Framework

In this commentary, then, Barth sets forth a theological ontology in which all earthly-historical reality is predicated upon and encompassed by the far greater, ontologically prior reality of the 'other side' which also exists as the presupposition which is determinative for all existence on this side of reality. Those events of fundamental cosmic significance such as the fall, the incarnation, and the death and resurrection of Jesus occur *there* first, and only subsequently become visible and real in this dimension of reality. Further, in accordance with the sovereign purpose of God, the entirety of earthly-historical existence is also placed within an overarching eschatological context so that over against the decentralising disintegrating powers of death at work in the world, the kingdom of God grows organically toward the consummation of God's saving intention.

Some commentators, of course, both in Barth's day and more recently, have conjectured regarding the sources of this theological framework. Hans Urs von Balthasar, for example, writes that Barth

> meant to proclaim glad tidings. The vision is enthusiastic and in its own way it unrolls the scroll of God's saving economy. But it makes use of a conceptual framework that owes more to Plato, right-wing (that is, religious) Hegelianism and religious socialism than it does to the Bible, Luther or Calvin.[66]

According to von Balthasar, 'pantheism manages to dissolve the creature both into God and into nothingness. In this theology, God is the "innermost, if scattered, *nature* of all things and of man"'.[67] The work as a whole is a 'radical philosophical mysticism', the theme of which is 'dynamic eschatology, the irreversible movement from a fatally doomed temporal order to a new living order filled with the life of God, the restoration (*apokatastasis*) of the original ideal creation in God'.[68] If von Balthasar's reading of *Romans I* were accurate, it would suggest the absorption of humanity into divine being with the

---

[65] McCormack, *Karl Barth's Dialectical Theology*, 158.

[66] von Balthasar, *The Theology of Karl Barth*, 64.

[67] von Balthasar, *The Theology of Karl Barth*, 66. The citation is from Barth, *Romans I*, 55.

[68] von Balthasar, *The Theology of Karl Barth*, 67, 64.

corresponding annulment of human agency and corollary loss of any serious notion of Christian and ecclesial existence. Von Balthasar's energetic and influential work established the central paradigm of interpretation for a generation of Barth scholars, including such as O'Grady and Willis. It is little wonder, then, that their descriptions of Barth's ethics are predominantly negative at this point.[69]

In like manner Henry also finds the origins of Barth's theological framework in philosophy, but argues that Barth has derived the categories of his thought primarily from Kant.[70] Nevertheless, Henry argues that Barth also effects a transformation of Kant's thought by the imposition of his theological ontology with the result that 'Kant and Barth travel the same road, but they start at opposite ends and travel in opposite directions.'[71] The result of this transformation, says Henry, is that now Barth's worldview bears striking resemblance to the philosophical idealism of Hegel.[72] This is not because Hegel had any direct influence on Barth's thought, but because both Barth and Hegel make similar transformations of Kant's thought.[73] Certainly Barth's familiarity and continued engagement with Kant cannot be dismissed.[74] Nevertheless, even Henry's description of Barth's relation to Kant indicates not so much dependence as critique. Again, more recent commentators have argued that although Barth retains some semantic links to Kantian thought, the actual use of his terminology and concepts owe more to Kutter than to Kantianism, and are employed more for rhetorical and critical purposes.[75]

Barth, of course, believed that his theological framework was predicated on

---

[69] More recently von Balthasar's interpretation of Barth has been overturned by the magisterial work of Bruce McCormack who has argued decisively against von Balthasar's thesis that Barth experienced two major turns in his career, in 1914 from liberal theology to 'radical Christianity', and around 1930 from dialectic to 'a genuine, self-authenticating' theology. See von Balthasar, *The Theology of Karl Barth,* 93. This book supports the position of McCormack by showing that while Barth's work certainly underwent profound development over the course of his career, particularly with respect to his grounding of theology in christology, its fundamental orientation and emphases were present in germinal form even during this early period.

[70] Henry finds a number of points of contact between Barth and Kant, most especially the correlation of *Jenseits/Diesseits* with the noumenal and phenomenal realms, and the central role given to the human will. 'Here,' says Henry, 'Barth appears to follow Kant almost to the letter.' See Henry, *The Early Development,* 134.

[71] Henry, *The Early Development,* 131, 133.

[72] Henry, *The Early Development,* 135-139, see also 206.

[73] Henry, *The Early Development,* 138.

[74] Henry notes that Barth gave a presentation on Kant's *Prolegomena to Any Future Metaphysics* on November 1, 1917—clear evidence of his continuing engagement with Kantian thought. See Henry, *The Early Development,* 113.

[75] See McCormack, *Karl Barth's Dialectical Theology,* 149, also 43-49. See also Archibald James Spencer, *Clearing a Space for Human Action: Ethical Ontology in the Theology of Karl Barth* (New York: Peter Lang, 2003), 140-141, 145-147.

the writings of Paul, explicated in accordance with his understanding of the task of hermeneutics, using the cosmological and metaphysical terminology of his day. Perhaps the best account of the influences discerned in the theology of *Romans I* is delineated by Barth's associate and biographer, Eberhard Busch, who suggests that Barth's commentary reflects a Herrmannian focus on the concepts of *life* and *actuality* (together with Beck's notion of how that life develops organically), the socialist insistence that God's purpose is the establishing of a *new world*, and the influence of one particular group of pietists (several Swabian pietist theologians and commentators; Blumhardt also lived and ministered in this area) who emphasised the reality and coming of the *kingdom of God*.[76]

It was the constellation of these ideas that influenced Barth's approach to the interpretation of Paul's letter to the Romans, and within which his vision of Christian and ecclesial existence was also nurtured. In the next section I take up an explication of that vision beginning with the troublesome issue of human agency in Barth.

The Question of Human Agency

The previous discussion of Barth's theological framework included a brief treatment of humanity under sin and the divine response to that sin in the death and resurrection of Jesus Christ by whom the eschatological victory of life is inaugurated. This discussion also raises a question crucial to a consideration of Barth's ethics, namely, whether his construal of the two-dimensional structure of reality, together with the objectivity with which events and decisions in the *jenseitig* dimension are determinative for occurrences in the *diesseitig* dimension, serves to diminish or even annul the reality of human agency. This section, therefore, addresses this question by examining how Barth conceives of human agency at this stage of his career in face of the objectivity of the fall in Adam and the redemption in Christ.

In the previous section we noted Barth's contention that sin is humanity's desire for autonomy over against God.[77] For Barth, as we saw, this sin is a supra-temporal decision of *humanity*, and as such it has become a 'presupposition of all happening'.[78] It is clear that here Barth, while he is careful to qualify what he does *not* intend, does depend on a notion of original sin whereby the free act of separation instigated by humanity against God lies at the base of all human thought and action, and is the source of all ongoing incidents of sin on the earthly-historical side of reality.[79]

Humanity, then, exists in a tension in which its sinfulness is both determined

---

[76] See Busch, *Karl Barth and the Pietists*, 30-35, 53-67.

[77] Barth, *Romans I*, 177.

[78] Barth, *Romans I*, 182.

[79] Barth, *Romans I*, 183.

(on account of the solidarity which exists between Adam and every other person) *and* freely chosen. The fall is the result of the 'misused freedom of humanity',[80] 'the division of will into divine and human will'[81] by which the nature of humanity is 'poisoned' by sin.[82] Sin itself is now an 'organic element' in the world,[83] the movement of the power of disorganisation which characterises the 'line of Adam' so that the same quest for autonomy which displayed itself in Adam breaks forth inevitably in the life of every person. Barth does not seek to explain precisely how present human sinfulness is linked to that of Adam's, except to say that

> [t]he one sin of humanity, which has become historical with [Adam], repeats, varies, and renews itself continually all through subsequent history, and we all loyally follow the way which he was the first to take.... The other-side hidden fatal determinant of our existence presses toward its consequence. We now stand objectively under the cosmic power of death. 'We are by nature children of wrath.'[84]

As it is the case that human sinfulness is both grounded *outside* the individual and yet is also freely chosen *by* the individual, so also with regard to salvation. Barth trenchantly insists that the individual experience of salvation is merely 'the smallest part of a *world*-event,...a matter of world history', something which has befallen us from entirely other dimensions.[85] To construe salvation in strictly individualist terms is the equivalent of seeking to value a single link in isolation from the chain of which it is part.

This salvation was decisively accomplished on our behalf by God's action in Jesus Christ, who is set over against the 'whole world of "fall" in which the "falling" of Adam lives to the full again and again' as the 'breakthrough of *his* plans, the vindication of *his* ways, the acquittal of the captive whole of men, the disclosure of a new history'.[86] In Christ is established a new presupposition which was activated through the obedience of Christ in his death, where his will—a free and wholly human will—is at one with God's will.[87] In Christ 'a changed disposition of the whole of life in its relation to the Origin breaks through (*durchbricht*) and becomes visible'.[88] God's gift to the world in Christ is that 'the *freedom* of humanity from fate is re-established with the same universal validity with which it was lost in Adam. As a gift from heaven it has

---

[80] Barth, *Romans I*, 302.

[81] Barth, *Romans I*, 197.

[82] Barth, *Romans I*, 178, 300.

[83] Barth, *Romans I*, 179.

[84] Barth, *Romans I*, 183-184.

[85] Barth, *Romans I*, 172-173.

[86] Barth, *Romans I*, 193-194.

[87] Barth, *Romans I*, 197-198.

[88] Barth, *Romans I*, 198.

come to us as the inauguration of a new relationship to life…a new causality in which a future slumbers which will be other than the past.'[89]

It is evident that Barth's soteriology is grounded in the objectivity of a world-reconciliation accomplished in Christ, not by way of penal substitution ('God is spiritually richer than that!'[90]) but by God's action of calling light out of darkness in the establishment of a new creation.[91] This objectivity, however, does not obviate the need for human decision. Rather, God's action has introduced a 'new causality' which frees the individual to reverse the decision of autonomy by which they have fallen away from God, and to follow Christ in his obedience to God. The liberation of the human will is not an automatic accomplishment or an enacted divine *fiat*, for, as Barth says,

> [t]he coming world comes not mechanically, but organically. And the means by which this is to occur is an anticipation of the goal to be reached: the free union of humanity with God, as it was accomplished in Christ and as it becomes possible and actual in those called by Christ.[92]

The objective pole of Barth's soteriology, then, is balanced by a subjective pole in which Barth makes genuine place for human agency, albeit an agency which can only function as it is freed by God. Thus Barth introduces the theme of Romans as follows:

> Our theme is our knowledge of God realised in Christ, in which God approaches us, not as an object but immediately and creatively. In this knowledge we not only see but *are* seen, not only understand but *are* understood, not only grasp but are *grasped*.[93]

It is clear that for Barth, the knowledge of God refers not simply to an objective knowledge, whereby one might know without participation in and with that which is known, but to a self-involving, relational knowledge. This knowledge arises out of divine-human encounter and has the character of response to divine initiative. Being grasped by God does not spell the end of human freedom but its genesis, for humanity in sin is not free but enslaved. Nevertheless, through the objective redemption accomplished for us in Christ, God has claimed humanity for himself, and in so doing has created a new possibility for humanity. In a remarkable passage Barth says, 'Now humanity may and can and should willingly become aware of itself once more! To be sure, we are imprisoned, but we are called to freedom and a lane is made for

---

[89] Barth, *Romans I*, 191-192.

[90] Barth, *Romans I*, 193.

[91] Barth, *Romans I*, 194. See pages 20, 113 and 301 for further examples of Barth's use of the imagery of new creation to describe God's salvific activity.

[92] Barth, *Romans I*, 21.

[93] Barth, *Romans I*, 19.

freedom. To which side will humanity say Yes?'[94]

In light of Barth's view of sin as the quest for autonomy, this is an astonishing statement. The quest for autonomy, for self-awareness and self-expression is original sin. Now, in accordance with the new presupposition created by the coming of Christ, humanity 'may and can and should' become self-aware. Barth says simply that once people are released from coercion they may become themselves once more since they are God's.[95] In the re-establishment of human dependence upon God, humanity finds not only freedom, but authentic existence as well.

As already noted, the means by which this remarkable transformation of the human will from captivity to liberty occurs is nothing less than a new creative act of God. His response to the desperate fallenness, chaos and brokenness of the world in general and humanity in particular is 'the inauguration of a new history...with a sea of darkness God begins, and he ends, by calling light out of darkness'.[96] Again, Barth writes of a new creation in the midst of the old world by which the new possibility is opened for humanity to live in fulfilment of God's will: 'God has spoken a second *Let there be!* by giving his own son in the old world: *the new human* who through his immediacy to God, an immediacy untouched by Adam's fall, was himself able to become the beginning of a new humanity and a new world.'[97]

This new world and the possibility contained in it breaks forth into individual human lives through the hearing of the gospel proclamation,[98] whereby

> [i]f one says Yes to the divine Yes which in Christ has been spoken to them, if they make use of the new eyes and ears which have been given to them through the power of God, if the faithfulness of God who cannot abandon the world and humanity encounters a newly awakened faithfulness in return, that is 'faith.' There salvation begins. There the world-turning founded in Christ continues.[99]

Barth's view of salvation in *Romans I*, then, includes a strong and positive affirmation of the reality and necessity of human agency. While it is certainly true that the knowledge of God which arises in faith is the result of divine creative activity, it is nonetheless a self-involving form of knowledge by which a free and definite response is called forth from the believer. For Barth, both the objective and subjective poles of salvation are necessary if God's righteousness is to be established on earth.[100]

---

[94] Barth, *Romans I*, 194-195.
[95] Barth, *Romans I*, 195.
[96] Barth, *Romans I*, 194.
[97] Barth, *Romans I*, 300-301.
[98] Barth, *Romans I*, 23.
[99] Barth, *Romans I*, 21.
[100] Barth, *Romans I*, 24.

Further, while it is undeniable that much development would occur in Barth's treatment of this theme over the course of his lifetime, we see already in this early period the beginnings of his distinctive ordering of divine and human agency. God and humanity are placed over against one another, not as equal subjects, but as subjects-in-relation in which human subjectivity is always derivative and contingent upon prior divine subjectivity. Barth's refusal to ground the divine-human relation in subjectivist terms from the human side does not entail the abolition of human agency, but its establishing on a different foundation. His manner of construing this relation with regard to salvation bears significant implications for his understanding of Christian life as we shall see shortly. But before turning our attention to his positive instruction with regard to Christian existence, it will be beneficial to examine his negative characterisation of religion and ethics in order to bring his positive statements into sharper relief.

Barth's Critique of Religion and Ethics

It comes as no surprise to find that the severe critique of religion and church seen in Barth's earlier works comes to fuller expression in *Romans 1* without any loss of his rhetorical flourish. In this work Barth continues his insistence that the dawning kingdom of God is not a human possibility, nor a development within existing life possibilities, but the inbreaking of divine power creating a new possibility of life.[101] Because this is so, the kingdom of God cannot be identified with any human movement, including especially the church, but also other groups and movements such as idealism, morality, pacifism or social democracy.[102]

For Barth, all human distinctions between the religious and the irreligious, the moral and the immoral are relativised in the presence of God: 'The difference between the mountain and the valley becomes meaningless when the sun at its zenith fills both with its light.'[103] Indeed, Barth is able to list the church along with 'mammon, war and the state' as a 'characteristic outbreak' of sin![104] Its history, a 'mishmash of error and violence', serves as proof that the church is itself implicated in 'the whole world of the fall in which the "falling" of Adam lives to the full again and again, the whole confusion of sin' and is thus part of the 'chaos over against God as in the beginning'.[105]

In a reference to the early days of his own pastoral career Barth recalls the triumphal attitude of the church and religion in 1909-12 which had become an 'immensely prominent power.' He alludes to the publication of the influential

[101] Busch, *Karl Barth*, 100.
[102] Barth, *Romans 1*, 42.
[103] Barth, *Romans 1*, 56.
[104] Barth, *Romans 1*, 186.
[105] Barth, *Romans 1*, 193-194.

Die Religion in Geschichte und Gegenwart (*Religion in History and the Present*), the student movement of John Mott, the World Missions Conference in Edinburgh in 1910, and the International Socialist Congress in Basel in 1912.[106] His complaint against these groups and movements was that God was expected to crown the valiant efforts of humanity with his blessing. Nevertheless

> everything was always settled without God....The fear of the Lord did *not* stand
> objectively at the beginning of our wisdom....From God's standpoint that is more
> of a hindrance than a help, since it continues to delude people about the need for
> the coming of *his* kingdom. Our 'movements' then stand directly in the way of
> God's movement; our 'causes' hinder his cause, the richness of our 'life' hinders
> the tranquil growth of the divine life in the world....The collapse of *our* cause
> must demonstrate for once that *God's* cause is exclusively *his own*. That is where
> we stand today.[107]

Barth rejected, therefore, the ecclesial triumphalism of the pre-war era, and with it, all forms of hero worship. In particular, he also launched an attack on Pietism, which he developed as the dominant foil for his thought regarding religious individualism.[108]

Barth's Polemic against Pietism

As already noted, Barth's interest in Pietism was evident at the very beginning of January, 1916, when he wrote to Thurneysen that he had been reading Ritschl's history of Pietism.[109] In November of the same year, soon after commencing his exegetical investigation of Romans, he writes again several times to Thurneysen regarding a Pietist evangelist named Jakob Vetter who had conducted a preaching campaign in Safenwil.[110] Barth found himself won over by Vetter's friendly humour, and writes that '*personally* he is most certainly an agreeable religious man'.[111] Nevertheless, his evaluation of Vetter's message is less amenable:

> But the things, the things—that for eight whole days he kept proclaiming up
> there—these are really *not* the gospel but rather a quite bad form of religious
> mechanics. If *this* were 'Pietism,' we would never again believe that there was
> even the slightest point of contact between us and the Pietists. Their intentions
> would really be something totally different from ours. This is psychologizing in

---

[106] Barth, *Romans I*, 400-401.

[107] Barth, *Romans I*, 401-402.

[108] Busch, *Karl Barth and the Pietists*, 40.

[109] Smart, *Revolutionary Theology*, 36.

[110] Smart, *Revolutionary Theology*, 39-40. The letters are dated November 15 and 20, 1916.

[111] Smart, *Revolutionary Theology*, 39.

its worst form, just a describing of 'Christian' spiritual experiences....No, that really isn't it.[112]

Barth reveals his own pastoral and evangelistic concern when he laments that, 'the result will probably be that a number of the men from now on will be *still more* inaccessible than ever'.[113] Vetter's campaign had the effect of motivating Barth to undertake an intensive study of Pietism lasting about six months, during which time his work on Romans slowed virtually to a standstill. Barth particularly read the biographies and theology of nineteenth century Pietist revivalists as a means to access and understand their concerns.[114]

The above citation is illuminating on several counts. First, and most importantly, it shows that Barth believed that there was a degree of overlap between the theological position he and Thurneysen represented and Pietism. Second, he implies that the form of religion represented by Vetter as Pietism is something less than (true) Pietism, a departure from the gospel for a form of religious mechanics and 'psychologism.' In his commentary on Romans, therefore, it is this particular form of revivalist Pietism that is most likely the focus of Barth's attack.

In his carefully nuanced study of Barth's relationship with Pietism, Busch suggests that Barth employed the insights of one particular stream of Pietism— the Swabian Pietists including Bengel, Rieger and Beck—in order to launch his attack against the kind of Pietism represented by Vetter.[115] Because of the centrality of the notion of the kingdom of God in the theology of the Swabian Pietists, a 'critical barb against "individualism" had been part of it for a long time'.[116] It is the form of Pietism represented by Vetter, therefore, which was of concern to Barth, and against which his polemics raged. Barth refers to 'the old individualistic horror of Pietism, whose dead ends and mistakes we have escaped in Christ'.[117] He rejoices that we may 'return from the psychological depression in which the horror lives, from the inferno of Pietism, where the demons are at work'.[118]

The problem with this form of Pietism, according to Barth, was its determined focus on the human soul, and its unrelenting concern for '*individual* breakthrough, *individual* conversion, *individual* sanctification, *individual* salvation, *individual* bliss'.[119] For Barth, *religious* individualism was simply another variety of the more thoroughgoing individualism which characterises

---

[112] Smart, *Revolutionary Theology*, 40.

[113] Smart, *Revolutionary Theology*, 41.

[114] McCormack, *Karl Barth's Dialectical Theology*, 136.

[115] Busch, *Karl Barth and the Pietists*, 60-65. As already noted, Blumhardt also belongs to this tradition.

[116] Busch, *Karl Barth and the Pietists*, 63.

[117] Barth, *Romans I*, 334-335.

[118] Barth, *Romans I*, 293.

[119] Barth, *Romans I*, 276.

human existence under the conditions of the Fall, and as such, it shares the same dark nature of the unredeemed world which is far from God.[120] Thus although the Pietists saw the need for redemption from the fallen and sinful world, because their model of spirituality shared the basic pattern of human sinfulness with the world, they could not achieve their desired goal. The 'religious mechanics' about which Barth complained to Thurneysen are nothing more than vain and all-too-human attempts to produce redemption by one's own doing. Such efforts, suggests Barth, may perhaps lead one 'to the higher realms of the earth, but not into the kingdom of heaven'.[121] God's kingdom is his own work and issues in the new world, which as a seed was planted in Christ. It is not the result of our own efforts, or of practices deriving from the old world. Only by being planted in Christ and thus 'growing organically' can we experience the new world.[122]

Barth was also critical of Pietism on account of its tendency to foster separation of itself from the world, rather than solidarity with it. In a famous statement he insists that he 'would rather be in hell with the world church than in heaven with Pietism....In this case Christ is with us in hell.'[123] There is little doubt that the ferocious irony of this phrase serves as a rebuke to the sectarian character of Pietism which accused those churches who accepted all and sundry into membership, of being 'of Satan'.[124] Barth assails the Pietist assurance of purity and salvation by insisting that Christ himself has chosen solidarity with the world rather than separation from it, and hence is amongst those rejected by the Pietists. In their moralistic attempts to secure salvation for themselves, they have distanced themselves from the Saviour and have thus failed to secure the very salvation they seek.

In Barth's ruthless critique of Pietism, therefore, we hear echoes of the themes he introduced in the works examined in the previous chapter, including his conviction that God alone establishes his kingdom, the 'worldliness' of God, and the strident critique of religious reductionism wherein religion and salvation are wholly concerned with individual and interior realities. For Barth, Christian and ecclesial existence can never be an attempt at one's own sanctity at the expense of the world that God has created, loved and redeemed. Christian life and ministry necessarily presupposes solidarity with and presence in the world if it is to be a legitimate and faithful representation of Christ. Barth's critique also reveals the close connection he observed between religion and morality, as we shall now see.

---

[120] Busch, *Karl Barth and the Pietists*, 43.

[121] Barth, *Romans I*, 408-409.

[122] Busch, *Karl Barth and the Pietists*, 46.

[123] Barth, *Romans I*, 363.

[124] Busch, *Karl Barth and the Pietists*, 44.

Immoral Morality

Barth explicates his understanding of this connection in his exposition of Romans 1:18-21, which he entitles simply, 'The Fall.'[125] In this section Barth analyses the character of the sin which has infected all humanity, and lays the foundation for his rejection of religion. In his discussion of Paul's contention that 'the wrath of God is revealed from heaven against all ἀσέβειαν καὶ ἀδικίαν of men,' Barth interprets ἀσέβειαν (wickedness or ungodliness) as a reference to humanity's irreligiosity, and ἀδικίαν (unrighteousness) to its immorality, and further suggests that the former is an outgrowth of the latter. The deepest basis of human opposition to God is found in humanity's self-exaltation against God which subsequently issues in idolatry.[126]

For Barth at this time, the root of sin was the positing of the self as its own centre of value, thereby usurping and rejecting the place of God. Because humanity refuses to acknowledge God *as God*, and insists on the contrary to have God on their own terms, they lose God himself. Instead of acknowledging its 'absolute dependence' on God by 'lying down honestly and submissively in his hand' humanity establishes itself *next to* or alongside God autonomous in its morality.[127] Humanity, therefore, has knowledge (*Kenntnis*) of God, but not 'effectual knowledge' (*Erkenntnis*).[128] That is, humanity has knowledge *about* God, but fails to enter into the reality of knowing and being known by God, into the dynamic and creative relation that occurs when his faithfulness awakens and finds the corresponding faithfulness of humanity. God, therefore, remains ever external and distant, and although humanity knows of God, it does not experience the transformative power of the 'effectual knowledge' of which Barth speaks.

This is not to suggest that Barth dismisses morality and ethics as irrelevant. In a discussion about the function of the law based on Romans 5:20-21, he acknowledges that the law, too, is a word of God, 'only not the last'.[129] As such, the law, and hence for Barth morality, has only penultimate significance. While morality may have projects and retrospective judgements, 'it has no word to speak through which non-being would be called into being. It is not creative....It does *not* contribute at the crucial point.'[130] Morality issues only in the effectual knowledge (*Erkenntnis*) of *sin*, not the effectual knowledge of God in which lies the creative and transformative power of God. Barth insists, therefore, that 'it must be declared: we boast of the world-redemption on the basis of the world-reconciliation, and we do not conceive of it in fact in terms

---

[125] Barth, *Romans I*, 24-32.
[126] Barth, *Romans I*, 26-27.
[127] Barth, *Romans I*, 25, 30.
[128] Barth, *Romans I*, 30.
[129] Barth, *Romans I*, 201.
[130] Barth, *Romans I*, 200-201.

of morality and immorality'.[131] The problem of morality is that it fails to consider the reality of our situation from the standpoint of grace: '*Must* we continually think in terms of morality, as if nothing had happened? *Must* we continually think from the perspective of Adam and Israel?'[132]

Barth's 'as if nothing had happened' is the key to his ethical thought. He steadfastly refuses to allow ethics or morality an independent sphere of deliberation. The event of God's grace in Christ *has* occurred and has thus created the new presupposition under which we now live. Barth continues, therefore:

> Grace *abounds*. It enters even as grace, as the free gift of God's act for us through the creation of a new situation, because of which the problem of morality becomes superfluous. In Christ, Adam and Israel are redeemed. And so morality cannot be the question which occupies us *in earnest*...but rather the question is whether we want to *accept* the reconciliation, *enter* into it, *be* in Christ, *place* ourselves on the foundation which has been laid. *Here* is the decisive question. *Here* we become earnest. *Here* our heart burns and our conscience afflicts us.[133]

For Barth, the question of human righteousness and human activity gives way before the righteousness and activity of God, although without the abolition of the former. Barth sets the question of human activity on an entirely new foundation so that human activity has the character of response to what God has done and continues to do. Clearly, his intent is to challenge the idealist notion that the human self may be constructed through the autonomous generation of moral imperatives.[134] His critique of ethical idealism is grounded upon his analysis of sin as the human quest for autonomy. As such, all human attempts to identify, define and perform the good are not only manifestations of the pervasive sin of humanity, but are also doomed to fail, because moral norms thus generated confront the person as an external demand which must be fulfilled by the individual, that is, as *law*. Thus, as McCormack has noted, 'idealistic morality can only postulate the good; it cannot bring it to life...ultimately [it] crashes on the rocks of the fact that the good cannot be done by the sinner (i.e. by the individual *qua* individual)'.[135]

In this respect, then, Barth's critique of morality corresponds to his critique of religion. Precisely because the dawning kingdom of God is neither a goal nor a result of human design or activity, there can be no confusing of divine renewal with human progress.[136] This refusal to allow an identification of divine and human activity serves a dual purpose. First, Barth disallows a

---

[131] Barth, *Romans I*, 200.
[132] Barth, *Romans I*, 202.
[133] Barth, *Romans I*, 202-203.
[134] Spencer, *Clearing a Space*, 145.
[135] McCormack, *Karl Barth's Dialectical Theology*, 168.
[136] Gorringe, *Against Hegemony*, 45.

religious legitimation of the status quo. While Christians have a responsibility to pay their taxes and to give honour to whom honour is due, they must go no further: 'Fulfil your duties without illusion, but *no* compromising of God. Payment of tax, but *no* incense to Caesar! Citizens initiative and civic obedience, but *no* combination of throne and altar, *no* Christian Patriotism.'[137] Second, and in contrast to this, Barth also disallows the identification of the kingdom of God with movements seeking social change. Thus, he continues, 'strike and general strike, and street-fighting if needs be, but *no* religious justification and glorification of it! Military service as soldier or officer if needs be, but under *no* circumstances army chaplain! Social democratic but *not* religious socialist! The betrayal of the gospel is *not* part of your political duty.'[138]

Thus, both conservative and radical alike are refused divine authorisation for their programmes and activities. Barth's refusal to provide religious legitimation for the bourgeois culture is of a piece with his critique of the church generally, and, in light of his socialist background, unsurprising. Also anticipated is the sharpening of his critique of Religious Socialism into a forthright repudiation of the theology of Ragaz. Barth rejects the supposition of Ragaz that the Religious Socialist movement was a vehicle by which the kingdom of God would be realised on earth, along with its underlying (bourgeois) conviction that the human agent is the subject of history.[139]

Barth likewise resisted the growing sentiment toward political revolution in the aftermath of the Bolshevik revolution of 1917. For Barth, the replacement of one form of state with another by way of armed insurrection was nothing more than a capitulation to the means and methods of the fallen aeon—the threat and actual use of coercive force—the result being the replacing of one unjust order with another of the same ilk.[140] Instead, Barth longed for 'the *absolute* revolution of God'[141] by which he means the overturning of all worldly values and dominion through the *divine* establishing of God's kingdom.

Ethical Idealism in Barth?

The question which forces itself upon us at this point is clear: does Barth's exclusion of both radical and reactionary ethics imply a quietist ethic and spirituality? Does his eschatological construal of reality render Christian and ecclesial existence essentially passive, a sombre waiting for the divine realisation of the kingdom of God? At times his rhetoric seems to suggest so:

---

[137] Barth, *Romans I*, 520.

[138] Barth, *Romans I*, 520-521.

[139] McCormack, *Karl Barth's Dialectical Theology*, 178.

[140] McCormack, *Karl Barth's Dialectical Theology*, 173-174.

[141] Barth, *Romans I*, 506.

'On the basis of the ultimate viewpoint which we must adopt *in Christ*, there are *no ethics*, there is only the movement of God.'[142]

Some scholars suggest that in *Romans I* Barth has not succeeded in setting forth a comprehensive ethic. McCormack, for example, regards Barth's reflections on ethics as belonging to the weakest sections of the commentary.[143] He suggests that this weakness is a developmental issue because Barth has not yet developed the means by which he might make clear how human action could correspond to divine action without removing the distinction between the two.[144] In his effort to reject every attempt to 'Christianize' particular political options, Barth fails to apply his new theological insight into the sovereignty of God consistently. Thus, according to McCormack, despite his thorough-going criticism of ethical idealism, Barth himself resorts to idealistic morality in his discussion of the 'ethics of the confused situation', in particular, his discussion of political realities in Romans 13:1-7.

In his exegesis of this passage Barth utilises a citation from Troeltsch to explicate the revolutionary stance of the believer with regard to the existing state, although he certainly departs from Troeltsch's intention: 'The conservative attitude (of Christianity)…was founded on a mixture of contempt, submission, and relative recognition. That is why, in spite of all its submissiveness, it destroyed the Roman state by alienating souls from its ideals.'[145] By refusing to accord ultimate status, and thus loyalty to the state, the believer relegates the state to a penultimate level and creates the presupposition for the kingdom of God, 'the *absolute* revolution of God'.[146] The state, along with all that is penultimate has already fallen into 'the process of dissolution' and Christians are to seek neither its preservation nor its destruction as a goal in itself.[147] Rather, they are to negate and subvert the state by denying its fundamental legitimacy.

Barth's use of the term *revolution* at this time is hardly coincidental. Nevertheless his characterisation of Christian life as revolutionary bears a very different hue to the revolutionary methods and ideals espoused and enacted by the socialists and communists. Barth writes, 'Your state and your revolution are in heaven.'[148] While Barth held great sympathy for the revolutionaries, and

---

[142] Barth, *Romans I*, 524.

[143] McCormack, *Karl Barth's Dialectical Theology*, 179.

[144] McCormack, *Karl Barth's Dialectical Theology*, 165-166.

[145] Barth, *Romans I*, 505. Barth's editor notes the citation as E. Troeltsch, *Die Soziallehren der christlichen Kirchen und Gruppen* (Tübingen 1912), 72.

[146] Barth, *Romans I*, 506.

[147] Barth, *Romans I*, 506.

[148] Barth, *Romans I*, 507. McCormack is no doubt correct in his assertion that in his exposition of Romans 13:1-7 Barth was engaging with Ragaz and Religious Socialism, despite the fact that the latter is nowhere named in the passage. In a letter to Thurneysen dated May 3, 1920, Barth writes in response to Ragaz' call for Switzerland to join the League of Nations, 'It is a frightening proof of the fact that I did not unjustly saw him up

refused to rule out Christian participation in an uprising against an unjust state, he still clearly favoured working within the parameters of the existing state, for the simple reason that it is impossible to overcome evil with evil. In the final analysis, political, and especially armed, revolution could not achieve the goals it set for itself.[149] The revolution of Christ is of a different order. Barth claims that Christianity

> is *more* than Leninism! So far as Christianity is concerned it is 'all or nothing' in the sense that its expectation is not…the aim or result of a development or a gradual ascent of humanity, but the discovery of a new creation or the content of a new knowledge (*Erkenntnis*). *This* programme cannot become the object of 'ethics.' The Christ-life must grow in its own power.[150]

Because no human action can in and of itself inaugurate the righteousness of the kingdom, revolution is doomed to supplant one evil system with another. It will share the same fundamental weakness of the system it replaces, namely a reliance on coercive power which stands in antithesis to the righteousness and freedom of the 'state of God'. According to Barth, a state established on such power is evil in itself.[151] What is required is the new creation that only God can produce, and which is at work in the movement of God. The stance of the Christian and the church toward the existing state is revolutionary in that it denies in principle the use of coercive power in favour of an order of mutual freedom and love.[152]

It is at this point that the inconsistency observed by McCormack in Barth's ethical vision surfaces, for believers cannot with good conscience involve

---

in Romans 13…' McCormack comments, 'With the publication of this virulent attack on Ragaz in the pages of *Romans I*, Barth's break with Religious Socialism was complete.' Less certain is McCormack's additional contention that the exposition is '*not* an *Auseinandersetzung* (argument) with Leninism as has been suggested by Friedrich-Wilhelm Marquardt' (McCormack, *Karl Barth's Dialectical Theology*, 173). According to Jüngel, Lenin's *State and Revolution* (1918) first appeared in German translation on November 20, 1918 (Eberhard Jüngel, *Karl Barth: A Theological Legacy* (trans. G. E. Paul; Philadelphia: Westminster, 1986), 159, and thus dismisses the possibility of influence on Barth's work which was submitted to the publisher in December of the same year. It remains possible, however, that Barth had access to it, or to an outline of its ideas prior to its translation, prior to the submission of his own manuscript. It is to be noted that he does explicitly refer to Leninism in the same paragraph as this citation, as we shall see momentarily. For further discussion see Friedrich-Wilhelm Marquardt, *Theologie und Sozialismus: Das Beispiel Karl Barths* (München: Chr. Kaiser Verlag, 1972), 127, Jüngel, *Karl Barth*, 96-97, 159, and Gorringe, *Against Hegemony*, 46.
[149] McCormack, *Karl Barth's Dialectical Theology*, 176-177.
[150] Barth, *Romans I*, 506-507.
[151] Barth, *Romans I*, 501.
[152] Barth, *Romans I*, 503-504. See also McCormack, *Karl Barth's Dialectical Theology*, 174.

themselves in politics, nor can they withdraw from the political arena in pursuit of a Christian asceticism. Barth has already lambasted the Pietists for their sectarian withdrawal into a supposed 'spiritual' realm of existence separate from the desperate realities of the world. Here, too, such withdrawal only serves to confirm the status quo and thus to implicate the Christian in the evil that presently exists. '"Personal life",' says Barth, 'is no longer the answer to world war and revolution....Whoever will not join in solidarity with what is happening on the outside will not save his own soul either.'[153] Thus the believer is cast into the fatally 'confused situation' where the only choice is between complicity in evil by engaging in politics or by avoiding it. It is impossible *not* to share the guilt which accrues to all political activity.[154] McCormack, as we have seen, finds in Barth's treatment of the 'confused situation' evidence that Barth lapses into Kantian idealism, failing to apply his insight into the sovereignty of God. The believer is caught in an impossible dilemma and must decide in accordance with the dictate of their conscience and their best judgement what they should do.[155] Gorringe suggests that Barth's refusal to offer prescriptive guidance for the confused situation, serves to protect the immediacy of the divine command.[156] While this suggestion has obvious merit, it overlooks the fact that if that were indeed Barth's intent here, he need not have been so pessimistic in the face of the so-called 'confused situation'.

The correctness of McCormack's judgement is also evident in the citations above where one's political involvement might include either civic obedience or street-fighting, depending on the dictates of one's conscience. Caught in the tragic situation where one cannot continue to support a legitimately constituted but unjust civic authority, but where one also recognises that revolution is inevitably mired in human injustice and unrighteousness, one must act boldly and decisively as the situation requires, inescapably involving oneself in the inherent evil of political striving for power, and trusting in God for the forgiveness of even 'our political sins'.[157]

Spencer follows McCormack at this point, but also suggests that part of the weakness is due to Barth's rhetorical purpose in *Romans I*, which is largely the

---

[153] Barth, *Romans I*, 489.

[154] McCormack, *Karl Barth's Dialectical Theology*, 176.

[155] McCormack, *Karl Barth's Dialectical Theology*, 165-166, 179.

[156] Gorringe, *Against Hegemony*, 45. A discussion of Barth's concept of 'the command of the moment' occurs below.

[157] Barth, *Romans I*, 510. It is also necessary at this point to reject Marquardt's contention that Barth maintained an 'anarchistic' position. See Marquardt, *Theologie und Sozialismus*, 133. While it is true that Barth does, in this work, view political activity as inherently evil, this applies as much to those who would seek to overthrow or abolish the state, as to the state itself. That Barth is able to commend civil initiative and obedience, military service and regular participation in democratic process as legitimate options for Christian engagement in political activity is indicative that he is not an anarchist.

negative task of a thorough critique of ethical idealism. Spencer suggests that although Barth does present an embryonic form of a divine command ethic, 'it is continually submerged in favour of this negative task'.[158]

In this section, then, we have observed that Barth ruthlessly critiques a particular expression of Christian and ecclesial existence—that which seeks its own sanctity and salvation in supposed separation from the evil of the world, and at the expense of engagement with the desperate realities of worldly life. He also aims his critique at a particular form of ethics—that which seeks to establish its own vision of the good independently of the goodness God has created and creates through his gracious work in Jesus Christ. This dual critique is obviously in service of a more positive statement of both religious practice and ethical existence. That Barth appears unable at this time to present a fully coherent ethical vision does not suggest that he has no sense of the nature and shape of Christian and ecclesial existence, or of the need Christians have for guidance in facing the dilemmas confronting them. In fact, careful attention to his work indicates that Barth had a quite specific, albeit underdeveloped sense of the shape of Christian life. The positive delineation of this vision is the focus of the final two sections of this chapter.

Life in the Third Dimension: Christian Existence in *Romans I*

It is evident that Barth's work of demolition in this commentary is in service of a work of construction. The preceding discussion suggests that Barth indeed had a particular understanding of the nature of Christian existence at this stage of his career. We have noted, for example, that Barth's soteriology rotates around both an objective and a subjective pole, and that the establishment of Christian existence requires a free exercise of human volition. Significant for our purposes here is the recognition that for Barth, Christian existence continues and develops in the same manner in which it began, that is, as faithful response to the prior and initiatory divine faithfulness which has come and comes to us in Christ.[159]

Barth's identification of the quest for autonomy as original sin, and his thoroughgoing critique of Pietist individualism, are alike instructive for highlighting the contours of his Christian and ecclesial vision. If the essential character of sin is humanity's refusal to 'simply be God's,' that is, 'to live directly, firmly, child-like, simply, actually in the spirit', then it is evident that Barth considers the Christian life to be characterised by precisely this form of demeanour.[160] The nature of Christian existence is recognition of God as *God*, and a corresponding falling down before God in free and glad submission. Nor does this require the super-heated piety of the Pietists, which is simply a variant

---

[158] Spencer, *Clearing a Space*, 144.

[159] Barth, *Romans I*, 21.

[160] Barth, *Romans I*, 178.

form of self-grounded spirituality. In a withering blast directed toward both liberal and Pietist humanity, Barth writes, 'He becomes his own delight and his own problem. He climbs too high into sublime spiritualisation and, shuddering, looks down into the depths of Satan and both times departs equally far from the innocence of the Holy Spirit.'[161] For Barth, genuine spirituality is characterised by faith which looks away from the self towards God.

Also evident from the discussion above is Barth's opposition to the Pietist strategy of withdrawal from the world which underlines his conviction that Christian and ecclesial existence is necessarily an existence in, amongst and for the world at large. Since Christ himself has chosen solidarity with the world, the church can do no other.

Similarly, his rejection of Pietist 'mechanics' and the ecclesial triumphalism of the pre-war period is predicated on his conviction that the kingdom of God comes 'organically' as a new creation which is wholly the work of God: 'Our "movements" stand directly in the way of God's movement; our "causes" hinder his cause, the richness of our "life" hinders the quiet growth of the divine life in the world....The Christ-life must grow in its own power.'[162] The form of Christian and ecclesial existence that corresponds to this divinely quiet action and growth is 'quiet waiting'.[163] If believers would 'stand before God in steady growth' they would have no further need of a 'heated piety'.[164] 'Do we still want always to be serious and solemn and mechanical,' asks Barth, 'where we simply ought to grow happily in Christ?'[165] Clearly, Barth has in mind the kind of quiet waiting he learned from Blumhardt, which is a waiting in service of hastening, and which, accordingly, is not to be construed in terms of a quietist ethic.

The Movement of God

Barth's complaint that 'our movements stand directly in the way of God's movement' leads us into the heart of his Christian and ecclesial vision in *Romans I*. We have previously noted that Barth's theological ontology in this work envisages a two-dimensional world, where the ontological priority lies with the *jenseitig* dimension of reality, and the whole is cast in an eschatological framework. As a result of human sin, the entire *diesseitig* dimension of reality has come under the terrible lordship of death which is itself a 'perverted, downward, centrifugal, disintegrating *movement*' which drives everything away from its centre in God.[166] It is precisely as a counter-

---

[161] Barth, *Romans I*, 178.
[162] Barth, *Romans I*, 401-402, 507.
[163] Busch, *Karl Barth and the Pietists*, 52.
[164] Barth, *Romans I*, 288.
[165] Barth, *Romans I*, 276.
[166] Barth, *Romans I*, 176, emphasis added.

movement against this movement of death and alienation that God has acted in Christ. In Barth's words, 'it is God who proceeds, not us. It is *power* which has proceeded from God in the resurrection of Christ from the dead.'[167] Barth insists that the sending of Christ was neither a necessary truth of reason nor an accidental truth of history. Rather it is understood only as a movement or counter-movement following the perverted movement within the first creation, a movement which has its origin not in history but in God himself. As the old aeon was inaugurated by the human seizure of divine prerogatives, so the new aeon was brought about by the forgiving descent by God into the midst of the old world.[168]

In Christ, then, God has initiated a *movement*, one in which God himself is in eschatological procession. It must be remembered, however, that Barth conceives of this procession in terms of actualistic breakthroughs, so that while it is ever pressing toward the realisation of the kingdom of God, its appearance in the *diesseitig* dimension is often in hiddenness, and hence it is not 'a state of affairs, nor an actuality, not a stable "reality!"…it is a matter of a course, a movement, a struggling and a triumphing'.[169] This is also the case with Barth's use of the image of Christ as the divine seed planted and growing in the world. The seed does not take on a life of its own as though it were capable of growth without continuous divine intervention.[170] Nevertheless, as Chalamet has shown, Barth's use of the organic image functioned to subvert his intent in this commentary. Although he used the organic imagery in order to emphasise the hiddenness of the kingdom, in the nature of the case, as the 'seed' (the kingdom) grows, its presence becomes less hidden and more obvious so that 'God's reality erupts into the old aeon and thus ceases to be hidden.'[171]

Nevertheless, the actualistic portrayal of the divine movement within history is also indicative of the fundamentally unstable character of Christian existence when viewed from the side of humanity. McCormack correctly notes that Barth's use of the two dimensions of reality

> serves as a circumlocution for two ways of being in the world which Barth refers to…as 'Adam' and 'Christ.' 'Adam' and 'Christ' stand for two movements: a movement away from an original relationship of fellowship with God (Fall) and a counter-movement of return to the 'Origin' (Reconciliation). These two movements are not to be conceived of as sequential, but rather as parallel and simultaneous.[172]

---

[167] Barth, *Romans I*, 19.

[168] Barth, *Romans I*, 302. See also, page 85.

[169] Barth, *Romans I*, 189-190.

[170] McCormack, *Karl Barth's Dialectical Theology*, 157.

[171] Christophe Chalamet, *Dialectical Theologians: Wilhelm Herrmann, Karl Barth and Rudolph Bultmann* (Zürich: Theologischer Verlag Zürich, 2005), 111-112.

[172] McCormack, *Karl Barth's Dialectical Theology*, 147.

Both the line of Adam and the line of Christ pass through every human existence in such a way that the person is continually confronted with the decision regarding whether they will live in accordance with the line of Adam and the verdict of sin and death, or with the line of Christ and the verdict of righteousness and life.[173] And while it is the case that the Christian is 'much more in Christ than in Adam',[174] it is also the case that their status before God is highly provisional, depending moment by moment on whether genuine faith is present.[175]

McCormack's note that these 'two ways of being in the world' are to be understood as 'parallel and simultaneous' also identifies what Barth refers to 'the crucial problem of human life: on which line we find ourselves and under which verdict we thus place ourselves'.[176] It is precisely at this juncture that Barth rejects the role of idealistic morality on the grounds that although it can indeed accompany the believer as a 'searchlight' in the struggle between the great realities of Adam and Christ, 'it has no word to speak through which non-being would be called into being. It is not creative....It does not contribute at the crucial point.'[177] Barth reasons that once morality is allowed to become an independent object of thought,

> [o]ur participation in God's victorious struggle…becomes endangered, because we lose the meaning of *the third dimension, of the movement itself.*…Because we do not want that, we do not grant an independent place to the moral question. It will find its answer in the context of the whole, in the movement.[178]

Here, finally, we gain the crucial insight into Barth's Christian and ecclesial vision in *Romans I*, as well as an understanding of his provocative, and often misunderstood statement that 'in accordance with the ultimate position we must take in Christ, there are no ethics. There is only the *movement of God.*'[179] Genuine Christian existence is being caught up in 'the third dimension', that is, being grasped and led by the Spirit in the eschatological movement and procession of God. For Barth in this period, Christian faith and life is not something a person *possesses*, nor is it something grounded in Christians themselves. Rather, it is the result of being grasped and placed into a new order

---

[173] Barth, *Romans I*, 197-198.

[174] Barth, *Romans I*, 237.

[175] McCormack, *Karl Barth's Dialectical Theology*, 157.

[176] Barth, *Romans I*, 198.

[177] Barth, *Romans I*, 200-201.

[178] Barth, *Romans I*, 201, emphasis added. See also page 550: 'The movement in which you stand embraces both elements of truth: you *are* in Christ, and you are simply *becoming* what you are. … In Christ you must learn to think in a three-dimensional way in accordance with the movement, and not two-dimensionally in the vulgar-idealistic sense of the "ethical."'

[179] Barth, *Romans I*, 524.

or context of being, as Barth insists:

> Grace is no 'experience.'…That is a prejudice of Pietism and a modern theology which…reads with Pietist glasses. Grace obviously will not be without experiences; but grace is primarily the divine presupposition, the new order under which we are placed, the altered world-context into which our lives are inserted.[180]

The Body of Christ

Rather than a stable or static possession, then, Christian life is the very act of the person's life as they are grasped by God and respond in faithfulness to the decision with which they are continually confronted. In response to the question, 'What shall I do?' Barth replies:

> Answer: Above all stop asking that question! Every word of this question is ambiguous and confused. For it abolishes freedom once again, placing itself *next to* the creative power of the good under which we are placed in Christ.…We are to remain in the 'body of Christ,' in the power of the resurrection inaugurated in him in which all moral obligation proceeds organically out of the new 'being in the Spirit,' in which the good is not something *problematic*, but rather only something which *occurs*.[181]

It is evident that Barth, in this text, casts Christian existence in a passive light. Here, it seems, it is not so much that people live the Christian life, as it arises in them and is lived through them. Nonetheless, in light of the preceding discussion, it is evident that Barth's distinctive ordering of divine and human volition cannot be ignored. The moral imperatives which characterise the good are not a dilemma to be investigated or agonised over, but rather 'proceed organically' from the power of the resurrection at work in the world, and 'occur' in the life of the one who 'abides' in it. This abiding, of course, is

---

[180] Barth, *Romans I*, 206-207. (*Gnade ist kein 'Erlebnis', keine 'Erfahrung'… Gnade wird freilich nicht ohne Erlebnisse und Erfahrungen bleiben.*) Again, however, Chalamet argues that Barth's use of the organic imagery subverts his intent that Christian life is not something 'possessed' by the Christian. He shows that Barth uses Kutter's terminology of the *immediate* to argue that 'there are now some people who again have God'. See Chalamet, *Dialectical Theologians*, 113-114, citing Barth, *Romans I*, 172. Chalamet demonstrates that in *Romans I* Barth's theology becomes undialectical as the divine movement enters history, becomes visible and grows in the world. There is an immediate apprehension of, and even possession of God as his kingdom becomes a 'thing' in this world. Ultimately, as we shall see in our discussion of *Romans II*, this is precisely why Barth felt it necessary to fully revise his commentary, and to expunge this sense of the immediate apprehension of God from his work. See the discussion in Chalamet, *Dialectical Theologians*, 105-115.

[181] Barth, *Romans I*, 263-264.

critical. Earlier in his treatment of Romans, Barth states that 'the righteousness of God, *where it finds faith*, transfers us into a movement which has a goal in view, into a growth which is full of promise as soon as it takes a path with us'.[182] The human agent, then, remains an active subject, but their activity is strictly responsive in nature, following and empowered by the prior divine activity.

Also of note in this citation is Barth's reference to the 'Body of Christ' and the 'new being in the Spirit'. In a further discussion of the 'Body of Christ' Barth clarifies and sharpens his understanding of the relation between human agency and the community of faith. Humanity in and of itself, including Christian humanity, is wholly incapable of performing the good, and it is only as a person abides in the 'Body of Christ'—that is, only as they empowered and moved by the Spirit—that the good can be accomplished in and through them. While it is true that the faith and activity of the individual is important, it is only a momentary expression of the movement, and not the movement itself, for 'the movement is not borne by the individual but by the Christian community'.[183]

By grounding the agency of the individual in the Body of Christ, Barth is not attacking human agency per se, but the notion of independent human agency and form of individualism which he identifies as sin. For Barth, 'it is not the *individual* who thinks, believes, and acts on his account and at his risk; rather, the "Body of Christ" thinks, believes, and acts in him and through him, in the measure in which it can do so in this moment'.[184] When he states that it is the 'Body of Christ' who thinks, believes and acts in the believer, it is understood first, as Christ himself, in the power of his resurrection at work in and through the community gathered around his name, and only then in and through the individual who is part of that community.[185] It is not the individual *qua* individual who does the good, therefore, but the individual as a participant in the Body of Christ.

Thus it is clear that for Barth, Christian existence is necessarily a corporate existence. It is also evident that when Barth refers to the Body of Christ, he is not simply making reference to the empirical or phenomenal church, for he goes on to say that

> [w]e are not an external, accidental fellowship [*Gemeinschaft*] like the state or the church [*Kirche*], which are established in authority and freedom *without* God and *without* love. We are the inner, necessary fellowship which exists and is maintained by a higher will. We stand under grace.[186]

---

[182] Barth, *Romans I*, 25, emphasis added.

[183] Barth, *Romans I*, 475.

[184] Barth, *Romans I*, 475.

[185] McCormack, *Karl Barth's Dialectical Theology*, 169.

[186] Barth, *Romans I*, 476.

For Barth, the Body of Christ is identified with the kingdom of God and the new world.[187] It refers to the *hidden* movement of God which leaves traces in the ongoing march of history, but which cannot be identified with any institution or cultural development within history, including the organised churches. It is composed of those who are gathered by the power of the resurrection when they obey the gospel—'an international people of God', and knows no boundaries between an arena called 'church' and another named 'world'.[188] This company already stands in the movement of God: 'No longer under judgement, but under grace, no longer in sin but in righteousness, no longer in death, but in life. That is the course of salvation which the power of God wills to take and will take, now with us and someday with the whole world. Now with us!'[189]

Barth's 'now with us' indicates his belief that even now, during which time the divine eschatological procession goes forth predominantly in hiddenness, the community of faith serves as a proleptic witness and paradigm of God's intent for the world at large. In this community the righteousness of God will come into visibility, albeit in an actualistic form. 'On earth as in heaven,' Barth says, 'God's work has begun to come to pass. In the midst of the world of flesh, an enclave of God's world has arisen.'[190] For those who are in Christ, the possibility of doing the good has become a 'genuine reality' on account of the 'power of God which appeared in the life of Christ' appearing once more 'in us as the members of his body'.[191]

The Nature of Barth's Ecclesial Ethics

The preceding section indicates that the heart of Barth's ethics in *Romans I* is located in the central concept of the divine *movement* inaugurated in Christ and proceeding through history as God himself is in eschatological procession encountering and gathering a people who serve as a proleptic witness and paradigm of his intent for the world generally. As Barth begins the positive delineation of his ethics it becomes evident why he claims that there are 'no ethics'. For Barth, there are no ethics because there is no possibility of any human action establishing that which is truly good: the establishing of God's kingdom is God's work alone, a work of new creation in the midst of the old world. The whole question of morality finds its resolution only in the movement and activity of God.

Such a vision of ethical existence, of course, raises the inevitable question as to whether it is actually a viable description of ethical existence or moral

---

[187] Barth, *Romans I*, 254.
[188] Barth, *Romans I*, 21.
[189] Barth, *Romans I*, 20.
[190] Barth, *Romans I*, 303.
[191] Barth, *Romans I*, 303-304.

community at all. Surely, the simple rejection of 'ethics' per se, and the complementary assertion that Christian existence is being caught up in the eschatological procession of God such that the good simply 'occurs,' is naïvely utopian. Has Barth constructed an impossible vision of Christian and ecclesial existence which fails to do justice to actual life in this present age in which the kingdom of God is *not* present in its fullness, and in which believers and non-believers alike must struggle with life in a fallen world? Is it sufficient to assert that the good will occur *organically* without provision of any moral instruction or guidelines?

In answer to questions such as these, McCormack argues that Barth was not blind to the need for moral guidance in the Christian life, and that close examination of his commentary reveals that Barth had an ethic after all, though he preferred not to call it that. Following Romans 12:1, Barth preferred to name his programme 'Christian exhortation'.[192] Similarly, Spencer maintains that Barth is trading on a semantic distinction between 'ethics'—a term he reserves for the characterisation of moral idealism—and 'exhortation,' a term he adopts to speak of a distinctly Christian form of moral exhortation in the new community of those in Christ.[193] The significance of this semantic distinction for Barth's ecclesial vision must not be understated. By identifying 'ethics' with idealistic morality which seeks to generate universally valid norms to govern human behaviour, and by then contrasting it with 'Christian exhortation,' Barth clearly indicates that the Christian community is to be guided by a *particular* ethics, that he envisages a distinctive *ecclesial* ethics in contrast to the universal imperatives of idealistic morality.

The Command of the Moment

Barth commences his exposition of Romans 12 with the question 'What is the will of God for us?' in the new situation created by the lordship of the 'Spirit of Life'. His response to the question posed is simple: 'The answer is already given to us…It says, stand in the victory of life (chapter 5), in grace (chapter 6), in freedom (chapter 7), in the Spirit (chapter 8).'[194] This counsel, however, is not something that can be routinely applied to all and sundry, but applies specifically and exclusively to those who are in Christ, in whom the 'new situation' is an actualised reality. It is in this context alone that 'Christian exhortation' is to be practiced—only amongst 'brothers and sisters, fellow travellers in the movement, those who find themselves with me in the same situation…for these I speak'.[195] Barth insists that outside of Christ, Christian exhortation has no meaning, and that it can only appear as law unless the

---

[192] McCormack, *Karl Barth's Dialectical Theology*, 170.
[193] Spencer, *Clearing a Space*, 147.
[194] Barth, *Romans I*, 462.
[195] Barth, *Romans I*, 463.

presuppositions of chapters 5-8 have become actual in the lives of the listeners.[196]

Not only is Barth's concept of exhortation specific to the Christian community, but it also functions in the immediacy of the situation confronted, and thus cannot be reduced to a system of rules or law. In his comment on Romans 12:11, Barth adopts a variant reading to translate the verse 'Obey the command of the moment!'[197] Christian obedience occurs moment by moment as believers seek to *be*, and *remain*, and *become* obedient to the *living* call of God. Only in this way is the will of God understood, comprehended and fulfilled.[198] In this context, it is crucial to recall the point made earlier, that this *being*, *remaining* and *becoming* obedient is primarily a function of the 'Body of Christ,' and only then of the individual who is a part of that body. It is, then, the community of believers together who seek the *living* voice of God.

This 'command of the moment,' issuing in the situation itself, is recognised by those who have been restored to a relation of immediacy with God, and whose minds have been 'renewed'. For Barth, a critical aspect of the fulfilment of God's will involves an intellectual pursuit: 'Adequate *thought* is the principle of transformation, which will enable you to become new and to represent something new toward the old world.'[199] 'Adequate thought' is thought obedient to faith, which for Barth aims at reflecting God's thoughts in a continuous begetting of the truth from truth itself. This process takes place in permanent confrontation with the reality of this world which is passing away.[200] Clearly Barth intends the society of believers to function as a community of discernment, seeking to hear in its actual confrontation and interface with the realities of life in the old aeon, the 'command of the moment'. Because the command of the moment is entirely *zeitgemäß*—contemporary, and in keeping with the immediate time and context—the action of the community in obedience to this command is also *zeitgemäß*.[201] Through a process of critical reflection, and 'through a prayerful following of the "real development of things…behind the curtain of time"',[202] the community is enabled to bear the particular character of God's people in the world.[203]

That God's people in the world are to bear a 'particular character' shows, significantly, that the command of the moment is not to be conceived of in an arbitrary or capricious manner. To the contrary, because God's will is

---

[196] Barth, *Romans I*, 463-464.

[197] See Barth, *Romans I*, 484. In the phrase τῷ κυρίῳ δουλεύοντες Barth follows Origen and substitutes καιρῷ for κυρίῳ, translating it *Dem Gebot des Augenblicks gehorchet!*

[198] Barth, *Romans I*, 524-525.

[199] Barth, *Romans I*, 470.

[200] Barth, *Romans I*, 471.

[201] Barth, *Romans I*, 486.

[202] McCormack, *Karl Barth's Dialectical Theology*, 171, citing Barth, *Romans I*, 486.

[203] Barth, *Romans I*, 470.

consistent, his command will also be consistent, following a particular trajectory or *Tendenz* from moment to moment. Further, because the divine will has a definite tendency, Christian norms which seek to apply that will in specific situations will also be characterised by that tendency.[204]

What are some of the features of this *Tendenz* which characterise the command of the moment, and hence also, the activity of the church? Barth takes it as virtually axiomatic that Christians are to have nothing to do with 'monarchy, capitalism, militarism, patriotism or liberalism': such a stance need hardly be asserted![205] Rather, in the midst of the old world of the flesh, the enclave of God must arise in which the power of God which appeared in the life of Christ must and will manifest and prove itself in the members of his body.[206] Two observations may be made here. First, Barth evidently views Christ himself as the paradigm of Christian existence, although not as a paradigm to be emulated as in a mimetic ethics. Rather, as believers are incorporated into the new being in the Spirit, the divine life which appeared in the life of Christ will once again come to expression in them. Moment by moment men and women must '*become* what they are in Christ', so that the turn of the ages from Adam to Christ might be provisionally realised in them anew.[207]

Second, it is also clear that Barth envisages the community of faith as a group within society which, carried along by the divine movement, stands, or better, *moves*, in contrast to the dominant cultural powers over against which it is placed. To fall into alignment with these cultural powers would be nothing less than a fall from grace back into the sinfulness of the world. 'How shall we who have died to sin,' Barth asks, 'continue to live in it?'[208] The movement of this people echoes and reflects the divine movement of grace which is a movement *from below*. For Barth, there can be no neutrality in this:

> You belong under all circumstances to the common people....God is certainly a God of the Jews *and* the heathen, but not a God of the powerful *and* the lowly, but rather, one-sidedly, a God of the lowly; not a God of the great *and* the small, but rather recklessly, a God of the small....The movement of the kingdom of God within social and cultural conflicts is...fundamentally and one-sidedly a movement from below. Those who participate in it must...be willing to stand below where everything depends on God. I can certainly become a Jew to the Jews and a Greek to the Greeks, but not a lord to the lords....Where idols are

---

[204] McCormack, *Karl Barth's Dialectical Theology*, 171.

[205] Barth, *Romans I*, 509.

[206] Barth, *Romans I*, 303-304.

[207] McCormack, *Karl Barth's Dialectical Theology*, 164.

[208] Barth, *Romans I*, 509.

erected, I may not be present. Over against everything that wants to be great I must take the standpoint of the small people, with whom God begins.[209]

The *Tendenz*, therefore, of a Christian action which reflects the being and activity of God will show itself as such by its echoing of the divine preference for the lowly, over against the mighty. Against the backdrop of revolutionary movements in his own milieu, Barth proclaims the revolution of Christ, whose revolution is nothing less than the dissolution of all dependencies save dependence on God. For Barth, the only legitimate dependency is dependence upon God, which is the foundation of true liberty.[210]

The freedom of which Barth speaks is *mutual* freedom. Life in Christ is characterised as a life for others. In accordance with his identification of individualism with original sin, and religious individualism as simply one variety of the larger species, Barth not only decentres the individual self by granting priority to the community as the Body of Christ, but also insists that genuine personal subjectivity cannot be 'a subjectivity imprisoned in itself' as was the fatal case with Adam.[211] Humanity resting only in itself and for itself is characteristic of life *without* God.[212] Thus, says Barth, we must not take our own freedom *too* seriously. Those the apostle refers to as 'strong in faith' (Romans 14:1) are those with the capacity to limit their own freedom in order to grant freedom to another.[213] Accordingly, the truly free subject is one who is free *for* others, who lives in and through others.[214] This too, then, will be reflected in the *Tendenz* of Christian activity. As God is at work liberating men and women from their self-relatedness and creating a community of fellowship and freedom, so Christian activity grounded in the divine movement will show itself to be such by its efficacy in producing fellowship and freedom.[215]

This notion receives additional treatment in Barth's comments on Romans 13:8-10 where he develops what he calls the 'positive principle' of his

---

[209] Barth, *Romans I*, 490. Paul Nimmo demonstrates that Barth retained this idea later in his career, using the language of 'certain prominent lines' which provide direction for Christian discipleship, and further argues that that these 'lines' are grounded in the divine being itself. The believer is 'ontologically determined' for obedience and humility in correspondence to the very essence of (the immanent) God revealed in Jesus Christ: 'We stand under the sign and direction of the cross...not so much [as] a matter of morals as "ontology".' See Paul T. Nimmo, 'Barth and the Christian as Ethical Agent: An Ontological Study of the Shape of Christian Ethics' in *Commanding Grace: Studies in Karl Barth's Ethics* (ed. Daniel L. Migliore; Grand Rapids: Eerdmans, 2010), 234-237.

[210] Barth, *Romans I*, 196.

[211] Barth, *Romans I*, 274.

[212] Barth, *Romans I*, 271.

[213] Barth, *Romans I*, 533.

[214] McCormack, *Karl Barth's Dialectical Theology*, 166.

[215] McCormack, *Karl Barth's Dialectical Theology*, 171-172.

programme, namely, love: 'Only love builds the new world, but love will surely build it....Love is the power of the resurrection through which the new creation comes.'[216] It is this love which, as a reflection of the love God has shown us in Christ, leads the believer into solidarity with the lowly and suffering, and into the formation of a community of fellowship and freedom. Elsewhere Barth refers to this community in the love of Christ as the community of the Spirit in which the righteousness of the kingdom of heaven grows.[217]

It is precisely this growth of the righteousness of the kingdom as expressed in the love of the community which Barth views as revolutionary. The Spirit who inspires and empowers this love is the power of the new world, and, Barth notes with an eye toward the political developments of his era, 'can at this present time be nothing other than revolution—precisely what we at the moment call revolution!'[218] In spite of his criticism of the religious socialism advocated by Ragaz, Barth had not given up hope for a 'true socialism' which would come into being, not through the revolutionary activities of human agents, but organically, as the 'healing unrest that is set in the heart by God' deepens and grows until the rising flood of the divine will itself 'break through the dams' and establish the 'state of God'.[219] The 'absolute revolution' of God comes through the power of the Spirit who is at work in the entire world and who brings life from the dead:

> Perhaps God at present, is in the process of leaving the old and uncertain socialism behind. Perhaps its historical hour has now run out, without bringing the world what it was to have brought....But more important than this dissolution will be another hour which fulfils history, when the now dying flow of Marxist dogma will illuminate a new global truth, when the socialist church will be resurrected in a socialist world.[220]

Conclusion

When, in the middle of 1916, Barth sat under his apple tree and opened Paul's letter to the Romans together with a few commentaries, he had no idea that his 'little notebook' in which he recorded his observations and insights would become the proverbial 'bombshell in the theologians' playground' and that as a result of its publication he would be offered a chair of theology at Göttingen University a few years later.

As I suggested in the conclusion to the second chapter, the primary emphases identified in Barth's initial work following his break with his liberal heritage came to a climax and received more complete expression in his first

[216] Barth, *Romans I*, 522.
[217] Barth, *Romans I*, 353.
[218] Barth, *Romans I*, 316.
[219] Barth, *Romans I*, 508.
[220] Barth, *Romans I*, 444.

commentary to the Romans. Here, once more, we find the same theological realism, the sovereignty and centrality of God, the critique of religion and especially religious individualism, and the notion of the organic development of the kingdom of God which characterised Barth's earlier works. We also find that Barth had a definite, albeit nascent, vision of Christian and ecclesial existence, and that this ecclesial dimension is an essential aspect of his theological work. Barth tackles Pietism, Liberalism and Idealism in a mighty struggle to demolish the vision of life and Christian existence presented by exponents of these groups in order to call the church and believers to a different order of existence. His polemics, therefore, function in service of a practical end, which was to recall the church from its disastrous assimilation to the idolatrous character of the prevailing culture to a more faithful praxis in accordance with the eschatological nature of the coming kingdom.

The nature and shape of ecclesial existence in *Romans I* also echoes the portrait provided in the earlier works. Once more Christian existence falls under the purview of the Holy Spirit as the immanent power of the coming kingdom. When Barth speaks of the church he intends the concrete fellowship of believers rather than the institutional or hierarchical church, the *Gemeinde* rather than simply *Kirche*. Christian existence is necessarily corporate, a fellowship of faith, love and freedom which stands in dependence upon God and in solidarity with the poor and lowly.

Barth's depiction of the Christian life also presupposes the free and responsive activity of human agents. The community is portrayed as a community of discernment seeking to hear and discern the command of the moment in order that God's will might be done amongst them. This obedience, while active and freely chosen, is not independent, however, but the work of the divine life evident in Jesus Christ coming to expression once more in the community and the individual by the Spirit. While the doctrine of the command of God in this phase of Barth's career is not nearly as developed or nuanced as it will become later, it is clear nonetheless that already he is developing his ethics in this direction. Gerhard Sauter has noted that the motif introduced here in *Romans I*—thought obedient to faith—is one which will in time 'pervade his entire oeuvre' incorporating not only his dogmatics, but his ethics also.[221]

The evident tension in Barth's treatment of the political responsibility of the Christian may reflect, as Gorringe suggested, an attempt to apply the command of the moment in impossibly trying circumstances. More likely, however, it is indicative, as McCormack and Spencer suggest, that Barth has not yet developed the theological resources that will enable him to treat the matter more adequately. Certainly in this work Barth endeavoured to lay out a comprehensive theological worldview and corresponding field of ethical

[221] Gerhard Sauter, 'Shifts in Karl Barth's Thought: The Current Debate between Right- and Left-Wing Barthians,' in *Eschatological Rationality: Theological Issues in Focus* (Grand Rapids: Baker, 1996), 134.

existence. The eschatological framework within which he developed this worldview was, however, ultimately inadequate for the task he set himself, and as a result he quite quickly jettisoned this framework in order to locate and develop a more useful one. While retaining an eschatological orientation in his work, Barth turned from the process or evolutionary eschatology seen in this commentary to a consistent eschatology, one which anticipates the climatic dénouement that only God can achieve, and which awaits humanity on the further side of death.[222] Instead of the dynamic eschatological procession of God occurring *within* history, now time and eternity would be set over against one another. Why Barth felt impelled to this shift is the focus of the next chapter.

---

[222] McCormack refers to this shift from a process to a 'radically futurist "consistent" eschatology' the most fundamental shift which occurred between the two editions of the commentary. See McCormack, *Karl Barth's Dialectical Theology*, 208-209. Note that McCormack credits Michael Beintker for developing the terminology of 'process eschatology' (155, 162-164, 208-209). See Michael Beintker, *Die Dialektik in der 'dialektischen Theologie' Karl Barths* (Munich: Chr. Kaiser Verlag, 1987).

CHAPTER 4

LIFE IN THE SHADOW OF DEATH?

> The only source for the real, the immediate, revelation of God is *death*. Christ unlocked its gates. He brought *life* to light out of *death*. *Out of death!* The word cannot be spoken significantly enough. The meaning of God, the power of God, begins to shine upon the men of the Bible at the boundary of mortality....Life comes from *death!* Death is the source of all.[1]

We have earlier noted that the end of the war did not signal the end of the tumult which had threatened to engulf Europe. The six months following the cessation of hostilities saw the establishment of the fledgling Weimar Republic in Germany, the violent repression of the attempted 'Sparticist' coup in Berlin, and the failed attempt at revolution in Germany.[2] Although Switzerland was spared these upheavals, the general strike of November 1918 caused great concern in the nation because of the possibility that more radical elements might commandeer the socialist attempts to force a change in governmental policy, and seek through violent means to force a change of government along Bolshevik lines. The uncertainty felt at this time is illustrated in comments written by Thurneysen to Barth on October 30, 1918: 'So where does the journey go from here? Towards world Bolshevism? Only one thing is clear to me: we must think of the kingdom of God consistently as "other" and keep our hope pure from all democratic and other "preliminary stages."'[3]

For his part, Barth continued his pastoral work and biblical investigations, as well as continuing his engagement in local political affairs. He wrote several statements for local distribution regarding Swiss socialism, warning the Socialist Party against joining the Third International, which was dependent on Russia, and, after a lengthy hiatus, resumed his lectures to his Workers'

---

[1] Karl Barth, 'Biblical Questions, Insights, and Vistas,' in *The Word of God and the Word of Man* (New York: Harper and Brothers, 1956), 77, 80.

[2] For a discussion of the historical background of this period see Eberhard Busch, *Karl Barth: His Life from Letters and Autobiographical Texts* (trans. J. Bowden; Philadelphia: Fortress, 1976), 106-109, and also Friedrich-Wilhelm Marquardt, *Der Christ in der Gesellschaft, 1919-1979: Geschichte, Analyse und Bedeutung von Karl Barths Tambacher Vortrag* (Munich: Kaiser Verlag, 1980), 7-37.

[3] Cited in Bruce L. McCormack, *Karl Barth's Critically Realistic Dialectical Theology: Its Genesis and Development 1909-1936* (Oxford: Oxford University Press, 1995), 187-188.

Association in February 1919 providing commentary on the political events of the day. He also continued to present formal lectures and to write occasional articles on theological issues during the immediate period following the war, which provide insight into his vision of Christian and ecclesial existence during this time of political turmoil and social instability.

This chapter begins by examining a short article Barth wrote upon the death of Christoph Blumhardt in August 1919 in which he compares the influence and legacy of Blumhardt with that of fellow churchman-politician Friedrich Naumann, who died the same year. For Barth, the two men represent the past and the future possibilities of Christianity. The second section considers a lecture given by Barth in Tambach, Germany in September 1919 at a conference for Religious Socialists, entitled 'The Christian's Place in Society.' Barth's lecture develops and extends his understanding of Christian existence within the theological framework unfolded in his commentary on Romans. The third work investigated in this chapter is another review article Barth wrote in early 1920, this time on the work of Franz Overbeck. The influence of Overbeck on Barth should not be under-estimated, for from Overbeck Barth gained the tools to sharpen his critique of the modern church and its theology. This influence is clearly discerned in the next lecture examined in this chapter, 'Biblical Questions, Insights and Vistas' which was given in April 1920 to a student conference in Aarau. In this lecture we have substantial evidence of Barth's development in the period between the two editions of his commentary. Barth has sharpened his understanding of the divine-human relation by bringing the concepts of divine election and 'crisis' into the foreground of his theological reflection. He provides an exposition of Christian and ecclesial existence in terms of witness, in which genuine piety is radically 'ec-centric' in orientation and grounded in the forgiveness of sins. In a surprising development, we also note a new awareness of and appreciation for the role of the individual in God's interaction with humanity. The final section of the chapter examines a series of seven sermons delivered by Barth to his Safenwil congregation in mid-1920. The value of these sermons lies in the insight they provide of how Barth sought to apply his developing theological framework in the context of local church ministry, including the notion of election and crisis, the dialectical structuring of the divine-human relation in terms of eternity and time, the new emphasis on the importance of the individual, and the attempt to ground ethical existence in the forgiveness of sins.

The works examined in this chapter show that while Barth's theology in the two years following the publication of *Romans I* underwent clear development, several aspects of his vision of Christian and ecclesial existence remained continuous with what had gone before. Nevertheless, the tightened eschatological horizon within which Barth now began to work also had the effect of reducing some of the rich descriptions of Christian and ecclesial existence found in his works from 1915-17. Thus, at the end of the chapter we find that we are left with several questions concerning the viability of his attempt to ground ethics in the forgiveness of sins, particularly in such turbulent times as those in which he and his congregation lived.

The Bourgeois Church: Measured and Found Wanting

On August 2, 1919 Christoph Blumhardt died and Barth used the occasion to write a short piece in recognition of his contribution, comparing him with Friedrich Naumann, another German pastor who had exercised enormous influence in the German church and who had also recently died.[4] In an interesting co-incidence Barth had met both men on the same journey when in April 1915 he attended his brother's wedding in Marburg. Naumann was an uncle of the bride. It was on the return journey to Switzerland that Thurneysen introduced Barth to Blumhardt, to whom Barth had the duty of conveying Naumann's greetings.

Still earlier, in July 1914, Barth had written a review article of *Die Hilfe,* a periodical founded in 1890 by Naumann, which had as its motto 'Help for God, help for one's brother, help for the State, help for oneself.' Barth began that article with an acknowledgement of the significant contribution towards social issues made by *Die Hilfe* over the years, but noted the changing attitude and stance of the editor in more recent times. By 1914 Naumann had consigned Christian belief and practice to personal piety and morality, with virtually no relevance to political life, and thus, according to Barth, pursued politics 'under the presupposition that there is no God.'[5] This, for Barth, was impossible since God cannot be excluded from any arena of life, and because genuine Christian hope is ultimately unable to make final peace with the world as it is. He expressed his disappointment in Naumann's political shift towards capitalism, nationalism and militarism, and refused the idea that 'a politics which simply capitulates before certain alleged realities is the only possible, the correct politics. We should expect more from God.'[6] This article, of course, was written just prior to the Socialists' capitulation to nationalism at the commencement of the war, which, as we have already seen, came as a profound disappointment to Barth.

The divide between Barth's position and that of Naumann also surfaced at the 1915 wedding where Barth met Naumann. One evening in conversation

---

[4] Karl Barth, 'Past and Future: Friedrich Naumann and Christoph Blumhardt,' in *The Beginnings of Dialectic Theology* (ed. James M. Robinson; Richmond: John Knox Press, 1968), 35-45. The original article appeared in the *Neuer Freier Aargauer,* XIV (1919), issues 204 and 205.

[5] Karl Barth, 'Die Hilfe 1913' *Christliche Welt,* August 14, 1914. Cited in George Hunsinger, 'Conclusion: Toward A Radical Barth,' in *Karl Barth and Radical Politics* (ed. G. Hunsinger; Philadelphia: Westminster, 1976), 198.

[6] Barth, 'Die Hilfe 1913'. This is cited in McCormack, *Karl Barth's Dialectical Theology,* 110.

Barth and Thurneysen heard Naumann remark that one now sees how well 'religion can be used for purposes of conducting the war'. The remark infuriated Barth: 'What do you mean "use religion"? Is that permissible? Can one do that?'[7] Hunsinger has rightly noted that it was intolerable for Barth that the sovereign God should be so misused by the contemporary church as to support the political horror of the war.[8] It was precisely this decadence of the church, represented so well by Naumann, which compelled Barth to break with the liberal tradition of academic theology and the form of ecclesial praxis it engendered.

In the present article Barth presents Naumann's life as an odyssey, tracing in outline the development of his career and thought.[9] Naumann had begun his ministry working with a well known charitable organisation in Hamburg before serving as a pastor in an industrial community in Saxony, and as an industrial chaplain in Frankfurt. In these positions he became familiar with the conditions of industrial workers and the emerging tenets of Social Democracy. In these early years of his career, claims Barth, Naumann was confronted with the radical message of the New Testament—the message directed towards the transformation of the world. As Barth saw it, however, Naumann shifted over the years from his understanding of 'the social Jesus' to what Barth calls 'a religious veneration of nature and of modern culture':[10]

> *Why not?* God speaks everywhere. But without his noticing it, everything that existed began to be surrounded with a peculiar halo of religion—the State and the Hohenzollerns and the Prussian military, the German citizen with his incomparable 'efficiency,' capitalism, trade, enterprise, in short, the whole Germany of Kaiser Wilhelm....Overnight the flag of 'Christian socialism' changed into that of a 'national socialism,' and in 1903 disappeared completely into the museum of 'liberalism.' Then came Naumann's journey to Palestine, on which he made the discovery that Jesus could not possibly have been the practical social reformer whom we need, for if he had been, the streets and roads in that land would be in better condition![11]

Barth describes Naumann's shift as a 'truly tragic second conversion' in which he moved from positive Christianity to modern theology, and from there again to what Barth refers to as Darwinism, or naturalism.[12] His emphasis on the immanence of God and revelation in nature and culture led to an enthusiastic fusion of religion and nationalist politics, which envisioned an industrialised Germany strengthened by her allies as 'the preliminary citadel of

---

[7] Hunsinger, 'Toward A Radical Barth,' 200.
[8] Hunsinger, 'Toward A Radical Barth,' 201.
[9] Barth, 'Past and Future,' 35-37.
[10] Barth, 'Past and Future,' 37.
[11] Barth, 'Past and Future,' 37-38.
[12] Barth, 'Past and Future,' 38, 36.

German world rule'.[13]

Barth locates the genesis of this transformation in Naumann's understanding of God. Instead of adhering to that which the New Testament calls 'God,' Naumann, according to Barth, now understood God in idealistic terms as the presupposition of life binding humanity with necessity to its nature and to the general laws of nature, and launching it into the struggle for existence and self-preservation.[14] Under the influence of idealism and naturalism Naumann had jettisoned any form of eschatological hope in favour of liberal notions of progress and power. In place of a faith that was bound to God and his purpose of transformation in the world, faith was the courageous taking up of the struggle for existence. In the end Naumann settled for an inscrutable God and a religion of the soul 'which may seek comfort and power in the world, but does not seek victory *over* the world'.[15] Indeed, as Hunsinger has suggested, the bourgeois theology of liberalism, having flattened the eschatological horizon and thus vitiating the concept of God from within, was wholly unable to imagine the transcendence of God over existing social conditions: capitulation in the face of political crisis was virtually inevitable.[16]

By contrast, Blumhardt, as we have previously seen,[17] embraced a thoroughly realist and eschatological view of God in his relation to the world. It was this which first attracted Barth to him when they met in 1915. Blumhardt stood not for religion but *God*, not for idealism but *reality*. His main contribution, according to Barth, was the recovery of eschatology:

> What appeared again in Boll that was new and in accord with the New Testament can be comprehended in one word: *hope*—hope for a visible and tangible appearing of the lordship of God over the world....to believe in 'God' meant, for the two Blumhardts, to take this comprehensive hope seriously, more seriously than all other considerations.[18]

This hope, for Barth, relativises all earthly 'realities' and is itself a critical hope which includes 'a comprehensive attack on the bases of present-day society, culture and church'.[19] Nevertheless, it is a hope that also inspires patient engagement in all of the affairs of human society and culture because in the coming kingdom of God all earthly reality will be transformed.

It is clear in this brief article that Barth continues to view the God-world relation in terms of the theology outlined in *Romans I*. He still longs for the

---

[13] Barth, 'Past and Future,' 40.

[14] Barth, 'Past and Future,' 38.

[15] Barth, 'Past and Future,' 39.

[16] Hunsinger, 'Toward A Radical Barth,' 203.

[17] See chapter 2, page 67 above.

[18] Barth, 'Past and Future,' 41-42. '(Bad) Boll' was the home of the Blumhardts' ministry.

[19] Barth, 'Past and Future,' 42.

new world[20] that is to be born out of the old,[21] and which will come into being as a result of *God's* activity, specifically, an outpouring of the Holy Spirit.[22] He retains the process eschatology of the commentary which conceives of the relation of God to the world as 'a mighty, historical process, a movement, a victorious struggle, which must end with the renewal of all things'.[23] He still regards socialism as the form of political praxis that most adequately represents the coming kingdom of God, although it is now the chastened affirmation of socialism that views it as a parable of the kingdom, rather than the presence of the kingdom itself.[24] He also eulogises Blumhardt's 'endless movement between hurrying and waiting' as a prophetic message which exemplifies authentic eschatological existence in this age.[25]

Finally, and of particular concern for understanding our topic, this article also echoes the critique of the church found in earlier works, and is in fact here particularly scathing because of the way in which Barth rhetorically associates the church with Naumann but not with Blumhardt. Barth begins his discussion of Naumann with the assertion that

> [t]he church was the home of this German member of the Reichstag....It was the orthodox Lutheran Church of Saxony, but that was accidental; it could just as well have been the Catholic or the Mohammedan—in any case, *the* church, for which the relationship of the world to the divine is an a priori, fixed, ordered, unchanging connection which merely needs religious explanation and transfiguration.[26]

When Barth aligns Naumann with the church, his critique and rejection of the Naumann is also an implicit critique and rejection of the church. This citation indicates, however, that Barth is not speaking of the church in an absolute sense, but as a reference to an undifferentiated sense of *religion*, or, in the context in which Barth is writing, to the modern church grounded in idealist theology. According to Barth, *this* church, which assumes a static connection between God and the world, and which is thus oriented towards the maintenance of the established order, does not understand the God of the New Testament who seeks the transformation of the world.[27] *This* church, as Naumann himself came to suspect in his early years when he read the New Testament 'with new eyes' and came 'very near to the sacred fire,' had fallen short of God's intention and was in need of repentance: 'Is it possible,' he asks,

---

[20] Barth, 'Past and Future,' 36.
[21] Barth, 'Past and Future,' 42.
[22] Barth, 'Past and Future,' 43.
[23] Barth, 'Past and Future,' 41.
[24] Barth, 'Past and Future,' 42.
[25] Barth, 'Past and Future,' 44-45.
[26] Barth, 'Past and Future,' 35-36.
[27] Barth, 'Past and Future,' 36, 38.

'that the godless Social Democrats (they were fighting against the church!) understood God better than the church did? Was it possible that the church needed to repent and turn to the God of the godless?'[28] Naumann, as we have seen, turned from this early insight and subsequently 'always remained the typical pastor'[29]—one firmly committed to the maintenance of the established order.

While Barth notes that Blumhardt also started out as a pastor, and that his work as director of the spa Boll 'was very nearly that of a pastor' in reality 'his path had nothing in common with the church'.[30] When he spoke of God, says Barth, he meant something very different to what the church meant. His new insight—the recovery of eschatological realism—'is all along the line and in all points down to the present day a total contrast to the general religion of churches and pastors of all denominations'.[31] Indeed, says Barth, the prophetic character of his life and message, as well as his practical devotion to socialism as the most important contemporary parable of the kingdom ensured that he remained an enigma to all those willing and able to feel at home in the church.[32]

Barth's unrelenting critique of the church in this article raises a question that must be faced: does his rhetoric here actually betray an anti-ecclesial motive in his theology? It is certainly true that it is not possible from this article to identify a positive ecclesial concern as the motive for his theology. Nonetheless, he gives indication that his critique is directed specifically against the kind of ecclesial existence represented by Naumann. Further, his approbation of Blumhardt is indicative, as we have previously seen, of the kind of Christian and ecclesial vision that Barth maintained in this period. To the extent, therefore, that the church has forsaken the reality of God and eschatological hope, and thereby compromised and accommodated itself to the form of this age which is passing away, it is to be rejected. Thus, it is the form of Christian and ecclesial existence represented by Naumann that Barth rejects as belonging to an era now past, not the church and Christianity generally. Once more, it is the praxis exemplified by Blumhardt which Barth holds forth as that which is authentic eschatological and prophetic existence, even while not specifically referring to it as Christian or ecclesial existence.

---

[28] Barth, 'Past and Future,' 36-37.
[29] Barth, 'Past and Future,' 36.
[30] Barth, 'Past and Future,' 40.
[31] Barth, 'Past and Future,' 42.
[32] Barth, 'Past and Future,' 45.

'The Christian's Place in Society'

Barth's Tambach Lecture

About the same time that Barth was writing his piece on Naumann and Blumhardt he was also preparing a lecture to be delivered at a September conference for Religious Socialists in Tambach (Thuringia), Germany. Initially Barth declined the invitation, preferring to stay in Switzerland, but when Ragaz (who was first choice for the speaker) pulled out, the organisers requested once more that Barth speak. The topic assigned to Barth for the lecture was 'The Christian in Society.'[33] For Barth, the kingdom of God and socialism stood over against each other, but he was concerned that Religious Socialism had equated itself with the arrival of the kingdom of God. He did not want to deliver a theological basis for zeal into the hands of a few zealots for social reform.[34] If the organisers had been more fully aware of Barth's position they may have chosen to invite someone else to their conference. As it was, they heard a lecture where it was made clear in no uncertain terms that such an identification is wholly illegitimate. Nonetheless, according to Busch, his address had an extraordinarily powerful effect on his hearers, not entirely positive, of course. When Ragaz heard what Barth had had to say he felt that Barth had 'vitiated the influence of the movement in Germany by "dialectical distortion"'.[35]

The lecture itself is a lengthy convoluted affair comprising five sections of dialectical argument. In a letter to Thurneysen Barth himself acknowledges that 'it has become a rather complicated kind of machine that runs backwards and forwards and shoots in all directions with no lack of both visible and hidden joints'.[36] Webster has described the lecture as 'not an easy work. At points it is simply unclear.'[37] He suggests the dialectical complexity of the form of the address is reflective of the content Barth is seeking to communicate, and that Barth is best understood not so much as constructing a position as attempting to

---

[33] Spencer's suggestion that Barth *changed* the title to 'The Christian's *Place* in Society' does not seem warranted although it reflects the title given to the lecture in Horton's translation (*The Word of God and the Word of Man*). Neither the lecture itself, its title in the new translation, nor the introduction to the lecture provided there, support this suggestion. See Archibald James Spencer, *Clearing a Space for Human Action: Ethical Ontology in the Theology of Karl Barth* (New York: Peter Lang, 2003), 98-99, and Karl Barth, *The Word of God and Theology* (trans. Amy Marga; London: T. & T. Clark, 2011), 31-69.

[34] Spencer, *Clearing a Space*, 99.

[35] Busch, *Karl Barth*, 111.

[36] John D. Smart, ed., *Revolutionary Theology in the Making: Barth-Thurneysen Correspondence, 1914-1925* (London: Epworth, 1964), 47. The letter is dated September 11, 1919.

[37] John Webster, *Barth's Moral Theology: Human Action in Barth's Thought* (Grand Rapids: Eerdmans, 1998), 20.

bring home to the reader a spiritual and intellectual process in which he found himself inescapably caught up.[38] Accordingly, Webster suggests that we read the essay backwards, from the fifth section into what is argued earlier, since it is only at the end that the full scope of Barth's argument emerges into view.[39] The contention that Barth utilised the dialectical form in order to engage his listeners in the spiritual and intellectual process in which he was caught up may well be true. To claim, however, that Barth is not constructing a position is to underestimate the intent of his rhetoric. While Webster's suggestion to examine the lecture backwards has undoubted heuristic merit, for our own purposes we will endeavour to read and interpret the lecture in accordance with the manner in which Barth delivered it, in order to appreciate the nuanced character of his presentation as he builds towards his climax. It will be seen that Barth clearly intended to lead his hearers towards a particular kind of ethical response, and will thus illustrate once more the ethical and ecclesial motive that is of a piece with his theological reasoning.

The Hope of the Christian: Divine and Human Action

Barth begins his lecture with a meditation on the title given for the lecture, identifying and discussing the concepts of 'Christian' and 'society'. He identifies society with various social orders and arrangements: marriage and family, civilisation and economics, art and science, the state, the party, and international relations. Each of these takes a familiar course in accordance with its own inner logic. The problem is that their familiar course is apparently wrong, says Barth, more so in light of the catastrophic events from which Europe is only now emerging. Indeed, in light of these realities, one could wish to withdraw from society, but, alas, one cannot. Barth perhaps gives voice to some of the cultural despair of the time when he mournfully says, 'we are still painfully aware that in spite of all the social changes and revolutions, everything is as it was of old'.[40] In view of this pessimistic assessment he asks whether there is any basis for hope in the present situation, the answer to which is simply, for Barth, *'The Christian'*. He goes on to say that

> [h]ere is a new element in the midst of the old, a truth in the midst of error and lies, a righteousness in the midst of a sea of unrighteousness, a spirituality within all our crass materialistic tendencies, a formative life-energy within all our weak, tottering movements of thought, a unity in a time which is out of joint.[41]

Barth very plainly identifies 'the Christian' as a promise of hope within the

---

[38] Webster, *Barth's Moral Theology*, 20. See also Spencer, *Clearing a Space*, 100.

[39] Webster, *Barth's Moral Theology*, 21.

[40] Karl Barth, 'The Christian's Place in Society,' in *The Word of God and the Word of Man* (New York: Harper and Brothers, 1956), 273.

[41] Barth, 'The Christian's Place,' 273.

present darkness which pervades the social realities of contemporary Germany. And not only a promise of hope, but that which is new, true, righteous, spiritual, and unified, a *formative life-energy*. This is a very high estimation indeed! But it must be noted that when Barth speaks thus of 'the Christian' he is not simply referring to the individual believer, nor to the church generally, nor to those specific believers who concern themselves with religion and social relations. Rather, 'the Christian is *the Christ*. The Christian is that within us which is not ourself but Christ in us.'[42] For Barth, this notion—*Christ in us*—is not reducible to a personal existential reality which we might identify, but is 'a presupposition of life' over, behind and beyond us, that is, encompassing our existence on every side, and which is in principle inclusive of all humanity.[43] As such, it cannot be used as a means of division whereby to identify those within and those without because 'the community of Christ is a building open on every side, for Christ died for all—even for the folk outside'.[44] Because this is true Barth deduces that, 'if Christ is in us, then society, in spite of its being on the wrong course, is not forsaken of God....So: we bid you hope.'[45]

Barth's opening salvo is, then, a proclamation of hope: that hidden like leaven within the darkness of a world which seems God-forsaken is *The Christian*. Immediately, however, he warns that the connection and relationship of the Christian with society is neither apparent nor easy. The two stand over against each other like two great 'magnitudes' which are inherently foreign to each other. Part of the blame for this must lie with the Christians themselves, who, on account of their own religious indigence have become aloof from society in their attempt to create and maintain an honourable religious domain. To this Barth declares that, 'the meaning of so-called religion is to be found in its relation to actual life, to life in society, and not in its being set apart from it. Holiness in itself is no holiness whatever.'[46]

Thus, on the one hand, Barth rejects an isolationist withdrawal of the Christian from society, and yet, on the other hand, he also appeals to the divine aseity to reject simplistic identifications of the Christian with society, as found in such hyphenations as Religious-Socialism or Christian-Democracy, as though the kingdom of God will be realised through existing mechanisms or movements within human culture. 'The Divine,' insists Barth, 'is something whole, complete in itself, a kind of new and different something in contrast to the world. It does not permit of being applied, stuck on, and fitted in.'[47] For

---

[42] Barth, 'The Christian's Place,' 273. Willis suggests that Barth is here utilizing a neo-Kantian notion of the Transcendental Ego. See Robert E. Willis, *The Ethics of Karl Barth* (Leiden: Brill, 1971), 15.

[43] Barth, 'The Christian's Place,' 273-274.

[44] Barth, 'The Christian's Place,' 274.

[45] Barth, 'The Christian's Place,' 275.

[46] Barth, 'The Christian's Place,' 276.

[47] Barth, 'The Christian's Place,' 277.

Barth, then, the attempt to identify the Christian's place in society by positing a unity between the two serves only to 'secularise Christ'.[48] Nor, in any case, will society itself permit such an identification, for 'society is now really ruled by its own logos; say rather by a whole pantheon of its own hypostases and powers'.[49] Not only does God assert his independence over against society, but society, under the demonic influence of its own idols, continues to assert its own independence over against God.

Neither is the relation between the two a matter of clericalising the society, or of making the church more relevant: 'for all our new patches, the old garment still remains the old garment'. Thus, Barth admonishes his audience, 'let us withstand the new temptation of ecclesiasticism!...God alone can save the world...and we shall deceive society about it if we set to work building churches and chapels and do not learn to wait upon him in a wholly new way.'[50]

Barth brings the initial section of his message to a conclusion by re-iterating what he perceives in the theme announced for his lecture. On the one hand, there is a great promise to be found in the present situation. On the other hand, however, there is an inevitable separation between the Christian and the society, 'a thorough-going opposition between two dissimilar magnitudes....This is our hope and our need both as Christians and as members of society.'[51] What solution may be found for this situation? Barth is unequivocal: 'Do not expect me to provide a solution! None of us may boast a solution. There is only one solution, and that is in God himself.'[52]

Before he takes up the main concern of his lecture, Barth inserts another section in which he introduces a discussion of his 'general standpoint,' beginning by suggesting that his position is not so much a *position* as 'an instant in a *movement*, and any view of it is comparable to the momentary view of a bird in flight'.[53] This movement, of course, is not to be identified with any particular human movement, but is rather

> a movement from above, a movement from a third dimension, so to speak, which transcends and yet penetrates all these movements and gives them their inner meaning and motive; a movement which has neither its origin nor its aim in space, in time, or in the contingency of things, and yet is not a movement apart from others: I mean the movement of God in history or, otherwise expressed, the movement of God in consciousness, the movement whose power and import are

---

[48] Barth, 'The Christian's Place,' 277.

[49] Barth, 'The Christian's Place,' 279-280.

[50] Barth, 'The Christian's Place,' 281.

[51] Barth, 'The Christian's Place,' 282.

[52] Barth, 'The Christian's Place,' 282.

[53] Barth, 'The Christian's Place,' 282.

revealed in the resurrection of Jesus Christ from the dead. This must be the gist of all our thinking about the Christian's place in society.[54]

Here we hear unmistakable echoes of the theology of *Romans 1*, and of Barth's contention that Christian existence involves being caught up into the divine eschatological procession inaugurated by the resurrection of Jesus Christ. He insists, though, that it is a mistake to think of the movement as an end in itself. What is important is neither a theory nor description of the movement, but becoming a participant in the *motion*. Such participation is possible only on the basis of the miracle of revelation, for we can do nothing to place ourselves into this movement.[55] He also emphasises that this movement is not to be equated with religious forms or experience, for Christ is 'the absolutely *new from above*; the way, the truth, and the life of *God* among men; the Son of Man, in whom humanity becomes aware of its *immediacy* to God'.[56] Rather, this movement 'penetrates and passes through all our forms of worship and our experiences; it is the world of God breaking through from its self-contained holiness and appearing in secular life; it is the bodily resurrection of Christ from the dead. To participate in its meaning and power is to discover a new motivation.'[57]

Clearly, then, Barth considers that the various human movements seeking social and cultural reformation are permeated by and find their true significance and coherence in this divine movement, although the initiative for this interplay between the divine and the human lies only on the divine side. While *we* cannot secure a way to bridge the separation between the human and divine worlds, God has no such limitation. He manifests himself in consciousness through 'compelling, revealing, immediately self-confirming insights and communications'[58] by which we are 'impelled to venture our lives... immediately and completely'.[59] Thus, to the miracle of revelation corresponds the answering miracle of faith, itself the work of God in us.

Of particular significance is the nature of this venture to which the human agent is impelled. Just as God's movement is a movement into the secular arena of human life, a movement into history and consciousness, so too those who are gripped by revelation 'prove their devotion to the holy by daring to relate it

---

[54] Barth, 'The Christian's Place,' 283. Note the slight difference of terminology here. In *Romans 1* the third dimension was the movement itself. Here the movement derives *from a* third dimension. In this lecture Barth has not developed the dual-dimensional conceptuality of the commentary, and the difference does not seem to bear any material freight.

[55] Barth, 'The Christian's Place,' 287.

[56] Barth, 'The Christian's Place,' 286.

[57] Barth, 'The Christian's Place,' 286-287.

[58] Barth, 'The Christian's Place,' 284.

[59] Barth, 'The Christian's Place,' 287.

directly to the secular life of man'.[60] They do so, however, in light of the newly-recognised fact that they can no longer submit themselves to earthly realities and powers as to 'ultimate independent authorities'.[61] In the event of their awakening to the soul's immediacy to God as their true Origin, they have been liberated from dependency to lesser authorities.

Further, and in a move that highlights the fundamentally ethical orientation of his theology, Barth insists that the divine movement into the world awakens people in such a way that they are caught up in the movement, so that their activity becomes an echo and instrument of the divine activity:

> There can be no awakening of the soul which is anything but a 'sympathetic shouldering of the cares of the whole generation.' This awakening of the soul is the vivifying movement of God into history or into consciousness, the movement of Life into life. When we are under its power, we can but issue a categorical challenge to all the authorities in life....We are engaged in Life's revolt against the powers of death that inclose it.[62]

The sphere of the human agent's activity is simply society in all its breadth. Barth notes the seeming universal unrest of his era and exhorts his listeners to view the 'strangely confused and ambiguous' movements of the time sympathetically, and in accordance with the belief that they are part of the inbreaking movement of God, and therefore, 'in the fear of God to enter into the movement of the era'.[63] By so doing they will participate in a critical opposition to life as it is in order that the victory of Christ—the new world accomplished in the resurrection—might advance amongst them. Barth refers to the resurrection as the Archimedean point where God applies the lever in order to lift the world. He insists that 'as a matter of fact we *do* share in the resurrection movement: with or without the accompaniment of religious feeling we *are* actuated by it....We *are* moved by God. We are conscious of God. God in history lives in us and about us.'[64]

Christian existence, therefore, is existence in hope of the ultimate victory of God even now coming to expression in history. Christian existence occurs in this time of transition. While Barth is careful to acknowledge the genuine seriousness and tragedy of the present circumstances, he is also adamant that the final word has already been spoken, that 'the advancing glory of God is already vouchsafed us'.[65] The world and history is in process, gathered into the transition from 'death to life, from the unrighteousness of men to the righteousness of God, from the old to the new creation. We live in society as

---

[60] Barth, 'The Christian's Place,' 287.
[61] Barth, 'The Christian's Place,' 289.
[62] Barth, 'The Christian's Place,' 290-291.
[63] Barth, 'The Christian's Place,' 294.
[64] Barth, 'The Christian's Place,' 296.
[65] Barth, 'The Christian's Place,' 297.

those who understand, as those who undergo, and as those who undertake.'[66] Consequently, Barth's view of Christian existence is one of active and hopeful engagement in the realities of this world. He deliberately crafts his theology in such a manner as to exclude ethical passivity and quietism.

The Posture of the Christian: Critical Affirmation

Having argued that the nature of Christian existence involves being caught up in the divine eschatological procession towards the realisation of the new world, Barth turns, in the third section of his lecture, to describe more clearly the posture of the Christian in their interactions with society and culture. He begins by contending once more that the kingdom of God cannot be identified with or limited to human movements of reform or revolution. Nor, on the other hand, can it be identified as a wholly future reality. Rather, the kingdom of God 'is the revolution which is before all revolutions, as it is before the whole prevailing order of things. The great negative precedes the small one, as it precedes the small positive. The original is the synthesis. It is out of this that both thesis and antithesis arise.'[67]

In this convoluted section Barth utilises an inverted form of Hegel's conception of thesis, antithesis and synthesis, as well as meditations on Colossians, Ecclesiastes and Jesus' use of parables in order to press one simple point: the initial posture of the Christian towards culture and society is one of critical affirmation:

> Insight into the true transcendence of the divine origin of all things permits, or rather commands, us to understand the particular social orders as being caused by God, by their connection with God. Naturally, we shall be led first not to a denial but to an *affirmation* of the world as it is....Only out of such an affirmation can come that genuine, radical denial which is manifestly the meaning of our movements of protest.[68]

Because 'all things were created by Christ and for him' (Col. 1:16), the world, even in its fallen condition, is God's world, and as such always retains a 'living and divine element' so that 'the new from above is at the same time the oldest thing in existence, forgotten and buried'.[69] Even the *regnum naturae* (kingdom of nature) is the kingdom of God although its glory is presently veiled. Because this is so, says Barth, we must accept that there are orders of creation in all social relations just as there are in the natural world. Christian existence begins, therefore, with a commitment of the self to 'the living and divine element which is always there; and this very committing of ourselves to

---

[66] Barth, 'The Christian's Place,' 297.
[67] Barth, 'The Christian's Place,' 299.
[68] Barth, 'The Christian's Place,' 299.
[69] Barth, 'The Christian's Place,' 300-301.

God in the world is our power of not committing ourselves to the world without God'.[70]

By affirming that the world was created *by* Christ and *for* Christ Barth is able to preclude both an ascetic denial of or withdrawal from the world, as well as an uncritical affirmation of the world as it is. Both of these constitute false one-sided options. The Christian posture as envisaged by Barth is one in which opposition to the world as it presently is (antithesis) arises precisely because the prevailing conditions of the sinful world (thesis) stand in opposition to the original intent of the creator (original synthesis). It is because Christians recognise the divine order of creation as intended in Christ, that they must take a position of opposition to that which is presently not in submission to the rule of Christ. Christians not only find in Christ the criterion for this world, but are themselves found in Christ. As such, they cannot take a position of neutrality with regard to the world:

> It is not ours to be onlookers; it is ours to take our appointed place in the world's march. We are forced to it by the consciousness of solid responsibility laid upon our souls for the degenerate world; we are forced to it by the thought of the creator who is and remains the creator even of our fallen world.[71]

Barth acknowledges that our work is certainly limited in its capacity to effect change in the world, but nonetheless encourages determined and happy participation in all the varied spheres of social and cultural life in hope that 'the spark *might* come from above, and the eternal be brought to light in the transitory'.[72]

As presaged in the preceding discussion, the Christian's posture toward the world is not simply that of affirmation, but includes criticism and denial as well. These two aspects of posture—affirmation and denial—are not brought into a harmonious balance but continue to interact in tension with each other, with denial at all times surpassing affirmation in worth and meaning. Thus Barth confesses that

> we live more deeply in the No than in the Yes, more deeply in criticism and protest than in naïveté, more deeply in longing for the future than in participation in the present....Our Yes toward life from the very beginning carries within it the divine No, which breaks forth as the antithesis and points away from what but now was the thesis to the original and final synthesis. That No is not the last and highest truth but is the call from home which comes in answer to our asking for God in the world.[73]

---

[70] Barth, 'The Christian's Place,' 300.
[71] Barth, 'The Christian's Place,' 308.
[72] Barth, 'The Christian's Place,' 308-309.
[73] Barth, 'The Christian's Place,' 311-312.

For Barth, the Yes which arises from the original synthesis issues in a louder and more urgent No against the form of the world in its present condition, in order that the original synthesis may be restored. Because we would say Yes to the intent of the creator we must also say No to that which is contrary to this intention. The No arises, therefore, from the Yes and functions in service of an ultimate Yes. Christian existence involves not only affirmation, but life in echo of the divine No uttered against the fallenness of this age.

Significantly, Barth hints that this No arises in prayer, in our calling upon God in and for the world. Under the impulse of divine movement we are moved forward as 'the kingdom of God advances to its *attack* upon society'.[74] Yet, although we are impelled and moved forward, we also participate voluntarily in the 'onward march of God in history'.[75] Precisely because God the creator is also God the redeemer, the Christian 'must enter fully into the subversion and conversion of this present and of every conceivable world, into the judgement and grace which the presence of God entails', lest they fall away from the truth and power of Christ and his resurrection.[76] In this context Barth explicitly turns his attention to the church:

> How terrible if the *church*, of all institutions, should not see this, but put her effort into maintaining for men a balance which they must finally lose!…*Have* we heard the call that we have heard? *Have* we understood what we have understood?—that the demand of the day is for a new approach in God to the *whole* of life?[77]

Thus Barth calls the church to 'make good that approach by frank criticism of particulars, by courageous decision and action, by forward-looking proclamation of truth and patient work of reform'.[78]

The Activity of the Christian: Sub Specie Aeternitatis

In the fifth and final section of the lecture Barth recapitulates the position he outlined in the previous sections, and reiterates the eschatological nature of the Christian's place in society. In a blunt summary statement he asserts that 'simple cooperation within the framework of existing society is followed by radical and absolute opposition to that society'.[79] Both postures are necessary and ongoing in the Christian's interaction with society and culture. Clearly Barth sets himself against political revolution and uprising in favour of democracy, and yet also calls for a revolutionary opposition to all that is not aligned with the original and coming synthesis. He anticipates that Christians

---

[74] Barth, 'The Christian's Place,' 313-314.
[75] Barth, 'The Christian's Place,' 316.
[76] Barth, 'The Christian's Place,' 318.
[77] Barth, 'The Christian's Place,' 318.
[78] Barth, 'The Christian's Place,' 319.
[79] Barth, 'The Christian's Place,' 320.

will criticise, protest, reform, organise, seek democracy, socialism, and even revolution, but that they must not expect that their endeavours will 'satisfy the ideal of the kingdom of God. That is really beyond us.'[80] All human endeavours are strictly provisional. The God in whom we find rest is also the God who stirs our unrest, and neither state in this age is final.

In a turn of phrase that indicates a shift from the theology of *Romans I*, and echoing his recent article on Naumann and Blumhardt, Barth refers to human activity as parabolic of the 'wholly Other' kingdom which belongs solely to God. Human action *represents* the Other, but can and does not in itself produce it. Christian and ecclesial existence derives its life from that Other, but this is a life wholly in a period of transition—there can be no thought of development from one side to the other for the synthesis we seek is in God alone.[81] Certainly the Christian is caught in the movement of God issuing from the resurrection of Jesus and the outpouring of the Holy Spirit at Pentecost. Nevertheless, says Barth,

> [i]f we understand ourselves rightly, we shall see that power to grow comes always from above and never from below. For the last thing, the ἔσχατον, the synthesis, is *not* the continuation, the result, the consequence, the next step after the next to the last, so to speak, *but*, on the contrary, is forever a radical break with everything next to the last.[82]

Thus, Christians are to 'throw their energies' into the business nearest to hand in order to make a new Switzerland and a new Germany, but this only looks forward to, and will not result in the creation of the New Jerusalem.[83]

Barth, then, concludes with Calvin to fix the place of the Christian in society within the *spes futurae vitae* (hope of future life).[84] Christian and ecclesial existence draws its life, motivation and energy from the hope given in the vision of the *regnum gloriae* (kingdom of glory). It considers its situation and makes its decisions *sub specie aeternitatis* (in the light of eternity), and is in this respect, a thoroughly eschatological existence. In its thought, speech and action it seeks to represent the coming kingdom, and works energetically for the character of that kingdom to be replicated in this age, but with the modest apprehension that the fullness of the kingdom belongs to God alone.

Following after God: A Community of Discernment

In this lecture, then, Barth reiterates for a new audience themes familiar from his earlier works. Once again we encounter his resolute theological

---

[80] Barth, 'The Christian's Place,' 320.
[81] Barth, 'The Christian's Place,' 322.
[82] Barth, 'The Christian's Place,' 324.
[83] Barth, 'The Christian's Place,' 323.
[84] Barth, 'The Christian's Place,' 324.

realism and his emphasis on the sovereignty of God. Once again Barth insists that the coming of God's kingdom is God's own work, and that human attempts, including religious attempts, in this direction cannot succeed. We also hear an echo of Blumhardt in Barth's admonition that the church need learn to 'wait' upon God in a 'wholly new way'. So, too, the earlier recognition that in binding us to himself, God liberates us from subjection to all other deities and powers is found in this lecture also. Finally, Barth continues to envisage an active Christian ethic. Although he has not yet developed the category of correspondence to describe the relation of divine and human action, his thought is already tending in this direction. Faithful human activity echoes the direction and priority of divine action, thus proving its devotion to the latter.

Of particular note in this lecture is the shift identified in Barth's eschatology when compared to *Romans I*. Although he continues to utilise the imagery of the third dimension and movement of God into history, it is apparent that Barth has begun to shift from the process eschatological framework of the commentary to a more consistent eschatology which anticipates the climax of history that only God can achieve. Christian and ecclesial existence remains thoroughly eschatological in its orientation, and the note of hope and optimism that characterised the former work, while somewhat attenuated, continues here.[85]

This examination of Barth's Tambach lecture also supports the present thesis, namely, that Barth's theology, far from having no place for ethical

---

[85] This point is debated in the literature. Hunsinger, for example, finds in this lecture that 'Barth *begins* to break with his earlier organic or developmental eschatology in favor of one conceived along more strictly dialectical lines.' See Hunsinger, 'Toward A Radical Barth,' 210, emphasis added. McCormack, however, demurs, arguing that the shift from a process eschatology to a consistent eschatology has not yet occurred. See McCormack, *Karl Barth's Dialectical Theology*, 202. I hold with Hunsinger that Barth has indeed *begun* to revise the eschatological model with which he explicates the relation or *diastasis* that obtains between God and the world—but only *begun*. In this lecture, as we have seen, we find statements which reiterate the organological model of *Romans I*, but also statements which are more indicative of a consistent eschatology. More recently Chalamet's study of Barth's use of dialectic provides strong support for Hunsinger's position. Chalamet contends that in the few months since the publication of *Romans I* Barth has revised significant aspects of his thought, rejecting the idea of *immediacy* with God with the warning 'Respect the distance!' See Christophe Chalamet, *Dialectical Theologians: Wilhelm Herrmann, Karl Barth and Rudolph Bultmann* (Zürich: Theologischer Verlag Zürich, 2005), 120. Indeed, for Chalamet, 'Respect the distance!' becomes the watchword of Barth's theology from the time of the Tambach lecture, and the characteristic feature of his theology in *Romans II*. For the sharp juxtaposition Barth makes of these terms, see Barth, 'The Christian's Place,' 286: 'Christ is the absolutely *new from above*...in whom humanity becomes aware of its *immediacy* to God. But keep (*wahren*) your distance! No mental apprehension of the *form* of this truth, however subtle that apprehension may be, can replace or obscure the true transcendence of its *content*.'

existence, actually functions towards the formation of moral community, and presupposes an active Christian and ecclesial existence. The knowledge that the kingdom of God is not the work of humanity does not excuse the Christian or the church from the need for active engagement in temporal affairs. Rather, through the event of revelation which includes within it the answering response of faith, the believer is impressed into the service of the kingdom of God.

The particular character of the Christian life as portrayed in this lecture stands in continuity with Barth's works surveyed earlier. Once more Barth refuses to prescribe normative Christian activity, although he is willing to hope for the 'possibility of comradeship and brotherhood on our earth and under our heaven'.[86] Likewise he extols such virtues as hope, courage, endurance, liberty and joy,[87] while also identifying false paths such as that taken by Naumann or an unnamed German theologian during the war who, on the basis of divine immanence, argued for 'the Life Within' rather than 'the Life Beyond'.[88]

Barth's unwillingness to provide prescriptive guidance for Christian activity is, of course, a source of concern for some interpreters of his ethics. In his analysis of this lecture, for example, Willis correctly notes that Barth has adopted a dialectical structure to frame his argument in order to enable an approach to the question of ethics without becoming committed to a particular stance or ideology. He also acknowledges that Barth's proposal does allow the possibility of concrete human action, but complains that 'what are needed are criteria or conditions enabling one to decide in particular cases, i.e. when the response at the human level is properly acceptance of existing structures, patterns, and norms, and when criticism, modification, or overthrow of these is required'.[89] Further, Willis is concerned that the *diastasis* posited by Barth between God and humanity renders human ethics 'at the outset *problematic*' by 'relativising all human activity' and placing a question mark 'at every point over its validity'.[90]

Here Willis not only misrepresents Barth, but fails to grasp the fluidity of Christian and ecclesial existence as Barth conceives it. Barth's concern in this lecture, as Spencer has noted, is not the justification of a particular politics (or, one might add more broadly, a particular ethics) but the theological circumscription of all political-social action.[91] In this lecture Barth continues the preliminary work of establishing the parameters of the divine-human relation, and the situating of the ethical agent within those parameters. In

---

[86] Barth, 'The Christian's Place,' 323.

[87] See Barth, 'The Christian's Place,' 319, 323.

[88] Barth, 'The Christian's Place,' 321. Note that Gorringe identifies the unnamed theologian as Emanuel Hirsch. See Timothy J. Gorringe, *Karl Barth: Against Hegemony* (Oxford: Oxford University Press, 1999), 51.

[89] Willis, *The Ethics of Karl Barth*, 20.

[90] Willis, *The Ethics of Karl Barth*, 21.

[91] Spencer, *Clearing a Space*, 107.

contrast to Willis' reading, Barth refuses to allow the human an independent status over against God, or to allow the divine-human relation to be reduced to a static relation in which God is effectively muted and initiative is given over to the human agent. For this reason, the divine-human relation is characterised as a *living* relation befitting the living God and the living human, and so it is not by accident that Barth adopts the image of a bird in flight as a motif of his Christian and ecclesial vision.

Has Barth, as Willis alleges, failed to provide any constructive ethical guidance for his listeners? It is certainly true that in later years Barth will indeed formulate his ethics in such a way as to allow a legitimate though subordinate role for ethical analysis and reason. Here, nonetheless, his concluding remarks are instructive:

> Our theme contains a question which must now be upon the lips of us all: What ought we then to do? It is true that many other questions, great and small, burning questions for which we are badly in need of an answer, are contained in this fundamental question and have not apparently been met by the fundamental biblical answer we have given. But they merely *seem* not to be answered. We are moved by the truth of Christ....We are grounded in God: why should eternity not then be set in our heart? And *sub specie aeternitatis*, why should we not know what is to be done? We can indeed do only one thing—not many. But it is just that one thing which *we* do not do. What can the Christian in society do but follow attentively what is done by *God*?[92]

Ironically, Barth asks the very question which in *Romans I* he insists we cease from asking![93] Once more, however, his answer is not given in terms of prescriptive virtues or activities, save the requirement of practical Christian discernment. Only here is it possible to resolve the dilemma of the correct practical relation of the Yes and the No. This relation, says Barth, cannot be resolved systematically, but only historically. That is, 'without being disturbed by the inconsistent appearance of it we shall then enjoy the freedom of saying now Yes and now No, and of saying both not as a result of outward chance or of inward caprice but because we are so moved by the will of God'.[94]

Barth again conceives of ethics in terms of the 'command of the moment' he elaborated in his commentary on Romans. Ethical existence finds its genesis in the liberty of believers before God, and his theological labour is directed toward a description of this divine-human relation. That Barth situates this guidance at the climax of his address, and laments that this is the one thing *we* do not do, is indicative of his motive towards the formation of moral community, a community of Christians who are enabled by the Spirit to take an active place in society because they are actively attentive to God in prayer and

---

[92] Barth, 'The Christian's Place,' 326-327.
[93] See page 119 above.
[94] Barth, 'The Christian's Place,' 325-326.

discernment. He remains convinced that earthly reality can be changed because *God* is actively at work and moving in the world. The task of the Christian is 'to learn the meaning of true revolution, to join in the revolution of the kingdom which is before all revolutions'.[95]

The Influence of Overbeck

In June 1920 Barth published a pamphlet entitled 'The Inner Situation of Christianity' which was later reprinted in the second volume of his collected essays and addresses.[96] The essay was an extended review of an edited collection of the literary remains of Franz Overbeck published posthumously in 1919.[97] Overbeck, who died in 1905, had been professor of New Testament and Early Church History at the University of Basel from 1870-1897. His most important work, published in 1873, was *Über die Christlichkeit unserer heutigen Theologie*, in which he offered 'a severe and trenchant critique of all historical Christianity' in contrast to the original foundation of the church in Christ and his apostles.[98]

Overbeck's professional aim had been to write a 'profane church history'— that is, a completely objective history of the church with all religious illusions and colouration stripped away. In the process of applying his historical method he discovered that apostolic Christianity had been intensely eschatological in nature, and concluded that in its beginning, Christianity derived its life from another world and thus stood in radical contradiction to everything in this world.[99] The church's loss of this animating eschatological faith in succeeding generations had two fundamental implications for Overbeck. First, with the loss of eschatological faith the church became a historical entity, an aspect of this world living in accordance with the ebb and flow of general historical forces, and thus a living contradiction to its original essence. Second, the unfulfilled hope of the *Parousia* in effect falsified the truth claim of original Christianity and thus also rendered the entirety of subsequent church history and Christian

---

[95] Gorringe, *Against Hegemony*, 51.

[96] Karl Barth, *Zur inneren Lage des Christentums* (München: Christian Kaiser, 1920). The essay was published under a new title as Karl Barth, 'Unsettled Questions for Theology Today,' in *Theology and Church: Shorter Writings 1920-1928* (New York: Harper & Row, 1962), 55-73.

[97] *Christentum und Kultur. Gedanken und Anmerkungen zur modernen Theologie* (*Christianity and Culture: Thoughts and Observations on Modern Theology*). The work was edited by friend and colleague Carl Albrecht Bernoulli.

[98] Thomas F. Torrance, *Karl Barth: An Introduction to His Early Theology 1910-1931* (Edinburgh: T. & T. Clark, 1962), 42. Overbeck's work has only recently been translated and published in English. See Franz Overbeck, *How Christian Is Our Present-Day Theology?* (trans. Martin Henry; Edinburgh: T. & T. Clark/Continuum, 2005).

[99] James D. Smart, *The Divided Mind of Modern Theology: Karl Barth and Rudolph Bultmann, 1908-1933* (Philadelphia: Westminster, 1967), 101.

theology false.[100] According to Overbeck, these implications were amply demonstrated in the nature of contemporary Christianity and its historicist theology which he assailed with iconoclastic fervour.

Overbeck denied the possibilities that Christianity can have a historical development, or that the historian can treat Christianity apart from culture. As soon as Christianity is treated as a historical reality its very essence has been denied. 'Historic Christianity,' says Overbeck, 'that is, Christianity subjected to time, is an absurdity.…To include Christianity under the concept of the historical, means to admit that it is *of this* world, and like all life has lived in the world in order to die.'[101] Overbeck developed the category of *Urgeschichte* (pre-history) to distinguish primal Christianity from all ensuing expressions of it. As McCormack has pointed out, *Urgeschichte* is a technical term, a *geschichtsphilosophische* (philosophy of history) category which insists on a hiatus, an unbridgeable chasm, between the originating events of early Christianity and all subsequent periods of church history. Overbeck developed the category and invented the term in order to demonstrate the hermeneutical limits governing all historical enquiry and thus to criticise the foundational assumptions of contemporary historical studies.[102]

The sharpness of his polemic alienated most of his contemporaries, and ensured that Overbeck remained something of a misfit in theological circles, a most unlikely theologian. In addition to being an outspoken critic of contemporary Christianity and theology, he was also a close friend of Friedrich Nietzsche, and, according to McCormack, inwardly an atheist whose historical studies had led to the loss of faith.[103] And although Barth recalls that 'one merely needed to mention [Overbeck] in Basel at that time to make everyone's hair bristle',[104] he nonetheless found in him an ally. In a letter to Thurneysen dated January 5th 1920, Barth wrote, 'our Melchizedek is probably—Overbeck. I may write something about him'.[105] By the end of February Barth had finished his essay.[106] In April the same year Barth visited Overbeck's widow and

[100] Neil B. MacDonald, *Karl Barth and the Strange New World Within the Bible: Barth, Wittgenstein and the Metadilemmas of the Enlightenment* (Carlisle: Paternoster, 2000), 10.

[101] Franz Overbeck, *Christentum und Kultur. Gedanken und Anmerkungen zur modernen Theologie* (Basel: Benno Schwabe & Co., 1919), 242, 7, cited in Barth, 'Unsettled Questions,' 61-62.

[102] McCormack, *Karl Barth's Dialectical Theology*, 229.

[103] McCormack, *Karl Barth's Dialectical Theology*, 226.

[104] Karl Barth, *The Theology of Schleiermacher: Lectures at Göttingen Winter Semester of 1923/24* (trans. G. W. Bromiley; Edinburgh: T. & T. Clark, 1982), 265.

[105] Cited in Eberhard Jüngel, *Karl Barth: A Theological Legacy* (trans. G. E. Paul; Philadelphia: Westminster, 1986), 56.

[106] Eberhard Busch, *Karl Barth and the Pietists: The Young Karl Barth's Critique of Pietism and Its Response* (trans. Daniel W. Bloesch; Downers Grove: Inter-Varsity Press, 2004), 73.

reported to Thurneysen,

> She is fully abreast of affairs, a lively, sensible old lady, who received me very warmly and portrayed her husband for me in a way that simply tallies to the hairbreadth with our conception of him. It will be alright for our booklet to appear since everything is in order....This is a splendid relationship that protects us against attack from the rear, is it not? Now we must both of us spit on our hands in preparation for new deeds. It is clear that the idol totters.[107]

Barth's rear-guard defence was certainly required. Thurneysen notes that when the pamphlet was published it became the cause of much head-shaking and opposition. Opponents asserted that his interpretation was based on insufficient knowledge of the real Overbeck.[108] Nevertheless, Thurneysen defends Barth, insisting that he did not misrepresent Overbeck but, 'seeing through his outward profession of scepticism to his real intentions' probably understood him better than Overbeck understood himself.[109] Despite this testimony, however, some contemporary scholars agree that Barth has co-opted Overbeck's trenchant polemics for his own purposes.[110] What was it, then, that Barth found—or thought he found—in Overbeck which excited his enthusiasm?

Between Overbeck and Blumhardt[111]

Before answering this question directly it is instructive to note the similarity between Barth's treatment of Overbeck and *Auf das Reich Gottes warten*— Barth's first essay on Blumhardt. Both essays take the form of an extended review on a publication of what might be considered 'fragments' of the authors in view. That is, neither work is a systematic presentation of a position, nor even a developed argument. Further, both objects of Barth's attention are also characterised by their opposition to contemporary theology and church. They are both contemporary religious personalities who are to some extent at least, ignored and even scorned by the prevailing theology. Nor is this association of Overbeck with Blumhardt arbitrary or accidental, for Barth himself makes explicit the connection between the two men:

---

[107] Smart, ed., *Revolutionary Theology*, 50. The letter is dated April 20, 1920.

[108] Eduard Thurneysen, 'Introduction,' in *Revolutionary Theology in the Making: Barth-Thurneysen Correspondence, 1914-1925* (ed. J. D. Smart; London: Epworth, 1964), 21.

[109] Thurneysen, 'Introduction,' 21. See also Torrance, *Karl Barth: An Introduction*, 42-43.

[110] See, for example, Jüngel, *Karl Barth*, 54, where Jüngel refers to Barth's interpretation of Overbeck at one point as 'rather a grotesque misunderstanding'. See also McCormack, *Karl Barth's Dialectical Theology*, 227, who insists that 'Barth's reading of Overbeck was certainly tendentious.'

[111] The phrase is borrowed and adapted from Jüngel, *Karl Barth*, 54.

Actually, Blumhardt and Overbeck stand close together; back to back, if you like, and very different in disposition, in terminology, in their mental worlds, in their experience, but essentially together. Blumhardt stood as a forward-looking and hopeful Overbeck; Overbeck as a backward-looking, critical Blumhardt. Each was a witness to the mission of the other.[112]

And so Barth begins his review with a question as to why contemporary theology refused to allow itself to be challenged by these two very different men who nevertheless bear the same message. His introduction is a call for theology to hear what it has so far refused to hear: a challenge to its vocation which threatens to capsize the ship. He suggests that Overbeck's *Christentum und Kultur* is

an inconceivably impressive sharpening of the commandment 'Thou shalt not take the name of the Lord thy God in vain.'…It is a dangerous book, a book filled with the apocalyptic air of judgement. It is a balance sheet, a book which calls the comprehending reader away from the fleshpots of Egypt into the desert, to a place of durance where he can neither gain nor possess, nor feast, nor distribute, but only hunger and thirst, seek, ask, and knock.[113]

Barth insists that the events and experiences of the previous years have clearly indicated that contemporary theology is illusory and bankrupt, that 'we have been living until now in a house built on sand; and that theology—if this venture "Theology" is to continue longer to exist—would do better to clench its teeth and take the road to the desert'.[114]

The remainder of the review is a defence and explication of this basic call for renewal. In the first section after the introduction, Barth outlines the essential framework of Overbeck's thought as he understands it from his literary remains. This framework has two primary aspects: the notion of 'super-history' (*Urgeschichte*) on the one hand, and death on the other. For Barth, *Urgeschichte* refers to the 'supra-temporal, unknowable, inconceivable super-history which is composed wholly of beginnings, in which the boundaries dividing the individual from the whole are still fluid', while death refers to the great unknown into which all humanity is going.[115] Human existence, and all human knowing, is utterly bounded by these great unknowns from which we arise and into which we go. That which is historical, which arises on its own account in the period between these two boundaries is necessarily *of* this world and thus has in itself no ultimacy, but is limited and relative. Barth interprets Overbeck's concepts of *Urgeschichte* and death with the more familiar imagery of creation and redemption, and views them as the critical basis upon which

---

[112] Barth, 'Unsettled Questions,' 56.
[113] Barth, 'Unsettled Questions,' 57.
[114] Barth, 'Unsettled Questions,' 57.
[115] Barth, 'Unsettled Questions,' 58.

three primary polemical discussions are founded. Barth treats each of these in turn.[116]

Overbeck's first polemic is directed against the formal possibility of historical Christianity, which as we have already seen, denies the possibility of the historical development of Christianity as well as the possibility of grounding contemporary Christianity upon historical scholarship. His second complaint targets the modern church and theology as a perversion of Christianity leading inevitably to its own demise. The roots of the declension lie in the loss of the eschatological horizon which was so central to original Christianity, and which set it in invariable opposition to all that is of the world. In contrast, the modern church seeks above all to establish itself in the world as an entity alongside other entities, and so is thoroughly accommodated to the prevailing culture, as revealed by its capitulation to nationalism and the 'religion of Bismarck'.[117] As a result modern Christianity is simply unchristian.

Finally, Overbeck's third protest is directed against modern theology, which he labels 'the Satan of religion'[118] and specifically against modern theologians who 'expect indeed "to put God daily into their bag"' and 'allow themselves "to play [with God and the human soul] like children with their dolls, and they have the same assurance of ownership and the right of disposal"'.[119] Because modern theology exists in service of a compromised and accommodated church, it is itself compromised and accommodated and in Overbeck's estimation, not 'Christian' at all. In fact, the logic of Overbeck's argument is that theology as an academic pursuit is impossible, for all that passes for theology can be subsumed more accurately under other branches of intellectual pursuit such as history, anthropology or morality, and that if theology had any intellectual integrity at all it would acknowledge it no longer existed and had in fact ceased to exist some time before.[120]

Thus, Barth found in Overbeck an ally for his own project, seeing that he, too, had come to reject modern theology and the kind of ecclesial existence it engendered. Overbeck not only confirmed Barth in his own trenchant criticism of the modern church and theology, but also provided additional resources that enabled Barth to develop his critique in new directions. One example is the substitution of the language and imagery of 'life' which characterised *Der Römerbrief* and Barth's earlier essays, with that of 'death'. With this move

---

[116] Barth has adopted Overbeck's term *Urgeschichte*, but clearly uses it in a different sense to what Overbeck did. As noted, for Overbeck the term refers to the historical impossibility of accessing the essence of originating events, for there always remains a gap between the origin of an event in history and later explications or interpretations of it. Barth, in contrast, uses the term to refer in a similar sense to the *jensitige* conception of history in his first commentary, which exists behind and under phenomenal history.

[117] Barth, 'Unsettled Questions,' 67.

[118] Overbeck, *Christentum und Kultur*, 12, cited in Barth, 'Unsettled Questions,' 69.

[119] Overbeck, *Christentum und Kultur*, 268, cited in Barth, 'Unsettled Questions,' 70.

[120] MacDonald, *Karl Barth and the Strange New World*, 15.

Barth continues to purge remnants of liberalism from his own theology, and denies that the presence of the divine in human existence and experience is immediately given. Death, which names the end of all human potentiality, is the source from which all that is of God flows.[121]

Another clear example is Barth's adoption of Overbeck's term *Urgeschichte*, to sharpen the eschatological framework with which he is working. The term was coined, as we have already seen, as a technical term describing a category in the philosophy of history. For Barth, however, the term functions as a *theological* category and indicates an ontological reality. Thus, 'the only possible abode of Christianity lies, so far as the past is concerned, not in history, but in the history before history, the super-history (*Urgeschichte*)'.[122] The life and faith of Jesus, Paul, the apostles are understood under the category of miracle and not, therefore, as arising as part of normal historical occurrence.

Thus, in place of the former emphasis on a process eschatology, is now found a more consistent eschatology. Again, it is not so much that Barth learnt a new eschatology from Overbeck, for Overbeck, while acknowledging the thoroughly eschatological conceptual world of Jesus and the early Church, denied that such a world view was possible any longer. What Overbeck did provide was an insistence that this eschatological world view was essential to genuine Christianity, a status forfeited by the modern church through its inability to conceive of itself in such eschatological terms. Barth, however, did not share Overbeck's pessimism at this point for he had already been instructed by Blumhardt. He already knew of 'a living Christianity whose "theology" was a proclamation of the kingdom of God which hinged on the resurrection of Jesus'.[123] It was no accident then, that his final sentence for the Overbeck review was a citation from 1 Corinthians 15: 42-43: 'It is sown in corruption, it is raised in incorruption; it is sown in dishonour, it is raised in glory; it is sown in weakness, it is raised in power.'[124] But whereas formerly Barth envisaged the resurrection as the inauguration of a life-process growing organically through history, he now views it as the action of God on the other side of all human possibility.

Overbeck provided Barth the means for radicalising the message of Blumhardt, for declaring even more stringently than he had in *Romans I* that although revelation can occur in history, it is not *of* history. In return, Blumhardt provided Barth the means for accepting Overbeck's critique of the current situation without falling into theological despair. It is quite clear that Overbeck did not believe that genuine theology was possible, and that he did believe in the 'gentle fading away of Christianity'.[125] Barth, however, argued

---

[121] Busch, *Karl Barth and the Pietists*, 75.
[122] Barth, 'Unsettled Questions,' 62.
[123] Jüngel, *Karl Barth*, 65.
[124] Barth, 'Unsettled Questions,' 73.
[125] Overbeck, *Christentum und Kultur*, 68, cited in Barth, 'Unsettled Questions,' 64.

that Overbeck was merely presenting the negative side of the point which now had to be set forth positively.[126] Indeed, he likens Overbeck to Jeremiah, and contends that Overbeck's analysis was itself 'from beyond', a 'fragment of super-history' appearing now as a prophetic message to a compromised church, escaping from the prophet 'almost against his will'.[127] If Christianity is to live once more, it must do so on a thoroughly new foundation, and it is this task that Barth sets himself and those who will hear him.

A New Christianity

Barth affirmed Overbeck's contention that 'modern theology was a species of non-theology' but rejected his corollary contention that theology in and of itself was impossible.[128] 'Our next task,' says Barth, 'is to begin the desert wandering....A theology which would dare that passage—dare to become eschatology—would not only be a new theology but also a new Christianity; it would be a new being, itself already a piece of the "last things," towering above the Reformation and all "religious" movements.'[129]

This citation makes clear that Barth was not only seeking a new theology, but a new Christianity, a new form of authentic Christian and ecclesial existence. Thus, while MacDonald's contention that 'all of Barth's theology is best understood within the horizon of the specific Enlightenment legacy of Hume and Overbeck's metatheological dilemma'[130] may well be true, it is not sufficient. Barth's concern was not only for the intellectual integrity of theology as an end in itself, but for the renewal of Christianity itself, for authentic Christianity, the 'new being' which is present *in* history, but which is not explainable in any historical terms including developments from the Reformation or other religious movements.

Indeed, while it is true that Barth's theological and ethical concerns must not be separated, it is at least arguable that in 1920 Barth's greater concern was with regard to the actual life of contemporary Christianity than for the theological question raised by Overbeck's critique. At this time he entitled his pamphlet 'On the Inner Situation of Christianity' and only later, with the publication of his second collection of essays eight years later, changed the title

---

[126] Barth, in a letter to a colleague December 23, 1940, cited in Busch, *Karl Barth*, 115.
[127] Barth, 'Unsettled Questions,' 65, 72.
[128] MacDonald, *Karl Barth and the Strange New World*, 18.
[129] Barth, 'Unsettled Questions,' 73.
[130] MacDonald, *Karl Barth and the Strange New World*, 23. MacDonald describes Overbeck's metatheological dilemma as the choice between 'doing non-theology or nothing' since theology in and of itself is formally impossible'. See MacDonald, *Karl Barth and the Strange New World*, 14-17. He goes on to say that 'Overbeck's dilemma is of immense importance to understanding Barth's theology: not only does it inform *Romans* II, it is the key to *Fides Quaerens Intellectum* and the *Church Dogmatics*. It is the key to *what it is* Barth is doing as a theologian.'

to 'Unsettled Questions for Theology Today.' For Barth, the 'inner situation of Christianity' has reference to the nature of Christian and ecclesial existence. This is seen in the review itself where Barth raises the issue of the inner situation of Christianity by means of a direct citation from Overbeck:

> 'A façade can lack an interior...on the other hand it is unendurable that an interior should present a false façade; and that is the case with present-day Christianity. But you cannot summon its interior as a witness *against* its exterior as though it could be found without it. And anyhow, no one has to listen to it....Those representatives of Christianity who currently appeal to its "inner life" are its worst traitors' (p.71). For 'the innermost and the real *need* of Christianity at the present time is the practice of it in life' (*Praxis*) (p.274).[131]

Barth concurs with Overbeck that the façade of modern Christianity is false, a betrayal of the interior essence of Christianity, and that its most pressing need is genuine praxis. Modern Christianity's thorough accommodation of its dogmatic heritage to modern thought 'erases the last traces which true Christianity still has left in life. What is accomplished serves wholly for the greater glory of the modern...and to the detriment of Christianity.'[132] This is particularly evident in the inability of the modern church to stand apart from and against modern German nationalism. In a paraphrase of Overbeck's concern Barth exhorts his reader to

> Consider...the religion of Bismarck (pp.148-59), which provides the most magnificent example of the way the world pleases itself and wins the applause of the representatives of religion. Therefore Bismarck is the best-known advocate of the indispensability of religion for all earthly effectiveness. He had religion simply in order to keep his hands free for secular work....His religion was erected on the basis of his self-esteem. Moreover, it was something which he had reduced to the size of a personal plaything and which he could lay aside at any time. But the fact that he could play with it and occasionally had a Christian notion was sufficient in the eyes of the modern advocates of Christianity to make him a Christian, even a model Christian....Thus Christianity has now been handed over to every holder of power. So cheap is today's canonization in the Christian heaven.[133]

These sentiments are, of course, simply echoes of those we have heard from Barth time and again since his initial break from his theological mentors. As a result of its thorough enculturation the integrity of modern theology and Christianity has been gutted with the result that religion and the church has been co-opted by the secular powers to legitimise national ideologies and agendas alien to its true essence. It is precisely this evisceration which led to

---

[131] Barth, 'Unsettled Questions,' 66. The page numbers refer to *Christentum und Kultur*.

[132] Overbeck, *Christentum und Kultur*, 67, cited in Barth, 'Unsettled Questions,' 67.

[133] Barth, 'Unsettled Questions,' 67-68.

the devastating capitulation of the church to Kaiser Wilhelm's war agenda in 1914 and which set Barth on his search for a new foundation for theology, which would in turn sponsor a more authentic form of Christian and ecclesial existence.

Two other features of Barth's review merit comment. The first is recognition once more of the pivotal place Blumhardt continued to play in the development of Barth's thought and ecclesial vision. In this review Barth placed Blumhardt back to back with Overbeck, seeing in them both the same criticism against modern Christianity from the central standpoint of eschatology. Criticism alone, however, is insufficient, and it is here that Blumhardt's hope-filled influence is decisive. Not only must the old be torn down but the new must arise, and for Barth, it is the theological and ecclesial vision inspired by Blumhardt that continues to provide the impetus for his search for a new foundation for theology and corresponding Christian and ecclesial existence.

The second feature of the review that merits comment is Barth's remarks regarding Pietism which indicate a development of perspective in the period which had elapsed since he wrote *Romans 1*. The first remark is a citation from Overbeck to the effect that 'Pietism is for me the only form of Christianity under which a personal relation to Christianity would be possible for me.'[134] By this Overbeck did not mean the kind of Pietism which was akin to other forms of modern Christianity seeking to discover God within the human psyche, but the more 'ascetic' forms of Pietism which stood aloof from modern culture and against the secularising of the faith.[135] Overbeck argued that such Pietism was actually closer to genuine Christianity than the modern orthodoxy which had arisen in Protestantism:

> The modern world is ready to do everything to make it possible to remain within the *illusion* of Christianity; and for that purpose, as it is easy to see, orthodoxy is more usable than Pietism....In modern life, Christianity is thirsting for life and so for Pietism. In modern Christianity, the modernity thirsts for orthodoxy since it has already drunk its fill of life; and so in modern Christianity, Christianity gets nothing to drink.[136]

While it remains to be seen how Barth will develop this reserved affirmation of Pietism, it seems evident nevertheless that Barth has learnt from Overbeck a way of viewing Pietism more positively than he was able when writing the commentary.

Overbeck's influence on Barth should not be underestimated. While Barth's

---

[134] Barth, 'Unsettled Questions,' 60. Barth has truncated Overbeck here. The full statement reads, 'For Ritschl the Pietistic form of Christianity is the most detestable. For me it is the only one under whose influence a personal relationship to Christianity would be possible for me' (Overbeck, *Christentum und Kultur*, 179).

[135] Busch, *Karl Barth and the Pietists*, 76-77.

[136] Overbeck, *Christentum und Kultur*, 274, cited in Barth, 'Unsettled Questions,' 67.

critique of contemporary Christianity had arisen independently, it received renewed force as a result of his engagement with Overbeck who bluntly avowed that Christianity and theology were in fact impossible under the conditions set forth in the modern church. Reading Overbeck convinced Barth that Christianity must of necessity be eschatological in its very essence. His concept of *Urgeschichte*, modified as it was by Barth, allowed him to insist even more stringently that revelation is non-historical in the sense that it does not arise as a result of historical process. Finally, his meditations on death also captured Barth's theological imagination, causing him to rethink the way he articulated his theological convictions. This influence came to expression very quickly as can be seen in a lecture given by Barth shortly after he completed this review.

'Biblical Questions, Insights and Vistas'

On April 17, 1920 Barth delivered a lecture to the Aarau Student Conference entitled 'Biblical Questions, Insights, and Vistas,'[137] and addressed the question, 'What does the Bible offer us toward an understanding of the meaning of the world?'[138] The venerable Adolph von Harnack, Barth's former teacher, was also present at the conference and had earlier addressed the same audience on the question 'What assured knowledge can historians provide for the interpretation of world events?'[139] Several days after the lecture Barth had opportunity to meet with Harnack who was clearly dismayed with Barth's lecture. In a written report of this meeting to Thurneysen Barth records that Harnack admitted that

> [i]t may be desirable that the church should be shaken *a bit*, but I do best to keep my conception of God to myself and not make an 'export article' of it. Finally I was branded a Calvinist and intellectualist and let go with the prophecy that according to all the experiences of church history I will found a sect and receive inspirations.[140]

This section investigates what Barth had said to so arouse Harnack, and which threatened perhaps, to inordinately 'shake' the church.

---

[137] The lecture is found in Karl Barth, *The Word of God and the Word of Man* (trans. D. Horton; New York: Harper & Brothers, 1956), 51-96.
[138] Barth, 'Biblical Questions,' 51.
[139] Busch, *Karl Barth*, 115.
[140] Smart, *Revolutionary Theology*, 50. The letter is dated April 20, 1920. The same letter also records Barth's meeting with Frau Overbeck, which took place during the same visit to Basel.

The Bible and the Knowledge of God

In the first section of his address Barth suggests that the immediate answer to the question posed is that the Bible's contribution is to offer us the knowledge of God as the origin, limit and creative unity of all knowledge and of the world's meaning. Accordingly, 'it is our part to confirm it in our own lives by labouring to relate ourselves, our daily task, and our hour of history to God the creator and redeemer'.[141] Barth's ethical concern is disclosed in these opening comments. Indeed he goes on to lament that 'the knowledge of God, instead of being the presupposition which gets *us* somewhere…comes to be a philosophical or mythological problem which one must try to get somewhere *with*'.[142]

This is the problematic of the knowledge of God, according to Barth in this lecture. Humanity generally is not outside the knowledge of God, but inside, for we cannot escape the reality that God is the origin of our existence: we cannot quite forget the soul's provenance or its original unity with God.[143] Yet humanity is not led by this innate knowledge of God to a full acknowledgement of God and his claim upon their lives. Rather, 'our individualism revolts against its comprehensiveness. The unredeemed mind of man, split off from the mind of the creator, denies its Origin, denies itself.'[144] Just as our primal acknowledgement of God is a 'last inevitability' grounded in God, however, so too is our thorough-going refusal of him. Barth grounds human alienation from God in God's No rather than any human or historical necessity. What, then, does the Bible have to say to people thus caught in the tension between an original Yes by which they are inescapably related to God, and an original No by which they inevitably refuse acknowledgement of him?

> With the Yes and the No, the No and the Yes in which we find ourselves, we are thrown into the perplexity, into the crisis, of the Scriptures.…Give no credence to any *secondary* reasons and explanations for the perplexity. When we ask the Bible what it has to offer, it answers by putting to us the fact of *election*.…The really vital core, the secret both of history and of our existence, is our response to the fact of election.[145]

Two aspects of this citation are significant. First is Barth's use of the term *crisis*, which features prominently in this lecture and becomes the major motif of *Romans II*. The term is not completely new in Barth's oeuvre, appearing once in *Romans I*, but the emphasis placed on it indicates a development of Barth's thought. In his first commentary Barth refers to the 'crisis…in which all

---

[141] Barth, 'Biblical Questions,' 51.

[142] Barth, 'Biblical Questions,' 52.

[143] Barth, 'Biblical Questions,' 55.

[144] Barth, 'Biblical Questions,' 53-54.

[145] Barth, 'Biblical Questions,' 58.

men and women of all classes stand again and again before God'.[146] *Crisis*, therefore, is descriptive of the situation of human persons when placed under the judgement of God.[147] It is precisely this sense that Barth intends in his usage of the term in this lecture.

The second significant aspect of this citation, Barth's grounding of the human condition in the problem of election, functions on two levels. First, in accordance with his fundamental commitment to the sovereignty of God, Barth refuses any theological description which reduces God to an object of human study. Thus election serves to assert and protect the sovereign aseity of God. Second, the concept also serves to indicate the fundamental nature of human and Christian existence. Barth rejects the concept of election as proposed by Augustine and the Reformers, opting instead for a more existential account:

> The idea of election is well adapted to the requirements of individual *freedom*: our responses cannot be determined once and for all: they are constantly to be made anew. Indeed, opposite responses are awakened *simultaneously* in a single individual. There is never so decisive a Yes that it does not harbour the possibility of the No: there is never so decisive a No that it is not liable to be toppled over into the Yes....From the Bible we may learn to soften the affirmations of our belief or unbelief, and perhaps to keep silence, until we perceive the true relation between God and ourselves.[148]

In this account of election human existence is a matter of being ever confronted by God. Sharp distinctions between those who are Christians and those 'outside' are blurred. Christian life is a life before God, being encountered by him in an ever-renewed call to faith and decision in which God holds the ultimate say.[149]

Genuine Biblical Piety

Barth begins the second section of his address with an affirmation of the human, historical and psychological character of the Bible, asserting that the humanity of the Bible is a given. Nonetheless he maintains that its composition was by particular human persons who had been thrown out of their course and

---

[146] Barth, *Romans I*, 441.

[147] McCormack, *Karl Barth's Dialectical Theology*, 210.

[148] Barth, 'Biblical Questions,' 58-59.

[149] For further discussion of Barth's doctrine of election see Michael D. O'Neil, 'Communities of Witness: The Concept of Election in the Old Testament and in the Theology of Karl Barth,' in *Text and Task: Scripture and Mission* (ed. Michael Parsons; Carlisle: Paternoster, 2005), 172-186, Michael D. O'Neil, 'Karl Barth's Doctrine of Election,' *The Evangelical Quarterly* 76.4 (2004): 311-326, and Michael D. O'Neil, 'The Mission of the Spirit in the Election of God' (Unpublished Dissertation for the Master of Theology (Honours), Murdoch University, Western Australia, 2001).

enabled to 'see the invisible and hear the inaudible'.[150] They had been captured and moved by something external to themselves, and thereby drawn into the movement itself. For Barth, 'this movement meets us in the Bible in an unescapable way'.[151] Thus, while he acknowledges the validity of such historical questions Barth is more concerned with the 'special *content* of this human document, the remarkable *something* with which the writers of these stories and those who stood behind them were concerned, the biblical *object*,'[152] which for Barth is nothing other than God:

> The Bible has only *one* theological interest and that is not speculative: interest in God himself....*God* is the new, incomparable, unattainable, not only heavenly but more than heavenly interest, who has drawn the regard of the men of the Bible to himself. He desires their *complete* attention, their *entire* obedience. For he must be true to himself; he must be and remain holy. He cannot be grasped, brought under management, and put to use; he cannot serve. He must rule. He must himself grasp, seize, manage, use....He is not a thing among other things, but the *Wholly Other*, the infinite aggregate of all merely relative others. He is not the form of religious history but is the Lord of our life, the eternal Lord of the world. *He* it is of whom the Bible speaks. And is he spoken of elsewhere? Certainly. But whereas elsewhere consideration of him is left to the last, an imposing background, an esoteric secret, and therefore only a possibility, in the Bible he is the first consideration, the foreground, the revelation, the one all-dominating theme.[153]

Two matters from this lengthy citation bear further reflection. First, it is plain that Barth has sharpened his characteristic emphasis on divine transcendence. Second, he emphasises the 'ec-centric' nature of biblical piety. I will look at each of these is turn. In his infinity and sovereignty God towers over all creaturely reality as the *Wholly Other*, and is as such the *content* of the Bible. All other interests, whether piety, experience, religion, religious history or church are *form* and must not be confused with the overriding focus of Scripture. These lesser interests function in the subordinate role of witness to the divine reality towards which they point, like the enlarged finger of John the Baptist in Grünewald's Isenheim altar piece.[154] And like John they must decrease:

---

[150] Barth, 'Biblical Questions,' 64.

[151] Barth, 'Biblical Questions,' 65.

[152] Barth, 'Biblical Questions,' 61.

[153] Barth, 'Biblical Questions,' 73-74.

[154] It is well known that for almost the entirety of his career Barth worked with a print of Grünewald's crucifixion scene above his desk, and that he often refers to it in his work. The pointing finger of John the Baptist, seen in this lecture as a descriptive image of the being and task of Christian and ecclesial existence, remained a fundamental motif in Barth's theology. Busch lists Barth's discovery of this painting as one of the formative influences of his theology in this period of his career. See Busch, *Karl Barth*, 116.

The prophet, the man of God, the seer and hearer, ceases to be, as that to which he unwaveringly points begins to be. The object, the reality, the Divine himself takes on new meaning; and the meaning of piety as such, of the function of the church as such, falls away. We may call this the characteristic insight of the Bible.[155]

Barth's identification of piety, religion, experience and church as *form* distinct from *content* functions to relativise them, prohibiting them from becoming things in and for themselves. This critique echoes and develops the similar critique he made in earlier works. In this lecture Barth insists that religion and church have a right to exist only when they continually do away with themselves.[156] But this is what the church refuses to do. Rather,

[s]he does not tolerate her own relativity. She has not the patience to wait; she lacks that spirit of the stranger and pilgrim, which alone justifies her coming into the world....Form believes itself capable of taking the place of content....Man has taken the divine into his possession; he has brought it under his management.[157]

Barth is emphatic: 'at the moment when religion becomes conscious of religion, when it becomes a psychologically and historically conceivable magnitude in the world, it falls away from its inner character, from its truth, to idols'.[158] For Barth, genuine biblical piety is conscious of its limits and relativity: 'In its essence it is humility, fear of the Lord. It points beyond the world, and points at the same time and above all beyond itself. It lives absolutely by virtue of its Object and for its Object.'[159]

Barth's refusal to grant religious experience and practice legitimacy as a thing-in-itself highlights the second matter of importance from the lengthy citation above. Not only has he sharpened the transcendence of God in relation to all creaturely reality, but he also emphasises the 'ec-centric' nature of biblical piety, and hence also, of Christian and ecclesial existence. God drew 'the regard of the men of the Bible to himself,' desiring 'their complete attention, their entire obedience'.[160] The biblical authors were captured, directed and drawn to a centre outside of themselves, and henceforth lived from that centre and toward that centre. For Barth, the true purpose of Scripture is to testify to this centre, directing humanity toward the same Object that had laid hold of the biblical authors. Likewise, the true purpose of biblical piety,

---

[155] Barth, 'Biblical Questions,' 75-76.
[156] Barth, 'Biblical Questions,' 67. Note that in this passage Barth speaks sometimes of 'religion' in a general sense, and sometimes of 'church' more specifically. Nevertheless the context indicates that when he speaks of religion he has in mind contemporary institutional Christianity.
[157] Barth, 'Biblical Questions,' 67-68.
[158] Barth, 'Biblical Questions,' 68. Overbeck's influence is evident here.
[159] Barth, 'Biblical Questions,' 69.
[160] Barth, 'Biblical Questions,' 74.

religion and church is also to point away from themselves towards God as the central reality of their existence. By construing the nature of genuine piety in this manner Barth again repudiates the inwardness, idealism and historicism characteristic of much Pietism and liberal Protestantism. These forms of ecclesial existence are those which have fallen away from their true character and from their truth to idols, and as such are indicative of 'false Christianity'.[161] In their place Barth intends the construction of an alternative framework designed to support and sustain a new form of Christian and ecclesial existence, one in which the entire being of the church derives from and is directed toward this supreme Object which has encountered it. God claims the 'complete attention' and 'entire obedience' of this people as his own.[162]

This radical orientation of the believer to an external centre secures the primacy of God over against the Christian and the church, and identifies the role or task of these in terms of witness. Or to say it in terms more closely aligned to Barth's in this lecture, the task of the believer and the church consists in being once more the pointing finger of Grünewald's John. The character of this witness includes the attributes of 'obedience, righteousness, love, open ears, thanksgiving, a contrite spirit and broken heart',[163] each of which stands in antithesis to the triumphant posture of the modern church. Genuine biblical piety will engender a church with 'the patience to wait,' displaying the 'spirit of the stranger and pilgrim' in the world,[164] and ready to decrease as God increases. It is this aspect of the character of witness that Barth takes up in the lengthy third and final section of the lecture. It is also in this third section of the lecture that we encounter most forcefully the changing structure of his theological framework.

The Wisdom of Death

Barth begins the third section of the lecture by again utilising Grünewald's

---

[161] Barth, 'Biblical Questions,' 75. See also Gorringe's assertion that 'because religion falsifies our experience of the world Barth's critique of religion is ideology critique'—Gorringe, *Against Hegemony*, 53.
[162] I have borrowed the concept of 'ec-centric' existence from a later period in Barth's career. See, for example, Karl Barth, *Church Dogmatics IV/3.2: The Doctrine of Reconciliation* (ed. G. W. Bromiley & T. F. Torrance, trans. G. W. Bromiley; Edinburgh: T. & T. Clark, 1962), 548. See also William S. Johnson, *The Mystery of God: Karl Barth and the Postmodern Foundations of Theology* (Louisville: Westminster John Knox, 1997), 176-183, and Nicholas M. Healy, 'Karl Barth's Ecclesiology Reconsidered,' *Scottish Journal of Theology* 57, No. 3 (2004), 293.
[163] Barth, 'Biblical Questions,' 70.
[164] Barth, 'Biblical Questions,' 67.

imagery,[165] this time to indicate that the witness of John, and thus of the church also, is to the *crucified* Christ:

> The only source for the real, the immediate, revelation of God is *death*. Christ unlocked its gates. He brought *life* to light out of *death*. *Out of death!* The word cannot be spoken significantly enough. The meaning of God, the power of God, begins to shine upon the men of the Bible at the boundary of mortality.[166]

For the Barth of this lecture, the entire witness of Scripture, culminating in the story of Jesus, reveals that witness is cruciform, tending toward death and self-dissolution. The biblical characters 'witness not to humanity but to the *end* of humanity'.[167] In place of the optimistic organic metaphor for the coming of the Kingdom in *Romans I* Barth now says:

> 'The axe is laid unto the root of the trees,' *consummatio mundi*, the dissolution of all things, the crumbling away of all being, the passing of this age—this is the meaning of the 'kingdom of God.'...To understand the New Testament Yes as anything but the Yes contained in the No, is not to understand it at all. Life comes from *death!* Death is the source of all.[168]

Once again Barth is emphatic: '*The affirmation of God, man, and the world given in the New Testament is based exclusively upon the possibility of a new order absolutely beyond human thought; and therefore, as prerequisite to that order, there must come a crisis that denies all human thought.*'[169]

That the new order of the kingdom is neither a possibility of the old order, nor a religious possibility,[170] is something Barth has reiterated often since his break with liberalism. In this lecture, however, Barth has sharpened this assertion with the insertion of *absolutely*, and the insistence on crisis as a prerequisite for that order. Humanity now stands before the closed wall of death, hardly aware of the new world that may be waiting behind it.[171] God himself awaits us beyond this boundary of our existence, the divine first being 'on the further side of the human last'.[172] Yet it is here, confronted in the New Testament by 'the wisdom of death,' that we discover at the same time that it is the most comprehensive wisdom of life.[173] Death, the threat and reality of

---

[165] Barth's threefold reference to Grünewald's painting provides the order and shape of the whole lecture. See the introductory comments to the lecture in Barth, *The Word of God and Theology*, 73.
[166] Barth, 'Biblical Questions,' 77.
[167] Barth, 'Biblical Questions,' 78.
[168] Barth, 'Biblical Questions,' 79-80.
[169] Barth, 'Biblical Questions,' 80.
[170] Barth, 'Biblical Questions,' 82.
[171] Barth, 'Biblical Questions,' 85.
[172] Barth, 'Biblical Questions,' 87.
[173] Barth, 'Biblical Questions,' 83-84.

dissolution as the crisis visited upon humanity, is comprehensively addressed and overcome in the resurrection of Jesus Christ. For Barth in this lecture, the Easter message of resurrection has five decisive implications: the sovereign victory of God over all the power of death; the entrance of eternity into time at that point which is therefore also the dawn of the new time; the miracle of the new world which includes the reconstitution of the moral subject; a new corporeality in which the totality of creaturely being is subject to the activity and power of God the redeemer; and finally, the resurrection as an experiential reality in the life of the God-fearing individual.[174]

Such is the comprehensive victory of the resurrection. Nevertheless Barth is forced to ask whether it is really true that *life* springs from *death*. Is the rhythm revealed in the passion and exaltation of the Messiah—from life into death, from death into life—really credible, rational and real?[175] Glib answers from religion and the church are wholly insufficient in light of the enormity of the death which has descended upon Europe. Indeed, 'if any utterance at all is in need of substantiation, attestation, and demonstration in corresponding moral, social, and political action, it is the biblical utterance that death is swallowed up in victory,' says Barth.[176] 'The only real way to *name* the theme of the Bible, which is the Easter message,' he continues, 'is to have it, to show it, to live it. The Easter message becomes truth, movement, reality, as it is expressed—or it is not the Easter message which is expressed. Let us be satisfied that all biblical questions, insights, and vistas focus upon this common theme.'[177]

Here Barth rejects the arrogant presumption of a church that claims it possesses the victory of God when so little of the reality of the resurrection is actually manifested 'in our conventional and self-reliant lives'.[178] Nor will the situation be remedied by the church continuing along its familiar paths of busy evangelism, social work or religious experience.[179] He insists that 'religion's blind and vicious habit of asserting eternally that it possesses something, feasts upon it, and distributes it, must sometime cease, if we are ever to have an honest, a fierce, seeking, asking, and knocking'.[180]

Barth applies Overbeck's 'wisdom of death' to the being and activity of the church. Only as the church confronts the relativity of its own existence, as it enters into the crisis common to all human being and activity, will it cease from the relentless pursuit of its own works and cry to God for his work. The actuality of the resurrection in the life and being of the believer and the church is sheer grace, 'an absolute *novum* and original *datum*, wherever its traces are

---

[174] Barth, 'Biblical Questions,' 87-95.
[175] Barth, 'Biblical Questions,' 84-85.
[176] Barth, 'Biblical Questions,' 85-86.
[177] Barth, 'Biblical Questions,' 86.
[178] Barth, 'Biblical Questions,' 86.
[179] Barth, 'Biblical Questions,' 85.
[180] Barth, 'Biblical Questions,' 86-87.

discernible....There are no transitions, intermixings, or intermediate stages. There is only crisis, finality, new insight. What the Bible brings us from beyond the grave is the perfect, the absolute miracle.'[181] It is for this reason that the church's first movement must be movement toward God in earnest prayer.

Also noteworthy in this lecture is Barth's description of the moral agent, who, as the recipient of the forgiveness of sins

> is constituted anew by virtue of his interconnection with the order of the kingdom of heaven, by virtue of his being counted unto God; the beginning of good is perceived in the midst of bad; the royal freedom of man is established by virtue of the royal freedom of God; the possibility is given of understanding all things in the light of God, of doing the greatest and the smallest deeds to the glory of God....Man, for all his limited, constrained and ephemeral existence, is at the same time 'in an all-exclusive way' dependent upon God, animated by God, and supported by God.[182]

For Barth, the forgiveness of sins represents 'the highest expression of the *totaliter aliter* (wholly other) which the Bible utters...even more astonishing than the raising of Lazarus'.[183] The raising of Lazarus represents resuscitation to the same form of existence as he previously had. In the forgiveness of sins the crisis confronting humanity is vanquished, with the result that the human agent is 'constituted anew'. The human subject is 'born anew, that is, "from above," and is conscious of itself in God'.[184] Ultimately this will issue in the utter renewal of the entirety of their being—a new corporeality in which nothing from 'below' remains. Meanwhile, it means the granting of possibilities hitherto unknown which will issue in the 'royal freedom of man,' that is, the restoration of the human agent into a correctly ordered relationship with God the creator and redeemer. In this freedom the 'beginning of good' may be perceived in the fields of moral and political reality.

Finally, we have noted already that at the outset of the lecture Barth laments the human individualism which separates us from God and frustrates the knowledge of God from coming to fruitfulness in our lives. Barth's repudiation of individualism, however, does not spell the dissolution of the individual per se, for in and through the resurrection it is the '*God-fearing individual*' who finds themselves addressed, and who is first to be touched.[185] It is the *individual* who is called to believe, to venture and to persevere. This person responds to the crisis which breaks upon humanity in the fear of the Lord, and their repentance consists in a 'radical change of mind, in a revaluation of all practical

---

[181] Barth, 'Biblical Questions,' 91-92.
[182] Barth, 'Biblical Questions,' 92.
[183] Barth, 'Biblical Questions,' 92.
[184] Barth, 'Biblical Questions,' 93.
[185] Barth, 'Biblical Questions,' 95.

values'.[186] But why *this* individual? Barth concludes his lecture at the same point where he began, that is, with the puzzle of election, and the implicit call to live responsively to the ever-renewed call and claim of God which confronts the human person.

In sum, this lecture evidences several definite points of Barth's theological development. Most notable is the absence of 'organic' language in his description of God's relation to the creation. But, to use the words of Helmut Gollwitzer, 'his turning away from J. T. Beck does not imply that he also turned away from the Blumhardts'.[187] Indeed, as may be expected, the continuing influence of Blumhardt is evident in this lecture, chiefly in the priority that Barth gives to the need for urgent, fervent prayer, and his criticism of a church that does not have 'the patience to wait'. Especially evident is the new influence of Overbeck, who Barth used to radicalise his eschatology by means of his emphasis on death as the crisis befalling all humanity. Indeed, Barth would later recall that his change of theological direction first became apparent in this lecture.[188]

In this lecture again, then, it is seen that Barth constructs his theology with an ethical horizon in view, and he seeks to shape the praxis of his hearers through the construction of an alternative theological perspective of reality. The primary element of this construction, which stands in continuity with his earlier work, is his insistence that human existence is radically 'ec-centric,' thoroughly and decisively oriented to a centre external to the individual subject. It is this feature of his theology which undergirds his depiction of human existence as ever-renewed existential response to the electing God, who is also creator and redeemer. It also functions to determine the fundamental character of Christian and ecclesial existence as *witness*. Nevertheless, it must be acknowledged that in this lecture his ethical vision is more concerned with formal categories, with the result that the material content of his Christian and ecclesial vision is relatively thin. Barth says more about waiting than hastening, a factor exacerbated by his grounding of the reconstituted moral agent in the forgiveness of sins rather than in the vital presence, movement and growth of the coming kingdom. His tightening of the eschatological horizon introduced a sombre, indeed pessimistic, note into his theology, and functioned to constrict his depiction of moral existence. Whether this new theological perspective is able to sustain his hitherto vibrant vision of Christian and ecclesial existence remains to be seen.

---

[186] Barth, 'Biblical Questions,' 82.

[187] H. Gollwitzer, 'Kingdom of God and Socialism in the Theology of Karl Barth,' in *Karl Barth and Radical Politics* (ed. G. Hunsinger; Philadelphia: Westminster, 1976), 94.

[188] Bernd Jaspert, ed., *Karl Barth~Rudolph Bultmann Letters 1922-1966* (Grand Rapids: Eerdmans, 1981), 156. The comment occurs in an autobiographical sketch penned by Barth in 1927.

Life in the Shadow of Death: Sermons on 2 Corinthians

Throughout this period Barth's pastoral responsibilities in Safenwil continued to demand his attention. This is true most particularly of his preaching responsibilities, which also continued to fuel his biblical investigations. We have noted already the role of Colossians and Ecclesiastes in his Tambach lecture. His letters to Thurneysen also indicate that Barth laboured over Ephesians, Psalms, the Acts and the Corinthian correspondence.[189] In a letter dated November 11, 1919 Barth writes:

> Yesterday and today I sat over 1 Corinthians 15, but I came to a dead stop in the earliest stages as I started to work through it thoroughly....The chapter is the key to the entire letter with its profound disclosures that have their source in ultimate wisdom, some of which have struck us recently like shocks from an electric eel. Not without effect.[190]

These epistolary references indicate the continuing and formative influence that Scripture had on Barth's theological development. His preaching ministry also provides another avenue by which to examine this development. A month after the Aarau lecture Barth again writes to Thurneysen, 'The Second Letter to the Corinthians sweeps over me like a torrent. Only the smallest part can flow on in the form of sermons.'[191] Seven of these sermons, however, were published in a joint collection of Barth and Thurneysen's sermons in 1924.[192] In these sermons the practical outworking of Barth's new emphasis can, to some extent at least, be seen, and so in this section I will examine these sermons with a view to explicating their contribution to our understanding of Barth's Christian and ecclesial vision. Because Barth's treatment of these themes is somewhat uneven across the particular sermons, in this section I will adopt a thematic approach

---

[189] See Smart, *Revolutionary Theology*, 46-52. See also Busch, *Karl Barth*, 108.

[190] Smart, *Revolutionary Theology*, 48. Busch (*Karl Barth*, 108) notes that during February 1919 Barth wrote a 'mini-commentary' on 1 Corinthians 15. During his Göttingen period (1924) Barth's lectures on 1 Corinthians were later published as Karl Barth, *The Resurrection of the Dead* (trans. H. J. Stenning; Eugene, Oregon: Wipf & Stock, 2003).

[191] Barth's comments to Thurneysen indicate that he was preaching from 2 Corinthians in late May and June 1920. See Smart, *Revolutionary Theology*, 51-52.

[192] Karl Barth & Eduard Thurneysen, *Come Holy Spirit* (trans. E. G. Homrighausen, K. J. Ernst & G. W. Richards; Edinburgh: T. & T. Clark, 1934), 205-287. Both Thurneysen and Barth contributed sermons to this volume, and while the author of particular sermons is not indicated, some evidence that the sermons on 2 Corinthians were Barth's work is given by his biographer who cites them as such. See Busch, *Karl Barth*, 114; cf. Thurneysen, 'Introduction,' 12. An additional sermon from this series (on 2 Corinthians 1:3-11) has been translated in Karl Barth & William H. Willimon, *The Early Preaching of Karl Barth: Fourteen Sermons with Commentary by William H. Willimon* (Louisville: Westminster John Knox, 2009), 111-121.

across the sermons rather than treating each sermon as a unit. My treatment of the sermons will unfold in three sub-sections. In the first, I investigate Barth's theological framework as it is expressed in these sermons, and find substantial evidence of his theological development in this period between the two editions of his commentary. The second sub-section unpacks Barth's growing awareness of the individual with respect to his or her participation in the activity of the kingdom of God. We shall see that Barth adopts the apostle Paul as a paradigm of Christian existence, and calls his congregation to be amongst those who walk in the way of Christ after Paul. In the final sub-section Barth outlines the nature of an ethics grounded in the forgiveness of sins and inhabiting the pathways of grace as he wrestles with a Christian approach to the particularly live issue of national reconstruction in the immediate post-war era.

Barth preaches to his congregation against the familiar background of the events unfolding in their world. Thus he speaks of 'living in a time when collapse threatens society' and of the 'break-up and collapse which mark our day'.[193] Yet he can also speak in light of the new hope springing forth as Europe and the world work toward reconstruction: 'Our age is seething with a feeling of high hope and with a spirit of new life.'[194] He remarks that 'tremendous forces are at work'. Over that summer five different international Congresses were convened in Switzerland alone. New associations, new attempts at international and inter-religious cooperation were being founded.[195] In light of this great threat and equally great hope, what response should Christians and the church make?

Touched by Eternity in the Midst of Time

Barth intends theology and church to be engaged in the broader issues of society and culture, and thus it is not surprising that his regular preaching occurs within the same ethical horizon that we have observed in his earlier lectures and works. Yet also apparent here are differences from what has gone before. There is virtually no trace at all of the organic metaphor for describing the activity and advance of God's kingdom in the world. In fact, Barth does not speak of the 'advance' of God's kingdom at all. Neither is socialism even mentioned—although this might be anticipated given the context of these addresses. What, then, is the theological framework of these sermons?

Prominent in these sermons are meditations on the human condition, of the 'loss of heart' and despondency which often characterises humanity, as well as

---

[193] See Karl Barth, 'A Narrow Way (2 Corinthians 2:5-11),' in *Come Holy Spirit* (Edinburgh: T. & T. Clark, 1934), 214, and Karl Barth, 'Moses-Time and Christ-Time (2 Corinthians 3:12-17),' in *Come Holy Spirit* (Edinburgh: T. & T. Clark, 1934), 231.

[194] Karl Barth, 'Behold, now! (2 Corinthians 6:1-2),' in *Come Holy Spirit* (Edinburgh: T. & T. Clark, 1934), 282.

[195] Barth, 'Behold, now!,' 283.

the human determination to do whatever is possible to rectify that which we see as wrong.[196] In an echo of the Aarau lecture Barth presents the human situation as a 'groaning' which arises from the *seeming* reality in which we live: 'We have seen the truth of our life, in one way or another, and its truth is death.'[197] While this is indeed true—'we are standing under a large, all-embracing and all-destroying Nay'[198]—it is not the ultimate source of our groaning. Rather, the true source of our groaning is the innate memory of the Yes within us, the memory of our origin which is also our goal and homeland.[199] Thus Barth continues,

> Here is the cause of our groaning. Do you understand now why you must groan? Yes, the present tabernacle must be broken down that the building from God may receive you. And you are groaning now not because the tabernacle is being broken down, but because the building from God has not yet taken you up....It is not death that is painful, but that we do not yet live....The cause of our anxiety is not the Nay; but the Yea which has been pronounced over us even before the Nay has come over us....If there were no God and if the heavenly habitation were not awaiting us, there would be no cause for groaning. But God has begun to trouble us with an anxious restlessness. He is the cause of our groaning; and therefore, we must groan.[200]

In these sermons, then, we hear a strong emphasis on the crisis that God is bringing upon humanity from above.[201] Humanity exists in the shadow of death, and it is only by way of death that we may find life—'through an extended cancellation, removal, limitation, and discarding of what we call life. True life begins where everything ends'.[202]

Yet it is also clear that humanity is not abandoned in its earthly existence, but rather already belongs to God and is addressed by God.[203] This divine address—the Word of God—is the gospel, which is addressed to common

---

[196] Karl Barth, 'The Inward Man (2 Corinthians 4:16-18),' in *Come Holy Spirit* (Edinburgh: T. & T. Clark, 1934), 254.

[197] Karl Barth, 'Confident Despair (2 Corinthians 5:1-8),' in *Come Holy Spirit* (Edinburgh: T. & T. Clark, 1934), 271.

[198] Barth, 'Confident Despair,' 270.

[199] Barth, 'Confident Despair,' 272.

[200] Barth, 'Confident Despair,' 273-275.

[201] Busch, *Karl Barth*, 114.

[202] Barth, 'Confident Despair,' 273. See also Barth on 2 Corinthians 1:3-11, in Barth and Willimon, *The Early Preaching*, 115, and Barth, 'The Inward Man,' 260: 'Where everything finds an end, there the inward man has his beginning. At the point where what we call life is fading away in the absolute mystery of death, there is our genuine life. Where our sight fails us and where we find only an abyss, darkness and the end as our portion in life, there it is where God makes himself known to man.'

[203] Karl Barth, 'The Freedom of the Word of God (2 Corinthians 2:14-17),' in *Come Holy Spirit* (Edinburgh: T. & T. Clark, 1934), 219-220.

persons in the ordinary circumstances of their lives, reminding them of the eternity which they have known but forgotten.[204] Here again the interplay between divine and human agency is evident, although as in the Aarau lecture, Barth predicates a sovereign freedom to the Word of God beyond the freedom of the human agent, grounding this greater freedom in the mystery of election. Thus,

> [t]he free Word of God always has some effect where men face it with their liberty. But it does not have the same effect in every instance, for man's liberty is also freedom. Only in freedom here and there, does God carry on his work. 'He chooses whom he will, and hardens whom He will.'...For heat has the power to melt but also to wither; light may illumine and cause blindness; wind can bring relief from heat and it can carry on its wings the winter's icy blasts.[205]

Barth speaks of the Word of God 'waiting for men who will give it attention'. This same word 'comes over them, and overcomes them. But it does not care to overcome them save in its own freedom and in their liberty.'[206] When a person, in the interplay of this divine-human encounter, gives their attention to and hears the Word of God, eternity touches time in the circumstance of their personal existence. In them 'the new man' is being born, who 'must also think and speak and act in a new way. He is completely severed from the old man and his whole kind.'[207]

In these sermons, then, Barth maintains the earlier emphasis on the divine freedom vis-à-vis humanity, although his structuring of this relation is now altered in order to secure this freedom more adequately. In the earlier works Barth conceived of a two-dimensional reality in which God's kingdom, planted as a seed in the resurrection of Christ, grew vigorously in the world as the kingdom advanced in accordance with the impetus of 'the other side'. Now the two dimensions stand in a more stark relation to each other, reconceived under the rubric of time and eternity. 'The very mystery and meaning of our existence,' says Barth, 'consists in this, that we are living in time and in eternity. But these two factors of our existence are not of equal strength.'[208] Eternity is ever present to time, casting its light over time in such a way that time is never without eternity. Nevertheless, Barth insists that 'there are no bridges leading back from...life to death. Time shall become as eternity; but never, never can eternity become as time. The earth shall become like heaven;

---

[204] Barth, 'The Freedom of the Word of God,' 221-222.

[205] Barth, 'The Freedom of the Word of God,' 227-228.

[206] Barth, 'The Freedom of the Word of God,' 220.

[207] Barth, 'The Freedom of the Word of God,' 224.

[208] Barth, 'The Freedom of the Word of God,' 221. Barth's reflections on time and eternity in this series of sermons reflect the new influence of Kierkegaard on his thought. See Karl Barth, *The Epistle to the Romans* (trans. E. C. Hoskyns; 6th ed. Oxford: Oxford University Press, 1933), 4.

but never, never even unto the end of time, can heaven become like the earth.'[209] Thus, while eternity encompasses time on every side, and even penetrates time, it remains distinct from time in its nature and essence. For Barth, time is 'eternity emptied, pauperised, despoiled; and eternity is time fulfilled'.[210] Time, in this sense, represents the world and humanity fallen away from God, empty, impoverished and spoiled. Its only hope is that it might somehow be taken up into eternity that it might be fulfilled, or as it were, healed and restored to its proper estate.

The question confronting us is now clear: how shall time become as eternity, earth as heaven, if the entirety of earthly existence lies under the doom of the divine No, the all-encompassing reign of death? This is the crisis under which humanity has its existence. Although Barth does not address this question directly it is possible to find in these sermons several indications of how he approached it, all of which serve to maintain the freedom of God in his relation to humanity. Barth begins with reference to Jesus Christ through whom 'eternity rushes into time as a mountain freshet rushes into its empty bed after a shower. The kingdom of heaven bursts upon earth as an army bursts into hostile territory.'[211] The coming of Christ has resulted in a decisive reconstitution of the human situation so that all humanity is claimed by God and belongs to him. Significantly, however, Barth insists on both a historical and a present fulfilment of time in the coming of Christ: '"When the fullness of time came, God sent forth his Son" and we must understand it so. That time was, *and is being*, fulfilled in this: that God is sending his Son.'[212] The fulfilling of time so that it may become as eternity is a continuing work of God. Here, however, in place of the organic language which was indicative of process, we find the language of proclamation, and of the *Paternoster*:

> *Thy* name be hallowed—in time where it is not yet holy. *Thy* kingdom come—in time where it is not yet established. *Thy* will be done—in time where it is not yet being done. In this Thine, Thine, Thine in contradistinction to all what is not yet Thine, the word of God, the Gospel, Jesus Christ, lives, moves and has his being. Yes, here is the place where Jesus Christ is standing. They are God's interests that he is minding and of which he reminds us. That we let ourselves be reminded of them is our salvation and our redemption. It is the end to which God's love for us tends. But we cannot be helped except as we help God. Here is God's end; his impetuous message which will meet us, strike us, that we also shall have a part in its fulfilment and that we also shall discover it and become aware and alive in resurrection. *We* are being led to the point where time and eternity meet. *We* are being asked if we will acknowledge eternity's advantage and preponderance over

---

[209] Barth, 'The Freedom of the Word of God,' 224.

[210] Barth, 'The Freedom of the Word of God,' 221.

[211] Barth, 'The Freedom of the Word of God,' 222.

[212] Barth, 'The Freedom of the Word of God,' 222, emphasis added. Note also Barth's shifting of the tenses in this sentence: 'God *is* sending his Son.'

time. We are being offered this insight that there is hidden behind all decay and death a greater advent and a larger life. We are given a perspective of the victory and perfection toward which our whole existence tends.[213]

Several points in this passage call for attention. First, Barth speaks of the message of God which will 'meet us, strike us, that we also shall have a part in its fulfilment'. Barth understands the proclamation of the gospel itself to be a means by which time comes to its fulfilment. This proclamation, though, is not simply a human activity. Barth insists that, 'The Word of God promotes itself. Its proclamation is God's own deed. Man merely attends; he is the ear, the heart, and head and mouth, and hand and foot.'[214] Barth uses the language of personal encounter to indicate that God addresses the human subject by means of the proclamation. In this encounter the person is confronted with realisation of a new reality and the demand and promise it brings. This renewal of vision constitutes the call of the person thus encountered by the gospel, and becomes the catalyst for a new existence as he or she is incorporated into the activity of God, and becomes part of the fulfilment he intends for creation and humanity.

Second, Barth also indicates that the human agent is incorporated not just generally into the activity of God, but specifically into the prayer of Jesus that they might become part of the fulfilment of his purpose. In the giving of the Lord's Prayer, and particularly the first three petitions, Jesus is minding God's interests, and reminding his followers of them. Further, Barth indicates that 'the Word of God, the Gospel, Jesus Christ, lives, moves and has his being' in this place where these petitions are presently being offered to God in prayer. Where the people of God join with Jesus in his cry for the hallowing of God's name, for the coming of the kingdom, for the doing of God's will, there 'is the place where Jesus Christ is standing', there it is that 'we are being led to the point where time and eternity meet'. Here again we observe the ethical horizon of Barth's theology, and see also the integral role that prayer has in his vision of Christian and ecclesial existence. Summoned by the gospel, we pray. In prayer we not only cry out to God for the coming of his kingdom, but are ourselves moved and become part of the answer of that prayer. Only in allowing ourselves to be reminded of God's interests, and in being moved in accordance with these interests, do we find salvation. Thus, for Barth, an election which does not issue in ethical response is not God's election.

Finally, it is clear in the passage cited above that the personal encounter which initiates our incorporation into the redeeming activity of God is freighted

---

[213] Barth, 'The Freedom of the Word of God,' 222-223.

[214] Barth, 'The Freedom of the Word of God,' 225. See also Willimon's comment on Barth's 'The Narrow Way' sermon: 'the most politically relevant thing we can do is to preach, to sign, to signal, and to witness to the new world that God is creating in Jesus Christ. This is the heart of Barthian "politics," and it is clearly the background for this sermon's comments about the peculiar, radically odd way that Christians can help the world.' See Barth & Willimon, The Early Preaching, 130.

also with cognitive content. We are reminded of God's interests. We are 'being offered this insight that there is hidden behind all decay and death a greater advent and a larger life. *We* are given a perspective...' In other words, the person encountered by God experiences an alteration of their worldview, a renewed vision of reality. Given his emphasis on 'thought obedient to faith' in *Romans 1*, it seems likely that Barth would argue that this renewed vision must be theologically construed and underpinned, but its genesis is grounded in the revelatory encounter of God.

In these sermons, then, Barth has begun to apply his new theological insights. The manner in which he construes the divine-human relation reflects a heightened sense of divine sovereignty, now explicated by means of a time-eternity dialectic and set within an embracing context of divine election. Humanity exists in the shadow of death confronted by the divine crisis befalling it from above and putting its entire life into question. Yet, for all this, humanity is not abandoned but addressed by God in promise and hope, most particularly through the proclamation of the gospel. Through this address particular people are encountered by God, and, touched by eternity in the midst of time, they are made new, given a new comprehension of reality and set on a new path of life. Crucial to this new manner of life is responsiveness to God's interests, and the act of prayer by which they are incorporated into the divine activity presently occurring in the world.

Called as an Individual

After his tirades against individualism, especially in *Romans 1*, it was curious to observe at the end of Barth's Aarau lecture, a positive account of individuals in their relation to God. In his sermon series on Second Corinthians Barth extends his reflections on this theme in his sermon on 4:7-15, entitled 'The Individual'.[215] This sermon has particular significance because Barth establishes Paul as an exemplar of 'the true life,' and thus as a paradigm of Christian existence.[216] 'For is there a man who is not equally necessary to God, as was Paul?' Barth asks. 'If only a man will understand the divine necessity of this kind of a life—and engage in living it. God has need of men who will lend their ears to his call, even if many others remain deaf to him.'[217] He continues,

> [i]t is simply a divine necessity and a law in God's kingdom that there shall be such individuals. God's relation to humanity is not fashioned after the principle of our political states where all citizens are equal before the law. Neither does God follow the rule of the army where a thousand men lift their right feet at the same moment when the regiment begins to march. God's relation to mankind is

---

[215] Karl Barth, 'The Individual (2 Corinthians 4:7-15),' in *Come Holy Spirit* (Edinburgh: T. & T. Clark, 1934), 242-253.

[216] Barth, 'The Individual,' 243.

[217] Barth, 'The Individual,' 244.

constituted in liberty. God does not start with mass movements. He begins with a few individuals; and even among them different stages and degrees of preparedness and alertness for divine service are possible.[218]

To be such a person is not a badge of merit, or a sign that God loves this one more than others. Nor does it implicitly suggest that those who remain deaf have a lesser status. They are distinguished from others as those 'who search and wait' for God's truth, and who 'surrender' to God.[219] Nevertheless, says Barth, God uses such individuals precisely because his eye is on the whole of humanity, and as such, they 'must be God's servants in his movement toward men'.[220] Such individuals become leaders of 'God's vanguard': 'amidst the sham life of their fellowmen, and for their benefit, they are living the true life that men ought to live'.[221] Thus, 'God employs individuals who offer themselves to his service; and of them more is required than of others.'[222]

Paul's cruciform life also serves as a pattern for Christian existence. The person who lives for God, suggests Barth, invites attacks upon themselves, for their 'very existence is an attack upon the world and its existing order, on what it prizes and values'.[223] Further, this person has no weapons they can use to defend themselves from these attacks but must simply 'stand and suffer'.[224] By participating in the sufferings and death of Christ, Paul, and those who follow him, become testimony to the dethroning of humanity, to the dethroning of what is highly exalted by humanity that God may be highly exalted. Those who serve Jesus as Lord cannot expect to be led on any road other than the one he trod.[225]

The corollary of this, of course, is that those who participate in the dying of Jesus shall also share in his resurrection, and therefore, this existence is borne along with joyfulness and hope in the promise of God. In his sermon on 2 Corinthians 5:1-8 Barth again returns to the example of Paul for the contemporary believer. Paul was empowered to participate in the sufferings of Christ *by* his vision of the resurrection. Although in the crisis of the cross every little light was extinguished and earthly life closed, in the resurrection true life appears from beyond death and a new great light arises from the darkness. Paul viewed life from the perspective of the resurrection, from the turning of God to humanity, and as a result,

[218] Barth, 'The Individual,' 244.
[219] Barth, 'The Individual,' 245.
[220] Barth, 'The Individual,' 245.
[221] Barth, 'The Individual,' 243-244.
[222] Barth, 'The Individual,' 246.
[223] Barth, 'The Individual,' 248.
[224] Barth, 'The Individual,' 248.
[225] Barth, 'The Individual,' 251.

He did not become a hermit with his insights...he did not lock himself up with a few chosen disciples...he did not rest, but lived, and fought, and suffered, and fell, and rose again, and triumphed with these insights, and filled the world, this dreary world of death with his victorious deeds and set it in motion to God's glory.[226]

The vision of the resurrection is thus an empowering vision calling men and women in whatever station they hold in life to embark on the way of Jesus in hope of sharing his resurrection. Although only few actually surrender to this call, it is clear that Barth is calling his congregation to be amongst this number.

This call is apparent also in the final sermon of the series as Barth asks rhetorically, 'Why should God be farther removed from us than from Paul and the Corinthians? Why should we not receive grace and salvation today?'[227] Again Barth casts the answer in terms of waiting, seeking and crying out for God, although 'when men have learned that they can only wait for God, they do no longer need to wait for him'.[228] He speaks of those gripped with a 'holy impatience' whose sincere question *Why not?* 'drives them on until they stand in God's presence'.[229] In this presence they can only continue to cry out, and in so doing experience the grace which not only gathers them up but also commissions them making them co-workers together with God, as Paul was.[230] Barth concludes his message with the exhortation that

[w]hen men like Paul come forth from the presence of Christ, God's time has come. What shall we say of our time? Look about you for such men!...Let it be your concern that we may have such men with us....Be such men yourselves, if you can! *Why not?* Why should we not be taught humility and find grace at the feet of the Christ? Why should not the righteous wait upon God in joy today? Is not everything prepared? Do you not hear what our time is telling us? Everything is prepared, if only we are prepared. Yes, Paul would call our time with the same call as he called yesterday. Give us again a Paul who speaks thus. A Christ who makes Paul speak as he spoke, we have....What are we waiting for? For a harvest where no seeding has been done? For fruit that grows by our hands? It is God who works, both to will and to do. Therefore work out your own salvation with fear and trembling![231]

Here, once more, the interplay between waiting and hastening is evident, although it is also placed within the new framework of the time-eternity dialectic. Barth is concerned that 'God's time'—the fulfilling of time by eternity—might be realised in 'our times'. His use of Paul as exemplar, and his

[226] Barth, 'Confident Despair,' 277. See also Barth & Willimon, *The Early Preaching*, 117-118.
[227] Barth, 'Behold, now!,' 284.
[228] Barth, 'Behold, now!,' 285.
[229] Barth, 'Behold, now!,' 285.
[230] Barth, 'Behold, now!,' 285-286.
[231] Barth, 'Behold, now!,' 286-287.

exhortation that the congregation seek the presence of Christ that they might come forth from that presence as Paul did, is clearly indicative that he does not conceive of Christian existence in quietist terms. He has already described the way of Paul in the world in terms of activity, struggle and ultimate triumph in which he 'filled the world, this dreary world of death with his victorious deeds and set it in motion to God's glory'.[232] This, too, is his call to his Safenwil parishioners: a life of activity which arises from a holy restlessness which drives them into the presence of Christ.

Forgiveness and Freedom

When he considers the direction this activity—Christian existence—is to take, Barth is also careful to warn his parishioners against taking a false path. In his sermon on 2 Corinthians 3:12-17 Barth identifies such a path, labelling it as 'Moses-time'.[233] The opening words of this sermon—'Your question is quite pertinent, is it wise to preach on these words?'[234]—suggest the possibility that his sermon arises out of dialogue, or perhaps criticism, occurring in his congregation as a result of this preaching series.

In his extended opening salvo Barth reflects on Paul's claim that 'we use great boldness of speech, and are not as Moses' (2 Corinthians 3:12-13). For Barth, to 'be as Moses' represents the bold imposition of law, and striving for order as a means of rebuilding society in chaotic times. It further implies an ethics of responsibility and diligent work in a time of moral corruption. The argument put to Barth seems to be as follows:

> The shadows of night are settling ever deeper on the hearts of peoples and nations. Must we not give all that we are and have to keep at least flickering a few candles of conscience and duty toward higher things, and if possible to relight a few that have been extinguished?…It really will not do to extinguish the light of laws which sheds a few rays in our twilight hours. It may be that, some time or other, a new day will fully dawn for us. Then we shall dispense with our artificial lights because the end to which they tend and point has come to pass. In the full splendour of that day-to-come we shall discard the makeshifts which served us in our twilight hours. But today we have certainly not reached the point where we can do without them.…We live in the twilight of an interim, and we do not know whether it is the dusk before an oncoming night or the dawn of a new day. But can we do better justice to the demand of our time than by accepting our present fate, becoming wanderers in the twilight, eating our bread in the sweat of our brows as

---

[232] Barth, 'Confident Despair,' 277.
[233] Barth, 'Moses-Time and Christ-Time,' 230-241.
[234] Barth, 'Moses-Time and Christ-Time,' 230.

did our first parents, and by clinging to law as Israel did in its wilderness-journey? Do you know of a better and more perfect way?[235]

Before Barth answers the question posed by his (assumed) interlocutor, he sets about destroying the presupposition upon which his protagonist's position is founded. The interlocutor may have correctly asserted that the present culture is bearing the rightful burden and sentence of its own guilt-worthiness, but their solution is inadequate:

> Have we not done enough, we ask, if we have finally become aware of the precariousness of our situation and if we feel our guilt and are ready to atone? No, Paul would say, you have really not done enough, even if you have repented, even if you shoulder your guilt and make restitution as best you can; and even if you should go to the jungles of Africa to atone there for the sins of our civilisation with a life of self-sacrifice; and if you give your body to be burned and all your goods to the poor. All these things you may do and perhaps you ought to do them; but not enough has yet been done. For none of them atones for your sin; none of them clears the road. All this is 'being as Moses,' and Moses does not redeem. If you go wrong here, it may well be that you are turning away from God by your very conversion.[236]

Barth's rhetoric applies classic reformational theology in the face of a theology and spirituality of works. He insists that the repentance of those who would thus 'be as Moses' is not genuine repentance, nor does it lead to genuine conversion. In this form of repentance the self never escapes its own orbit but remains fundamentally oriented to itself, in spite of its submission to an external law. The self *uses* the law as a means of its own preservation and deliverance. But it is impossible to redeem oneself, or to escape the legitimate divine wrath which has fallen upon the society by the works of the law. It is likewise impossible to build a new world by our own efforts, even should we be aware of things which must be done. Thus Barth cries out,

> Oh, that we would let ourselves be brought to the point where we shall lay aside, not only our folly and sin, but also our conversion, our awareness, all our resolutions and faculties, our whole 'being as Moses' with this confession: No, what must be done, if we are to be truly free from our chains and burdens, has not yet been done with all that we have done and are doing. We have lighted candles in the darkness; it had to be done; but the New Day has not dawned with them....Something that we cannot acquire from ourselves must be given us; no, not something, but everything;...The best must still be given us, and this is it: to turn to the Lord.[237]

---

[235] Barth, 'Moses-Time and Christ-Time,' 231-232, 233.

[236] Barth, 'Moses-Time and Christ-Time,' 234-235.

[237] Barth, 'Moses-Time and Christ-Time,' 236-237.

In this sermon Barth wrestles with the categories required to ground Christian existence in the forgiveness of sins, refusing to allow any form of self-grounded Christian existence. That which we must have must be given to us, for we are incapable of supplying it for ourselves. In this sense, Christian existence is entirely gratuitous, including its very inception and reception: even our turning to the Lord is gift given to us, by which '*we* are called; *we* are addressed; before *our* eyes the veil is being removed; and *we* see through and into the mystery of him who is perfect—into the mystery of our help and salvation!'[238] Genuine repentance radically reorients the self to a new Lord— Jesus Christ not Moses—not according to works, but in faith, which '*God* works in our hearts through his Spirit.'[239] Through this gift of faith the believer is granted a participation in the victory and liberty of Jesus Christ and may thus 'make a real fight for self-discipline and purity' being freed from the fear and dominion of 'fate,...death and devils'.[240]

Barth's attempt to ground Christian existence in the forgiveness of sins does not mean he relinquishes engagement with the ethical arena, for

> the great truth of the Moses-time is not simply invalidated when our veiled face begins to behold a new vision....Now, if ever, we see how fearfully godless the world is and how necessary it is for her to break away from it. And we shall also be making attempts to bring it to pass. We shall rise from our slumbers. We shall rekindle the candles of faith in a dark world and breathe life into our dead Christianity....Because [Jesus Christ] is here, Moses has passed away. Because Christmas has come, what we *will* with eager zeal, transitory though it may be, has the promise of a large fulfilment. Before this we are standing; but before this there is no standing still.[241]

We see, then, that Barth does not reject the 'lighting of candles' in an absolute sense, but rather anticipates that the Christian community will be actively engaged in the same kind of works that others are, but the underlying motive and form of its engagement will fundamentally differ. The Christian community may participate in lighting the candles of national reconstruction, but will do so specifically with an eye toward reconstruction in light of the world to come rather than simply a reconstruction of the old world of godless darkness and oppression. Being freed from the fear of 'fate, death and devils' the believer is freed to engage the questions confronting the age with courage and grace. For example, as a result of being forgiven it has learned the way of forgiveness. For Barth,

---

[238] Barth, 'Moses-Time and Christ-Time,' 237.
[239] Barth, 'Moses-Time and Christ-Time,' 240.
[240] Barth, 'Moses-Time and Christ-Time,' 240-241.
[241] Barth, 'Moses-Time and Christ-Time,' 237, 239.

[f]orgiveness saves. Forgiveness reconciles. Forgiveness must permeate our politics again; forgiveness and not moral codes; forgiveness and not Moses-zeal! For forgiveness alone makes it possible for us to live together. Forgiveness alone heals wounds. Forgiveness does not make void the laws of God; no indeed, it teaches us to keep them.[242]

As 'the company of people among whom Christ will live on earth until he can reveal himself fully',[243] it is imperative that the church learn to conduct its affairs in love and forgiveness, not only that the head of the church is not disgraced, but also that it might exhibit an alternative way of life in a society threatened with collapse because parties in conflict do not and cannot forgive.[244]

Finally, we see in these sermons a reiteration of the notion of the command of the moment as a way characterising the nature of Christian life:

> God's way of grace is like a mountain trail between two abysses, high up above the lowlands....At every moment only one right step is possible for us, and we must take it. Every other possibility is in reality an impossibility which must end with our precipitous fall into one or the other of the two abysses.[245]

Neither is this way of grace an easy path, for it contains no comfortable spots or resting places. 'We can only incessantly push on,' says Barth, 'paying strict attention only to the steps we are to take.'[246] Barth thus characterises the Christian life as a 'daring venture',[247] a life of obedience to the 'voice of God with its ever-new demands'.[248] The believer is free, but must also be flexible on account of the command which comes anew in every moment, and whose coherence is in God alone.[249]

In conclusion, it is unquestionable that in this preaching series Barth was seeking to form his congregation into a community that actively pursued a life founded in a theological vision of the resurrection, even if that life should take the form and shape of the cross. Although for Barth the community has a certain priority over the individual, nevertheless the individuality of each person cannot be forfeit. Individuals are living subjects who must actively exercise their volitional powers in response to the awakening and empowering grace of the God who encounters them, and to whom they cry. He exhorted his parishioners to live the 'true life' in the midst of a world filled with sham. This

---

[242] Barth, 'Moses-Time and Christ-Time,' 240-241.

[243] Barth, 'A Narrow Way,' 214.

[244] Barth, 'A Narrow Way,' 210, 214-215.

[245] Barth, 'A Narrow Way,' 205.

[246] Barth, 'A Narrow Way,' 206.

[247] Barth, 'The Inward Man,' 262.

[248] Barth, 'A Narrow Way,' 213.

[249] Barth, 'A Narrow Way,' 211.

true life is a life of prayer and activity, of love and forgiveness, courage, purity and hope, and of obedience to the command of the moment. We see in this series of sermons the beginnings of an ethics grounded in the forgiveness of sins, and resulting in the formation of moral community, a community of reconciliation and holiness, and a community which actively seeks to bear witness to the truth of this forgiveness in the broader social context. Fundamental to this ethics is the concept of liberty, which arises from faith and issues in courage, and hope, by which the human agents actively work in anticipation of the larger fulfilment which will occur through the activity of God who makes all things new, and thus, who alone is able to bring into being the new world for which we hope.

Conclusion

The works examined in this chapter provide a clear indication that Barth's theological understanding underwent significant development and change in the two years following the completion of his first commentary on Romans. This development is particularly noticeable with regard to the shift in his eschatology and the prominence of the concept of election, both of which serve to strengthen the objective sovereignty of God over against humanity. The optimistic imagery of life proceeding organically towards eschatological consummation has given way to the more sombre and pessimistic imagery of death as the crisis befalling humanity.

These developments do not, however, suggest complete discontinuity with what has preceded. Barth's characteristic emphasis on divine sovereignty remains, as does the eschatological orientation of his theology, despite the shift in the model used to explicate it. So, too, the severe critique of modern Christianity and idealist theology continues and indeed increases here. In addition, many of the features which characterised his vision of Christian and ecclesial existence in 1915-1918 remain evident in this time of transition and development. There is within these works a surprisingly positive account of the moral agency of the individual in respect of God, although this agency remains firmly anchored in a subordinate and responsive position vis-à-vis divine agency. Barth's notion of the command of the moment is repeated here and corresponds to his understanding of election. So, too, the importance of prayer is reiterated as foundational for authentic Christian existence, which is construed as an 'ec-centric' existence, a life radically oriented to a centre outside of the self in allegiance and obedience.

While Barth again refuses to provide prescriptive guidance with regard to the character of Christian existence and moral community, he does provide an array of virtues that he evidently considers 'typical' of Christian and ecclesial existence. These include attributes of faith, love, liberty, courage, humility, righteousness, obedience, open ears, thanksgiving, contrition and hope. Further, the individual and community exist not for themselves or their own blessedness but for the sake of the world. Their activity echoes the divine movement into the world for the sake of the world, and they exist as a witness to and a parable of God's kingdom. Barth exhorts the Christian community to 'live resurrection' but to do so as a cruciform community in hope of God's ultimate vindication and victory. They are the vanguard of God's kingdom called upon to live the 'true life that men ought to live' amidst the sham life of their compatriots and for their benefit.[250]

Thus, Barth's theological development in this period did not function to evacuate his Christian and ecclesial vision of its major contours and substance. Nevertheless, some questions remain. First, does Barth's heightened emphasis on the objectivity of divine sovereignty over against humanity undermine his hitherto carefully construed relation between divine and human agency? Second, Barth's trenchant criticism of the church has become even more severe in this period. Given the tightening of the eschatological tension that exists between time and eternity, can he delineate a viable ecclesiology which in turn shapes a genuine ecclesial praxis? Third, the situating of ethical life under the rubric of the forgiveness of sins appears to restrict the nature and scope of ethical existence. Will Barth's grounding of the moral agent in the forgiveness of sins sustain the kind of robust vision of Christian and ecclesial existence that characterised his earlier works? In the second edition of his commentary to the Romans, these themes of Barth's new theological framework find their fullest exposition. We now turn to that work to see how Christian and ecclesial existence comes to expression under this new regime.

---

[250] Barth, 'The Individual,' 243-244.

CHAPTER 5

DER RÖMERBRIEF (1922):
A THEORY OF PRAXIS

In reality the entire direction of Barth's thought leads to *praxis:* to faith as the praxis-determining element, not to faith as the enabling of dogmatic utterances—the latter is only a stage on the way to praxis. *Analogia fidei* corresponds at the theoretical level to 'parable' at the level of social praxis; the former is necessary in that it grounds and secures the correct occurrence of the practice of the Christian life.[1]

The attempt to provide a succinct account of Barth's thought as it unfolds in his second commentary on Paul's letter to the Romans might be likened to the attempt to swallow an elephant! G. C. Berkouwer has remarked that this book is the most difficult and demanding of all Barth's works.[2] As we shall see shortly, the book was written in great haste as Barth prepared to leave his pastoral ministry in Safenwil and take up a new appointment as lecturer in Reformed theology at Göttingen. Despite the pressure under which he worked, however, the commentary itself is robust and sinewy, displaying a profound theological vision and bristling with creative insights and imagery. Nevertheless, it will also be seen that the questions raised at the end of the previous chapter are particularly acute in this commentary, because of the new theological framework Barth brings to his work. Indeed, had this framework been applied consistently, it would not only have threatened but actually evacuated human agency and Christian and ecclesial existence of any genuine possibility and meaning. As it is, however, we find that Barth compromises his own framework at critical points with the result that he still manages to provide an account of human agency and to find 'space' for genuine Christian and ecclesial existence.

---

[1] H. Gollwitzer, 'Kingdom of God and Socialism in the Theology of Karl Barth,' in *Karl Barth and Radical Politics* (ed. G. Hunsinger; Philadelphia: Westminster, 1976), 97.

[2] G. C. Berkouwer, *A Half Century of Theology: Movements and Motives* (trans. L. B. Smedes; Grand Rapids: Eerdmans, 1977), 40. Kenneth Oakes has recently produced a reader's guide for Barth's *Romans*: Kenneth Oakes, *Reading Karl Barth: A Companion to Karl Barth's Epistle to the Romans* (Eugene: Cascade Books, 2011). Unfortunately, Oakes' highly recommended book only came into my possession as this book was going to print.

This chapter begins with a summary of the circumstances that led to the composition of this work, before turning to examine the content of the commentary in two parts. In the first part I endeavour to follow the road of thought that Barth treads in chapters 1-11, briefly outlining the major features of Barth's theological vision before focussing on matters of particular relevance to our topic in this book, in particular the nature of human faith in response to revelation, Barth's ecclesiology, and the nature of grace as both indicative and imperative. The section on the imperative of grace is particularly significant for it is at this point that Barth compromises his theological framework in order to establish the grounds upon which he might explicate his ethical vision. That he finds it necessary to compromise his theological framework precisely at *this* point is indicative of the serious ethical intent he brings to his theological reflection. This intent becomes explicit in the second part of the chapter where I examine Barth's exposition of Romans 12-13 in which he treats ethics and certain ethical issues specifically. Finally, because of its chronological and material proximity to Barth's *Romans*, I examine one last lecture, 'The Problem of Ethics Today' which Barth gave during this period of his career.

Review and Revision

In late October 1920 Barth decided to rewrite his commentary on Romans rather than approve a reprint of the original work. In a letter to Thurneysen dated October 27 Barth announced:

> And now a strange and decisive bit of news: when Gogarten, with whom I had so many good conversations by day and night, was gone, suddenly the *Letter to the Romans* began to shed its skin; that is, I received the enlightenment that, as it now stands, it is simply impossible that it should be reprinted; rather it must be reformed root and branch....I have already wired to Munich a 'Halt!' in this regard. But better this delay than that the first version (which now all at once I find overloaded, bloated, etc., wherever I look into it) should continue to give rise to misunderstandings and errors.[3]

Barth's 'enlightenment' was predicated upon two things. First, his theological development had resulted in a sense of personal dissatisfaction with the original work so intense that 'it is simply impossible that it should be reprinted'. Second, it became evident to Barth that his intention in the first edition had been misunderstood at least to some extent by his readers and reviewers. Indeed, in the preface to the second edition Barth is explicit: 'I am bound to say that the more favourable reviews have been the most valuable in compelling me to criticise myself. Their praise has caused me such dismay that I have had sometimes to express the matter otherwise, sometimes even to adopt

---

[3] John D. Smart, ed., *Revolutionary Theology in the Making: Barth-Thurneysen Correspondence, 1914-1925* (London: Epworth, 1964), 53-54.

an entirely different position.'[4] Not all the reviews of Barth were favourable, of course. In July 1920 Adolf Jülicher gave a polite but damning review of Barth's commentary,[5] labelling it a 'practical exposition' rather than a 'strictly scientific exegesis' and taking Barth to task on a number of exegetical points.[6] According to Jülicher, Barth is a pneumatic,[7] whose approach to the relation of spirit and history is 'exactly' that of Origen and the Gnostics, and most especially Marcion who 'held the same position as Karl Barth in his exegesis of Paul'.[8] This judgement was echoed by Karl Ludwig Schmidt, and also by Harnack, who compared Barth to Thomas Münzer. The young Rudolph Bultmann dismissed the book as 'enthusiastic revivalism'.[9]

Nonetheless, it was the positive reviews which, as we saw in the citation above, proved most troubling to Barth, because they indicated that his work was being read in ways which were not true to his intention. In a letter dated May 21, 1919 Barth writes to Thurneysen, 'In the *Brosamen* [*Crumbs*] of the Evangelical Fellowship in Bern there has appeared a review of *Romans*...astonishing in its approval, with the exception of chapter 7.'[10] To Barth, it seemed incredible that such a conservative Pietist group would respond so positively to the commentary. The misunderstanding which arose around the commentary did so primarily because of Barth's use of organological language to describe the relation between God and the world. Philipp Bachmann, for example, wrote that the 'religious relationship of a human being to God.,.appears to him [Barth] with particular emphasis under the viewpoint of the *immanence* of God in the human soul.'[11] From Bachmann Barth learned that his primary metaphor in *Romans 1* was insufficiently

---

[4] Karl Barth, *The Epistle to the Romans* (trans. E. C. Hoskyns; 6th ed. Oxford: Oxford University Press, 1933), 4.

[5] Adolf Jülicher, 'A Modern Interpreter of Paul,' in *The Beginnings of Dialectic Theology* (ed. James M. Robinson; Richmond: John Knox, 1968), 72-81. Note Barth's response to Jülicher's review in his letter to Thurneysen dated July 14, 1920: 'There! Yesterday afternoon Jülicher's long-heralded 42-centimeter shell landed here' (Smart, *Revolutionary Theology*, 52). See also Gogarten's response to Jülicher's review: Friedrich Gogarten, 'The Holy Egotism of the Christian: An Answer to Jülicher's Essay: "A Modern Interpreter of Paul",' in *The Beginnings of Dialectic Theology* (ed. James M. Robinson; Richmond: John Knox, 1968), 82-87.

[6] Jülicher, 'A Modern Interpreter of Paul,' 72-73.

[7] Jülicher, 'A Modern Interpreter of Paul,' 77.

[8] Jülicher, 'A Modern Interpreter of Paul,' 78.

[9] Eberhard Busch, *Karl Barth: His Life from Letters and Autobiographical Texts* (trans. J. Bowden; Philadelphia: Fortress, 1976), 113.

[10] Smart, *Revolutionary Theology*, 46.

[11] Philipp Bachmann, 'Der Römerbrief verdeutscht und vergegenwärtigt: Ein Wort zu K. Barths Römerbrief,' *Neue kirchliche Zeitschrift*, no. 32 (1921): 520, cited in Bruce L. McCormack, *Karl Barth's Critically Realistic Dialectical Theology: Its Genesis and Development 1909-1936* (Oxford: Oxford University Press, 1995), 181.

dialectical because it risked the eschatological reservation and threatened to transform faith into sight.[12] Likewise Emil Brunner, whose review was the first to appear in print, understood Barth to be addressing 'that part of our souls which is not imprisoned in the temporal and finite, but has remained an undisturbed reservoir for the voice of God, undistorted by the "culture" and adaptation to the world of merely human knowledge'.[13] In fact, it was precisely those aspects of the commentary lauded by Brunner which Barth cut from the second edition, as Robinson has perceptively noted.[14]

The issue at stake was the apparent relational nexus posited between God and humanity suggested by the organological language used in *Romans I*. This 'native' relationality, of course, was precisely the very core of the liberalism Barth had sought to dismiss. He had intended to dismantle the very subjectivism that Brunner was now affirming, and began to realise that the conceptuality employed in the first edition of the commentary was not able to bear the freight intended for it: a full revision was necessary if the objective sovereignty of God was to be fully and properly delineated.[15] According to Chalamet, all the sentences which betrayed a kind of *theologia gloriae* in the first edition required substantial correction by a thoroughgoing *theologia crucis* in the second. The romantic terminology of the first edition had proven unable to *respect the distance*. A more critical thought was required.[16] As such, the

---

[12] Christophe Chalamet, *Dialectical Theologians: Wilhelm Herrmann, Karl Barth and Rudolph Bultmann* (Zürich: Theologischer Verlag Zürich, 2005), 130.

[13] Emil Brunner, 'The Epistle to the Romans by Karl Barth: An Up-to-Date, Unmodern Paraphrase,' in *The Beginnings of Dialectical Theology* (ed. James M. Robinson; Richmond: John Knox, 1968), 65. See also page 68 where Brunner speaks once more of 'that divine reservoir in us'. Hart documents a quite extensive interaction that occurred between Barth, Brunner and Thurneysen in November and December 1918 around Barth's commentary as he was preparing the final proofs for publication. See John W. Hart, *Karl Barth Vs. Emil Brunner: The Formation and Dissolution of a Theological Alliance, 1916-1936* (New York: Peter Lang, 2001), 14-21. It is clear that even at this earliest stage of their theological relationship significant differences separated the two men.

[14] James M. Robinson, 'Introduction,' in *The Beginnings of Dialectic Theology* (ed. James M. Robinson; Richmond: John Knox, 1968), 20.

[15] For a discussion of Barth's intent in the first edition of *Romans* to dissolve the liberal notion of a 'native' community of divine and human being, see George Hunsinger, 'Conclusion: Toward A Radical Barth,' in *Karl Barth and Radical Politics* (ed. G. Hunsinger; Philadelphia: Westminster, 1976), 205-211. Note, however, Hunsinger's comment that 'in the 1919 edition, Barth had succeeded only in transferring the relational nexus from the internal experience of the individual to the external experience of history' (Hunsinger, 'Toward A Radical Barth,' 206). The comments by Brunner and Bachmann noted above indicate that Barth did not, in the first edition, actually succeed in loosening his theology from this remnant of liberal theology.

[16] Chalamet, *Dialectical Theologians*, 131, 133-134. See also Willimon's comments in Karl Barth & William H. Willimon, *The Early Preaching of Karl Barth: Fourteen*

second edition was for Barth a much bolder attempt to construct a theology 'which may be better than that of the nineteenth century and the beginning of the twentieth in that it is concerned quite simply with *God* in his independent sovereignty over against man, and especially the religious man, and that seeks to approach God as we believe that we can see him in the Bible'.[17]

Barth set to immediately on the revision of his commentary working at an intense rate so that by the first week of December he was already wrestling with the difficult issues of Romans 3:25, and by mid-February the following year had finished the work up to the end of chapter five.[18] In addition to the publisher's complaint that he must wait for the revision,[19] on January 31, 1921 Barth learnt that the Reformed Churches wanted to appoint him to a newly established chair of Systematic Theology in Göttingen, an appointment he eventually accepted and which increased the pressure to finish *Romans* quickly. In August he wrote that 'this hot summer will ever be unforgettable to me. I amble like a drunk man back and forth between writing desk, dining table, and bed, travelling each kilometre with my eye already on the next one.'[20] The manuscript was finally complete by September 26, 1921, and within a week the Barth family had packed up their belongings for the move from Safenwil to Göttingen.[21]

Before engaging the content of *Romans II* it is well to pause for a moment and consider the *form* of Barth's work. An examination of the various prefaces to each succeeding German edition of his *Romans* commentary reveals Barth providing an extraordinary discussion justifying his hermeneutical method. It is evident that from the time of its initial publication many people have regarded *Romans II* as something other than a *commentary*, and that he is providing an account of his own dogmatic thought which is only very loosely concerned with the text of Paul's letter.[22] In October 1932, however, in the preface to the

---

Sermons with Commentary by William H. Willimon (Louisville: Westminster John Knox, 2009), 119: 'Is that not one of the major reasons why we preachers preach—to lessen the gap between us and God? In this sermon [on 2 Corinthians 1:3-11, January 18, 1920], Barth tries to widen the gap. It is as if Barth claims that nearness with God begins with respect for the distance between us and God and that for us to think that we have at last succeeded in becoming tight with God is to prove how badly we have misunderstood God.'

[17] Cited in Busch, *Karl Barth*, 119. For the original citation (a comment made in 1963) and its context see, Karl Barth, *Fragments Grave and Gay* (trans. Eric Mosbacher; London: Fontana, 1971), 97-98.

[18] See his comments to Thurneysen in Smart, *Revolutionary Theology*, 55-56.

[19] Smart, *Revolutionary Theology*, 54.

[20] Smart, *Revolutionary Theology*, 59.

[21] See Busch, *Karl Barth*, 120, and Smart, *Revolutionary Theology*, 60.

[22] See, for example, the reviews by Rudolph Bultmann, 'Karl Barth's *Epistle to the Romans* in its Second Edition,' in *The Beginnings of Dialectic Theology* (ed. James M. Robinson; Richmond: John Knox, 1968), 100-120, and Adolf Schlatter, 'Karl Barth's

English edition of the commentary, Barth states that his 'sole aim was to interpret Scripture' and that he felt himself 'bound to the actual words of the text, and did not in any way propose to engage...in free theologizing'.[23]

No doubt this immediate and long term appraisal of Barth's commentary was due in no small part to the very distinctive way in which his commentary differed in substance and style from other biblical commentaries written by his contemporaries. There is also little doubt that this difference is due to his hermeneutical approach to the biblical text.[24] Barth sought to hear the Word in, through and under the words of the text, to stand, as it were, alongside Paul in order to see what Paul saw and hear what Paul heard.

What did Barth see as he watched with Paul? He saw the sovereignty of God in his relation to humanity and the strange outworking of his saving purpose. He found the climax of Paul's argument in Romans 11:32, and used this text—rightly or wrongly—as the lens through which he read the remainder of the letter. Barth's comments on this text are revealing:

> *For God hath shut up all unto disobedience, that he might have mercy upon all....*it is precisely this conclusion which brings into prominence the grim disturbance underlying the whole Epistle, and not this Epistle only. Our understanding or our misunderstanding of what Paul means—and not only Paul— by the key words, God, Righteousness, Man, Sin, Grace, Death, Resurrection, Law, Judgement, Salvation, Election, Rejection, Faith, Hope, Love, the Day of the Lord, is tested by whether we do or do not understand this summary. How are we to spell out the meaning of those great words? In what context are we to interpret them? Well! It is this passage which provides the standard by which they can be measured, the balance in which they can all be weighed.[25]

Barth found in this text the key by which to unlock the entire Epistle:

> For by it the final meaning of 'Double Predestination' seeks to make itself known. Pregnant with meaning is the divine *shutting up*; pregnant also is the divine *mercy*. Most significant is the first *all*; most significant also is the second

---

Epistle to the Romans,' in *The Beginnings of Dialectic Theology* (ed. James M. Robinson; Richmond: John Knox, 1968), 121-125. Both reviews were originally published in 1922.

[23] Barth, *Romans II*, ix.

[24] For an excellent introduction to the issues involved with Barth's approach to Paul's letter to the Romans, including the manner in which it is a *commentary*, see John Webster, 'Karl Barth,' in *Reading Romans through the Centuries: From the Early Church to Karl Barth* (ed. Jeffrey P. Greenman & Timothy Larsen; Grand Rapids: Brazos, 2005), 205-223.

[25] Barth, *Romans II*, 421.

*all....*Here it is that we encounter the hidden, unknown, incomprehensible God, to whom nothing is impossible, the Lord, who is as such our Father in Jesus Christ.[26]

While it most certainly remains an open question whether Barth correctly or even adequately interpreted Paul's *Romans*,[27] or whether his use of this particular text as the organising principle of his commentary is legitimate, it will become evident that the issues identified here regarding the hidden and incomprehensible God who deals with humanity after this manner of judgement in order that he might have mercy upon all are the very issues around which Barth has structured his commentary. Whatever our answer to the question just posed, it remains essential to gain a purchase on Barth's orientation to the Epistle, and it is also a salutary reminder not to expect him to address topics in a commentary which might well find more detailed exposition in a formal theological treatise.

Barth's reading of Paul's letter to the Romans views it as an organic whole, which nonetheless has a movement of thought which may be traced. Having followed Paul's argument to its climax in chapter 11 with its concluding doxology, he begins his exposition of chapter twelve by considering the relation of the remaining chapters to what has preceded:

> We are not now starting a new book or even a new chapter of the same book. Paul is not here turning his attention to practical religion, as though it were a second thing side by side with the theory of religion. On the contrary, *the theory, with which we have hitherto been concerned, is the theory of the practice of religion.* We have spoken of the mercies of God, of grace and resurrection, of forgiveness and Spirit, of election and faith....But the ethical problem has nowhere been left out of account....We have not been searching out hidden things for the mere joy of so doing....the concrete situation—this has always been our starting-point. In following the road of thought, this it is which has caused us to enter dark recesses. The need of making decisions of will, the need for action, the world as it is—this it is which has compelled us to consider what the world is, how we are to live in it, and what we are to do in it.[28]

From the start, says Barth, his focus has been on 'the concrete situation'. There is no division between dogmatics and ethics, theory and practice; rather, the theory *is* the theory of the practice of religion. Immediately, then, Barth reminds us that his theology is intentionally and inescapably *moral* theology. Of course for Barth, 'the concrete situation' and 'the world as it is' are understood in very idiosyncratic ways. The 'concrete situation of the world as it is' is not understood by the accumulation of facts and knowledge garnered by

[26] Barth, *Romans II*, 421.
[27] See Stephen Neill, *The Interpretation of the New Testament, 1861-1961* (London: Oxford University Press, 1964), 201-212, especially 208, for a discussion of this point.
[28] Barth, *Romans II*, 426-427, emphasis added ('...daß eben die „Theorie" von der wir herkommen die Theorie der Praxis ist.').

observation of life as it occurs around us. Such a procedure is desperately insufficient because it is not privy to the *truth* of our situation as Barth understands it. The concrete situation of the world as it is, is the reality that we live in a world created by and for God, a world which has sinfully fallen away from him, and which has been redeemed by him through Jesus Christ, and which under the guidance of his sovereign providence hastens towards the consummation of his purpose. All human existence, including Christian and ecclesial existence, occurs within the overarching reality of *this* concrete situation, and is only understood and viable to the degree it conforms with this reality. With these thoughts in mind we may now begin our investigation of 'the theory of the practice of religion' that Barth lays out in his commentary.

Romans 1-11: The *Theory* of Praxis

The Sovereignty of God

Barth's exposition of Paul's Epistle to the Romans opens with a focus on the gospel which 'proclaims a God utterly distinct from men'.[29] The gospel is neither event, experience nor emotion, but rather 'the Word of the Primal Origin of all things' which addresses and confronts humanity with a demand for participation and cooperation. It is a 'communication which presumes faith in the living God, and which creates that which it presumes'.[30] The content of the gospel is Jesus Christ who is the point of intersection between this world which has fallen out of its union with God, and 'the world of the Father, of the Primal Creation, and of the final Redemption'.[31]

Already in the first pages of the commentary both the commonality and the distinction of this commentary to its predecessor become evident. In both commentaries Barth seeks to impress upon his readers the sheer transcendence of God vis-à-vis humanity, the solidarity of all humanity in its culpability before God, as well as the eschatological structure of the divine-human relation.[32] But while the eschatological structuring of the divine-human relation

---

[29] Barth, *Romans II*, 28.
[30] Barth, *Romans II*, 28.
[31] Barth, *Romans II*, 29.
[32] Eberhard Busch, *Karl Barth and the Pietists: The Young Karl Barth's Critique of Pietism and Its Response* (trans. Daniel W. Bloesch; Downers Grove: Inter-Varsity Press, 2004), 78-80. According to Smart, 'the *Romans* of 1922 represents not so much a revision of the 1919 commentary as a reaction against it. It is a turning point almost as sharp as the earlier one in 1914.' See James D. Smart, *The Divided Mind of Modern Theology: Karl Barth and Rudolph Bultmann, 1908-1933* (Philadelphia: Westminster, 1967), 109). The centrality of the three concerns identified above, together with their being common to *both* editions of Barth's commentary, suggests that Smart's contention is overstated.

constitutes a common feature of the two works, it is also evident that it is here that the major distinction between them is found. It will be recalled that in the former commentary the resurrection of Jesus initiated the life-process of the new creation within history. In the later commentary Barth avers that 'the resurrection is the emergence of the necessity of giving glory to God....In the resurrection the new world of the Holy Spirit touches the old world of the flesh, but touches it as a tangent touches a circle, that is, without touching it.'[33]

Barth's famous use of this mathematical metaphor functions in service of the heightened eschatological framework he has brought to this exposition, whereby he strives to remove any possibility of historicising divine revelation or of psychologising the human response of faith to that revelation. In place of the organic imagery of the first commentary which emphasised the interiority of God to all reality, and the growth and progress of divine activity in the world, Barth now insists that 'our world is the world within which God is finally and everywhere—outside'.[34] Indeed, 'the kingdom of God has not "broken forth" upon the earth, not even the tiniest fragment of it'.[35] The world of God is utterly beyond the circumference of the circle; the world of humanity, time and things is entirely bounded by the circumference, which is nothing less than the reality of death and dissolution. Thus, the world of God, of eternity, is entirely closed and inaccessible to humanity, and although humanity still bears a faint memory of its Primal Origin, all that can really be known of God is that God is the Unknown One.[36]

In a distilled summary of his exposition of the initial eight chapters of Paul's Epistle to the Romans Barth provides an outline of the major features of the theological framework he brings to this work:

> God, the pure and absolute boundary and beginning of all that we are and have and do; God, who is distinguished qualitatively from men and from everything human, and must never be identified with anything which we name, or experience, or conceive, or worship, as God; God, who confronts all human disturbance with an unconditional command *Halt!*, and all human rest with an equally unconditional command *Advance!*; God, the Yes in our No and the No in our Yes, the First and the Last, and, consequently, the Unknown, who is never a known thing in the midst of other known things; God, the Lord, the Creator, the Redeemer:—this is the Living God. In the Gospel, in the message of salvation of Jesus Christ, this hidden, living God has revealed himself as he is. Above and beyond the apparently infinite series of possibilities and visibilities in this world there breaks forth, like a flash of lightning, impossibility and invisibility, not as some separate, second, other thing, but as the truth of God which is now hidden,

[33] Barth, *Romans II*, 30.
[34] Barth, *Romans II*, 318. See also Timothy J. Gorringe, *Karl Barth: Against Hegemony* (Oxford: Oxford University Press, 1999), 58.
[35] Barth, *Romans II*, 102.
[36] Barth, *Romans II*, 46-48.

as the Primal Origin to which all things are related, as the dissolution of all relativity, and therefore as the reality of all relative realities. Though—nay rather, because—human life is temporal, finite, and passing to corruption, it is revealed in the gospel that the glorious, triumphant, existential inevitability of the Kingdom of God cannot be hidden. It is made manifest that the knowledge of God—faith working through love—is presented to men as the possibility which, though realised at no particular moment in time, is, nevertheless, open to them at every moment, as the new and realisable possibility of their being what they are in God—his children—cast, as men of this world, under judgement, looking for righteousness and awaiting redemption, but, under grace, already liberated.[37]

In this passage Barth raises a number of issues which could be fruitfully investigated. In the discussion which follows we will limit our examination to the primary issues of divine sovereignty and revelation. Because Christian and ecclesial existence have their genesis in the event of revelation, following sections will take up reflection on the nature of human reception of and response to revelation.

For Barth, the awesome sovereignty and aseity of God are primary. Nonetheless, although God is so utterly sovereign and so utterly distinct from all things human, he is not to be construed as *absolutely* ineffable, for although it is impossible for humanity to discover or attain the knowledge of God in and of themselves, the ineffable God gives himself to be known in the act of revelation. In this way Barth can insist that the way of knowing God proceeds always and only from above to below and never the reverse. Indeed, even when God gives himself to be known by humanity, this knowledge of God never passes over to become a human possession. Even *in* his revelation God remains ever beyond human reach. Thus Barth speaks of revelation as 'the possibility which, though realised at no particular moment in time, is, nevertheless, open to them at every moment'. Revelation therefore has the character of miracle, a humanly-impossible event breaking forth at every moment like lightning from above.

Barth's concern in this commentary was not an abstract formulation of divine ineffability, but the relationship of *this* God to humanity, a relationship which continues even in spite of human sin.[38] Nevertheless, Barth's emphasis on the divine ineffability, together with his actualistic construction of revelation renders an authentic concept of Christian and ecclesial existence problematic. This problem is further exacerbated by the stringent time-eternity dialectic Barth used to explicate the theological vision of this commentary. It has long and often been acknowledged that Barth's claim in the preface of his commentary correctly identifies the abiding concern he brought to his

---

[37] Barth, *Romans II*, 330-332.
[38] Busch, *Karl Barth and the Pietists*, 82.

exposition:[39]

> If I have a system, it is limited to a recognition of what Kierkegaard called the 'infinite qualitative distinction' between time and eternity, and to my regarding this as possessing negative as well as positive significance: 'God is in heaven, and thou art on earth.' The relation between such a God and such a man, and the relation between such a man and such a God, is for me the theme of the Bible and the essence of philosophy.[40]

This distinction between time and eternity, Creator and creature, God and humanity forms the central motif of Barth's exposition. As we have seen, for Barth, this *diastasis* or distance is both ontological and epistemological.[41] Thus, as McCormack has correctly noted, Barth sought to locate God 'beyond the realm of any and every conceptuality readily available to us, whether through a *via negativa* or a *via eminentiae* or a *via causalitatis*. The being of God lies on the far side of the "line of death" which separates the world of time, things and people, together with every conceptuality bound to it, from the eternal.'[42]

For Barth, it is precisely this reality—the 'line of death,' and our existence on *this* side of the line apart from God—which constitutes the *Krisis* that befalls all humanity whether religious or not. It is important that this prominent motif in Barth's commentary—*Krisis*—be carefully interpreted. Berkouwer is surely correct in asserting that for Barth the term is a *theological* description of the all-encompassing judgement of God befalling humanity, and that it does not arise as a result of historical, social, cultural or political pessimism on account of the first World War.[43] Rather, as Berkouwer points out,

---

[39] See, for example, David L. Mueller, *Karl Barth* (Waco: Word, 1972), 24, and Hart, *Karl Barth Vs. Emil Brunner*, 28. For a more complete discussion of Kierkegaard's influence on Barth during this period, see McCormack, *Karl Barth's Dialectical Theology*, 235-240. For a discussion of Barth's relationship to Kierkegaard over the course of his career, see Julia Watkin, *Kierkegaard* (London: Continuum, 1997), 99-101.

[40] Barth, *Romans II*, 10. It is certainly true that in *Romans II* the accent on the negative significance of this relation far outweighs the positive with the result that the positive significance of the relation has often been undeveloped or overlooked. That Barth genuinely intended the positive significance of this relation is, of course, the point of this book.

[41] Hart, *Karl Barth Vs. Emil Brunner*, 29.

[42] McCormack, *Karl Barth's Dialectical Theology*, 248.

[43] G. C. Berkouwer, *The Triumph of Grace in the Theology of Karl Barth* (trans. H. R. Boer; Grand Rapids: Eerdmans, 1956), 25-33. Compare Gorringe's claim that 'the *point* of the infinite qualitative distinction, almost universally misunderstood in Anglo-Saxon circles as a typically Calvinist attack on human sin, is political'. See Gorringe, *Against Hegemony*, 57. While conceding that Barth's use of this dialectic and the accompanying image of *Krisis* does have political implications, Gorringe fails to convince that the political motive was Barth's foremost intent.

[t]he *Krisis* is not intended as a self-evident and automatic negation of man and of all things human, it does not indicate an ontological disposition of the creature as such. Rather, it functions in Barth's theology as a means of unmasking man's own righteousness....The proclamation of the absolute *Krisis* is not a theme of despair, but it opens the only possible way to salvation by shutting off all others. Therefore the *Krisis*, seen from God's point of view, is the reverse side of grace.[44]

Barth utilises the image of the *Krisis* to press his conviction that humanity can never claim the knowledge or experience of God in such a way that they become the possessors of that knowledge, as though God has become an object over which they exercise mastery. *All* human knowledge and experience, and especially *religious* knowledge and experience, arise as elements of this world and are thus subject to the *Krisis*, to death and final dissolution as the great barrier which reduces every human work and hope, together with everything of 'the world of time and things'[45] to nothing but ashes. All humanity finds its common end here and without the miracle of resurrection there is no human possibility of knowledge of God or fellowship with him. Death is the boundary and limit of humanity, an impassable barrier beyond which no human work or hope or righteousness can proceed. There are no avenues by which human beings might reach beyond themselves to lay hold of the divine glory and salvation. Nor are there any means by which religious persons might exalt themselves over against other people as though they had attained a superior status: all alike remain subject to the *Krisis* of dissolution befalling humanity. The universality of the divine *Krisis* functions in service of the establishing of the particularity of the gospel: God alone is the Saviour, and if humanity will be saved it will be as a result of his activity and not their own.

This, of course, is the message of the gospel. The line of death is also a line of grace.[46] Although there remains no human possibility whatsoever of crossing the line of death from this side to that, God is able to cross from that side to this, and has done so and does so. This divine activity of revelation calls forth corresponding though subordinate human action: the response of faith. Because this response of faith signals the commencement of Christian existence, we

---

[44] Berkouwer, *The Triumph of Grace*, 30-31. Although Webb correctly notes that Barth's use of the *Krisis* metaphor has an epistemological function, and that 'the closest Barth does come to a definition is in saying that the *Krisis* is, in the end, God's wrath against original sin', he still prefers to view Barth's use of the metaphor more as a rhetorical device: 'This metaphor is, therefore, ironic: while it seems to say something about God, it really says nothing at all.' See Stephen H. Webb, *Re-Figuring Theology: The Rhetoric of Karl Barth* (New York: State University of New York, 1991), 58, 67-69, 73).

[45] Barth, *Romans II*, 91.

[46] See Barth's sermon 'The Great "But"' in Karl Barth & Eduard Thurneysen, *Come Holy Spirit* (trans. E. G. Homrighausen, K. J. Ernst & G. W. Richards; Edinburgh: T. & T. Clark, 1934), 20.

now turn to examine how Barth conceives it.

Divine Revelation and Human Faith

Revelation is God's action in the world from the other side, a punctiliar action that nonetheless leaves an imprint as a testimony to its occurrence. Barth develops a series of metaphors to describe the impact of revelation, all of which are strongly expressive of divine absence rather than presence.[47] Thus Barth speaks of the tangent which touches the circle—without touching it, of the impress of a signet ring, of the crater which remains after the bomb has exploded, of an empty channel or canal which once ran full of water, of the void at the centre of the wagon wheel, and so on.[48] In this way Barth sought to preclude any possibility of the continuity of revelation or of the other world generally onto the plane of history and time, and so protect the divine subjectivity not only as the source of revelation, but as the subject who retains control of revelation throughout the entire process of its unveiling and reception.[49]

Thus, even in the event of revelation God remains utterly beyond us. That which remains after the event of revelation is neither 'history, time or thing'.[50] That is, the impress of revelation is not revelation itself. Nor is the medium of revelation to be confused with the revelation itself, even if that medium is Jesus Christ![51] Thus Barth can aver that 'Christ is not one of the righteous'[52] and that apart from the resurrection by which Jesus is declared to be the Son of God, he 'has no more significance or insignificance than may be attached to any man or thing or period of history in itself'.[53] For Barth,

[t]he revelation which is in Jesus, because it is the revelation of the righteousness of God, must be the most complete veiling of his incomprehensibility. In Jesus, God becomes veritably a secret: He is made known as the Unknown, speaking in eternal silence; He protects himself from every intimate companionship and from all the impertinence of religion. He becomes a scandal to the Jews and to the Greeks foolishness.[54]

Jesus, in his life and in his death is not the *medium* of revelation, but its *veil*.

---

[47] John C. McDowell, *Hope in Barth's Eschatology: Interrogations and Transformations Beyond Tragedy* (Aldershot: Ashgate, 2000), 78.
[48] See, for example, Barth, *Romans II*, 29, 30, 88, 254.
[49] See McCormack's discussion of Barth's intent to protect the divine subjectivity of revelation in McCormack, *Karl Barth's Dialectical Theology*, 249-251.
[50] Barth, *Romans II*, 29.
[51] See Barth, *Romans II*, 29.
[52] Barth, *Romans II*, 57.
[53] Barth, *Romans II*, 30.
[54] Barth, *Romans II*, 98.

It is only as the light which shines forth from his resurrection illuminates his life and his passion that revelation occurs. The cross itself is a veil which hides the reality, presence and faithfulness of God. It is here, where Jesus enters 'the deepest darkness of human ambiguity', where he 'stands among sinners as a sinner', where he 'sets himself wholly under the judgement under which the world is set' that the righteousness and faithfulness of God is found.[55] Here, where the death of Jesus signals the negation of every human possibility or claim—*My God, my God, why hast thou forsaken me?*—is the end of humanity and the revelation of the faithful God who indeed has not forsaken humanity but who at this point has inaugurated the new era of his saving righteousness.[56] But this end, and this faithfulness is not self-evidently known, but is perceived only when the veil is lifted and the light proceeding from the resurrection discloses the meaning of this man's death. That this unveiling and disclosure occurs at all is pure miracle. So desirous is Barth of locating revelation beyond the reach of human capacity that the cross and the resurrection alone form the locus of God's revealing activity—and even this is perceivable only as God makes himself known. McCormack suggests that Barth, at this time, 'was haunted by the fear that his readers might once again turn the veil into a medium which functions as such, under its own steam, thus failing to preserve the critical distance separating revelation and medium'.[57]

It is immediately apparent that Barth's formulation of revelation at this point of his career is problematic, at least threatening if not destroying the possibility of a real incarnation.[58] Also imperilled is the possibility of a genuine Christian and ecclesial existence, for how is such existence possible when Barth so stridently disallows the extension of revelation onto the plane of history and time? How is the formation of moral community possible when even the recipients of revelation nonetheless remain subject to the all-embracing *Krisis* befalling humanity, never actually attaining to any righteousness or knowledge of God? Thus, once more, Barth's emphasis on the ineffability of God, together with his actualistic formulation of revelation renders Christian and ecclesial

---

[55] Barth, *Romans II*, 97.

[56] Barth, *Romans II*, 97. See also Barth, *Romans II*, 105: 'Consequently, in Jesus also atonement occurs only through the faithfulness of God, *by his blood*: only, that is to say, in the inferno of his complete solidarity with all the sin and weakness and misery of the flesh; in the secret of an occurrence which seems to us wholly negative; in the extinguishing of all the lights—hero, prophet, wonder-worker—which mark the brilliance of human life, a brilliance which shone also in his life.'

[57] McCormack, *Karl Barth's Dialectical Theology*, 251.

[58] It was only in May 1924 while lecturing at Göttingen that Barth found the means to grant the incarnation its proper place in his theology. At that time his discovery of the *anhypostatic-enhypostatic* dogma of the ancient church enabled him to retain the critical distance between God and humanity in revelation without reducing the event of revelation to a mathematical point. See McCormack, *Karl Barth's Dialectical Theology*, 327-328.

existence problematic.

Because Barth conceived his task so thoroughly as the work of 'clearing away the debris' the tonality of his work was iconoclastic and one-sided.[59] In 1956 Barth would criticise the 'powerful one-sidedness' of *Romans II* which led to an 'almost catastrophic opposition of God and the world, God and humanity, God and the church'.[60] He also admitted that the eschatological basis upon which the commentary was built was 'too strong, arbitrary and independent'.[61] We have already noted, however, that Barth's intent in this commentary was to set forth both the negative *and* the positive significance of the infinite qualitative distinction between God and humanity. That his emphasis fell decidedly on the former in no way requires the obliteration of the latter. As McDowell has noted, 'It is inadequate to read Barth's eschatology as a purely negatively critical mode of discourse and a mere cipher for the repudiation of all that is finite, serving therein to codify the divine-human *diastasis*.'[62] Indeed, careful attention to Barth's commentary does indicate that even in this work he found a place for human agency and Christian and ecclesial existence, as we shall now see.

When Barth considers the subjective aspect of the event of revelation he does not shrink from using the language of experience:

> How is it that there exist any far-seeing and intelligent men—real men, living in the real world—who, like the Jews of the time of Jesus, have *caught a glimpse* of the Last Things, and to whom waiting upon God, upon God alone, is well known? In such men a miracle has occurred above, behind, and in them. They have *encountered* the grace of God; have *met* the incomprehensibility of God, as Job did—out of the whirlwind. *They were terrified* in their ungodliness and unrighteousness and were *shaken* out of their dreaming....[T]hey *heard* the indiscoverable, *saw* the negation of God! *Felt* the barrier of the judgement, the paradox of existence, and, hopeful in their distress, divined the meaning of life. *They came to themselves in fear and awe and trembling* and in—'clarity of sight.' In the presence of God *they were compelled* to stand still. What, then, is all this?...The encounter of grace depends upon no human possession....He who has been chosen by God cannot say that he has chosen God.[63]

In language reminiscent of his earlier works Barth construes the event of

---

[59] See Archibald James Spencer, *Clearing a Space for Human Action: Ethical Ontology in the Theology of Karl Barth* (New York: Peter Lang, 2003), 150-151, and McDowell, *Hope in Barth's Eschatology*, 76.

[60] Karl Barth, *The Humanity of God* (trans. J. Weiser & J. N. Thomas; Louisville: John Knox, 1960), 38-39.

[61] Karl Barth, *Church Dogmatics II/1: The Doctrine of God* (ed. G. W. Bromiley & T. F. Torrance, trans. W. B. Johnston, T. H. L. Parker, H. Knight & J. L. M. Haire; Edinburgh: T. & T. Clark, 1957), 635.

[62] McDowell, *Hope in Barth's Eschatology*, 83.

[63] Barth, *Romans II*, 59, emphasis added; cf. 273.

revelation as personal encounter in which the human agent is graciously confronted with the reality of God in his judgement and mercy. In the 'eternal "Moment" of apprehension,...in order that our vision may have space to perceive, not what men think and will and do, but what God thinks and wills and does', we are 'encountered' by the truth 'from beyond a frontier we have never crossed; it is as though we had been transfixed by an arrow launched at us from beyond an impassable river'.[64] The agent of this encounter is the Holy Spirit: 'As a tumbler sings when it is touched, so we and our world are touched in faith by the Spirit of God, who is the eternal Yes....He is the miraculous factor in faith, its beginning and its end....He creates the new subject of the man who stands upright in the presence of God.'[65]

Thus for Barth, faith is a miraculous *effect*, occurring in a person as a result of the gracious election of God through the Holy Spirit. Indeed, in his discussion of Romans 4 he refers to faith as 'absolute Miracle...pure Beginning...primal Creation'.[66] 'He who says *God*,' intones Barth, 'says *miracle*':

> God encounters the soul as 'either-or'; and this involves acceptance or rejection, affirmation or denial, waking or sleeping, apprehension or misapprehension. We, however, are capable only of rejecting, denying, sleeping, and misapprehending. ...In so far as there is human comprehension and affirmation of God, in so far as spiritual experience is directed towards God, receives its impress from him, and possesses the form of faith, there has occurred what is impossible, the paradox and the miracle.[67]

This divine work is not a single operation which once accomplished endures forever, but, reflecting the actualistic structuring of revelation, is and must be ever-renewed in the eternal 'Moment' which is, as we have already seen, open to us at every moment of time. Faith, then, is the consequence of existential response to the presence and reality of God as he makes himself known to us 'in the moment':

> Faith is the ground, the new order, the light, where *boasting* ends and the true righteousness of God begins. Faith is not a foundation upon which men can emplace themselves...not a system under which they can arrange their lives....*The law of faith* is the place where we are established by God. There, there is nothing but God himself, God only; and there the place is no place; for it is the

---

[64] Barth, *Romans II*, 237-238. Note that Barth uses the concept of the eternal 'Moment' no fewer than 80 times in his commentary—almost as often as the term *Krisis* (93 times). For usage relevant in this context see especially, Barth, *Romans II*, 109-112, 331. The two concepts are related: it is the revelation of God occurring in the Moment which precipitates the *Krisis* at the existential level.

[65] Barth, *Romans II*, 157-158.

[66] Barth, *Romans II*, 140.

[67] Barth, *Romans II*, 120.

'Moment' when men are moved by God, by the true God, the Creator and redeemer of men and of all human things; the 'Moment' when men surrender themselves and all that they are to God. The 'Moment' of the movement of men by God is beyond men, it cannot be enclosed in a system or a method or a 'way.' It rests in the good pleasure of God, and its occasion is to be sought and found only in him.[68]

Once more Barth protects the divine sovereignty of revelation by grounding both its origin and reception in the concept of election, and by locating its dynamic within the time-eternity dialectic. Those whose lives are thus awakened by God find themselves standing in a place which is 'no place'. Just as God's election 'all hangs in the air' as 'pure, absolute, vertical miracle',[69] so the person awakened to faith has 'been lifted up into the air, so that we have no standing-place except the protection of God'.[70] Christian faith and salvation, therefore, bears the character of the resurrection, that is, of an 'impossible possibility': 'The righteousness of God is our standing-place in the air—that is to say, where there is no human possibility of standing—whose foundations are laid by God himself and supported always by him only; the place where we are wholly in his hands for favour or disfavour.'[71]

Further, as was the case with his lecture on 'Biblical Questions, Insights and Vistas,' so here: Barth utilises the concept of election to establish the priority of divine initiative and agency over human initiative and agency. He does not thereby abolish human agency but once more orders it in the particular manner we have previously noted. Human agency is genuine, just as human experience is genuine. Nevertheless, it ever remains subordinate to the greater and primary agency of God.

Here, however, another evident problem arises with regard to our topic. By defining faith as miracle, and by situating Christian existence 'in mid-air' and referring to it as an 'impossible possibility', Barth appears to jettison any possibility of a genuine Christian *life*, for if the extent of faith is limited to the moment of revelation it is clear that there can be no *life* of faith. Thus, despite his attempt to secure a place for authentic human response, such agency remains threatened by the theological framework Barth has employed. Nevertheless, Barth has more to say as regards the nature of faith.

The Critique of Religion and the Nature of Faith

Further insight into Barth's conception of the nature of faith and its implications for Christian and ecclesial existence at this juncture of his career may be gained by briefly noting how his critique of religion comes to

---

[68] Barth, *Romans II*, 110.

[69] Barth, *Romans II*, 60.

[70] Barth, *Romans II*, 163.

[71] Barth, *Romans II*, 94. See also pp. 58 and 292-293 for further use of similar imagery.

expression in the present work. Here, as before, Barth is relentless in his attack on human religion, although he also manages to find a positive role for it. In fact, religion, though a thoroughly human reality ever subject to the dissolution of the *Krisis*,[72] arises as a result of recollection of prior revelation and exists as a testimony to revelation once given.[73] In *Romans II* Barth is able to refer to religion as 'the unavoidable reflection in the soul—in experience—of the miracle of faith which has occurred to the soul. The church, from which we can never escape, is the canalisation in history of that divine transaction in men which can never become a matter of history.'[74] As the canal where the waters of revelation once ran; that is, as the impress of revelation, religion exists and finds its true purpose and validity in being a sign or witness to the reality which lies beyond the horizon of this world and this age.[75] Religion, then, has a particular and positive mission:

> The utter godlessness of the course of history does not alter the fact that it is marked everywhere by peculiar impressions of revelation, by opportunities and open doors, which, when seen from God's side, can summon men to recollection and knowledge. Whenever men wait upon God, they possess a mission and a character *indelebilis*, even though God be shrouded from their eyes and from the eyes of all in utter incomprehensibility…God never reveals himself to no purpose. Where there is *law*, even if it be nought but burnt out cinders, there is a word of the faithfulness of God.[76]

Two problems arise for religion, however. The first is religion's inability to reach and attain that towards which it points. Despite being an impress of revelation, religion, as a human reality, is not spared the all-encompassing *Krisis* befalling humanity: the line of death passes through religion also.[77] Religion may provide a context in which humanity can await the Moment of revelation, but it cannot produce or attain that Moment itself.[78] Second, and for Barth this is the heart of the matter, religion is ever tempted to become a thing in itself, to dwell within the empty canal and become busily engaged in preserving the impress.[79] Not content to be simply a sign pointing away from itself toward that other reality, it seeks to become a significant reality in its own

---

[72] Barth, *Romans II*, 127.

[73] Barth, *Romans II*, 65, 230.

[74] Barth, *Romans II*, 129. Note that Barth's reference to religion and church in this context is not limited to Christianity but is inclusive of all religious expression, particularly in its more formal or institutional aspects.

[75] Barth, *Romans II*, 129.

[76] Barth, *Romans II*, 80.

[77] Barth, *Romans II*, 127.

[78] Barth, *Romans II*, 138

[79] Barth, *Romans II*, 66.

right.[80] True religion, however, can be no more than a sign pointing to that which eternally precedes it, and which extends infinitely beyond it. As soon as religion or the church claims to possess the reality to which it points, as soon as it seeks or boasts to be anything more than a void in which the gospel reveals itself, it has embraced the *No-God* of this world, and fallen under the sentence of judgement.[81] Whenever the characteristic marks of Christianity become possession and self-sufficiency rather than deprivation and hope, 'there emerges, instead of the community of Christ, Christendom, an ineffective peace-pact or compromise with that existence which, moving with its own momentum, lies on this side [of the] resurrection'.[82]

Religion acts upon humanity 'like a drug which has been extremely skilfully administered'.[83] By means of religion humanity seeks to inoculate itself against the righteousness of God by parading its own righteousness. The religious person seeks a place to stand where they are protected from the impending *Krisis*. But this is precisely the great sinfulness and deception of religion:

> Transforming time into eternity, and therefore eternity into time, they stretch themselves beyond the boundary of death, rob the Unknown God of what is his, push themselves into his domain, and depress him to their own level. Forgetting the awful gulf by which they are separated from him, they enter upon a relation with him which would be possible only if he were not God. They make him a thing in this world, and set him in the midst of other things.[84]

It is of signal importance that we recognise that it is *this* form of religious activity that Barth assails. *This* form of religion, to which 'men cling...with a bourgeois tenacity...must die'.[85] The great problem with this form of piety is the *unbroken* confidence of its practitioners, who believe it to be 'deathless and unshattered'.[86] Thus, Barth characterises the 'mature and well-balanced man, standing firmly with both feet on the earth, who has never been lamed and broken and half-blinded by the scandal of his life' as a godless man.[87] Clearly his targets here, as in the first commentary, are the respectable bourgeoisie of Liberalism and Pietism who use religion as a means of attaining and proclaiming their own righteousness.[88] For Barth, however, a faith which is not

---

[80] Barth, *Romans II*, 129.

[81] Barth, *Romans II*, 36, 74, 136-137.

[82] Barth, *Romans II*, 36-37.

[83] Barth, *Romans II*, 236.

[84] Barth, *Romans II*, 244.

[85] Barth, *Romans II*, 238.

[86] Barth, *Romans II*, 238.

[87] Barth, *Romans II*, 235.

[88] Busch has shown that, in contrast to the first edition of the commentary, Barth 'no longer has any vital interest in *pursuing* a discussion with Pietism' in his second edition (emphasis added). This is not to say, however, that he had no *critique* to bring against

a 'standing in mid-air,' a faith which is not inherently 'broken' is not genuine faith.[89]

In this commentary Barth also adopts the image of 'unbrokenness' to describe the fallen existence of humanity. Such humanity is 'unbroken' in heart and mind and as such is incapable of rightly understanding the true nature of existence or of constructing truly moral conduct.[90] It marches confidently along 'the unbroken road' in the wisdom of night towards dissolution and death, not knowing that 'there is no other relation to God save that which appears upon the road along which Job travelled'.[91] Humanity will remain 'unbroken' unless and until they are confronted by the reality of God in the moment of *Krisis*.

But while Barth uses this image primarily as a description of fallen humanity, he also applies it, as we have seen, to the attempt of the religious person to remain 'unbroken' in the world, of the one who seeks to find a place of security where one may be sure of one's own rightness over against others, because they assume a sure and comprehensive knowledge of God. Religion seeks to 'discover and pursue a road which is unbroken by any radical negation and which claims to stretch from human nature to the divine nature'.[92] But such an existence is now impossible for those enlightened in the Moment of revelation, and the way of direct and unbroken apprehension of God must be abandoned at all points.[93]

It is at this point that we are led to the core of Barth's thought regarding the nature of faith. For Barth, faith is nothing other than human fidelity encountering the faithfulness of God.[94] What this means in practice, however, is perceived only at the cross. We have earlier noted Barth's contention that the faithfulness of God is revealed in the utter negation of all human possibility represented in Jesus' death on the cross, for in his death Jesus has forsaken every human possibility by which he might lodge a claim against God, and is

---

the Pietists. Again, Busch does acknowledge that 'a definite critique of Pietism is also found in the second *Epistle to the Romans*'. See Busch, *Karl Barth and the Pietists*, 90, 94.

[89] For Barth's use of the imagery of 'standing in mid-air' see, for example, Barth, *Romans II*, 58, 60, 94, 163, 230, 292.

[90] See, for example, Barth, *Romans II*, 48-49, 291. It is important to note Barth's dual use of the 'unbroken' imagery here, of *both* the attempt of the religious person to remain 'unbroken' in this world and so shield themselves from the *Krisis*, *and* as a description of the 'unbroken' (*ungebrochene*) heart and mind of humanity in its fallen condition. Fallen humanity is 'broken' in its alienation from God, certainly, but this 'brokenness' is consequent upon their 'unbroken' self-confident and self-chosen 'wisdom of death'. See Karl Barth, *Der Römerbrief (Zweite Fassung) 1922* (Zürich: Theologischer Verlag Zürich, 1940; 17th Abdruck, 2011), 25-26.

[91] Barth, *Romans II*, 48; cf. 52-54, 307.

[92] Barth, *Romans II*, 210.

[93] Barth, *Romans II*, 291, 355.

[94] Barth, *Romans II*, 32, 39, 42.

upheld by God alone. According to Barth, 'his entering within the deepest darkness of human ambiguity and abiding within it is *the* faithfulness. The life of Jesus is perfected obedience to the will of the faithful God.'[95] For Barth, then, faith is the relinquishing of every support whereby humanity might seek to support itself. It entails our bowing, in free and full acknowledgement of our sinfulness and blameworthiness and of the justness of his judgement, under the divine judgement that legitimately falls upon us.[96]

In this way Barth has posited Jesus in his death as the paradigm and analogy of Christian faith and existence. Faith is the antithesis of possession and is characterised rather by non-possession. There is 'no such thing as mature and assured possession of faith: regarded psychologically, it is always a leap into the darkness of the unknown, a flight into empty air'.[97] Barth speaks of faith as a void, and as a hollow space. It 'means motionlessness, silence, worship—it means not-knowing'.[98] Faith corresponds to the fear of the Lord arising from the *Krisis* befalling the individual in the Moment.[99] Thus, 'faith is to fear and love God above all things; to fear and love him as he is, and not as we think him to be. Faith is to bow ourselves under the judgement by which the whole relationship of God and man is governed....Faith is born in fear and trembling from the knowledge that God is God.'[100]

Christian faith, then, is ever the matter of divine miracle confronting and awakening the human agent to the fear and love of God. Christian existence in faith takes the form of an uncertain pilgrimage in which the person is 'wholly directed towards God and towards him only'.[101] Such a person must be prepared always for 'surrender and dissolution, ready always to decrease in honour, ever tireless in descending the ladder of renunciation and death. To be pilgrims means that Christians must perpetually return to the starting-point of that naked humanity which is absolute poverty and utter insecurity.[102] Nor may Christians find comfort or significance in self-abnegation as though their *negative* experience and work has religious merit and may function as a foundation or evidence of faith:

> The man who boasts that he possesses something which justifies him before God and man, even if that something be his own insecurity and brokenness, still retains confidence in human self-justification....No work, be it most delicately spiritual, or be it even a work of self-negation, is worthy of serious attention. In fact, our experience is that which we have not experienced; our religion consists in the

[95] Barth, *Romans II*, 97.
[96] Barth, *Romans II*, 83, 367.
[97] Barth, *Romans II*, 98; cf. 206.
[98] Barth, *Romans II*, 201-202; cf. 88.
[99] Barth, *Romans II*, 136-137, 151, 167.
[100] Barth, *Romans II*, 367, 411; cf. 39.
[101] Barth, *Romans II*, 132.
[102] Barth, *Romans II*, 132.

dissolution of religion; our law is the complete disestablishment of all human experience and knowledge and action and possession.[103]

This section has endeavoured to show that Barth's critique of religion functions to illuminate the cruciform nature of human faith and agency in his theology. But once more the question must be put regarding the adequacy of Barth's construal of these concepts. It is already apparent that Barth's tightening of the eschatological horizon results in a stringent ordering of the divine-human relation in which any possibility for genuine Christian existence beyond the *Moment* of revelation is seriously imperilled. Obviously this poses a great difficulty for the present work which seeks to show that Barth has developed his theology with the specific aim of forming and shaping moral community. In fact, if the above citation is accepted at face value, that is, if it is actually the case that 'our religion consists in the dissolution of religion; our law is the complete disestablishment of all human experience and knowledge and action and possession', then it appears that the Barth has reduced the 'space' for human activity to the point of revelation alone, and that no elongation of this existence onto the plane of time and history can occur. This leads to the conclusion that, as it presently stands, Barth is unable to provide a coherent account of Christian existence. Whether this is the case with regard to his understanding of *ecclesial* existence is the focus of the next section.

The Church in Romans II

In his examination of the church in Barth's commentary Colm O'Grady opines that 'his doctrine on the Church is but another facet of his presentation of the one main theme....simply the description of God and man infinitely qualitatively distinct, yet related *solo Deo*'.[104] According to O'Grady, this has dire implications:

> Since Christianity is completely unhistorical and eschatological, and the crisis of everything historical, it follows that a visible, historical Church can have no 'part' in it. A visible Church is for him nothing but man's greatest 'titanic' achievement, the ultimate manifestation of his opposition to the Gospel....As a result, Barth's whole 'ecclesiology' is nothing but a denial of the Church, an out-and-out attack on the existing historical Church.[105]

O'Grady's claim that 'Barth's whole ecclesiology is nothing but a denial of the Church' overstates the case. We have already seen that Barth can posit a positive role for the church in the divine economy as the impress of revelation,

---

[103] Barth, *Romans II*, 110.
[104] Colm O'Grady, *The Church in the Theology of Karl Barth* (London: Geoffrey Chapman, 1968), 21, 34.
[105] O'Grady, *The Church in the Theology of Karl Barth*, 34-35.

that is, the sign and witness to the revelation which has previously occurred, and a location where people may wait in hope for further revelation. Nevertheless, it must be acknowledged with Kimlyn Bender that this role was 'so limited as to make a coherent ecclesiology impossible'.[106] Bender continues:

> Completely absent in the *Romans* commentary is a positive and constructive account of the church as a new community in the world, or a discussion of the church in the traditional terminology of its being the people of God, the body of Christ, or the fellowship of the Holy Spirit. Nor is there any sustained discussion of the church's teaching, worship, or practices from a positive standpoint. Perhaps most conspicuously absent is any type of connection between the resurrection and the church in the light of this event. In the *Romans* commentary the church seems to be a community of sin that *precedes and opposes* the resurrection more than a new community that is established *in the light of and through* the resurrection. In short, Barth seems to have emphasised the division, or *diastasis*, between the kingdom and the church to such a degree as to have neglected their positive relation, identifying the church's visibility and historicity with its sin in an over-simplified manner.[107]

It is possible to respond to Bender's observation with the counter-observation that Barth was writing a *commentary* rather than a treatise on ecclesiology, and so it is not surprising that these more systematic concerns remain unaddressed.[108] To do so, however, avoids the evident emphasis on ecclesiology that Barth wished to bring to his commentary, especially in his treatment of chapters nine through eleven of Paul's Epistle. In a quite significant departure from the first edition of his commentary, Barth entitles his comment on these chapters the 'The Tribulation of the Church,' 'The Guilt of the Church' and 'The Hope of the Church,' respectively.[109] Bender's criticism, then, of the way in which Barth has constructed his ecclesiology within the

---

[106] Kimlyn J. Bender, *Karl Barth's Christological Ecclesiology* (Aldershot: Ashgate, 2005), 36.

[107] Bender, *Karl Barth's Christological Ecclesiology*, 36.

[108] It is noteworthy, however, that even in his later career Barth resisted discussion of the church in these terms. In his 1948 address at the Amsterdam Assembly which saw the establishment of the World Council of Churches, Barth declares that, 'No matter how sincere, all praise of the Church as the Body and Bride of Christ, as the City, Colony, People, and Flock of God then becomes spurious and untrustworthy, for all these New Testament insights and words are related to the living congregation of the living Lord Jesus Christ, and to it alone. No matter how earnest, all discussion of the nature and unity of the Church, its order and task, its inner life and its commission in the world then leads into uninteresting dead-ends. It is to be feared that no matter how honourable and zealous, all concern about the Church not focused concretely on this reality must ultimately be in vain.' See Karl Barth, *God Here and Now* (trans. Paul M. van Buren; 2003 *Classics* ed. London: Routledge, 1964), 75-76.

[109] In the first edition the chapters are entitled simply 'Tribulation,' 'Guilt' and 'Hope.'

constraints of the divine-human *diastasis* is not without some justification. While it is correct, however, to assert that he has not provided a comprehensive and coherent ecclesiology, it is not the case that his account amounts to a 'denial of the church,' as O'Grady has asserted. Rather, Barth employed the eschatological *diastasis* between God and humanity as a critical tool to demolish any form of synthesis or identification between the church and culture and so to provide the 'space' for the emergence of a new form of Christian and ecclesial existence.

Barth begins his discussion by accusing the church of a thorough-going attempt to domesticate God and the gospel:

> The Church is situated on this side of the abyss which separates men from God...the place where the eternity of revelation is transformed into a temporal, concrete, directly visible thing in this world....In the church, faith, hope, and love are directly possessed, and the Kingdom of God directly awaited, with the result that men band themselves together to inaugurate it, as though it were a *thing* which men could have and await and work for. To a greater or lesser extent, the Church is a vigorous and extensive attempt to humanize the divine....From this it is obvious that the opposition between the Church and the Gospel is final and all-embracing: the Gospel dissolves the Church, and the Church dissolves the Gospel.[110]

Barth thus insists that the church as a human and historical reality stands in solidarity with every other human possibility, that is, as subject to divine judgement. The tribulation of the church consists in the fact that although it is 'that visibility which forces invisibility upon our notice, that humanity which directs our attention towards God',[111] the church itself can never actually apprehend or possess or convey the reality of God regardless of its claim to the contrary. Barth defines the church as 'the fellowship of men who proclaim the Word of God and hear it'. Nevertheless, because of the inadequacy of human lips and ears 'the Church is condemned by that which establishes it, and is broken in pieces upon its foundations'.[112] Thus, the Word of God is the *theme* of the church by which it is both established and condemned, and divided into the 'Church of Esau' and the 'Church of Jacob'.

When Barth speaks of the Church of Esau he is speaking of the human, visible and historical church. It is to this church that Barth refers when he so stridently warns of the opposition between church and gospel, and declares that 'the Gospel dissolves the Church, and the Church dissolves the Gospel'.[113] Barth sees in the historical and institutional church a thorough-going attempt by humanity to defend itself against the righteousness of God by the establishing

---

[110] Barth, *Romans II*, 332-333.
[111] Barth, *Romans II*, 337.
[112] Barth, *Romans II*, 341.
[113] Barth, *Romans II*, 332-333.

of its own righteousness, and the pursuit of its own self-grounded life and success.[114] Such behaviour amounts to a betrayal of God and the gospel. Thus, not only is the church the Church of Esau, but also of Judas, Ahab and Jezebel![115] It betrays God and the gospel by refusing to acknowledge and bow before the fiery judgement of God's supreme righteousness. Its guilt is precisely its failure to give God the honour due to him by acknowledging the qualitative distinction between God and humanity, the 'recollection' of which is 'the life of the church'.[116] Instead it 'enthrones piety' in an attempt to present itself worthy of mercy, and 'needs to be continually reminded of the most serious of all symptoms. It was the Church, not the world, which crucified Christ.'[117]

The Church of Jacob, on the other hand, is no church in time: it is 'the unobservable, unknowable, and impossible Church, capable neither of expansion nor of contraction; it has neither place nor name nor history'.[118] The Church of Jacob is the invisible church which exists only in the miracle and moment of revelation. Barth clearly applies the major structural motif of his commentary to his concept of the church so that the Church of Jacob is understood as touching the Church of Esau as the tangent touches the circle: that is, without touching it. In the secret of predestination God has determined that all humanity are united under judgement: 'In its presence they all stand on one line—for Jacob is always Esau also, and in the eternal "Moment" of revelation Esau is also Jacob....But this victory is hidden from us in every moment of time. We cannot escape the duality, since the visible Jacob is for us Esau, and we can only conceive of Jacob as the unobservable Esau.'[119]

Because the Church of Esau is the Church of Jacob only in the moment and miracle of revelation, it can never presume to be the Church of Jacob, or to possess the reality or blessing of God in itself. Barth makes this move, however, not in order to deny the church, but to undermine the church-culture synthesis which had developed in Europe prior to the War; to 'dethrone' the church and to clear the space for the emergence of a different kind of ecclesial existence. According to Barth, once the church is dethroned it *may* be justified *if* in being dethroned it is also the recipient of revelation. 'The Gospel which we proclaim,' says Barth, 'is that this does occur, has occurred, and will occur; and that this occurrence is Truth. When the Truth occurs...the Church—the whole Church and every Church—has not been cast off. The Church of Jacob is already *at this present time* in the midst of the Church of Esau.'[120]

---

[114] Barth, *Romans II*, 344, 368-369.
[115] Barth, *Romans II*, 391, 394.
[116] Barth, *Romans II*, 365.
[117] Barth, *Romans II*, 398, 389.
[118] Barth, *Romans II*, 342.
[119] Barth, *Romans II*, 347-348.
[120] Barth, *Romans II*, 396.

As demonstrated in the previous section, Barth's critique of religion functioned to illuminate his understanding of the nature of human faith and agency. So here, Barth's rhetoric functions, not to deny the possibility of a genuine and faithful church, but to establish the only conditions by which it might emerge. God troubles and disturbs the church and, on account of its guilt, hands it over to tribulation in order that it may thereby be *opened* to God, which is the goal of its tribulation.[121] And, as was also the case in the previous section, genuine ecclesial existence is the product of a faith given in the moment of revelation, and issuing in a love and fear of the Lord that calls earnestly upon God and keeps his commandments, while it remains ever conscious that in and of itself, it is the Church of Esau.[122]

When Barth speaks of the possibility of the faithfulness of the church, therefore, he does so under the rubric of repentance:

> Were the Church to appear before men as a Church under judgement...it would be the Church of God. The Church, however, which sings its triumphs and trims and popularises and modernises itself, in order to minister to and satisfy every need except the one!; the Church which, in spite of many exposures, is still satisfied with itself, and, like quicksilver, still seeks and finds its own level; such a Church can never succeed, be it never so zealous, never so active in ridding itself of its failings and blemishes. With or without offences, it can never be the Church of God, because it is ignorant of the meaning of repentance.[123]

In typical fashion Barth construes repentance in dialectical terms. He refers to repentance as a *presupposition* required of the church as a means by which the church might encounter God, and yet also insists that this is not a presupposition that the church can accomplish in and of itself.[124] Rather, it is 'the new orientation of all possible human activity'.[125] The Word has drawn near to humanity and *is* near to us, but

> because it is the Word of Christ, it is beyond our hearing and beyond our speaking; for, to hear it and to proclaim it—we must wait. Weighed down by the ambiguity of our existence, we must await....The Word is nigh unto us. Wherever we cast our eye, the dynamite is prepared and ready to explode. But if there is no explosion, or if something less final takes place, can we not take just the smallest risk which is, in fact, the greatest? Are we always to prefer a thousand other days to one day in the outer courts of the Lord? Shall we never permit our hands to be empty, that we may grasp what only empty hands can grasp?...Impossibility

---

[121] Barth, *Romans II*, 402-403.
[122] Barth, *Romans II*, 342-343, 366-368, 411.
[123] Barth, *Romans II*, 370.
[124] Barth, *Romans II*, 379-380, 386.
[125] Barth, *Romans II*, 380.

presses upon us, breaks over us, is indeed already present. Impossibility is more possible than everything which we hold to be possible.[126]

It is clear that Barth does, in some sense at least, believe that the church is able to present itself before God *in hope*. The church may, and indeed, *must* be a community who wait upon God in hope that revelation may occur once more.[127] Furthermore, it may present itself before God with empty hands, having released from its grasp everything in which it has hitherto trusted, acknowledging its own guilt worthiness before God, bowing before his judgement in hope of his mercy.

For Barth, repentance is the ever renewed and ever necessary acknowledgement of the sovereignty and righteousness of God over against all human righteousness, the relentless honouring of God in 'his pre-eminence over all human eminence'.[128] It is

preparedness to enter upon the divine, seasonable, eschatological possibility, to bow before the wrath and before the mercy of God, to be accessible to the one-sided, passionate, and exclusive claim which God makes upon men. Repentance means being open to the strangeness of resurrection and to the free and boundless initiative of faith.[129]

It involves the church in a persistent denial of every attempt to establish its own righteousness, or its own relevance in the eyes of the world or of humanity. Only then is the church 'what men look for in it and expect from it. The Church is the place of fruitful and hopeful repentance; and it is nothing else.'[130]

Repentance also includes obedience, which means 'being committed to a particular course of action, a readiness to surrender individual freedom of movement to the free movement of God, a readiness to offer up everything that the known man of the world supposes to be important and necessary and right'.[131] Barth characterises the obedience which is congruent to the gospel as *freedom*, but it is the limited freedom wherein the human agent is free to 'move along the same road backwards and forwards again and again without ever standing still' between judgement and mercy, following as it were, the free and uninterrupted motion of a pendulum.[132]

In sum, humanly speaking and apart from God, the church has no hope.[133]

---

[126] Barth, *Romans II*, 380-381.
[127] Barth, *Romans II*, 414-415.
[128] Barth, *Romans II*, 373.
[129] Barth, *Romans II*, 386.
[130] Barth, *Romans II*, 377-378.
[131] Barth, *Romans II*, 386-387.
[132] Barth, *Romans II*, 387.
[133] Barth, *Romans II*, 393.

By means, however, of his concept of double predestination, Barth grounds the hope of the church in God alone. The one God who hands the church over to tribulation after the manner of the crucifixion of Jesus, and who so frees himself from every human claim, is also the one God who according to his own free grace brings forth in the church the resurrection of Christ.[134] Rejection issues in election, but only in hope. The one God slays in order to make alive, condemns in order to justify, hands over to the judgement of death in order to bring forth salvation unto life. In this way the church embodies and witnesses to the general situation of all humanity. Although the pinnacle of human endeavour with regard to God, it finds itself judged, rejected, cast down to hell, and yet—reconciled.[135] The church, therefore, is the theatre in which the judgement and grace of double predestination is set forth so that humanity may be 'made aware that there is always in its midst a place where the consequences of its inherent possibilities are fully worked out, and where its proved impossibility makes room for the appearance of the possibility of God. And so we know that rejection is not the final word either for humanity as a whole or for the Church.'[136]

Interlude: An inconsistency in Barth's Theology

The problems which we have noted in previous sections are present also in Barth's discussion of the church. It is simply the case that Barth's use of the infinite qualitative distinction to structure the divine-creaturely relation, and his restriction of the inter-play of divine and human agency to the actualistic moment of revelation reduces the event and reality of both Christian and ecclesial existence to a mathematical point which must be ever-renewed at the good pleasure of God. There is no ground for the extension of Christian and ecclesial faith and life onto the plane of history, and no possibility of growth, progress or development in sanctification or vocation. Rather, the Christian life is a dreary existence confined to walking back and forth on the same road time and again, caught in the endlessly recurring pendulum-cycle of judgement and mercy. And while it may be said that Barth does have a role for the church in the world, this role is admittedly very bleak and uni-dimensional. So too, while there is a profound insight into the cruciform nature of faith, and its expression as the fear and love of God, the sharp limitation in which it is set is more akin to despair than to hope.

In short, Bender's assertion that 'in the *Romans* commentary the church seems to be a community of sin that *precedes and opposes* the resurrection more than a new community that is established *in the light of and through* the

---

[134] Barth, *Romans II*, 404.
[135] Barth, *Romans II*, 392-393, 406, 417.
[136] Barth, *Romans II*, 406.

resurrection' appears justified.[137] Given that this theological framework forms the theory of practice, it is unclear just what practice might arise from it, save a dismal, isolationist and passive 'waiting' of the community on God—a waiting that cannot issue into a hastening or activity, but can only linger until God finally establishes the fullness of his kingdom.

At this point, however, we are happily confronted with the inconsistency in Barth's theology that was mentioned at the beginning of this chapter. According to Bruce McCormack, given the manner in which he constructed his dialectic of time and eternity, Barth 'should not have been able to say that revelation and the new humanity project themselves into time—but he did'.[138] Similarly, Smart has noted that 'the tangent was really meant to do more than merely *touch* the circle....In short, *Urgeschichte* becomes a reality in time.'[139] In blunt terms, Barth's construal of the divine-human relation in *Romans II* does not work, or, to state the matter differently, it works too well. If Barth were to apply his theological framework in *Romans II* with utter consistency there would be no possibility of Christian and ecclesial existence, no possibility of a *life* of faith, of progress in sanctification, of moral community.

Does this mean that those interpreters who accuse Barth of denying the church and eradicating human agency are actually correct in their assessment? No, for as McCormack and Smart point out, Barth is not content to colour within the lines he has drawn, but strays outside them. Thus, while it may be appropriate to judge his work strictly in accordance with the theological framework he established, Barth did not adhere strictly to this framework. This is evident in the one significant passage in his exposition of Romans 1-11 where Barth does turn his attention to consider the life of the believer: Romans 6:11-23.[140] So we, too, turn our attention to consider his treatment of this theme in this passage.

The New Subject and the Imperative of Grace

In the preceding treatment of divine revelation and human faith, we found that the moment of revelation involves the action of the Holy Spirit whereby the human recipient of revelation is constituted anew as a new subject 'who stands upright in the presence of God'.[141] Barth uses the imagery and terminology of the 'new man'—the new subject or new humanity—to refer both to the new situation of all humanity as a result of the coming of Christ, and

---

[137] Bender, *Karl Barth's Christological Ecclesiology*, 36.

[138] McCormack, *Karl Barth's Dialectical Theology*, 264.

[139] Smart, *The Divided Mind*, 115.

[140] It should not surprise us that Barth reserves his discussion of Christian life and obedience until Romans 6:11, for this is the first instance of an imperative in Paul's Epistle.

[141] See page 198 above; Barth, *Romans II*, 158.

to the individual awakened in the moment of revelation. This distinction is significant for it helps illuminate how Barth conceives the movement from the indicative to the imperative of grace.

In the indicative of triumphant grace the new subject refers to the ontological restoration of humanity into right relationship with God, whereby *all* are now set at liberty from the fallenness of the world and placed under divine affirmation.[142] This new subject, who 'has no existence except non-existence'[143] is the 'new man...who is righteous before [God] and in whom he is well pleased, the man in whom God again discovers himself as a father discovers himself in his child'.[144] In the moment of revelation the individual is confronted by this transcendent, existential reality:

> Upon the threshold of my existence there appears, demanding admittance—the new man of the new world, the new man in Christ Jesus, justified and redeemed, alive and good, endowed with attributes which are not mine, have not been mine, and never will be mine. This new man is no visible figure in history, no metaphysical phantom of my imagination; he is no other, second person, with whom I may be compared; he claims to be me myself, my existential, unobservable, EGO. In God I am what I am.[145]

This recipient of revelation is the new subject who has been 'lifted up into the air' and who has 'no standing-place except the protection of God' and who may be 'what he is not...a new subject related to a new object' so long as they 'remain still in fear and trembling, in awe and gratitude'.[146]

Barth's use of the 'new subject' to refer both to the ontological restoration of all humanity to divine affirmation, and to the individual awakened by the Holy Spirit in the moment of revelation suggests that he is making a functional distinction between that which is ontological and that which is ontic.[147] Ontological statements refer to the being of something and the range of possibilities open to it. Ontic statements refer to the being of something in its

---

[142] Barth, *Romans II*, 182.

[143] Barth, *Romans II*, 163.

[144] Barth, *Romans II*, 207.

[145] Barth, *Romans II*, 229.

[146] Barth, *Romans II*, 163.

[147] I am indebted to John Colwell for this distinction. See John Colwell, *Actuality and Provisionality: Eternity and Election in the Theology of Karl Barth* (Edinburgh: Rutherford House, 1989), 273, n.30. For a further discussion of this theme within the context of Barth's doctrine of election in *The Church Dogmatics*, see Michael D. O'Neil, 'The Mission of the Spirit in the Election of God' (Unpublished Dissertation for the Master of Theology (Honours), Murdoch University, Western Australia, 2001), 47. Admittedly, Barth's pneumatology in *Romans II* is very thin, especially in relation to its later development, so that the attribution of ontic renewal to the Spirit is difficult to sustain. Nevertheless the ontological-ontic conceptuality is present in this work, albeit in nascent form.

actual relations with other entities. To speak onticly is to presuppose the ontological, whilst the reverse is not so. Thus, in the death and resurrection of Jesus Christ God has effected an ontological alteration of the human situation whereby all humanity is constituted anew whether they ever experience this reality existentially or not. The possibility exists that they may be actually amongst those who are confronted and claimed in the moment of revelation. This, however, is not certain, for it is only those who 'are led to apprehend [their] Sonship by the Spirit' who are thus brought into the orbit of a new relation with God.[148] Thus in his comment on Romans 8:15, Barth affirms that

> this Spirit of Sonship, this new man who I am not, is my unobservable, existential EGO. Thence I am known, directed, enlivened, and beloved. In the light of this unobservable EGO I must now pass my visible and corporeal life. In its light I must live within the realm of that old duality, pressed against the narrow gate of critical negation where the fear of the Lord must be the beginning and end of my wisdom. I must live in the darkness, but not now without the reflection of light uncreated; God's prisoner, but as such his freedman; his slave, but as such his Son; mourning and yet blessed. I must still cry unto him who confronts me only as unknown and undiscoverable, as the enemy who has vanquished me, and as the judge who has sentenced me to death—but nevertheless, crying to him, *Abba Father*....For assuredly, in such crying the possibility of God is secreted: assuredly it is possible, when human action has become quite thin and transparent, for the glory of God to shine through it or, maybe, to rend it asunder.[149]

In this remarkable passage we see that Barth does allow the impact and effect of revelation to pass onto the plane of history and time, even to the extent of declaring a certain human action—the cry of worship and prayer—to be an action which may become transparent to the glory of God. Again, it is 'wholly congruous,' says Barth in a discussion of divine grace toward humanity based on Romans 5:15, 'that the positive relation between God and man should assume positive form among men in Christ's world....Through the death of Christ men are made new and are translated into the realm of life.'[150] In an evident echo of Luther's language, though not his meaning, Barth declares that, 'though mankind has become the slave of all things, yet in the death of Christ men are lord of all....they stand as individuals under the law of liberty through the grace of Christ.'[151] Barth goes on characteristically to express the eschatological reserve under which this liberty occurs:

> We have as yet only been declared free;...our actual redemption cannot be identified with any concrete happening in history. Here, too, men do not pass

---

[148] Barth, *Romans II*, 298.

[149] Barth, *Romans II*, 297-298.

[150] Barth, *Romans II*, 178, 179-180.

[151] Barth, *Romans II*, 180. See also Timothy F. Lull, ed., *Martin Luther's Basic Theological Writings* (Minneapolis: Fortress, 1989), 596.

beyond the threshold of the Kingdom of God....Yet they do stand hopefully on
the threshold; and, because they have hope, they do not wholly lack the
anticipatorily present reality of what is hoped for.[152]

The new subject created by the Holy Spirit in the event of revelation stands
on the threshold of the kingdom of God as a partaker of divine grace—in hope.
This grace is the divine disposition whereby 'we are no longer treated by God
as sinners'.[153] Accordingly,

> grace...means neither that men can or ought to do something, nor that they can or
> ought to do nothing. Grace means that God does something. Nor does grace mean
> that God does 'everything'. Grace means that God does some quite definite
> thing....Grace means that God forgives men their sins.[154]

Yet, as the above citation also suggests when it says that believers do not
'wholly lack the anticipatorily present reality of what is hoped for', grace is
also more than pronounced forgiveness, being the power of the resurrection
which at all times impinges upon the present existence of humanity, crossing
the 'threshold' of our world from that side to this, 'the act of God by which the
new man shall be and is, and by which also he is free from sin'.[155] The visible,
concrete existence of humanity is overshadowed and overturned by the
invisible, future, yet truly concrete existence of the believer as they now exist in
God through their union with Christ by faith.[156] Faith is a venture which must
be risked, says Barth, 'seeing what God sees, knowing what God knows,
reckoning as God reckons'.[157] By grace and in faith the believer may, and
indeed, *must* live as the new subject they are in God for the indicative of this
grace passes over into an imperative.

Grace for Barth, therefore, is not only the forgiveness of sins and the power
of the resurrection impinging on our lives, but also the mighty claim of God
upon our lives whereby God lays hold of us for his purpose and will: 'Grace is
the royal and sovereign power of God, the existential presentation of men to
God for his disposal, the real freedom of the will of God in men.'[158] Grace has
introduced a 'fissure and disturbance' into the being of the person between the
former subjectivity and the new, so that their bondage to sin has been
decisively broken, and their existence has been co-opted for the service of

---

[152] Barth, *Romans II*, 180.

[153] Barth, *Romans II*, 191.

[154] Barth, *Romans II*, 215.

[155] Barth, *Romans II*, 195, 197.

[156] Barth, *Romans II*, 199-201.

[157] Barth, *Romans II*, 206.

[158] Barth, *Romans II*, 213.

righteousness.[159] Thus, grace is a categorical imperative, a call, command and order which cannot be disobeyed.[160] By grace the new subject is awakened to a new responsibility. Barth uses military language to describe this responsibility: 'I am the warrior under grace, the new man, who can neither admit nor submit to the tyranny which sin exercises over me and over my mortal body....I am, consequently, in full revolt against it. I can be no neutral observer of the conflict between grace and sin.'[161]

Barth also rejects any dualism between grace and sin, as though God's claim and action is limited to only one aspect of the life of the individual. God's grace claims the whole of the person, the totality of their existence, and there remains no aspect of their person or life which lies beyond the bounds of God's claim. There is no dualism between visible and invisible, tangible and intangible: '[Grace] cannot hand visible life over to sin in order that it may be satisfied with the righteousness of some "other" invisible and intangible life....Grace seizes visible life and demands that it be presented to righteousness.'[162] Nor is there any dualism between life in this present age, and some future age, but rather, 'the barrier between them has been removed. Grace, as the invisible truth, cannot but press to concretion....Grace means: *thy will be done in earth as it is in heaven.*'[163] As those in a 'state of grace,' and who now 'stand under the imperative of grace'[164] believers

> must serve righteousness with the same members, with the same visible concreteness, with which they hitherto served uncleanness and iniquity. They must bring sanctification into concrete existence....They must glorify God with their bodies....There is demanded of them—of each single person—a different being and having and doing.[165]

In fact, if the disturbance of grace does not so work within the human agent that they long for and stretch out toward a life of sanctification to such a degree that true righteousness begins to break visibly through in the members of their bodies—grace is not grace.[166]

Barth is well aware of the tension which exists between the language he is

---

[159] Barth, *Romans II*, 219, 226. See also Torrance's discussion of grace in Barth's *Romans II* in which he says that 'grace...means that God reckons man's whole existence to be his and claims it for himself and therefore constitutes the positive *re-ligio* or re-binding of man to God' in Thomas F. Torrance, *Karl Barth: An Introduction to His Early Theology 1910-1931* (Edinburgh: T. & T. Clark, 1962), 69.

[160] Barth, *Romans II*, 207.

[161] Barth, *Romans II*, 209.

[162] Barth, *Romans II*, 221.

[163] Barth, *Romans II*, 222.

[164] Barth, *Romans II*, 219, 221.

[165] Barth, *Romans II*, 222.

[166] Barth, *Romans II*, 223.

using in this section, and the ruling conceptuality of *Romans II*. The possibility of the emergence of the visible and concrete sanctification of human life is not a human possibility. The *reality* he seeks to describe belongs to an order wholly distinct from every other human reality, and any concrete expression of it in the order of human being and having and doing is strictly a matter of miracle, of new creation. The divine imperative, however, is not unjustly demanding something which humanity has *absolutely* no possibility of fulfilling, for the imperative is grounded in the indicative. Although its fulfilment is not a human possibility, in the power of grace it becomes possible in the moment of revelation, which as 'lightning…sets our existence ablaze, illuminates at once our being and knowing, our thinking and speaking, our will and its execution, the motions of our souls and the achievements of our bodies, the aims we yearn after and the purposes we attain'.[167] In the moment of revelation we gain knowledge of God's sovereignty and our own sinfulness and contingency, an awareness of our origin and the purpose and hence of the meaning of our existence, and so also insight into the nature of good and evil.[168] The criterion by which iniquity is known is simply, death. That which issues from 'the vitality of mortality', which finds it origin, logic and telos in death, which spreads and is dedicated to death, is iniquity. Contrariwise, that which has its origin, logic and telos in life, which is devoted even imperfectly to life, may survive the fiery test of divine judgement and so be shown to be righteous.[169]

Finally, in the climax of his exposition on this chapter, Barth also acknowledges that those whose lives are enlightened by revelation, and who have come to understanding of the criterion of good and evil 'are again and again compelled to draw up a list of sinners and righteous men and to make a catalogue of what is permitted and what is forbidden. They are bound to attempt a system of ethics.'[170] Although it might be anticipated that Barth would condemn this activity, he does not. Instead, he insists that such attempts are *human* responses to revelation and as such always remain contingent, no more than *attempts* to understand the divine righteousness. As a means to the attainment of righteousness, of course, they are vain. Is the entire exercise therefore vain? Barth does not suggest this. It seems he considers ethics—and in this case, even the provisional attempt to construct an ethics—to be always necessary yet always contingent, leaving the possibility open, at least in this instance, that such lists and categories may have a heuristic function within the community of faith.

Given the importance of this notion for the thesis that Barth develops his

---

[167] Barth, *Romans II*, 227.

[168] Barth, *Romans II*, 226-227.

[169] Barth, *Romans II*, 227-228.

[170] Barth, *Romans II*, 228. Hoskyns' use of the word 'system' in his translation is unfortunate. Barth typically excoriates any attempt to develop a 'system' of ethics, and does not use the word in this passage (see the translation in the text below).

theology with the formation of moral community in view, it is necessary to respond to a significant rejection of this view. David Clough insists that the English translation of this passage in Barth is misleading, and that Barth has not, in fact, said that those enlightened by grace are to make an attempt at a system of ethics: 'In fact, Barth says that it is ordinary persons, who live in a "twilight world" where they cannot see the chasm between good and evil, who are condemned to this unrelenting search for an ethical system. Those under grace rely instead on the "power of obedience," which is the "power of the resurrection".'[171]

Certainly the passage is difficult, and translator Edwyn Hoskyns has attempted to render it more simply in English by inserting certain persons as the grammatical subject in several of his sentences, in place of Barth's more abstract language. In fact, it is only the final sentence of the paragraph which has a human grammatical subject, the subjects of the previous sentences being 'sin and grace', 'no bridge', 'the clarity', 'the abyss', 'its presence' (that is, the presence of the abyss), and 'the knowledge of God' respectively. Thus, strictly speaking, it is neither those enlightened by grace nor, as Clough suggests, those who inhabit the twilight world of ungraced humanity who are the subject of the attempt of an ethic. A more literal rendering of the passage runs as follows:

Just as death and life cannot stand together, beside one another or as links of a chain one after the other, so neither can sin and grace. *No* bridge leads across the abyss that is opened here. The clarity, which is brought about here does not tolerate *any* confusion. Right across the fissures of 'good' and 'evil,' 'worthy' and 'unworthy,' 'holy' and 'unholy,' which cannot bring about clarity and distinction in the twilight world of ungraced humanity, runs the abyss [which functions] as the orientation of a [the?] *new* order and as *the* unambiguous criterion. Its presence makes the attempt at an *ethic*, which is a list of sinful and just, prohibited and commanded (i.e. dead or living) life purposes, an absolutely necessary task, only to make an ethic that is meant to be more than an *attempt* absolutely impossible. This is because the knowledge of God, in which this orientation takes place and this unambiguous criterion of what is sinful and what is just is brought about, brings about human *knowledge* ever anew by dissolving *human* knowledge. The fact that we recognise and grasp the possibility of the impossible as our own task is the power of obedience in which we *stand*, because it is the power of the *resurrection*.[172]

---

[171] David Clough, *Ethics in Crisis: Interpreting Barth's Ethics* (Aldershot: Ashgate, 2005), 40.
[172] I gratefully acknowledge the assistance of Alex Jensen, in untangling this difficult passage, here reproduced in its entirety:

So wenig Tod und Leben zugleich, nebeneinander oder als Glieder einer Reihe hintereinander sein können, so wenig Sünde und Gnade. Über den Abgrund, der hier aufgerissen ist, führt *keine* Brücke. Die Klarheit, die hier geschaffen ist, duldet *keine*

The logic of Barth's sentences is that the abyss which opens up between death and life, sin and grace cuts across all conceptions of good and evil, worthy and unworthy, and holy and unholy and thus renders impossible any bridging, confusion, mixture or blending of these polarities. Those inhabiting 'the twilight world of ungraced humanity' are thus left without any genuine means of clarity or distinction regarding them: they do not possess the criterion of good and evil given in the moment of revelation. For those enlightened in the moment of revelation, however, the abyss functions as an orientation to the new world and as *the* unambiguous criterion. Its presence requires the attempt at an ethic and simultaneously renders any such attempt which seeks to be more than an *attempt* invalid.

Who, the question must be asked, are those who must make this attempt ever and again—those 'graced' or 'ungraced'? That this new orientation takes place 'in the knowledge of God' surely indicates that Barth means, contrary to Clough's assertion, that it is the graced who undertake this task. This view is further confirmed in the final sentence of the passage in which Barth quite explicitly says, 'The fact that we recognise and grasp the possibility of the impossible as *our own task* is the power of obedience in which we stand, because it is the power of the resurrection.'[173] Thus, while the formulation of a 'system' of ethics is quite impossible, it is nevertheless, for the Barth of *Romans II*, an impossibility rendered possible—and necessary—for those who by grace may comprehend the criterion disclosed by revelation, so long as it remains clear that all such attempts are no more than *attempts*, that is, that every such 'system' is recognised as radically and inherently contingent, standing ever and always in need of reformulation.

Further evidence might be adduced that Hoskyn's rather free translation of this passage is in accord with Barth's intent in this work. In the midst of Barth's discussion of the imperative of grace is a brief though significant passage in which he acknowledges the necessity of moral formation if the community is to

---

Vermischung. Quer hindurch durch die Risse von ‚Gut' und ‚Böse,' ‚Wert' und ‚Unwert,' ‚heilig' und ‚unheilig,' die in der Dämmerungswelt des unbegnadeten Menschen – keine Klarheit, keine Scheidung zu schaffen vermögen, geht als Orientierung *neuer* Ordnung, als *das* eindeutige Kriterium dieser Abgrund. Sein Vorhandensein wird den Versuch einer *Ethik*, einer Tafel der sündigen und gerechten, verbotenen und gebotenen (weil toten oder lebendigen) Lebenszwecke immer wieder zur unerbittlich notwendigen Aufgabe machen, um eine Ethik, die mehr als *Versuch* sein sollte, immer wieder ebenso unerbittlich zu verunmöglichen. Denn die Erkenntnis Gottes, in der sich jene Orientierung vollzieht, in der jenes eindeutige Kriterium des Sündigen und des Gerechten erzeugt wird, schafft immer wieder menschliche *Erkenntnis*, indem sie *menschliche* Erkenntnis aufhebt. Daß wir die Möglichkeit des Unmöglichen begreifen und ergreifen als unsre eigene Aufgabe, das ist die Kraft des *Gehorsams*, in der wir *stehen*, weil sie die Kraft der *Auferstehung* ist. See Karl Barth, *Der Römerbrief 1922*, 229.

[173] Translated as above, emphasis added.

realise its calling as the people of God. We have seen that those claimed by grace can no longer live their lives in servitude to sin, for they 'stand under the imperative of grace' and hence must take their place as God's servants.[174] This will hardly occur, however, without 'pastoral exhortation' whereby people are

> summoned to repentance, and the forgiveness of sins is spoken over them as the Word of God. They are bidden to think of themselves as existentially under grace, as belonging to God, and as brought within the sphere of the resurrection. Looking on him who has been crucified on their behalf, they are bidden to— believe; yes! to believe in their power of obedience. This is the venture which must be dared. How is it possible to speak of the grace and of the Kingdom of God, if each man be not persuaded that the description concerns him and that he is under grace and within the Kingdom? How is it possible to pronounce the truth that the grace of God concerns all men, if it be not boldly applied to each particular man?[175]

We have previously seen in his first commentary on Romans, that Barth was not unaware of the need for moral formation in the Christian community, although he preferred to name such formation 'Christian exhortation'.[176] So here, under the same nomenclature, Barth clearly intends that some form of spiritual and moral formation occurs within the Christian community such that believers are enabled to *reckon* as God reckons. Without this formation and pastoral exhortation believers will be unequipped to embark on the daring venture of faith asked of them. Using the passive voice to describe what must transpire in the lives of believers, Barth says that, 'we must be enabled to discover that we are no more of this evil world, no more under its power'. He continues, 'We must be set in radical opposition to it, and in such a manner that in the conscious tribulation of discovering its mere this-worldliness and negativity we discover also the promise, and in apprehending our deprivation we also apprehend our hope.'[177]

Barth desires that the believer be 'enabled to discover' their new identity in God and the promise that he gives, and to consciously wrestle with the 'this-worldliness' of the world until they are set in radical opposition to it. These sentences indicate that the kind of formation Barth proposes would require extensive theological instruction and exhortation, as well as substantial reflection upon the daily realities of human life and society. Further, the truth of grace is to be pressed upon each one so that each person understands both the blessing and the responsibility of divine grace. It is in this context that Barth then speaks of grace which 'cannot but press to concretion' but which is 'bound to move from the indicative of the divine truth concerning men to the

---

[174] Barth, *Romans II*, 221, 239.
[175] Barth, *Romans II*, 218.
[176] See the discussion on page 122 above.
[177] Barth, *Romans II*, 222.

imperative by which the divine reality makes its demand upon them. They must will what God wills, as hitherto they have not!'[178] Here again, as we have recently seen, 'They *must* serve righteousness....They *must* bring sanctification into concrete existence....They *must* glorify God with their bodies....There is demanded of them—of each single person—a different being and having and doing.'[179]

And yet, in accordance with the dialectical manner in which Barth has constructed his understanding of the imperative of grace, they will no doubt also be instructed in the nature of faith as a response to grace. That is, that genuine responsiveness to God is to appear before him ever and again with empty hands, refusing to rely on one's performance or achievement, but ever awaiting the fresh encounter of God by which our life is once again illuminated in the lightning event of revelation.

Barth describes the manner of this formation in terms of proclamation, exhortation, and, unexpectedly, a reminder of the experiences of grace that Christians have encountered. Surprisingly, he also allows this formation to occur using the 'language of romanticism', that is, direct language which describes the immediacy and actuality of divine forgiveness so that the reality of God's gracious provision may truly grip the hearer: 'broken men, we dare to use unbroken language'.[180]

In sum, then, the movement of the indicative to the imperative has significance out of proportion with its length in Barth's exposition, for here we see clearly Barth's intention to provide 'space' for a positive account of Christian and ecclesial existence in his commentary. The movement from indicative to imperative also indicates the movement of eternity into time and onto the plane of history as grace presses for concretion. It further indicates a movement beyond the general ontological alteration of the human situation as a result of the coming of Christ, to the ontic renewal of certain individuals in the gracious power and presence of the Holy Spirit who constitutes them anew. These individuals, awakened and claimed by divine grace in the power of the Holy Spirit, are exhorted to make the sanctification of human life visible, exhibiting a 'different being and having and doing'. As such, they are also called to be a community enabled to distinguish, though only provisionally, between good and evil, and to be set in radical opposition to the world. Whilst Barth does not use the language I have adopted, it is difficult to see how his

---

[178] Barth, *Romans II*, 222.

[179] Barth, *Romans II*, 222, emphasis added.

[180] Barth, *Romans II*, 220-221. Of course, it need hardly be noted that Barth's entire commentary functions in terms of the kind of exhortation he advocates in his reflections on Romans 6! It is the argument of this chapter, and of this book generally that Barth lectures and writes in order to stir the Christian community to a manner of life befitting the reality of divine grace given us in Jesus Christ, including the nature of faith that corresponds to the action of God.

exposition can be can be seen as anything other than an attempt at the formation of moral community. That he would expect his readers to be anything less is barely conceivable. As such, the argument of this book, that Barth deliberately develops his theology with an intention to form moral community and shape Christian and ecclesial existence receives strong confirmation at this point. Admittedly, this confirmation is at the expense of claiming that Barth is inconsistent in the application of his own theological ontology. Nevertheless, the fact that this inconsistency occurs at *this* point— where he considers the moral existence of the believer and community—serves only to underline the significance of this ethical motive in his theology.

This does not eliminate all the questions that have been raised, however. The discussion thus far at least indicates how stringent Barth has become in the space he allows for human initiative and activity. Even given the fact that Barth himself does not adhere strictly to his theological framework, the quite rich descriptions of human agency and moral community found in some of his earlier works have all but disappeared, with the exception of the short exposition on the imperative of grace. Further, Barth has also, in this revised edition of the commentary, removed ethical discussion from some sections where it is found in the first edition. It may be recalled, for example, that in *Romans I* Barth treats the entry of the Law in Romans 5:20-21 as an occasion to discuss the 'question of morality' and develops his idea of the 'third dimension', of the believer being caught up in the eschatological procession of God. In *Romans II*, by contrast, the verses are now grounds for a discussion of the earth-bound nature of religion—which must now be abandoned.[181]

Thus, serious questions in *Romans II* remain, if not about the bare possibility of ethical existence, at least about the nature and scope of such existence. Thus far this chapter provides an outline of the 'theory' Barth sought to present to his readers. The theory, of course, is not intended as an end in itself but is rather 'the theory of praxis'. We now turn, therefore, to the second major section of Barth's commentary: his exposition of chapters twelve to thirteen of Paul's Epistle where he specifically and extensively addresses what he refers to as 'the problem of ethics'.

Romans 12-13: The Theory of *Praxis*

The Problem and Presupposition of Ethics

For Barth, the problem of ethics consists in the question *What must we do?* and humanity's evident incapacity to answer that question in any kind of definitive manner. Nor is it a secondary or inconsequential problem, one we might easily dismiss or fruitfully ignore. Rather, it is pressed upon us

---

[181] Barth, *Romans II*, 184.

constantly in the actual tension of our daily existence, and most particularly in our interactions and confrontations with the *other*, who Barth also refers to as our *neighbour*.[182] For the Christian the problem is often especially acute, for the believer naïvely anticipates that God's will may be clearly apprehended and applied, and is troubled when this is not the case. In fact, it is precisely this problem which drives us to perceive the reality under which we live and to seek the knowledge of God. Accordingly, David Clough has rightly seen that the problem of ethics functions in Barth's *Römerbrief* to provoke the *Krisis* by the way it generates innumerable questions that only God can answer.[183]

This was certainly the case for Barth, who, as we have seen in the introduction to this chapter, declares that 'the whole concrete situation' was the starting point for his reflections in Paul's Epistle to the Romans. That is, 'the need of making decisions of will, the need for action, the world as it is—this it is which has compelled us to consider what the world is, how we are to live in it, and what we are to do in it'.[184] He rejects the notion that he has engaged in extensive theological reflection 'for the mere joy of so doing,' or that it has been an exercise in abstract thought.[185] Barth insists rather that

> it is our actual observation of life as it is that thrusts us back upon the necessity of hearing and speaking the Word of God. So also, it is our pondering over the question, 'What shall we do?' which compels us to undertake so much seemingly idle conversation about God. And it is precisely because our world is filled with pressing, practical duties; because there is *wickedness in the streets*; because of the existence of the daily papers; that we are bound to encounter 'Paulinism' and the Epistle to the Romans.[186]

These statements forcefully affirm the ethical nature of Barth's theology and provide further evidence in support of my contention that Barth practiced theology with a view to form and shape Christian and ecclesial existence. Further, Barth considers that he is following Paul himself in this emphasis, for Paul's Epistle is itself 'nothing but *exhortation*,' and that the whole conversation between Paul and the Romans forms one long reminder of the vast disturbance which has taken place.[187]

This claim stands in contrast to that of Neil MacDonald who has argued that the crisis to which Barth responded in *Romans II* was 'fundamentally a *theological* crisis' and secondly, that 'Overbeck's dilemma [that one either practices non-theology or gives up the attempt at theology altogether] is *the*

---

[182] Barth, *Romans II*, 425, 442.
[183] Clough, *Ethics in Crisis*, xiv.
[184] Barth, *Romans II*, 427.
[185] Barth, *Romans II*, 427.
[186] Barth, *Romans II*, 438.
[187] Barth, *Romans II*, 439.

final horizon of *Romans II* and not just *a* horizon.'[188] I do not wish to diminish the important contribution MacDonald has made to our understanding of Barth, and agree with him that Barth was consciously writing with Overbeck's challenge in the forefront of his mind. I argue, however, that these passages indicate Barth's *ethical* concern was the more immediate horizon within which he approached his commentary. Of necessity, however, the ethical problem drove him, as he indicates, back to God and to a fresh hearing and speaking of the Word of God. At *this* point, Overbeck's dilemma arises: how may we speak of God, of his will, and of his commandment in light of the criticism that Overbeck brought against theology?

Barth approaches his discussion of ethics by outlining the orientation and major structural features of his ethical method. His major presupposition is expressed quite simply: 'God is God: this is the presupposition of ethics.'[189] This seemingly simple assertion, however, is laden with significance. Barth insists that the entire theological ontology portrayed in his exposition of Romans 1-11 functions as the presupposition of ethics. In other words, the presupposition of dogmatics is also the presupposition of ethics: *Soli Deo gloria!*[190]

This presupposition requires that ethical thought, like dogmatic thought, be dialectical in its form. Barth is firm that 'genuine thought must always be broken thought' for when our thought is comprehensive and unbroken 'it is quite certain that we are not thinking about life; we are not thinking, that is to say, about the *Krisis* in which human life is in fact being lived'.[191] Thus Barth argues that, 'Pure ethics require—and here we are in complete agreement with Kant—that there should be no mixing of heaven and earth in the sphere of morals. Pure ethical behaviour depends upon its primal origin, an origin which needs to be protected by a determination on our part to call God God and man man.'[192] No human activity whether thought, will or deed—including even those activities which occur as a result of the inspiration or empowering of the Spirit—can claim divine justification: all are subject to the same *Krisis* which proved determinative in the arenas of theological epistemology and soteriology.

This is not to say, however, that human activity cannot actually *be* righteous—simply that we cannot claim this for our activity. By his use of dialectic, Barth intends to destabilise human confidence in its own goodness

---

[188] See Neil B. MacDonald, *Karl Barth and the Strange New World Within the Bible: Barth, Wittgenstein and the Metadilemmas of the Enlightenment* (Carlisle: Paternoster, 2000), 54, 59. It is possible to respond to MacDonald's thesis using his own idiom: 'Quite so! Barth was writing in view of Overbeck's dilemma, but Barth is *Barth!*' See also Clough, *Ethics in Crisis*, 21.

[189] Barth, *Romans II*, 439.

[190] Barth, *Romans II*, 431.

[191] Barth, *Romans II*, 425.

[192] Barth, *Romans II*, 432.

and capacity for ethical conduct. This is the function of the negative pole of his dialectic. But the positive pole, although certainly attenuated in *Romans II*, must be heard. The positive pole does not deny the reality of human finitude and incapacity in the ethical arena, nor does it overturn it through the provision of some new standpoint from which we might now have confidence. Rather, as Clough has noted,

> [i]t tells us that our ability to act virtuously is balanced on a knife-edge, or hangs from a single thread. But it tells us that if we can accept this instability, if we can embrace an existence in which we are not in charge of our destiny and do not make the rules, if we can repent of our desire to eat the fruit of the tree in the middle of garden and be like gods, then we can perform responsible, significant, genuinely human actions.[193]

When Barth turns to consider the possibility of human ethical behaviour he begins by recalling the imperative of grace from Romans 6: 'Sanctify yourselves! Be servants of God!'[194] He now explicates this demand in terms of Romans 12:1 saying that

> [t]o *sanctify* something means to separate and prepare it that it may be presented and offered to God. This is more precisely defined in the conception of *sacrifice*. The exhortation which is grounded upon the mercies of God and is directed towards men is summed up in the demand that men should present their bodies— that is, their concrete, observable, historical existence—as a *sacrifice*.[195]

For Barth, this self-offering which is the 'primary ethical action' may also be termed worship or *repentance*. Repentance involves the recognition of the 'vast ambiguity' of our existence, whereby we affirm and bow in adoration of the righteous judgement of God.[196] Repentance, as such, is not a work which qualifies as 'good' or a credible position upon which we may stand, but rather, is the ever-renewed, never completed dissolution of any such claim or position. It is a continual act of 'rethinking' by which we are re-oriented time and again in submission toward God.

That Barth characterises repentance in terms of 'rethinking' is a move to be noted. Repentance is not construed in religious or ritualistic terms, as though certain activities might be undertaken, and so become, in themselves a means of ethical justification. By construing repentance as rethinking Barth calls the believer and the community to return time and again to the kind of theological reflection exemplified in Paul's Epistle to the Romans (and in his own commentary?), whereby they acknowledge afresh in each new circumstance the

---

[193] Clough, *Ethics in Crisis*, 36.
[194] Barth, *Romans II*, 239.
[195] Barth, *Romans II*, 430-431.
[196] Barth, *Romans II*, 437.

fundamental presupposition of dogmatics and ethics, and the theological realities of their 'concrete situation'. It is also likely, as we shall see shortly, that such rethinking will also include *what* these theological realities mean and call for in the particular circumstances being confronted by the community.

The value or power of repentance lies in the re-presentation of the human agent as a sacrifice to God for his service and glory. Repentance, understood as rethinking, operates as a precursor to action,

> for it is the place where the turning about takes place by which men are directed to a new behaviour....Like the turning of a key in a lock, it is the prelude to a new action, to that conduct which is marked by the divine protest against the great illusion, and through which the light of the coming Day shines clear and transparent.[197]

Barth's mention of 'the divine protest against the great illusion' introduces his concept of the 'secondary ethical action' which he associates with the phrase *not to fashion yourselves according to the present form of this world, but according to its coming transformation* (Romans 12:2, his translation). Secondary ethical actions presuppose and arise from the primary ethical activity of repentance, and bear the two-fold witness unveiled in the citation above: they may take the form of a protest against 'the great illusion', against the form and idols of the present world, or they may be an expression of the 'coming Day'.[198]

Barth notes three things about the character of these secondary ethical actions. First, these actions arise out of the act of rethinking in which 'sufficient wisdom is given men to choose the road which is for the moment the right road'.[199] Once more we observe Barth's assertion that ethical activity occurs 'in the moment' as God's people present themselves to him. This occasionalist orientation of Barth's ethics stands in contrast to modes of ethics where the good may be predetermined apart from the presenting issue, and without the centrality of worship and prayer that Barth brings to the moment of ethical decision. It is noteworthy, however, that the ethical agents receive 'wisdom to choose the right road' rather than simply a bare command. This indicates that the ethical decision, at least as Barth construes it in this instance, involves genuine human engagement and reflection—rethinking—as part, though not the determinative aspect, of the ethical decision.

Second, Barth is emphatic that secondary ethical activities are and remain wholly human in nature, and that at best they can only point to and represent the action of God. They may function as sign-posts or parables, bearing witness to the glory of God, but whether this does in fact occur is entirely in his hands

---

[197] Barth, *Romans II*, 436, 437.
[198] Barth, *Romans II*, 434.
[199] Barth, *Romans II*, 437.

and not ours.[200] This is the risk of faith to which believers are called. Impressed into service by grace, they cannot remain still. But nor can they be assured that their service is accepted. They may only offer their life and service as a sacrifice, claiming nothing for themselves. 'All human duties and virtues and good deeds are set upon the edge of a knife. They hang on a single thread', says Barth. He asks, therefore, 'is the man who practices them and cherishes them really prepared to sacrifice them; really prepared to see in them no more than demonstrations, and thus to give glory to God?'[201]

Finally, Barth suggests that the ethical nature of a particular activity or virtue depends 'upon the light which shines in it', upon whether the human agent has 'been overcome' in accordance with the coming transformation of the present age.[202] Therefore,

> there is no human action which is not in itself fashioned according to the form of this world; and yet there are actions which seem almost to bear in themselves the mark of the divine protest against the great error. There is no human action which is in itself fashioned according to the transformation of this world; but there are actions which seem so transparent that the light of the coming Day is almost visible in them....So it is that every human position, every far-reaching, deeply penetrating human achievement, is to be sought out and recommended, for it is an urgent testimony to the power of the Spirit.[203]

In this passage Barth clearly acknowledges the possibility that in the midst of all human activity there may be a 'fruit of the Spirit, a fruit of the light, a doing which is justified by God'.[204] The situation of ethics may be tenuous at best, 'set upon the edge of a knife' but there remains—even in *Romans II*—the possibility of genuinely human, genuinely good acts which testify to the glory of God 'that he may be known as—Lord'.[205]

One final aspect of Barth's exposition requires comment before bringing this section to a close. At the beginning of this section we noted that the problem of ethics arises in confrontation with the human *other*. In his discussion of the body metaphor in Romans 12 Barth writes, 'But the parable does, of course, remind the individual of the fact of the community. That is to say, it reminds him of the existence of other individuals. And, indeed, the ethical problem— *what shall we do?*—appears at the point where the existence of these 'others' itself emerges as a problem.'[206] The ethical significance of the other does not lie in any phenomenal distinction or external reality—such factors are irrelevant.

---

[200] Barth, *Romans II*, 432-435.

[201] Barth, *Romans II*, 433.

[202] Barth, *Romans II*, 434.

[203] Barth, *Romans II*, 434-435.

[204] Barth, *Romans II*, 293-294.

[205] Barth, *Romans II*, 435.

[206] Barth, *Romans II*, 442.

What is important is that 'every man is a parable of the *oneness* of men—in God'.[207] Most especially, 'the *believers*—men in relation to God—are therefore, in their full-grown and in no way attenuated individuality, *one body, one individual* in Christ. They are not a mass of individuals....but The Individual, The One, The New Man. This *one*, this Body of Christ, it is which confronts us in the problem of the 'other' in the fellowship of the believers.'[208] Thus Barth is able to suggest that 'the *other*—the neighbour—who stands at the side of each one of us is the uplifted finger which by its 'otherness' reminds us of the *wholly other*,' and further, 'the community is that fellowship which reminds us of the Fellowship which is the *oneness* of every man and of all mankind in the unsearchableness of God'.[209]

In light of this Barth asks, 'Is the foundation of Ethics to be found, then, in the constitution of the community as Fellowship? Yes; for this is what these verses mean.'[210] Although the community remains the visible Church of Esau, it is capable of reflecting the coming light:

> This light need not be altogether hidden, and indeed is not altogether hidden; for wherever men are gathered together—*perhaps* their particular community is constituted by reference to the One—there men are found to be wrestling with the ethical presupposition, hoping for it, suffering for it—and this cannot be all to no purpose.[211]

It should now be evident that the discussion of this section serves to confirm my argument that Barth does envisage a definite form of Christian and ecclesial existence, and that he developed his theology with an explicit intention to form moral community. The question, however, of the material content and shape of that existence and community is still unclear. Thus far Barth has been satisfied to set forth the formal characteristics of a theological ethics, which as we have seen in previous chapters, has been his priority in all his work. This is not to say that in the *Römerbrief* Barth provides no indication of what this content might look like. As he continues his exposition of Romans 12 and 13 we find Barth not only wrestling with major ethical issues relevant to his historical context, but also suggestions as to the directions and shape of Christian and ecclesial existence. His exposition of the content of these chapters is the focus of the next three sections.

---

[207] Barth, *Romans II*, 445.

[208] Barth, *Romans II*, 443-444.

[209] Barth, *Romans II*, 444.

[210] Barth, *Romans II*, 449.

[211] Barth, *Romans II*, 450. Barth's *perhaps* is his way of still providing space for God in sovereign freedom to deal with his people as he might. See Barth, *Romans II*, 446.

Positive and Negative Possibilities

In his exposition of the second half of Romans twelve, Barth provides an account of positive and negative ethical possibilities, and in so doing provides some reflection at least on the material content of theological ethics. Some care is required here if Barth's meaning and intent is not to be misunderstood. By '*positive* ethics' Barth means, 'that volition and action which constitute a negation of the *form of this world*, a behaviour which contradicts its erotic course, and which protests against its great error'.[212] Similarly, he defines '*negative* ethics' as 'things that are willed and done, which, being congruous to the *transformation of this world*, stand in a positive relation to the Coming World'.[213] Thus, 'positive' ethics function in terms of negation while 'negative' ethics stand in a positive relation to the new world! This apparent confusion of terms may, however, be overcome when it is understood that Barth uses the terms *positive* and *negative* to refer to the mode of action undertaken by the ethical subject. That is, 'positive' ethics indicate definite actions undertaken whereas 'negative' ethics indicate a definite 'not-doing' or withdrawal of action.

Barth characterises the form of the world in terms of *Eros*, a deceptive force which impels humanity to see, to create, to shape and to possess, all without perception into the true nature of the surrounding world.[214] The great error of the erotic course of the world is precisely its failure to recognise the Other in the other, or to acknowledge the fundamental presupposition that God is God. Over against *Eros* as 'the supreme, positive ethical possibility' stands *Agape*, 'the love of one man for another'.[215] Barth refers to *Agape* as the recollection that in the encounter with the other we are faced with the reality of the hidden God—even if that other is our enemy![216] In this encounter 'the primary act of worship must be extended, or rather translated, into the secondary act of love towards our brother men. Indeed, it is precisely by this extension or translation of worship that the honour of God is demonstrated.'[217] For Barth, then, love toward God can only be genuine to the extent that there is a corresponding extension of love toward humanity. Conversely, love toward humanity functions as a parable and witness of the believer's love toward God, and of God's love toward this other human object of the believer's love.[218]

Agape must not be understood as some form of generally possible loving activity. In order to be a positive ethical activity which contradicts and protests the erotic course of the world, love must take the form of an offering or

---

[212] Barth, *Romans II*, 451.
[213] Barth, *Romans II*, 461.
[214] Barth, *Romans II*, 453-454.
[215] Barth, *Romans II*, 451.
[216] Barth, *Romans II*, 453, 474.
[217] Barth, *Romans II*, 452.
[218] Barth, *Romans II*, 452.

sacrifice within human relations that arises because of that Other encountered in the neighbour. The dialectic observed in Barth's treatment of love is indicative of the manner in which he treats all such positive ethical actions. The activity in and of itself is not constituted as an *ethical* activity unless and until it is an action that arises from the primary ethical activity of worship and repentance, and is directed towards the honour of God. Thus even love, which Barth denominates as 'the supreme positive ethical possibility' is no absolute virtue, nor can there be an 'absolute exhortation to love'. Rather, these positive possibilities are and always remain *relative* ethical possibilities, and can never function other than as parables which point to the new and coming world.[219]

This is the case with other positive virtues and practices that Barth extols from Romans twelve: brotherliness, service, honour, hope, patience, perseverance in tribulation and in prayer, hospitality, solidarity with others and blessing are all included as examples of positive ethical possibilities. Each constitutes a protest and contradiction against the form of the world, but only to the extent that they are directed toward the honour of God. Barth correlates the two tables of the Decalogue to the primary and secondary ethical actions, and insists that these secondary activities are only legitimate to the extent that 'our ethical behaviour bends backwards from the commandments of the second "Table" to those of the first, from secondary ethical actions to the primary ethical action'.[220] Thus Barth insists that

> [a]ll possibilities, negative or positive…are human possibilities, and are, as such, open to question; for they are subject to the right which must be reserved for God alone; they are liable to the judgement of the first 'Table' and to the *Krisis* of the passage from death to life. Indeed, they are ethical possibilities only because they are strictly related to their Primal Origin. Destroy this relationship, seek their essential nature in what they are in themselves or in what they contain in themselves, and their ethical character is done away.[221]

The honour of God as the presupposition of ethics remains the criterion by which any activity is judged as truly ethical. Apart from this criterion, which is never at human disposal, all attempts at ethical conduct remain subject to the *Krisis*. Moral activity, then, can never be understood as more than a sacrifice. The Christian community must attempt ethical behaviour, but it may never presume upon it, as though the behaviour is justified in itself, or as though it provides them with some ground by which they may proclaim their own superiority or worthiness in respect to others.

When Barth turns his attention to discussion of negative ethical possibilities, he begins by laying out a 'rule' for Christian ethics (despite his claim that 'these words do not seem to refer, at least in the first instance, to the universal

[219] Barth, *Romans II*, 453.
[220] Barth, *Romans II*, 454.
[221] Barth, *Romans II*, 461.

rule that governs all human doing and not-doing').[222] The words he refers to are Paul's exhortation to 'set not your mind on high things, but condescend to things that are lowly' (Romans 12:16). Barth goes on to indicate the significance of this rule saying, 'from the dialectic of this rule, that is to say, from the Rule in the rule—*Soli Deo gloria*!—the great contradictions emerge, world-denial and world-acceptance, enthusiasm and realism, the wisdom of death and the wisdom of life'.[223]

Barth utilises this text to argue powerfully for a preference for things which are lowly on the grounds of an analogy of the cross whereby

> [i]n the haphazard happenings of this life the things that are lowly have, at least relatively, a greater parabolic capacity than have those things that are set on high....Seen in the light of the Resurrection, every concrete thing that we appreciate as life and fullness, as great and high, becomes primarily a parable of death; death, however, and everything that is related to death—weakness and littleness, decrease, deprivation and lowliness—become a parable of life....This is the great disturbance of men.[224]

Accordingly, Barth counsels non-support and non-enthusiasm for projects characterised by some human eminence, confidence or boastfulness, even if they appear as movements, developments or ideals traditionally well aligned with Christianity, such as morals and religion, marriage and family. The grave danger Barth seeks to avoid is the church becoming a chaplain for the state or for secular causes, and in so doing becoming complicit in the construction of idolatrous towers of Babel.[225] For should it ever presume that it can enact and enforce any form of 'objective righteousness' it shall have become guilty of 'Titanism' and have seized the sceptre of God.[226] The calculated not-doing of the believer and the Christian community becomes a testimony against the human presumption that it can establish the new world of God's kingdom by its own endeavour.

Having established the principle Barth now radicalises it, so that this preference becomes a critical tool in the hands of the church, and the possibility that the church may develop an established position with respect to any particular societal group or movement is undermined. Barth draws a contemporary illustration to press his point: whereas in previous years the proletariat might well have been considered lowly, recent events, including especially the Russian revolution, have indicated that they are now busily

---

[222] Barth, *Romans II*, 461.

[223] Barth, *Romans II*, 465.

[224] Barth, *Romans II*, 462.

[225] Barth, *Romans II*, 462-463. The text does not actually mention Babel, but the reference is common in Barth's earlier works, and seems intended here. Compare McCormack, *Karl Barth's Dialectical Theology*, 279.

[226] Barth, *Romans II*, 473.

engaged in tower-building. Therefore, and in a turn which appears as a marked reversal of his stance in the first edition of the commentary, Barth wonders whether the time has now arrived

> [t]o condescend to things which are lowly, to arise, that is, and plunge into the world—to marry and care for wife and children, to enter politics—not merely on the side of the socialists!—to hold art in high esteem, to be cultured, and perhaps, with the last grim comedy of life, to become—a Churchman. The theses of Christianity here become its antithesis; for it is possible for the parable of death, though it be but a parable, to overstep itself.[227]

Barth therefore insists that no 'position' can ever be assumed, but a constant return, reorientation and relation to our Primal Origin is required.[228] That which previously was regarded as lowly and as the object of Christian preference or inclination has now set itself to become a human eminence, with the result that conservatism and reaction are now considered more radical and ethical than radicalism.

By radicalising his rule Barth has introduced a fundamental instability and relativity into the nature of Christian ethics. The extent to which this is the case is seen in the fact that Barth can even go so far as to declare 'the possibility that from time to time God may be honoured in concrete human behaviour which contradicts the second Table must...be left open'.[229] Barth intends by this relativising of all ethics to undermine every attempt—Christian attempt included—to construct and occupy a new human eminence with the consequent triumph and sorrow that such attempts produce.[230] Nevertheless, the relativity that Barth introduces to ethics is not a capricious relativity. Rather, it is an insistence that in each concrete circumstance the believer and the community take up the necessity of their primary ethical activity, that is, worship and repentance, that they might once again be granted 'sufficient wisdom...to choose the road which is for the moment the right road'.[231] The 'knowledge of God,' says Barth, 'directs us to God; it does not direct us to some human position or to some human course of action.'[232]

Barth goes on to provide several other negative ethical possibilities, including non-retaliation to provocation and evil, a refusal to engage in conflict

---

[227] Barth, *Romans II*, 464.

[228] Barth, *Romans II*, 465.

[229] Barth, *Romans II*, 451.

[230] Barth, *Romans II*, 466.

[231] Barth, *Romans II*, 437. Barth's own shift in emphasis regarding revolution between the first and second commentaries provides an example of how he applied this principle in his own life and thought. While Barth's attitude toward the state in both editions has not altered, the prevailing circumstances demanded a different response in 1921 than in 1918-19. See McCormack, *Karl Barth's Dialectical Theology*, 282.

[232] Barth, *Romans II*, 471.

and war which is almost—though in accordance with the freedom of God not quite—absolute, and finally, a repudiation of vengeance towards an enemy. Such 'withdrawal' from activity, that is, such purposeful and deliberate 'not-doing' gives place to positive ethical activities which in turn serve to testify to and announce the forgiveness and peace of the Coming World.[233]

Before moving onto the next section, it is necessary to consider a bold and quite unexpected pronouncement made by Barth at the conclusion of his reflections on Romans 12:16:

> though its purity is nowhere to be found, Christianity is human behaviour purified of all biological, emotional, erotic factors. Christianity is the final protest against every high place that men can occupy. For this reason it is the absolute ethic (*absolutes Ethos*), and for this reason it proclaims the Coming World.[234]

There is more than a little irony in the fact that Barth can refer to this ethics as 'absolute' given the way in which he has continually assailed the proposition of normative ethics, and given also the manner in which his interpreters have sometimes accused him of lacking any ethics. Even his comments on this verse have, as we have seen, insisted that ethics is fundamentally unstable and relative. What, then, does he mean when he declares that Christianity is an 'absolute ethics'?[235]

We must tread carefully here. Barth is *not* claiming that a *human system* of Christian ethics is absolute. He makes this clear in the same paragraph:

> This relativity of the ethics of grace is the axe laid at the root of *our own haphazard conceits*. The root from which our conceits spring, the secret which lies behind all human exaltation, is disclosed in the persistent regularity with which men crown themselves with the security of some absolute answer (*die absoluten ethischen Antworten*). By putting an end to all absolute ethics, Christianity (*Das christliche Ethos ist als das Ende aller absoluten ethischen Antworten*) finally puts an end to all the triumph and sorrow that accompanies the occupation of any human eminence....We are deprived by *the* Truth of the energy with which we immerse ourselves in *a* truth.[236]

For Barth, *every* formulation of ethics—including Christian ethics—can be no more than an *attempt*, for every such formulation remains subject to the *Krisis* befalling everything on this side of the line of death. No Christian ethics can 'harden' into a fixed position, into a 'concrete, observable thing' for the simple reason that life itself is never a stable reality, nor human activity. Christian ethics functions as the *end* of all such 'absolute ethical answers'.

---

[233] Barth, *Romans II*, 467-475.

[234] Barth, *Romans II*, 467.

[235] Because previous readers of a draft of this chapter have indicated concern with the idea of 'absolute ethics' in Barth, I will examine his use of this phrase more carefully.

[236] Barth, *Romans II*, 466; cf. Barth, *Der Römerbrief 1922*, 491.

Rather than answers,

> the absolute character (*die Absolutheit*) of Christian ethics lies in the fact that they are altogether problematical. Their evolution consists simply in the fecundity with which it puts forth more and more questions to which God Himself alone can be the answer....Christian ethics can only...bear witness that there is an answer.[237]

Over and again Barth refuses to give any ground for 'tower-building' in the name of Christian ethics. 'Death is the inevitable lot of everything which lies on this side of the discouragement of our courage.'[238]

> We must never forget the freedom with which Christianity allots its 'Yes' and its 'No.' It sets up and it tears down; it recalls the emissary it has dispatched; it gives and it takes away. Its purpose, however, remains always the same. It acts always in accordance with the same rule. Opposing what is *high*, it befriends what is lowly; loaning men *certitudo*, it permits them, for the honour of God, no *securitas*; measuring our time by the eternity of God, it allows us no established rights, gives us no rest, and preserves no strict continuity in its own action. Does it frighten us to discover how completely all that we are and do moves within the sphere of relativity?[239]

This relativity is 'our relationship to our Primal Origin'.[240] Although our position can never be 'fixed' and is ever subjected to the most thorough-going relativity, yet there is an abiding orientation and relation to God. As is often the case with Barth, what he takes away with one hand, he carefully restores, albeit in a reconstructed form, with the other. Thus, he continues:

> Human behaviour that has not passed through purgatory can never be ethical, it is simply *Bios, Pathos, Eros*; it is not governed by necessity, but simply haphazard and fortuitous;...it is not of God, but is capable of some explanation that is merely psychological, if not psychiatric. Christian ethical behaviour—in so far, of course, as it is not dramatized into a concrete, observable thing—is *the* Courage compared with which all *our* courage is just cowardice. By breaking down all 'individualism', Christianity establishes the Individual. Though its purity is nowhere to be found, Christianity is human behaviour purified of all biological, emotional, erotic factors. Christianity is the final protest against every high place that men can occupy. For this reason it is the absolute ethic, and for this reason it proclaims the Coming World.[241]

---

[237] Barth, *Romans II*, 465, 466; cf. Barth, *Der Römerbrief 1922*, 489, 491.

[238] Barth, *Romans II*, 467.

[239] Barth, *Romans II*, 465.

[240] Barth, *Romans II*, 465.

[241] Barth, *Romans II*, 467. See Barth, *Der Römerbrief 1922*, 491: Christliches Ethos ... ist die transzendentale (nie und nirgends als „Reinheit" erscheinende!) Reinigung des Handelns von allen biologischen, pathetischen, erotischen Elementen, der schlechthinige

Here, then, is the context of Barth's extraordinary and unexpected claim. In this statement Barth hints of an action or behaviour which has passed through the purgatorial fire, having experienced as it were, a 'transcendental purification' by which it is constituted as an 'absolute ethics' and thereby proclaims the Coming World. What kind of act is this? Once more, Barth is insisting on the primary ethical responsibility of worship and repentance, which functions, as we have previously noted, as

> the prelude to a new action, to that conduct which is marked by the divine protest against the great illusion, and through which the light of the coming Day shines clear and transparent.[242]

Perhaps the best way of interpreting Barth's meaning in these passages is to recognise first, that such an 'absolute ethics' nowhere *appears*, even to the person or persons performing the action. For them it is a venture of faith that must be risked, a sacrifice offered to the transcendent holiness of God and is known, as such, only by God. Second, the action so offered is constituted as an 'absolute ethics'—even in its imperfection and impurity—because it corresponds to the ultimate Truth 'by which human society is in fact constituted'.[243] Third, and most significantly, Barth is here referring to concrete 'human behaviour' (*Handelns*) and must not be understood as referring to a 'system' of Christian ethics. These singular acts become, by virtue of the 'light of the coming Day' that shines in them, a 'proclamation' or a witness to the coming world. This is the point of Barth's continued emphasis upon the relativity of all ethics in the preceding citations. He is clearing the ground of incorrect concepts of an 'absolute ethics' in order to prepare the way for the possibility that some acts arising from the primary ethical responsibility might become such a proclamation. Finally, Barth's language in this case is certainly idealistic, and undialectical, but perhaps that is the point: when it comes to 'pastoral exhortation' he allows the use of the 'language of romanticism': 'broken men, we dare to use unbroken language'.[244]

The 'Great' Negative Possibility

As Barth turns his focus to comment on the opening verses of Romans thirteen, which deal with the believer's relation to the 'powers that be,' he introduces a discussion of the *great* negative possibility, which is concerned with that 'collective attitude and behaviour in relation to the plurality of neighbours' rather than the 'demonstration to the honour of God effected by the

---

Protest gegen jede von *Menschen* eingenommene Höhenstellung – und eben darum und darin absolutes Ethos, eben darum und darin Verkündigung der kommenden Welt.
[242] Barth, *Romans II*, 437.
[243] Barth, *Romans II*, 469.
[244] Barth, *Romans II*, 220-221; see pages 219-220 above.

behaviour of particular individuals towards their neighbours'.[245] The human agent not only confronts the Other in the other as an individual, but also encounters vast corporate entities which claim to hold the answer to the ethical question and dilemma. According to Barth, 'these concrete, visible powers claim...to be, not merely things in human life, but that order and direction which constitute the solution of the problem....These powers demand recognition and obedience, and we have to decide whether we shall or shall not yield to their demand.'[246]

Barth identifies the powers as such entities as Church and State, Law and Society, Family and Science. These powers or 'orders,' however, must not be identified with *the* Order as though they possessed inherent divine legitimation. Rather, they are ordained of God as 'a pregnant parable of the Order that does not exist....The evil of the existing order bears witness to the good, since it stands of necessity as an order contrasted with *the* Order. Precisely in this contrast the existing order bears involuntary witness to *the* Order.'[247] For Barth, the evil of the existing order lies in its predisposition to function as a bulwark against the sovereign claim of God upon humanity by lodging its own claim for the allegiance and obedience of humanity that rightly belongs to God alone. As a result, Barth questions the right of governments to exist at all:

This whole pseudo-transcendence of an altogether immanent order is the wound that is inflicted by every existing government—even by the best—upon those who are most delicately conscious of what is good and right. The more successfully the good and the right assume concrete form, the more they become evil and wrong.[248]

Given this state of affairs it might be anticipated that Barth would reiterate the revolutionary stance of his first commentary on these verses. This, however, is not the case. Indeed, although Barth admits to having 'no material interest in Legitimism' he also confesses that he is 'most anxious about the man who embarks on revolution'.[249] The ground of his anxiety is simply stated: the revolutionary, as one who understands the fundamental requirement of negation; as one with insight into the corrupt nature of present earthly authority; as one imbued with a vision of a new and different order, stands far closer to the truth than does his or her reactionary counterpart who has no sense of deficiency or negation with respect to the present order.[250] While Legitimism functions to preserve the present evil order, the revolutionary seeks its overthrow and the establishment of a new and better order which is presumably

[245] Barth, *Romans II*, 477.
[246] Barth, *Romans II*, 477.
[247] Barth, *Romans II*, 485.
[248] Barth, *Romans II*, 479.
[249] Barth, *Romans II*, 477.
[250] Barth, *Romans II*, 478.

more attuned to the hope of the coming world.

It is precisely at this point, however, that Barth spies the mortal weakness of the revolutionary. For while the revolutionary aims at the true Revolution which ushers in the new world, he or she can actually only attain to the establishment of another earth–bound and in principle evil regime or structure, for the establishment of the kingdom of God remains the impossible possibility, beyond the reach of any human act. 'Even the most radical revolution,' says Barth, 'can do no more than set what *exists* against what *exists*....Revolution has, therefore, the effect of restoring the old after its downfall in a new and more powerful form.'[251]

Further, the taking up of arms against the existing order reveals that the revolutionary has 'adopted the possible possibility of discontent and hatred and insubordination, of rebellion and demolition' which is a decisive indication that they have been 'overcome with evil' rather than 'overcoming evil with good' (Romans 12:21).[252] In light of the reality of the time-eternity dialectic, then, both the legitimist and the revolutionary remain subject to the *Krisis* befalling the political realm. The legitimist is implicated in the evil of the present age and stands as a rebel against the inauguration of the coming kingdom, while both the means and the accomplishment of the revolutionary are subject to divine wrath, for they cannot but participate in the corrupt nature of fallen humanity. Caught, then, on the horns of this dilemma, what is the revolutionary to do? Barth's counsel is that the revolutionary turn toward the action of God: 'What more radical action can he perform than the action of turning back to the original root of 'not doing' — and *not* be angry, *not* engage in assault, *not* demolish?...There is here no word of approval of the existing order; but there is endless disapproval of every enemy of it.'[253]

Barth describes the great negative possibility in terms of *subjection*: 'Though subjection may assume from time to time many various concrete forms, as an ethical conception it is here purely negative. It means to withdraw and make way; it means to have no resentment, and not to overthrow.'[254] To exercise subjection as Barth intends it, is not facile submission to the will of the existing powers, but a deliberate posture which refuses to recognise the legitimacy and claim of these powers, and so 'starves' them of their 'pathos'.[255]

Barth develops the notion of subjection strictly in accordance with the believer's relation to the existing social powers. Over against these powers, both reactionary and revolutionary, the believer maintains the calm, critical posture of a so-called 'good citizen' who understands the penultimate nature of all human activity, and so refuses to invest it with any sense of ultimacy. Thus,

---

[251] Barth, *Romans II*, 482, 483.
[252] Barth, *Romans II*, 481.
[253] Barth, *Romans II*, 481.
[254] Barth, *Romans II*, 481.
[255] Barth, *Romans II*, 483.

the powers of revolution are also deprived of their pathos, enthusiasm and claim to be a 'high place'.[256] Subjection means 'no more than that vengeance is not our affair. It means that the divine minus before the bracket must not be deprived of its potency by a series of anticipatory negations on our part....The real revolution comes from God and not from human revolt.'[257] Thus, in this commentary Barth places far greater emphasis upon the concept of waiting than of hastening, and in this instance subjection amounts to waiting. The work of not-doing is an 'action' oriented toward the Primal Origin as the human agent waits for that work which only God can accomplish. Insofar as they do this they become 'ever more and more invisible, inaudible and undimensional'.[258]

The 'Great' Positive Possibility

It is evident that if the ethical posture that Barth develops here as the great negative possibility were elevated to become the primary ethical principle of the Christian community, it could only result in an ethic which is sectarian and isolationist, and in the withdrawal and complete disengagement of the believer and the community from the wider society.[259] It is important, therefore, that Barth's notion of subjection not be understood as such a principle, as though there were no positive ethical possibilities, and as though the waiting was not for the sake of hastening. Thus, when Barth turns in his exposition to Romans 13:8-14 he introduces the new section of his work by insisting that the wall represented by a determined 'not doing' is not inviolable, but may be breached by the equally determined *positive* activity of loving one's neighbour:

To every man we should owe love. It is not permitted us to excuse ourselves for the absence of love by saying that, since we live in the shadowy region of evil, we can only bear witness to the Coming World by 'not doing.' Even in the world of shadows love must come into active prominence, for it does not stand under the

---

[256] Barth, *Romans II*, 485.

[257] Barth, *Romans II*, 485. Barth adopts the mathematical image of the minus sign outside the brackets to indicate the manner in which the *Krisis* negates whatever is in the bracket – in this case, all existing social powers. The negation that the revolutionary achieves remains *inside* the bracket and results in the establishment of a new order which remains subject to the fundamental negation of the *Krisis*. See Barth, *Romans II*, 482-483.

[258] Barth, *Romans II*, 487.

[259] See, for example, the criticism of Charles Villa-Vicencio, who accuses Barth of quietism in Charles Villa-Vicencio, 'Karl Barth's "Revolution of God": Quietism or Anarchy?' in *On Reading Karl Barth in South Africa* (ed. Charles Villa-Vicencio; Grand Rapids: Eerdmans, 1988), 45.

law of evil. Love of one another ought to be undertaken as the protest against the course of this world, and it ought to continue without interruption.[260]

Barth, of course, has already given attention to love as a positive ethical possibility in his discussion of Romans 12:9, referring to *agape* as 'the supreme positive ethical possibility'.[261] In this context, however, love is the *great* positive possibility, by which Barth distinguishes love 'as the combination of all positive, that is to say, protesting, possibilities' from single, individual acts of love.[262] 'We define love as the "Great Positive Possibility",' says Barth,

> because in it there is brought to light the revolutionary aspect of all ethical behaviour, and because it is veritably concerned with the denial and breaking up of the existing order....Inasmuch as we love one another we cannot wish to uphold the present order as such, for by love we do the 'new' by which the 'old' is overthrown.[263]

In the passages just cited we see that for Barth, love is an essential activity which 'must come into active prominence', a 'protest against the course of this world', a revolutionary activity concerned with the 'denial and breaking up of the existing order', the *new* by which the *old* order 'is overthrown'. Love and all that proceeds from it is, according to Barth, a demonstration that the form of this world is passing away, and that the kingdom of God is coming.[264] Indeed love is *the* solution to the ethical question: 'What shall we do? To this question we now answer — *Thou shalt love thy neighbour as thyself*, inasmuch as "he that loveth the other hath fulfilled the law," does the truth and is therefore proceeding along the "more excellent way."'[265] Love, therefore, is the truly revolutionary activity, the positive human activity which corresponds to and fulfils all human not-doing, for in the *Thou shalt!* is summed up every divine *Thou shalt not!* The person 'who has been compelled to that "not-doing" which is his turning back to God is once again impelled by God to action'.[266]

Barth's contention that love of the neighbour constitutes *the* solution to the ethical dilemma must not be understated. In a remarkable meditation on Paul's text Barth goes on to insist that

> [i]n the concrete fact of the *neighbour* we encounter, finally and supremely, the ambiguity of our existence, since in the particularity of others we are reminded of our own particularity, of our own createdness, our own lost state, our own sin, and our own death....Here a decision must be sought as to whether the impossible

---

[260] Barth, *Romans II*, 492.

[261] Barth, *Romans II*, 451.

[262] Barth, *Romans II*, 493.

[263] Barth, *Romans II*, 493.

[264] Barth, *Romans II*, 501.

[265] Barth, *Romans II*, 494.

[266] Barth, *Romans II*, 496.

possibility of God—which lies beyond all human possibility—is or is not a mere phantom of metaphysics; whether, when we speak of the presupposition of all things that are capable of analysis and description, when we speak of the outpouring of the Holy Spirit in our hearts, we are or are not merely dreaming; whether our apprehension of the final Yes in the final No is or is not merely a wild guess; whether our knowledge of God is or is not simply the 'renunciation of knowledge' (Kierkegaard); whether the Unknown God has spoken to us in Jesus Christ; whether our being touched by the freedom of God, the establishing of our personalities, our proceeding along the still more excellent way, are existential events. The decision lies in our answer to the question—Do we, in the unknowable *neighbour*, apprehend and love the Unknown God? Do we, in the complete Otherness of *the other*—in whom the whole riddle of existence is summed up in such a manner as to require its solution in an action on our part—hear the voice of the One?...If I hear in the *neighbour* only the voice of *the other* and not also the voice of the One—that is to say, if I do not detect in him both question *and* answer,—then, quite certainly, the voice of the One is nowhere to be heard.[267]

In short, the entire truthfulness of Christian confession and of Christian and ecclesial existence finds its criterion in the love of the neighbour. In the neighbour we are confronted with the riddle of our existence *and* with its answer which can only be expressed 'in an action on our part.' If the criterion of all secondary ethical activities is that they arise from and are directed toward the honour of God, it is also true that all such activities will reflect the nature of love if they are genuinely ethical. Here again we see Barth's insistence that love for God will overflow and find its essential demonstration in the love people show for one another.[268]

Again it must be emphasised, however, that the activity of love as a genuinely ethical action is not a human or religious possibility, but is that 'impossible possibility' which only becomes possible through the activity of the Holy Spirit in the Moment.[269] As such, the occurrence of love is always a miracle, a genuinely human action that nevertheless 'springs from supreme knowledge; for he who loves is he who has been touched by the freedom of God.'[270] In saying this, however, Barth does not intend to diminish the urgency of the duty or the responsibility of the Christian community to practice this love. Instead, in this context he provides a development of the notion of the Moment of revelation, and in so doing intensifies the ethical demand which confronts the community in every moment. Barth understands Christian and ecclesial existence as situated in the midst of a radical temporality in which *every* moment in time is a parable of the eternal Moment, and indeed bears within itself 'the unborn secret of revelation'. In *every* moment of time

---

[267] Barth, *Romans II*, 494-495.

[268] Barth, *Romans II*, 452.

[269] Barth, *Romans II*, 497-498.

[270] Barth, *Romans II*, 498. Cf. 493.

humanity is confronted with the overhanging wall of eternity. The Christian, therefore, must 'become aware of the dignity and importance of each single concrete temporal moment, and apprehend its qualification and its ethical demand'.[271] *Every* moment in time 'apprehended and comprehended in its transcendental significance' is an occasion for the incomprehensible action of love.[272] Thus, even though love is only possible in the Moment of revelation, Barth insists that because we live in the flux of time, 'if we do not love within a succession of moments, we love not at all'.[273] Knowing the Moment in the moment, and having been loved in Christ, the only response left to the believer is to act, to love.[274] Those who take up this duty to practice love for one another fulfil the law, do the truth, and are 'therefore proceeding along the more excellent way'.[275]

This, then, is the climax of Barth's treatment of ethical issues in his Romans commentary. While Barth's answer to the ethical dilemma does not issue in specific rules, concrete behaviours or normative character requirements, his proposal that the ethical dilemma may find its solution in a love of the neighbour which fulfils the law indicates that such love is the paradigm within which the answer to the question may be found in every temporal moment. David Clough rightly observes that in his exposition on this passage (that is, Romans 13:8-14) Barth moves beyond his previous position that judged it impossible to provide any answer to the ethical dilemma. Here, remarks Clough,

> Barth is driven beyond a simple thesis and antithesis by the Pauline texts that portray love as the consummation of all things. To be sure, this escape from paradox and duality is an eschatological reality, rather than a present one. We can hope for this consummation, however, rather than remaining agnostic as to whether God's Yes or No will be finally determinative. The hope of this realm beyond the dialectical tension of the crisis is the most positive possibility we have yet seen in *Romans II*.[276]

Barth has thus traced the climax of Paul's argument to this point in chapter thirteen where love is the fulfilment of the law. While one might anticipate an exposition on Romans 14-15 to provide rich fodder for ethical reflection, particularly with respect to the corporate life of the community, Barth's

---

[271] Barth, *Romans II*, 501.

[272] Barth, *Romans II*, 497.

[273] Barth, *Romans II*, 498.

[274] Barth, *Romans II*, 501.

[275] Barth, *Romans II*, 494.

[276] Clough, *Ethics in Crisis*, 21. Clough has rightly seen that even here, Barth 'respects the distance' for although he is driven beyond the simple thesis and antithesis, yet the synthesis remains an eschatological reality, found only in God, only in hope. Cf. Chalamet, *Dialectical Theologians*, 135.

treatment of these final chapters of Paul's Epistle does not proceed in this direction. Although he admits that 'there can be no doubt that, according to the Epistle to the Romans, there is demanded of us a quite precise manner of life' which he characterises as 'free detachment',[277] his interpretation of Romans 14-15 subverts any attempt on the part of the reader to adopt this manner of life as an ethical platform upon which they might confidently stand:

> Once again our brokenness is broken. Paul against 'Paulinism!' The Epistle to the Romans against the point of view adopted in the Epistle! The Freedom of God against the manner of life which proceeds inevitably from our apprehension of it! Such is the amazing facing-about which takes place in the fourteenth chapter of the Epistle to the Romans....Once again, therefore, at the end of the Epistle to the Romans...there is presented to us the impenetrable ambiguity of human life— even of the life of the Christian and the Christian community.[278]

Simply put, the *Krisis* breaks forth even upon those adopting the manner of life that issues from the Epistle, so that there is no escaping the precarious status of ethical existence which ever remains poised on the edge of a knife.

To conclude: Barth's treatment of the great negative and positive possibilities in his exposition of Romans 13 is very significant because it clearly indicates his understanding of Christian and ecclesial existence as an *active* life, despite the apparent passivity of his exposition on subjection as 'not-doing'. The 'not-doing' of the believer is in relation to the idolatrous claim of existing powers; in relation to God, however, it is an action that corresponds to the primary ethical requirement of honouring God alone. Further, as we have seen, this not-doing is for the sake of the entirely radical action of love which is made possible by the prior action of the Holy Spirit. Thus, in his construction of the great negative and positive possibilities, we find a similar structuring between the two elements as we found in Barth's earlier structuring of the elements of waiting and hastening, in which the waiting was for the sake of the hastening. Here, too, the not-doing is for the sake of the doing. Finally, far from undermining human ethical activity, in this section we observe that Barth's time-eternity dialectic serves to radicalise the human ethical situation so that *every moment* confronts the human agent as an ethical demand.

Conclusion: *Romans II* and the Ethics of Grace

Barth characterises the ethics of *Romans II* as an 'ethics of grace',[279] the form of life and community that comes to expression as grace 'presses for concretion'. Throughout his commentary he has endeavoured to sketch and describe the moral field in which ethical existence and moral community

---

[277] Barth, *Romans II*, 503.
[278] Barth, *Romans II*, 504-505.
[279] Barth, *Romans II*, 466.

actually occurs, the ultimate reality which conditions human existence. This is not to say, however, that Barth fails to provide any concrete guidance with respect to ethical life. Rather, as we have shown, he developed his theology with an explicit concern to enable his readers to respond to the ethical issues of the immediate post-war context in which he wrote. To this end he details an array of 'positive and negative' ethical possibilities that include behaviours and actions, attitudes and virtues which the community may exhibit in their lives. But even here, Barth is careful to insist that none of these practices or virtues are inherently normative, but are ethical only to the extent that they arise from and are directed toward the honour of God. They remain *secondary* ethical activities subject always to the primary ethical activity of repentance. Nor can the practitioner ever assume that their activity is justified, for their action is ever a sacrifice awaiting a justification which comes from God alone. It is also apparent, though not surprising given the overall *critical* purpose of Barth's commentary, that his exposition places more emphasis on the negative possibilities than the positive.[280]

In some respects then, it is more accurate to describe Barth's commentary as a work of meta-ethics rather than ethics proper. His work details the arena in which ethical reflection and decision occur, the various factors which impinge upon the ethical subject and moral community, the posture of this subject and community with regard to God and the world and to all internal and external reality, and finally, the directions that ethical behaviour will take. If any aspect of Barth's ethics might be considered as having normative value, it is the insistence on repentance and worship as the primary ethical responsibility, arising simply from the fundamental presupposition of ethics: *Soli Deo gloria*. Thus Barth posits a normative *way* in which ethics is to proceed, and a normative *posture* of the ethical agent rather than a normative behaviour, character, virtue or habit. This posture includes a radical orientation to God in worship and repentance, a radical orientation to the other as the locus of our encounter with God, and a radical orientation to the Moment—which impinges upon us at every moment—as the occasion in which the ethical demand is pressed upon us.[281]

The previous chapter explored Barth's theological development after the publication of the first edition of his commentary on Romans and finished by posing three questions regarding the impact of this development on Barth's ethics. The questions posed were as follows:

---

[280] McCormack, *Karl Barth's Dialectical Theology*, 279-280.

[281] It is salutary to recall Oden's comment that 'the strength of Barth's ethics is not in any sort of deliberative, calculative criteria for moral choice. If that is all that one is looking for under the heading of "ethics," then surely Barth will be a consistent disappointment. ... The real strength is in what might be called its "theologically interpreted radical contextuality".' See Thomas C. Oden, *The Promise of Barth: The Ethics of Freedom* (Philadelphia: J.B. Lippincott, 1969), 74-75.

1.　　Does Barth's heightened emphasis on the objectivity of divine sovereignty over against humanity undermine his hitherto carefully construed relation between divine and human agency?

2.　　Given the tightening of the eschatological tension that exists between time and eternity, can Barth delineate a viable ecclesiology which in turn shapes a genuine ecclesial praxis?

3.　　Does his grounding of the moral agent in the forgiveness of sins sustain the kind of robust vision of Christian and ecclesial existence that characterised his earlier works?

Having surveyed the theological ontology of *Romans II* together with the ethical implications of this ontology we are now in a position to address these questions. With respect to the first question, it is clear that Barth's construal of the relation between divine and human agency remains remarkably similar in *Romans II* to the relation developed in his earlier works. Although the moral self is certainly de-centred, and the grounds of genuine ethical activity are strictly limited; although the heightened eschatological horizon renders *all* human activity subject to the *Krisis*, including Christian attempts at ethical behaviour arising from worship, prayer, repentance and ethical deliberation; although genuine ethical action is always subordinate to and responsive to the prior divine action, nevertheless this study has shown that there can be no doubt that there remains, even in *Romans II*, an authentic though limited form of human agency in which the human agent may enact morally responsible particular behaviours in hope that they will be accepted as ethical by God. That this will be the case cannot, of course, be presumed, 'for the world is the world and men are men. Questionable at all times is human conduct whether it be delicate or coarse....Nevertheless, we are then the beloved of God.'[282]

With respect to the second question, we have seen that Barth does not, in fact, delineate a comprehensive ecclesiology in this commentary, and that substantial elements belonging to this dogmatic locus are left untreated. Further, his dialectical treatment of ecclesiological themes means that the church, like the human agent, is radically de-centred and made, even in its attempts at obedience, ever subject to the *Krisis*. This does not mean, however, that Barth cannot develop a coherent account of ecclesial existence and praxis, although it is certain that the account he does develop lacks the breadth, depth and definition that will begin to emerge later in his career. In this commentary the praxis of the community, like that of the individual agent, is strictly limited. Its primary ethical conduct is ever the activity of worship and repentance from

---

[282] Barth, *Romans II*, 502.

which may then issue various forms of 'secondary' ethical behaviour appropriate to the specific moment and particular context in which the community finds itself. Its determination to radically orient itself to the reality of God in each moment frees the church from its cultural captivity and assimilation to pursue its own distinctive form of praxis.

With respect to the final question, Barth's grounding of the ethical subject in the forgiveness of sins does not preclude the ethical agency of the moral subject, but details the only grounds by which that agency may issue in genuinely ethical conduct. In such a scenario, *intent* is everything, although even here, one can never presume that one's ethical intent is justified. Any attempt at obedience which seeks to be more than a sacrifice of oneself for the honour and love of God fails to achieve its goal. Having once established this basic premise, however, and given the qualifications raised in the answer to the first question, there is no reason why Barth's ethical vision in *Romans II* cannot sustain a robust, though carefully nuanced, expression of Christian and ecclesial existence.

What shape might we anticipate this expression of Christian and ecclesial existence to take? Clearly Barth believes that the Epistle to the Romans claims the reader for a quite definite manner of life which he characterises as 'free detachment.'[283] Such free detachment issues both from the devastating reality of the ever-present *Krisis* that overshadows our existence, and from the hopeful reality that in Christ we have been so wholly claimed by God and bound to him that we have been set in a relative independence to every other competing claim or value. 'If then,' says Barth, 'we are to live in Pauline fashion we must dare to live freely.'[284]

Perhaps this detachment is best seen in Barth's development of the negative ethical possibilities, the deliberate *not-doing* by which the Christian community bears witness to the coming world by refusing to grant legitimacy or pathos to present social powers and conditions. But, as we have seen, in this detachment the believer and the community is freed for the doing of the positive ethical possibilities, particularly love, which is a radical orientation toward God as he encounters us and makes himself known to us in the other. Love is the very climax of ethical behaviour, the ultimate positive ethical possibility which we owe to every person in every moment.

But love is not the only characteristic of the moral community. The discussion in this chapter shows that Barth anticipates the life of the community to be also characterised by faith and hope, each of which is understood in quite radical terms. The hope of the community is radical inasmuch as it knows its *only* hope lies in the gracious activity of God on its behalf. Knowing that its

---

[283] Barth, *Romans II*, 503. See also page 504: 'It is, of course, true that a quite definite manner of life is demanded in the Epistle....It is true, also, that freedom is the essential meaning of the manner of life which is here required.'
[284] Barth, *Romans II*, 503.

existence occurs 'under the beetling crag of his *Krisis*' the community 'hurries and tarries' in light of the judgement and hope set before it.[285] Faith, too, is a radical orientation toward God in accordance with the analogy of Jesus' death on the cross which signifies the relinquishing of every support whereby humanity might seek to support itself, and of every claim which we might lodge against God. Instead, faith as the disposition of the believer and the community 'is simply open-hearted preparedness and willingness to receive' in 'fear and trembling, awe and gratitude'.[286]

Further, the manner in which Barth has structured his ethics presupposes a community of *exhortation*, a community gathered in worship and prayer constantly 'rethinking' itself in relation to God and its specific historical context. Barth also allows the community to engage in extensive ethical deliberation so long as it remains aware that any and all conclusions or systems deriving from such reflection remain radically contingent, subject to continual rethinking and even negation in the freedom of God. Thus, the community may never, even for a moment, presume that it has attained to ethical righteousness or established a position upon which it might stand. In a memorable image Barth asks, 'Dost thou see the stone rising in the midst of the stream? Well, put just one foot on it, and that only for a second, and then—jump. That is the only way to reach the other side.'[287]

'Free detachment', therefore, is applied by Barth even to those who seek to live such a life. The community must live in 'free detachment' even from itself and its own attempts at righteousness, for the life of free detachment is itself subject to the *Krisis*.[288] So it is that in his treatment of the final major section of Romans (14:1-15:13), Barth subverts the very manner of life he sees demanded of us in the Epistle. As Mark Lindsay has very aptly said, 'in the context of ethical praxis, it is clear why Barth's *Romans II* was, and remains, a bombshell. When it explodes, it shatters every human standpoint, including itself.'[289]

***

In this chapter we have demonstrated that Barth wrote his second commentary on the Epistle to the Romans with an explicit intention to form moral community and to shape Christian and ecclesial existence. That Barth addresses issues of immediate ethical concern in his historical context, particularly those issues of love and community, peace, war, revolution, and the

---

[285] Barth, *Romans II*, 163.

[286] Barth, *Romans II*, 163.

[287] Barth, *Romans II*, 521-522; cf. 524.

[288] Barth, *Romans II*, 512.

[289] Mark R. Lindsay, *Covenanted Solidarity: The Theological Basis of Karl Barth's Opposition to Nazi Antisemitism and the Holocaust* (New York: Peter Lang, 2001), 113.

relation of the believer and the church to the state and to other secular powers, is also suggestive that he sought to shape the faith and praxis of his readers. While it is true that his exposition with regard to ethics is again concerned primarily with formal categories, and as such fails to provide rich descriptions of ethical praxis, he has not left his reader without some instruction regarding the directions ethical praxis will take. This chapter has also addressed concerns that Barth's time-eternity dialectic in *Romans II* serves to preclude the possibility of genuine human ethical conduct. Indeed, if the dialectic were strictly applied it would appear that such ethical conduct would be impossible. We have demonstrated, however, that these concerns are mitigated by Barth's failure to apply his dialectic strictly. That this failure occurs, especially in contexts of ethical discussion, is indicative of the seriousness with which Barth intends his theology to be read as *moral* theology concerned with the formation of moral community, and the shaping of Christian and ecclesial existence.

Postscript: 'The Problem of Ethics Today'

Eleven months after he completed his manuscript of *Romans II*, Barth delivered a lecture in five different German towns entitled 'The Problem of Ethics Today'.[290] Although strictly speaking, this lecture belongs to Barth's Göttingen period, it will be beneficial to provide a brief overview of Barth's address at this point, first, because of the chronological proximity of this address to *Romans II*, second, because it shares the same title as the opening section in Barth's treatment of ethics in that commentary, and finally, because of its relevance to my own project.

That Barth still inhabits the thought-world of the *Römerbrief* period is evident by his frequent use of the *Krisis* motif in this lecture, particularly in the first section where it is used some eleven times, by his use of Kierkegaard to subvert the ethical idealism of modern Protestantism, and by his continuing use of other motifs such as the eternity-time dialectic and the forgiveness of sins as the primary ethical datum. Nevertheless, at several places in the lecture there are hints of further theological development. Barth's immersion in dogmatic theology due to his teaching responsibilities at Göttingen is beginning to exert a greater influence on his thought.

The lecture has four major sections, plus a shorter fifth section that functions as a conclusion. Barth commences his lecture by insisting that the problem of ethics arises as 'man finds himself seeking the inner meaning and law of his conduct, the truth about his existence'.[291] When the question regarding things as

---

[290] See Karl Barth, 'The Problem of Ethics Today,' in *The Word of God and the Word of Man* (New York: Harper and Brothers, 1956), 136-182. For dates and details regarding the various lectures, see the introduction to the lecture in Karl Barth, *The Word of God and Theology* (trans. Amy Marga; London: T. & T. Clark, 2011), 131-134.
[291] Barth, 'The Problem of Ethics,' 136.

they are merges with the ethical question regarding how they might and ought to be, the *Krisis* is precipitated and the human agent is brought face to face with the riddle of their own existence. Nor can it be otherwise: it is impossible to approach the whole question of life and ethics from the perspective of a spectator, for

> we are compelled to conceive ourselves as living doers....The fact remains that man as man is irresistibly compelled to acknowledge that his life is the business for which he is responsible, that his desires require examination, and that the might-be is sometimes the ought-to-be which is the *truth* about truth, the ultimate governor of conduct.[292]

Immediately, then, Barth sets the parameters for his lecture. First, the problem of ethics is fundamental to human life, an ontological question grounded in the actual conduct of daily existence.[293] Second, and as a consequence of this, no neutral vantage point may be secured whereby one might calmly and objectively survey the ethical field. By construing the nature of the ethical question in this manner Barth is undoubtedly turning his sights once more against the ethical idealism of modern Protestantism in order to lay the foundations for a new account of human agency.[294] Finally, because the reality of things-as-they-are *never* attains to the what-ought-to-be, the problem of ethics subverts every form of human thought and conduct with the growing realisation that we are *not* good, and hence the *Krisis* by which the human agent is cast into the hands of God.

In this lecture Barth construes the good in terms of a transcendent moral realism. The *What* in the question *what must we do?* is not part of this world as we know and conceive it. According to Barth, 'our question reaches toward a good which lies beyond all existence. Every random and temporal *What shall we do?* contains a *What* to which no random and temporal *That* can give a satisfying answer, because it is a last and eternal *What*.'[295] When a person or

---

[292] Barth, 'The Problem of Ethics,' 137-138.

[293] Gorringe, *Against Hegemony*, 89. Gorringe's further comment that, 'here again, as in *Romans*, theory arises from praxis' (89) is problematic for two reasons. First, this is not the meaning of Barth's statement in his *Romans* commentary. To say that theology 'is the theory of praxis' is to insist that theology sets the shape, direction and agenda for praxis, and finds its telos in ethical expression. Second, Gorringe's formulation provides space for the development of another form of natural theology arising from human experience. This is something Barth was seeking to purge from his thought at this period of his career.

[294] See Spencer, *Clearing a Space*, 110-121, especially page 110: 'It is in this address that Barth directly takes up the Kantian understanding of moral ontology and makes judgments about it....what Barth is doing in "The Problem of Ethics Today" is nothing less than an undoing of the idealist tradition so that he can erect a more theological account of human agency.'

[295] Barth, 'The Problem of Ethics,' 138, 141.

community ask the question they find themselves confronted by 'an Eye looking at [them] from beyond all worlds' and are assailed by the knowledge that their every act is weighed and judged. In the very asking of the question the human agent 'annihilates himself' for in his inability to attain the good required of him, he perishes.[296] Nor is asking the question an optional activity. Rather, it is 'fundamental, *first, a priori* in the situation; it takes *us* up'.[297] This is the unavoidable situation in which humanity finds itself. This is the *Krisis* in which humanity is faced with God and must perish.

In accordance with the topic of his address 'The Problem of Ethics *Today*,' Barth, in the second section of the lecture, situates the ethical problem within the contemporary socio-economic and political context of post-war Germany. While the question *What shall we do?* is one which persists in every age, the present circumstances give it a particular force and urgency. According to Barth, the pre-war era of ethical optimism and certainty has disappeared forever. No longer is it possible to ignore the 'unavoidable and *ultimate* character of the perplexity, embarrassment, and uncertainty under which man is placed by the ethical question'.[298] Indeed

> [t]he naïve belief in those better days essentially simplified the question about the good....It was then a pleasure to study ethics. Fundamentally, it was a matter not of asking *what* to do, as if that were not known, but rather of finding out whether philosophy or theology, Kant or Schleiermacher, provided the more illuminating formula for the obvious—for it was obvious that what to do was to further this infinitely imperfect but infinitely perfectible culture.[299]

As in earlier works, so here Barth rejects the church-culture synthesis that had arisen in modern Protestantism whereby ethics became an exercise in the legitimising of the status quo. He accuses the ethics of the Ritschlian school as being those of the 'bourgeoisie growing prosperous' with the expansion of empire, and those of Troeltsch as an accommodation of Christianity to the emerging German economic civilisation.[300] In other words, the answer to the ethical question was simply that 'we ought to do *this*—something which, in the state, in society, or in the church, was already being done before the question was asked'.[301] For Barth, the failure of this approach is evident. The war has revealed the emptiness and vanity of such human ethical constructs, and ethics is now seen as 'entailing a *judgement* about man as we know him—even about *moral* man as we know him'.[302]

---

[296] Barth, 'The Problem of Ethics,' 140.
[297] Barth, 'The Problem of Ethics,' 141.
[298] Barth, 'The Problem of Ethics,' 144.
[299] Barth, 'The Problem of Ethics,' 145.
[300] Barth, 'The Problem of Ethics,' 145.
[301] Barth, 'The Problem of Ethics,' 145-146.
[302] Barth, 'The Problem of Ethics,' 147.

The problem of ethics not only reveals the sickness which afflicts humanity, but shows that it is a 'sickness unto death'.[303] That the pre-war generation could approach the ethical question with such apparent ease was due in part to a theological reductionism in which the theological metaphysics of scripture and the church fathers were considered superfluous and rejected in favour of a simpler gospel 'reduced to a few religious and moral categories like trust in God and brotherly love'.[304] Barth, revealing a little of his developing theological perspective, now suggests that they are faced with a reality in which 'the difficult asseverations of the Christian dogma of the old style correspond far more closely to the actual situation than does our predecessors' confident assertion that "following Jesus" is a simple task'.[305] Accordingly, 'the era of the *old* ethics is *gone* forever....over against man's confidence and belief in himself, there has been written, in huge proportions and with utmost clearness, a *mene, mene, tekel*'.[306]

Barth concludes this section of his address with a plea to his audience not to use a false dialectic to resolve this difficulty and pre-empt the judgement under which humanity has fallen. By now the movement which had grown up around him had become popular, so that 'everywhere there are nooks and crannies where, intelligently and unintelligently, it simply buzzes with Yes! and No!, dialectic, resurrection, God is God, and all the other catchwords'.[307] Barth is concerned that some will view his lecture as a language game requiring a logical symmetry attainable by the mere positing of the Yes!, whereby the problem of ethics is simply transcended. But such a response does not 'correspond with reality'. Although 'the problem of ethics may sometime paradoxically resolve itself into justification and new possibility', says Barth, 'to *us* it reveals more clearly the negative of life, the judgement upon humanity'.[308]

In the third, central section of the lecture which begins with a proposition that is then developed in two further subsections, Barth intensifies his interrogation of modern Protestant ethics. The proposition is simply put: 'I say that the problem of ethics is a responsibility that cannot be borne: a deadly *aggression* against man.'[309] In the first subsection Barth unpacks his understanding of this aggression in terms of the asking *subject*, and in conversation with the ethics of Kant. Barth rejects Kant's conception of the autonomous moral personality whose will is strictly desirous only of *ultimate*

---

[303] Barth, 'The Problem of Ethics,' 150.
[304] Barth, 'The Problem of Ethics,' 147. The allusion to Harnack is unmistakable.
[305] Barth, 'The Problem of Ethics,' 148.
[306] Barth, 'The Problem of Ethics,' 149.
[307] Smart, *Revolutionary Theology*, 106. The statement is an excerpt from a circular letter dated July 7, 1922.
[308] Barth, 'The Problem of Ethics,' 151-152.
[309] Barth, 'The Problem of Ethics,' 152.

goals and is grounded in the 'intelligible world of freedom' on the basis that such a moral subjectivity is impossible: 'we know that no such *moral* personality has ever stepped into *our* world over the threshold of the world of freedom. No such man has ever lived or will ever live....There is no such thing in time or space as a human will determined by pure practical reason.'[310] Further, Kant's insistence that the human agent is claimed by such an impossible demand requires a correspondingly impossible act of faith with the following assumptions: first, that God is the guarantor of this moral order which contradicts the lived experience of humanity. Second, that the human agent has the capacity to make this impossible demand their own, and finally, that the human agent may then approach its actual fulfilment in the concrete experience of their lives.[311]

Underlying Barth's criticism of Kant's theory of the autonomous moral subject are two anthropological concerns. First, Kant, and the tradition which followed him are far too sanguine concerning the moral capacities of humanity, and have failed to give adequate recognition to the reality and pervasiveness of sin as the determinative factor of human existence since the Fall. The tradition has assumed an unwarranted degree of human freedom.[312] Second, Barth rejects the notion of moral autonomy as 'a kind of absolutizing of the self and its reflective consciousness....it is precisely this—the image of moral reason as a secure centre of value, omnicompetent in its judgements—that the ethical question interrogates'.[313]

For Barth, then, the problem of ethics is a deadly aggression against the moral subject as understood in modern Protestantism, because it confronts the moral subject with an impossible demand. Rather than establishing the ethical agent, the ethics deriving from Kant function only as a criticism of all ethics, and shows that such an account of moral agency is impossible.[314] Barth has taken Kantian ethics on its own terms and subverted one of its central tenets.

In the second subsection Barth considers the same issue, this time with regard to the ethical *objective*. The ethical question not only raises the difficulty concerning the human agent, but also the goal towards which human conduct is directed. Barth has already noted Kant's contention that ethics is concerned with *ultimate* rather than secondary objectives, and indeed, accepts this contention although he insists that the ultimate objective with which ethics is concerned be interpreted eschatologically. Thus, he is adamant that 'ethics can no more exist without millenarianism, without at least some minute degree of

---

[310] Barth, 'The Problem of Ethics,' 154.

[311] Barth, 'The Problem of Ethics,' 155-156.

[312] For an analysis of Barth's understanding of sin in the *Römerbrief* period, see Torrance, *Karl Barth: An Introduction*, 63-71.

[313] John Webster, *Barth's Moral Theology: Human Action in Barth's Thought* (Grand Rapids: Eerdmans, 1998), 36.

[314] Barth, 'The Problem of Ethics,' 156.

it, than without the idea of a moral personality'.[315] Ethics concerns far more than the individual: it has corporate or communal dimensions and is concerned with the goal of history. The question of the good is only asked seriously when it is accompanied by some idea as to how the good is to be realised in history.[316] Nevertheless, in relation to the ultimate goal set before it, humanity is powerless to bring it to pass for

> there is nothing in the whole range of human possibilities, from popular indifference to mystical absorption in the All, which is capable of realising the moral objective, the goal of history....Man cannot begin to answer the ethical question in actual life. He can only continue to recognise that he is wholly incapable of commanding an answer.[317]

Thus once again Barth attempts to subvert Kantian ethics, in this case the notion of the ultimate goal toward which ethical conduct is directed, and to demonstrate that ethics is a 'deadly aggression' against the human agent, whereby they stumble and are broken upon their own vision of the good. Those who ask the question about the good condemn themselves because the only answer to the question is that they are *not* good, and that from the standpoint of the good they are powerless.[318] Is there no possibility, then, of ethical existence, and more specifically, of Christian and ecclesial existence? As so often in earlier works, so here: once Barth has cleared the field of opposing viewpoints, he sets forth the framework of his own more positive proposal. In view of the 'dialectic of the thought of God' the No inherent in the problem of ethics functions in service of the divine Yes.[319]

In the fourth section of the lecture, then, Barth begins by insisting that the purpose of the 'all-inclusive critical negation under which we and our world exist' is to provoke the crisis whereby 'we understand the whole unbearable human situation, espouse it, take it upon ourselves. We are to *bend* before the doom revealed in the problem of ethics. It is through the unescapable severity of this doom that we come upon the reality of *God*.'[320] In the face of our utter inability to determine and form an adequate answer to the ethical question, we find 'the answer to all our questions is *God* and *God's* conduct toward *us*'.[321] Over against the presupposed autonomy of the moral agent of ethical idealism, Barth insists that 'the meaning of our situation is that God does not leave us and that we cannot leave God. It is because *God himself* and *God alone* lends our

---

[315] Barth, 'The Problem of Ethics,' 158.
[316] Barth, 'The Problem of Ethics,' 161.
[317] Barth, 'The Problem of Ethics,' 166.
[318] Barth, 'The Problem of Ethics,' 167.
[319] Barth, 'The Problem of Ethics,' 167.
[320] Barth, 'The Problem of Ethics,' 167-168.
[321] Barth, 'The Problem of Ethics,' 169.

life its possibility that it becomes so impossible for us to live.'[322] For Barth, humankind lives *coram Deo*, in inescapable relation to God even as sinners, so that there is no possibility of inhabiting the objective seat of a spectator as an autonomous ethical subject, as though God were not the immediate Subject to whom humanity is responsible.

It is precisely by bending before this doom, before this 'wholly negative and annihilating crisis' that the human agent becomes a participant in 'the justification, the promise, and the salutary meaning which are hidden there'.[323] As was the case in *Romans II*, however, so here—human participation in justification is strictly by means of promise: 'The new creation of man, the renewal of the unrenewable old man is a *justificatio forensis, justificatio impii*, a surpassing paradox; and so also is the positive relation of God's will to man's conduct.'[324] The final phrase of this citation must not be overlooked for there is no diminishing of the distance which separates human activity from divine righteousness: all human activity continues to bear the imprint of the fall, so that there is no salvation apart from the continuing grace of the forgiveness of sins.[325] Nevertheless, Barth is explicit in his avowal of this possibility:

> Since there is such a thing as forgiveness (which is always forgiveness of *sin!*), there is such a thing as human conduct which is justified. There is an *obedience unto salvation* which begins when we come down from our high places, from our High Place…and declare a thorough-going religious and moral disarmament. There is an effective *brotherly love* which provides a 'service' different from the Christian charity with which we are familiar; it begins with our forgiving our debtors—with empty hands!—as we also are forgiven. And if there is forgiveness, there are *worse* and *better* goals: there is such a thing as conscious choice and the establishment of a definite habit for the better. There is such a thing as cooperation in the tasks of industry, science, art, politics, and even religion; *civilisation* possesses its own true dignity, not as the very order of creation made manifest but as a *witness*, a quite earthly *reflection*, of a lost and hidden order….In brief there is such a thing as the *possibility*—and possibility here means *necessity*—of saying Yes both to the ethical question and to its *answers*— and in a way not sicklied o'er with doubt and pessimism.[326]

Clearly Barth does not assail the concept of ethics in order to annul the possibility of ethical existence. Nor has he sought to reduce the ethical subject to utter passivity, or to annihilate their agency. His intent is consistent with what has been observed throughout this period of his career: to re-establish

---

[322] Barth, 'The Problem of Ethics,' 169.

[323] Barth, 'The Problem of Ethics,' 170.

[324] Barth, 'The Problem of Ethics,' 170. See, for example, Barth, *Romans II*, 93. The two Latin terms refer to 'forensic justification' and 'justification of the ungodly,' respectively.

[325] Barth, 'The Problem of Ethics,' 171.

[326] Barth, 'The Problem of Ethics,' 172-173.

human agency on a new foundation. In this lecture as in the *Römerbrief*, the primary ethical activity consists in repentance.[327] From this primary response may then arise the kinds of responses indicated in the passage cited above. Noteworthy also is the pattern of human ethical activity, which is reflective of and witnesses to prior divine activity. Although Barth does not use the term 'correspondence' to characterise the nature of human activity in relation to divine, it is evident that this form of conceptuality is present here. While it also remains evident that these activities as thoroughly *human* deeds are at best only imperfect reflections of the divine activity, through the forgiveness of sins they are accepted before God.

Clear also is Barth's intent to form moral community. In a passage that anticipates his later development of the doctrine of God,[328] Barth portrays the Christian millennial hope as the cry to allow 'freedom in love and love in freedom [as] the pure and direct motive of social life, and a community of righteousness its direct objective'.[329] He calls for an end to paternalism, exploitation and oppression, class differences, national boundaries, war, violence, and the use and abuse of unrestrained power. He calls for a 'civilisation of the spirit [to] take the place of a civilisation of things, human values [in] the place of property values, brotherhood [in] the place of hostility'.[330] While this is certainly a vision of the *ultimate*—millennial—goal, Barth anticipates that it will find some measure of expression as the community struggles for relative ends in the 'humdrum purposes of every day'.[331] An ethics of grace grounded in the forgiveness of sins has no place for 'a cheap quietism' for 'forgiveness is found only in *God*, and God found only in the sense of *need* into which the problem of ethics plunges us, and the salutary sense of need only in the midst of real *struggle*'.[332]

Barth concludes this section of his lecture with another defence of his use of dialectical language, a protest against those who accuse him of empty intellectualism, and a warning that the resolution of the dialectic does not lie in human hands, but in God's. The truthfulness of the possibility of grace, of 'a life justified in its sanctity and obedience'[333] does not lodge in the dialectical manner in which Barth has set them forth. It is not true just because he or anyone else states that it is so. Its truthfulness is lodged in the freedom of God's election, and the human agent, like a shipwrecked sailor, can only ever and

---

[327] Barth, 'The Problem of Ethics,' 169.
[328] See Barth, *Church Dogmatics II/1*, 257, where Barth speaks of 'the being of God as the One who loves in freedom'.
[329] Barth, 'The Problem of Ethics,' 160.
[330] Barth, 'The Problem of Ethics,' 160.
[331] Barth, 'The Problem of Ethics,' 160. See also Webster, *Barth's Moral Theology*, 37.
[332] Barth, 'The Problem of Ethics,' 172.
[333] Barth, 'The Problem of Ethics,' 177.

again 'cling to the rocks which would have wrecked him'.[334]

Barth thus opens his conclusion with the wry statement that his audience could hardly expect him now to add a 'happy ending' for 'there is none for *me* to add'.[335] The 'circle' of his survey of the problem of ethics has reached its limit. Just at this point, however, something new remains to be said: a new circle, external to the present circle intersects the circle of the problem of ethics. This is the circle of faith and revelation which might also be termed *Jesus Christ. He* is the turn of the dialectic from No to Yes, from doom to grace and from death to life.[336] For Barth, Jesus Christ is the solution to the ethical dilemma, not as religious withdrawal from the arena of ethics and engagement with the world, but as the eschatological promise and reality of redemption of the world, and as the present justification even of our own imperfect and terribly limited ethical activity. Paul and the Reformers, says Barth, preached Jesus Christ as the solution to the ethical problem:

> Solution is certain because salvation is certain....Salvation is certain because the new man is present from above, bringing the new heaven and the new earth, the kingdom of God....This is the reason they preached the forgiveness of sins as the fundamental answer to the ethical question. But note that forgiveness always takes the way *from God to man* and never otherwise.[337]

In another hint of his development Barth also insists that Jesus Christ is to be understood not in terms of theological idealism, but dogmatically, in accordance with the traditional creeds of the church, in accordance with the reality that he and he alone is the divine act of redemption for humanity and the world. The answer to the problem of ethics is grounded in God's action understood in terms of resurrection from the dead and new creation. But while human activity can never achieve the comprehensive renewal of all things, it may and indeed *must* take relative and limited steps in that direction.

In this important lecture, then, we again find that Barth has a definite place for human ethical action, and envisages the church as a particular community with a particular ethos. We also find a possible reason for the largely formal character of his ethics. In an interesting aside Barth affirms the need for a comprehensive vision of the future such as is found in the socialist idealism of Ragaz:

> As a matter of fact, many of Ragaz' critics have an ideal for the future which differs from his only in that their field of vision, being perceptibly shortened, has a somewhat different colouring. If they find satisfaction in believing, for instance, in the future of Germany or the church or missions, may they not, must they not,

---

[334] Barth, 'The Problem of Ethics,' 178.
[335] Barth, 'The Problem of Ethics,' 179.
[336] Barth, 'The Problem of Ethics,' 180.
[337] Barth, 'The Problem of Ethics,' 180-181.

go on to draw the circle of their hopes with a somewhat longer radius or from a slightly different centre?....*All* ideas as to the goal of history are 'imaginative' and so are all of today's ideas as to the next steps which might lead thither. The *essential* elements in both the near and the distant goals, so far as they are ethical, *must* be very much the same.[338]

Barth argues that the means, methods and journey toward the ultimate goal may differ from group to group. What is important is that the community move toward this goal and that the elements of the goal are present within the movement as they progress toward it. It is also apparent that Barth *purposely* avoids ethical prescription, allowing the individual and community freedom to answer the ethical question in accordance with their uniqueness,[339] which also is in part, predicated upon their particular vision of the future. Curiously, then, Barth gives place to moral imagination in the process of ethical discernment. Perhaps it is this freedom of the individual and community which lies behind Barth's reticence to propound a specific material content in his ethical programme. By providing a description of the moral space in which the agents and community have their existence, and of the ultimate goal toward which their existence is directed; by indicating the lines and patterns of the divine activity toward and on behalf of humanity; by humbling human pride and releasing them from the presumption of responsibility for the establishing of the new creation, Barth has freed the individual and the community for responsible though relative ethical action that bears witness to the divine activity and to the coming world, in accordance with their sense of a specific call, emerging and encountering them as they wait upon and seek God in worship, prayer, reflection and discernment in their own particular time and location.

---

[338] Barth, 'The Problem of Ethics,' 159.
[339] Barth, 'The Problem of Ethics,' 160-161.

CHAPTER 6

THE CHURCH AS MORAL COMMUNITY: CONCLUDING REFLECTIONS

> The ethical problem has nowhere been left out of account. The questions, 'What shall we do?'—'How are we to live?' have nowhere been excluded. We have not been searching out hidden things for the mere joy of so doing....the whole concrete situation—this has always been our starting point....The need of making decisions of will, the need for action, the world as it is—this it is which has compelled us to consider what the world is, how we are to live in it, and what we are to do in it.[1]

My purpose in this book has been to demonstrate that Karl Barth's theology was always a theology in service of ethics, specifically, an ecclesial ethics which sought to shape the actual life and conduct of the church. From his dispute with the theological liberalism of his training occasioned by the *ethical* failure of his mentors, to the explicit assertions of *Romans II*, the ethical problem was, in fact, part and parcel of all his theological reflection. Certainly with regard to his own audience, Barth preached, lectured and wrote with a view to helping his hearers and readers discern the patterns and pathways of faithful response to God in ethical matters of immediate relevance and consequence. To that extent at least, Barth's theology and ethics were a contextual theology and ethics.

This study has further suggested that Barth's work, at least in part, might be regarded as a work of meta-ethics rather than ethics proper, in that his primary concern is to describe the moral field in which ethical existence occurs, rather than to prescribe a range of normative behaviours, virtues, decisions or habits. This feature of Barth's ethical programme has long proved problematic for some of his interpreters, many of whom seek more specific ethical guidance than Barth was willing to give. As we have seen, however, Barth did, in fact, delineate the nature and direction of an ecclesial ethics, providing some quite rich descriptions of genuinely ethical existence. In the first section of this final chapter, then, I reiterate the nature of Barth's ecclesial ethics by outlining the shape of his ethical vision with regard to Christian and ecclesial existence. This section highlights six central features that characterise Barth's ethical vision in

---

[1] Karl Barth, *The Epistle to the Romans* (trans. E. C. Hoskyns;, 6th ed. Oxford: Oxford University Press, 1933), 427.

the *Römerbrief* period. The second section of the chapter extends and deepens this analysis by insisting that Barth's ethics are *necessarily* an ecclesial ethics, and that this orientation is neither accidental nor incidental but an essential implication of his theological commitment to the work of the Holy Spirit. The second section also shows how Barth continued to utilise the motif of waiting, hastening and prayer as an important expression of ethical existence over the course of his career.

Karl Barth's Ecclesio-Ethical Theology I: The Shape of his Vision

In these chapters I have traced the development of Barth's vision of Christian and ecclesial existence in broadly chronological terms from his dispute with the liberal theology of his heritage circa 1915, to the publication of his second commentary on Paul's Epistle to the Romans in 1922. In what follows I will provide a more synthetic summary of our findings rather than a simple reiteration of the conclusions of each chapter, and will show that Barth's vision revolves around six central ideas.

An Ethics of Grace

The first central idea is that genuine ethical existence is predicated on the forgiveness of sins and is as such, an ethics of grace. While this theme received dramatic emphasis in *Romans II* and the lectures immediately prior to this work, it was nevertheless present as a primary feature even of Barth's earlier works. Already in his sermon 'The Righteousness of God,' God's will is viewed as 'wholly other' and his righteousness is so utterly beyond human achievement that nothing remains for humanity in its fallen state other than 'a re-creation and re-growth'.[2] In this respect, Barth's theology is an echo of the twenty-eighth thesis of Luther's Heidelberg Disputation that 'the love of God does not find, but creates, that which is pleasing to it'.[3]

---

[2] Karl Barth, 'The Righteousness of God,' in *The Word of God and the Word of Man* (New York: Harper & Brothers, 1956), 24.

[3] See Martin Luther, 'Heidelberg Disputation (1518),' in *Luther's Works Volume 31: The Career of the Reformer 1* (ed. H. J. Grimm; Philadelphia: Muhlenberg, 1957), 57. Note that Barth does not actually cite this Disputation in any of the works examined in this thesis. Compare Wannenwetsch's account of Luther's ethical thought: 'There is no single key to Luther's moral theology....If one should attempt to formulate a common rule in terms of a grammar that governs the various language games, it would perhaps be ideally expressed in what Luther himself called "vita passive" – a concept that could be rendered "living a receptive life". Christian ethos and ethics should conceive of everything that is to be done and left undone as being shaped by God's own activity: marked by a passivity that can be highly active, transcending the inherited antinomy between the active and contemplative lives' (see Bernd Wannenwetsch, 'Luther's Moral

Grace, in Barth's early theology, has a variety of nuances as we have seen throughout the thesis. Grace refers variously to the new ontological situation created in Jesus Christ, to the forgiveness of sins by which we are pardoned and stand before God in utter liberty, to the power of the resurrection at work within believers effecting the creation of a new subject, and to the mighty claim of God lodged against our lives. As such, grace is both indicative and imperative, pardon and empowerment.[4] Grace means the effecting of a new relationship of human agents with God, as well as the ontic renewal and visible sanctification of individuals as the same grace presses for concretion in the power of the Holy Spirit. By grace God has bound his people to himself in order to make them free of every other power, fate, lordship or bondage. It is this liberty before God exemplified in the forgiveness of sins which is the genesis of ethical existence. Because the establishing of God's kingdom is God's own work, a work of new creation in the midst of the old world, and because there is no possibility of any genuinely good human work apart from grace, Barth rejects every human attempt to develop a self-grounded ethics. Genuine ethical existence is wholly gratuitous, wholly a work of divine grace whereby we are freed to be what God has created and calls us to be: his children.

A Responsive Ethics

Second, Barth's ethics are best understood as an ethics of divine initiative and human response. The works examined in this book have demonstrated that fears that Barth's ethics of grace effectively annul legitimate human agency are unfounded. At every point we have seen that Barth finds place for genuine human action and agency. His construal of human agency, however, is markedly different from that of modernity deriving from Descartes and Kant. For Barth, human agency is legitimate only to the extent that it is subordinate to and dependent upon the prior and greater agency of God. This distinctive ordering of divine and human agency does not abolish the latter but provides the only means by which it is truly freed from the enslaving consequences of sin and thus enabled to become genuinely *human*. This distinctive ordering of divine and human agency further means that Barth's ethics have the character of response to the gracious initiative, call and command of God both at the inception of, and throughout the continuation of Christian life. Barth does not reject human agency per se, but models of human agency which set the moral agent in independence alongside, above or against God and which are thus

---

Theology,' in *The Cambridge Companion to Martin Luther Cambridge Companions to Religion* (ed. Donald K. McKim; Cambridge: Cambridge University Press, 2003), 133-134).

[4] See J. Couenhoven, 'Grace as Pardon and Power: Pictures of the Christian Life in Luther, Calvin and Barth,' *Journal of Religious Ethics* 28.1 (2000): 63-88.

insufficiently sensitive to the theological realities of creation, fall and redemption as Barth understands them.

Contrary, then, to some critics, Barth repudiates a quietist or sectarian ethics and insists that Christian and ecclesial existence presupposes an active life in response to the reality and command of God which is determinative of all existence. While Barth's doctrine of the divine command is still under-developed in this phase of his career, it is evident that the later development of this theme in his theology is built upon foundations originally laid here.

An Eschatological Ethics

Third, Barth has developed an eschatological ethics oriented towards the coming world and in contradiction to the fallen nature of human existence in the present age. We have noted that Barth's intention was always to insist that because God's kingdom is God's work alone, its presence or coming cannot be identified with, predicated upon or instigated by any human activity, including especially the activity of the church. Nevertheless, his model of eschatology in the years 1915-1918 compromised this theological conviction so that the Holy Spirit's activity resulted in the emerging enclave of God bearing a direct testimony to the presence of the kingdom. From 1919 on, however, his more stringent eschatology ensured that such direct identification between human activity and the presence of the kingdom was no longer possible. In both periods, however, the essential orientation of Christian and ecclesial existence was the same, and involved a vital *waiting* for the coming kingdom. Yet as this study has amply demonstrated, this waiting does not require a passive or quietist ethics. To the contrary, Barth learnt from Blumhardt that a genuine waiting for the eschatological kingdom must issue in a hastening toward that kingdom. In addition, such hastening exhibits and reflects the duality of the divine No and Yes toward the world, incorporating both the element of protest against the nature and course of the present age, as well becoming a sign or foretaste of the coming world. While it is certainly true that in this period of his career Barth's emphasis fell decidedly on the No, it is also true that the No functioned in service of an ultimate Yes, and as such his ethics are fundamentally an ethics of hope. The ground of this hope is, of course, the resurrection of Jesus which is the genesis and presence of the new world.

An Ethics of Witness

Closely associated with eschatological ethics is Barth's fourth central idea: his notion of ethical existence as witness to the kingdom of God. The community testifies to the coming kingdom by its existence as a contrast community to the greed, injustice, violence, militarism and isolation of the present world. In *Romans I* it is the enclave in which the power of God which appeared in Christ comes to expression once more in the members of his body, so that the community lives and moves in contrast to the dominant cultural powers amongst which it has its existence. In *Romans II* witness is the primary category Barth uses to explicate the ethical posture of the community in its relation to the world and to the coming kingdom. The church does not possess or mediate divine grace, but exists as a sign pointing away from itself toward the true reality from which its existence derives. As such, the church can never be more than the witness exemplified by Grünewald's John, and should it seek to be so, it actually forfeits the true nature of its being. Thus Barth portrays Christian and ecclesial existence as ec-centric, an ever-renewed response to the ultimate external reality towards which it points.

The witness of the Christian community is also cruciform and corresponds to the being and activity of God, especially as revealed in Jesus Christ. Accordingly, the praxis of the community was of particular import for Barth, and indeed a cause of great concern for him. His early appreciation of socialism was predicated upon his belief that socialist praxis corresponded to the nature of the kingdom as expressed in the life of Jesus in stark contrast to the culturally compromised praxis of mainstream religion. Against the assimilation of the church to the nationalist and bourgeois presumptions of the prevailing culture, Barth calls the church to an alternative praxis which enters into solidarity with the poor and lowly in accordance with his vision of the eschatological kingdom of unity, freedom and equity. Against the pretensions of the revolutionary he calls the church to bear witness to the true revolution which comes from God alone, by practicing love towards enemies and by becoming a community of forgiveness and reconciliation. In both instances he calls the church to live in accordance with its own integrity as *God's* people and with a praxis that corresponds to *his* activity and to the promise of the coming kingdom. In both instances he also envisages that the church forsakes reliance on earthly forms of power because it entrusts itself fully to the power and hope of the resurrection.

A Communitarian Ethics

The fifth central aspect of Barth's moral vision is that his ethics is an ethics of community. Barth highlights the communal nature of Christian existence with his rejection of the individualism which characterised his cultural milieu, and more profoundly, with his theological depiction of the other as the locus of our encounter with God. He characterises the community as the enclave or vanguard of the new world, a proleptic witness of God's intent for the entirety of human society.

Throughout the study I noted the severe criticism of the church and religion in which Barth engages, and argued that Barth's critique of the church is that of an insider. Barth's polemic against the cultural assimilation and captivity of the contemporary church functioned in service of a positive goal, namely, to call the church to a new faithfulness as a distinct community which lives in

accordance with its own integrity as *God's* eschatological people. Barth
envisaged the community not in terms of the institutional church, but as a
Gemeinde awakened by the Spirit through the event of revelation, and gathered
as a community of worship, prayer and discernment awaiting the command of
the moment by which its character and activity might be formed and guided.
The waiting of the community is not viewed as a formless or arbitrary waiting,
for the community is also a community of exhortation and moral instruction as
believers attend to the proclamation of Scripture, as well as to careful analysis
and scrutiny of contemporary events in light of the eternal and ultimate realities
arising from theological reflection. Barth's great hope was that the life of the
coming world and genuine sanctification would come to visible expression in
Christian communities as they gave themselves to God in prayerful, penitent
hearing, reflection and waiting. It is also clear that Barth envisaged that the
community would in some sense be a community of virtue bearing its own
particular character in the world. Thus we have repeatedly noted the many
occasions in these works when Barth identified particular characteristics he
considered typical of genuine Christian and ecclesial existence. For example,
Barth speaks of faith and faithful obedience, purity, goodness, brotherhood,
courage, endurance, joy, hope, gratitude, open ears, contrition, humility and, of
course, love, as virtues which will typically come to expression as the believer
is encountered by God and responds in faith by the power of the Holy Spirit.

A Universal Ethics

Finally, Barth's ethics are a universal ethics. This claim is almost counter-
intuitive given the manner in which his ethics is decidedly an ecclesial ethics
grounded in the gracious revelatory activity of the Holy Spirit, and strictly
oriented toward God in prayer, worship and repentance. Nevertheless, it is my
claim that Barth's ethics, while decidedly an ecclesial ethics, are also a
universal ethics and are certainly not to be considered as sectarian. Throughout
the period examined in this study Barth rejected any kind of Pietist or monastic
withdrawal from human society and to the contrary, demanded the church's
thorough-going solidarity with and engagement in the common life, and social
and political affairs of the wider community. Further, while it is certainly true
that this ethics can pertain only to those people for whom the indicative
presuppositions of Romans chapters five to eight have become actual,[5] because
these presuppositions describe the true nature of ultimate reality and thus the
moral field in which all human existence actually occurs, the ethics arising
from these presuppositions are universal in their relevance. The manner of life
which is to come to expression in the Christian community is, therefore, that
which is appropriate and valid for all humanity. For this reason Barth can
confidently exhort his parishioners to live 'the true life that men ought to live'

[5] Barth, *Romans I*, 463-464. See also page 122 above.

amidst the sham life of their compatriots and for their benefit.[6]

In sum, this study has shown that Barth developed his theology with a view to forming moral community, that is, with a specific intention to shape the way Christians and Christian communities actually conduct their affairs in this world. His ethics are an ethics of grace in which human moral existence is grounded in the gratuitous activity of God on humanity's behalf; a responsive ethics with a distinctive ordering of divine and human agency, in which the latter is always subsequent to and dependent upon the former; an eschatological ethics oriented to the coming kingdom of righteousness and freedom inaugurated by the resurrection of Jesus from the dead, which thus also protests the present course of human society as it exists in contradiction to the eschatological vision of the new world; an ethics of witness which testifies to the ultimate reality within which our existence occurs, and to the being and activity of God which alone can establish the kingdom in its fullness; a communitarian ethics in which the Christian community, because it is bound to one Lord, is freed from all other dependencies to exist as a distinct and contrast community within the broader society, and finally, an universal ethics that purports to delineate the truly virtuous life because it is grounded in and responsive to the true nature of ultimate reality. Of these six central aspects of Barth's vision of Christian and ecclesial existence in this period of his career, the first is primary. The attempt to adopt these central aspects as a programme to be applied for ethical existence is entirely to misconstrue Barth's most fundamental insight: true ethical existence is a gift. It is not a programme of particular activities to be adopted or a form of life to be cultivated as though those activities or form of life were inherently moral. Rather, genuine Christian and ecclesial existence emerges when the Holy Spirit graciously encounters and awakens the human agent to a new awareness of ultimate reality and in so doing empowers that person to respond in faithful and immediate obedience. In the next section I will show that it is this particular work of the Holy Spirit which renders Barth's ethics a necessarily *ecclesial* ethics. I will also provide a brief indication of how these central aspects of Barth's ecclesial ethics are drawn together in the pivotal activities of waiting, hastening and prayer.

Karl Barth's Ecclesio-Ethical Theology II:
Why Barth's Ethics are Necessarily an *Ecclesial* Ethics

Chapter one of this study argued that unless Barth is read carefully and in accordance with his own presuppositions and theological commitments, misunderstandings of his theology are virtually inevitable. This is particularly the case when we seek to think with and after Barth in ethical matters. For

---

[6] Barth, 'The Individual (2 Corinthans 4:7-15)' in Karl Barth & Eduard Thurneysen, *Come Holy Spirit* (trans. E.G. Homrighausen, K.J. Ernst & G.W. Richards; Edinburgh: T. & T. Clark, 1934), 243-244.

example, we have noted that apart from his carefully nuanced theological ontology Barth's ethics are simply incomprehensible, and that failure to read Barth's ethics in light of this ontology is the fault which has, perhaps more than any other factor, resulted in the many misinterpretations of Barth's ethics that have arisen both during and after his lifetime.

Thus we have continually been made aware of the primary aspects of Barth's theological ontology, most particularly his emphasis on the sovereignty of God, and the eschatological structuring of the God-world relation. In fact, Barth's characteristic emphasis on divine sovereignty, which emerged with great forcefulness in this period of his career, is the primary presupposition underlying the entirety of his theological and ethical project.[7] God is a being whole and complete in himself before, beyond and over against humanity. Only as interpreters are willing to acknowledge the legitimacy of this theological and moral ontology will they make sense of Barth's ethics.

But this insistence on the divine aseity is not the only presupposition operative in Barth's theology. Another fundamental presupposition that emerges in this period and which finds continual expression throughout the entirety of his career is his reliance upon the work of the Holy Spirit. In this section I deepen and extend the simple claim that Barth has developed an ecclesial ethics, by showing that the ecclesial orientation of his ethics is neither accidental nor incidental. Rather, the very structure of his theology, shaped as it is by a fundamental reliance on the work of the Holy Spirit, renders his ethics *necessarily* and *essentially* an *ecclesial* ethics.

If Barth's vision of Christian and ecclesial existence rests upon the crucial work of the Holy Spirit, it comes to primary expression in the responsive activities of waiting, hastening and prayer. These practices, already prominent in Barth's early works examined in this study, continue to play a fundamental role in his ethical thought in later years. Thus this section also provides a brief indication of how Barth developed these motifs in his later career, and how they function as the nexus of the various central elements of his ecclesial ethics surveyed in the previous section.

---

[7] John Webster has suggested that 'The *Church Dogmatics* as a whole is one lengthy exposition of the statement which in a very particular way is "at once the basis and the content of all the rest"…that "God is". One of the ways in which the *Dogmatics* can be construed is as a massively ramified reassertion of the aseity of God.' See John Webster, *Barth's Ethics of Reconciliation* (Cambridge: Cambridge University Press, 1995), 2-3, citing Karl Barth, *Church Dogmatics II/1: The Doctrine of God* (ed. G. W. Bromiley & T. F. Torrance, trans. W. B. Johnston, T. H. L. Parker, H. Knight & J. L. M. Haire; Edinburgh: T. & T. Clark, 1957), 257-259). Webster is careful, however, to make a crucial qualification: Barth's construal of the aseity of God is only correctly understood in relation to Jesus Christ and the covenant established between God and humanity in him. As such, 'the *Church Dogmatics* is also all along the line an anthropology'.

The Work of the Holy Spirit

Just as Barth's ethics are unintelligible apart from an apprehension of his theological and moral ontology, so they are often misunderstood as a result of the failure to see that his ethics are predicated on the crucial work of the Holy Spirit. As I noted in the conclusion of the preceding section, genuine Christian and ecclesial existence emerges when the Holy Spirit graciously encounters and awakens the human agent to a new awareness of ultimate reality and in so doing empowers that person to respond in faithful and immediate obedience. In this book we have noted this crucial activity at a number of points. For example, in 'The Strange New World in the Bible' we saw that it is the work of the Holy Spirit to make visible the newness of the kingdom of God here in the present world. So too in *Romans I* the Holy Spirit is the immanent power of the coming kingdom vigorously bringing forth the life of the kingdom here and now. In *Romans II* the agent of the divine-human encounter who establishes human agents in faith and obedience is the Holy Spirit. He is the miraculous factor in faith. He it is who touches our world and our lives in the moment of revelation and creates the new subject who stands upright in the presence of God. It is his work to bring forth the impossible possibility of genuine love in human relations which is the climax of ethics and the fulfilling of the law.

This emphasis on the crucial work of the Holy Spirit continues as a fundamental presupposition of Barth's theology throughout his career, and as such exercises a determinative function in regard to his ethics. Barth's understanding of the Spirit's activity in connection with ethics and Christian life receives substantial treatment prior to the *Dogmatics* in his Münster *Ethics* of 1928-29, as well as an important though more compact treatment in his 1929 lectures published under the title *Zur Lehre vom Heiligen Geist*.[8] In the latter work, for example, Barth argues that Christian life is *created* life as the human person in their creaturely and individual existence is 'opened, prepared and made fit by God for God'.[9] He argues further that it is the work of the Holy Spirit to grant us *con-scientia* (co-knowledge) with God, that we might genuinely apprehend the knowledge of the Father's will. In the Holy Spirit we are granted the voice of conscience to speak to us, and as a result we speak and act and live.[10]

Again, in the *Dogmatics* when Barth seeks to detail the origins of Christian life and righteousness, he turns to exposition of the Holy Spirit's activity: 'The work of the Holy Spirit is that our blind eyes are opened and that thankfully and

---

[8] See Karl Barth, *Ethics* (trans. G. W. Bromiley; Edinburgh: T. & T. Clark, 1981), and Karl Barth, *The Holy Spirit and the Christian Life: The Theological Basis of Ethics* (trans. R. B. Hoyle; Louisville: Westminster/John Knox, 1993).
[9] Barth, *The Holy Spirit and the Christian Life*, 6-7.
[10] Barth, *The Holy Spirit and the Christian Life*, 65.

in thankful self-surrender we recognise and acknowledge that it is so.'[11] That this is a conviction that Barth held to the end of his life is clearly seen in his exposition of the 'Baptism with the Holy Spirit' in his final publication.[12] Here, time and again, Barth characterises the Christian life under the nomenclature of 'mystery' and 'miracle', adopting terms previously used to indicate the mystery of the incarnation of Christ, and the miracle of his virgin birth and human existence by means of the Holy Spirit.[13] Use of this terminology has the effect of situating the reality of the Christian life under the purview of the Holy Spirit. In so doing Barth does not intend to restrict or diminish the reality of human agency and volition, but rather to insist that the divine irruption into human life is never predicated on anthropological or historical grounds, but remains always and ever the work of the Holy Spirit. In this sense, then, Christian life, like Christian theology generally, is as Barth insisted in *Romans II*, situated 'in mid-air'.[14]

Is this not precisely the problem, critics might ask—that Christian life and theology is thereby rendered irrational? It can be argued readily that recourse to the Holy Spirit simply introduces circularity into Barth's argument, for who can testify to the divinity of the work of the Holy Spirit's witness save the Holy Spirit? Bruce McCormack acknowledges this difficulty:

> Because the reality which Christian faith presupposes (as it undertakes theological reflection) is not disclosed to all but only to faith, there will still be a sense in which *the credibility of Barth's entire procedure rests upon the experienced reality of that internal testimony of the Holy Spirit which gives rise to faith in the Church* and, therefore, upon an experience which is not universally shared. Subjectivism is a danger; make no mistake. But it is Barth's view that the only adequate safeguard against the threat of subjectivism will be found in the

---

[11] Karl Barth, *Church Dogmatics I/2: The Doctrine of the Word of God* (ed. G. W. Bromiley & T. F. Torrance, trans. G. T. Thompson & H. Knight; Edinburgh: T.& T. Clark, 1956), 239.

[12] Karl Barth, *Church Dogmatics IV/4: The Doctrine of Reconciliation (Fragment)* (ed. G. W. Bromiley & T. F. Torrance, trans. G. W. Bromiley; Edinburgh: T. & T. Clark, 1969).

[13] See, for example, Barth, *Church Dogmatics IV/4*, 3, 5, 17, etc. For Barth's use of the terms 'mystery' and 'miracle' to refer to the incarnation and the virgin birth of Christ, see Barth's discussion of 'The Miracle of Christmas' in Barth, *Church Dogmatics I/2*, 172-173 and also Karl Barth, *Dogmatics in Outline* (trans. G. T. Thompson; London: SCM Press, 1949), 95-100. See also the parallelism established between the Spirit as the origin of both Jesus' human existence and the existence of the Christian community in Karl Barth, *Evangelical Theology: An Introduction* (trans. G. Foley; Grand Rapids: Eerdmans, 1963), 54-55.

[14] Barth, *Evangelical Theology: An Introduction*, 48-54. See also pages 198-199, 201 above.

objectivity of a God who discloses Himself in such a way that He remains Lord of the epistemic relation.[15]

McCormack correctly identifies the illuminating work of the Holy Spirit as a fundamental presupposition operative in Barth's theology. He also recognises that the credibility of Barth's entire programme rests upon this notion, and further acknowledges that this is a particular rather than universal experience. Dependence upon this presupposition does not, however, render Barth's programme irrational. What it does indicate is that Barth is operating with a different model of rationality than that of his critics.[16] McCormack thus continues:

> No doubt, David Friedrich Strauss was right when he said that the internal testimony of the Holy Spirit was the Achilles heel of Protestant theology. No human apologetic, not Pannenberg's or anyone else's, can strengthen us at this our point of greatest weakness. God alone can do that. '...there at its [Protestant theology's] weakest point, where it can only acknowledge and confess, it has its indestructible strength' (*CD* I/2: 537).[17]

This refusal of any presupposition other than the reality of God has a fundamental implication for Barth's ethics: they are necessarily an *ecclesial* ethics, grounded in the activity of the Holy Spirit who in the act of creating faith also creates the church and calls forth the obedience which is characteristic of the people of God. Although Barth in his early period has not yet developed the trinitarian underpinning of his theology, its essential orientation is here present, albeit in nascent form.[18] For Barth, our knowledge of and incorporation into the divine reality is not a human work, but the work of God the Holy Spirit. The fact, however, that the Spirit is not limited to working solely within the realm of the church, and is ever pressing the church into a living solidarity with the world, shows that this ecclesial ethic is not to be construed in a sectarian sense.

The Centrality of Prayer

If Barth's vision of Christian and ecclesial existence rests upon the crucial

---

[15] Bruce L. McCormack, 'Barth in Context: A Response to Professor Gunton,' *Scottish Journal of Theology* 49, no. 4 (1996): 497, emphasis added.

[16] For a discussion of the kind of rationality at work here, see Michael D. O'Neil, 'Ethics and Epistemology: Ecclesial Existence in a Postmodern Era,' *Journal of Religious Ethics* 34, no. 1 (2006): 21-40.

[17] McCormack, 'Barth in Context,' 497.

[18] This is particularly evident at the climax of 'The Strange New World Within the Bible.' See Karl Barth, 'The Strange New World within the Bible,' in *The Word of God and the Word of Man* (New York: Harper and Brothers, 1956), 48-50.

work of the Holy Spirit, it comes to primary expression in the responsive activities of waiting, hastening and prayer. As in the previous sub-section, I will show that Barth's emphasis in this period on waiting, hastening and prayer finds continual expression throughout his career.[19] Barth's use of the waiting and hastening motif surfaces at various places in the *Church Dogmatics*, generally in eschatological contexts as might be expected. For example, in his discussion of the time of revelation, Barth insists that the entirety of Christian existence—including Word and sacrament, faith, sanctification and justification, Christian identity, the activity of the Holy Spirit, and much more—can only be understood as eschatological existence. Because of this reality 'the Church of the New Testament lives in this time-consciousness; that is, it is the Church of those who "wait" and "hasten."'[20] In this context the waiting and hastening of the church refers to its steadfast endurance of the present as it awaits the fulfilment of revelation, and to the thorough ordering of its present existence in light of the coming Judge.

Barth's most prominent discussion of this concept, however, occurs outside the *Dogmatics*, in the Münster *Ethics* of 1928-29, and in his final lectures on dogmatics preserved in *The Christian Life*.[21] In the former series of lectures, Barth treats the concept under the rubric of 'The Command of God the Redeemer,' in association with the topics of hope and conscience.[22] Having carefully delineated what he intends when speaking of conscience, Barth says that 'when conscience speaks to people, it involves a categorical command to wait'. Similarly, 'when conscience speaks to people, it also involves a categorical command to hasten'.[23] Against the criticism that this is contradictory Barth argues:

> Waiting *and* hastening, says scripture (2 Pet. 3:12). Even the fact that scripture uses two words here indicates already that for our ears the one command splits into two....All the more important is it for all of us, then, to realize that it is the

---

[19] The importance of this motif in Barth's ethics is acknowledged in the title of Biggar's treatment of Barth's ethics. See Nigel Biggar, *The Hastening That Waits: Karl Barth's Ethics*, Revised ed. (Oxford: Clarendon, 1993).

[20] See Barth, *Church Dogmatics I/2*, 68-70. See also Karl Barth, *Church Dogmatics IV/2: The Doctrine of Reconciliation* (ed. G. W. Bromiley & T. F. Torrance, trans. G. W. Bromiley; Edinburgh: T. & T. Clark, 1958), 605-606, and especially, Karl Barth, *Church Dogmatics IV/3.2: The Doctrine of Reconciliation* (ed. G. W. Bromiley & T. F. Torrance, trans. G. W. Bromiley; Edinburgh: T. & T. Clark, 1962), 939-942, where Barth speaks of the 'prophetic character' of Christian hope.

[21] In a sense, these two lecture series on theological ethics serve as bookends for the entirety of Barth's mature theology, that is, the *Church Dogmatics*. Although no more than an accident of history, it is nonetheless symbolic of the ethical orientation of the entirety of his work.

[22] Barth, *Ethics*, 473-475, 487-492.

[23] Barth, *Ethics*, 487.

one revolutionary voice of conscience, the voice of hope, which on two sides points and pushes those who hear it beyond things as they are in the kingdoms of nature and grace.[24]

As in the earlier works on Blumhardt, so here. Waiting and hastening is viewed as a revolutionary activity, instigated by the Holy Spirit who grants to God's children the reality of conscience, and who thus presses believers 'beyond things as they are in the kingdoms of nature and grace'. Indeed, Barth questions whether 'we have really heard the command of conscience if we are not really anointed with a single drop of enthusiastic oil, if what we do is only conservative and not also revolutionary'.[25]

Crucially, not only does Barth ground this notion in Scripture, but it is clear that he also intends a precise ordering of the two elements: the hastening is preceded by and arises out of the waiting. For Barth, only in this order, only when the command to wait, surrender and rest is taken seriously, can the hastening be considered genuine obedience. In these lectures waiting is carefully nuanced to mean an inner work which orients the entire person towards their future as it will be revealed in the person of the Redeemer and of the coming kingdom of glory, thus resulting in a fundamental questioning of the present form of the world. Barth says 'demolition is required of me, for finally all this is inner work, work on myself, which makes the waiting into hastening'.[26]

> We have to *breathe* in the atmosphere of the redemption hidden in the future. We have to *act* in the experience of the coming Redeemer. We are ordered to fight, to build, to work, to organise, to fashion things. The same conscience which drove us inside relentlessly drives us outside. Responsibility is responsibility that something should happen. We cannot build up the kingdom of God or bring it in by force. But when it comes we cannot be idle. We are summoned to go to meet it. Our waiting can take place only in our acting, our hastening.[27]

These statements find remarkable echoes in the lectures which make up *The Christian Life*. In these final lectures on the ethics of reconciliation toward the end of his life, Barth asserts that Christians are summoned by God's command to revolt against the dehumanising disorder of the world, and therefore to entry into conflict.[28] The decisive action of their revolt consists in their calling upon God for the establishing of his kingdom in accordance with the second petition of the Lord's Prayer. Nevertheless, this decisive—*vertical*—action, if it is

---

[24] Barth, *Ethics*, 488.
[25] Barth, *Ethics*, 491.
[26] Barth, *Ethics*, 488.
[27] Barth, *Ethics*, 490-491.
[28] Karl Barth, *The Christian Life: Church Dogmatics IV/4 (Lecture Fragments)* (trans. G. W. Bromiley; Edinburgh: T. & T. Clark, 1981), 206, 211.

genuine, will incorporate a host of other congruent *horizontal* actions.[29] Where such prayer is present, Barth claims,

> there the vitality and force of little hopes for the present of a person and of people will not be lacking....what kind of waiting for the new heaven and the new earth in which [righteousness] dwells, what kind of praying that prayer [would it be], if we were not motivated thereby to do resolutely what we can here and now on this side in orientation and with a view to God's side, to the great there and then of his kingdom, and to do this without claim or illusion, not trying to anticipate what only God could begin and only he can finish, but rising up to fight for human righteousness and order in the midst of disorder and in opposition to it.[30]

Later in the same series of lectures Barth will again address this notion of 'little' hopes. Because the establishing of the kingdom for which Christians pray is properly God's activity, Christians are absolved from the impossible responsibility of establishing the kingdom and its righteousness in their own power. They are not, however, thereby absolved from their own activity, but rather with their prayer, Christians are 'with great strictness required and with great kindness freed and empowered to do what they can do in the sphere of the relative possibilities assigned to them....They may and can and should rise up and accept responsibility to the utmost of their power for the doing of the little righteousness.'[31] In another important echo of the early work on Blumhardt, Barth says that to wait for the kingdom

> cannot possibly mean that they are commanded or even permitted to be idle in the meantime;...No, they *wait* and *hasten* toward the dawn of God's day....They not only wait but also hasten. They wait by hastening. Their waiting takes place in the hastening. Aiming at God's kingdom, established on its coming and not on the status quo, they do not just look toward it but run toward it as fast as their feet will carry them. This is inevitable if in their hearts and on their lips the petition 'Thy kingdom come' is not an indolent and despondent prayer but one that is zealous and brave.[32]

In these citations we see the close association that Barth intends between the motif of waiting and hastening, and that of prayer.[33] In his article on

---

[29] Barth, *The Christian Life*, 212.

[30] Barth, *The Christian Life*, 213.

[31] Barth, *The Christian Life*, 265. See also Dirk Smit, '"The Doing of the Little Righteousness": On Justice in Barth's View of the Christian Life' in *Loving God with our Minds: The Pastor as Theologian* (ed. Michael Welker & Cynthia A. Jarvis; Grand Rapids: Eerdmans, 2004), 120-145.

[32] Barth, *The Christian Life*, 263.

[33] Other works which deal with prayer as an aspect of Barth's ethical thought include Webster, *Barth's Ethics of Reconciliation*, especially 174-213, John Kelsay, 'Prayer and Ethics: Reflections on Calvin and Barth,' *Harvard Theological Review* 82, no. 2 (1989),

Blumhardt's devotions (*Auf das Reich Gottes warten*) Barth indicates a growing appreciation of the role of prayer when he suggests that 'our cause, our hope, is at the moment served better with prayers than with treatises' and that pleading before God for the coming of his kingdom is the highest and most promising thing a believer could undertake.[34] By the late twenties Barth can refer to prayer as 'the primal and basic form of human action in which man looks and reaches beyond his reality as a creature and as a sinner saved by grace, in which he acts as ἔνθεος, i.e., as one who belongs to God'.[35] For Barth at this time, prayer is an eschatological act which gives to human existence 'the character of openness: openness to what is ahead'.[36] Prayer, in fact, is the form of waiting in which we are encountered by the Spirit and granted the gift of conscience and the divine command, that we might hasten in a new obedience. Thus, Barth goes on to say that

> [i]n prayer—and not for nothing is 'Come, Creator Spirit' the prayer that includes within itself all prayer—we ask God not only that he would view us in a very different reality from merely that of his creatures and his sinners saved by grace, but also that he would give us this reality, the reality of people of the Spirit....In the superabundance of *this* action we have concrete fellowship with God our Redeemer, we have a conscience.[37]

The emphasis on prayer is found also in the *Dogmatics*. In the exposition on the doctrine of election, for example, Barth identifies prayer—as it was exemplified in the life of Jesus—as the telos of election, and as the fulfilment of creaturely existence:

> God's eternal will is the act of prayer (in which confidence in self gives way before confidence in God). This act is the birth of a genuine human self-awareness, in which knowledge and action can and must be attempted; in which there drops away all fear of what is above or beside or below man, of what might assault or threaten him; in which man becomes heir to a legitimate and necessary

---

and Eberhard Jüngel, 'Invocation of God as the Ethical Ground of Christian Action: Introductory Remarks on the Posthumous fragments of Karl Barth's Ethics of the Doctrine of Reconciliation,' in *Eberhard Jüngel: Theological Essays* (ed. J. Webster; Edinburgh: T. & T. Clark, 1989). For additional studies in Barth's theology of prayer see also Han Chul-La, 'A Comparison Between Calvin and Barth on Prayer,' *ATA Journal* 1, no. 1 (1993), Matthew Boulton, 'We Pray By His Mouth: Karl Barth, Erving Goffmann, and a Theology of Invocation,' *Modern Theology* 17, no. 1 (2001), as well as the essays by Hesselink, McKim, Migliore and Saliers, in Karl Barth, *Prayer* (trans. S. F. Terrien; 50th Anniversary ed. Louisville: Westminster John Knox, 2002).

[34] Karl Barth, 'Action in Waiting for the Kingdom of God,' in *Action in Waiting* (ed. Society of Brothers; Rifton, NY: Plough, 1969), 22-23.

[35] Barth, *Ethics*, 473.

[36] Barth, *Ethics*, 474.

[37] Barth, *Ethics*, 478.

and therefore an effective and triumphant claim; in which man may rule in that he is willing to serve.[38]

More exalted acclamation regarding the priority and potency of prayer could scarcely be found. Authentic human existence finds both its genesis and its apex in the act of prayer. Prayer is an invitation from God for us to participate in the rule and reign of God's kingdom, both now and in the life to come, but to do so in accordance with the creaturely limits which characterise humanity.[39] Barth found in the notion of invocation (*Anrufung*) a material concept for Christian existence, which not only provided shape for the Christian life, but did so in a way which maintained the careful delineation and ordering between divine and human agency, that is, 'a moral ontology and a moral anthropology in which dependence is not diminishment and resolute action is not self-assertion'.[40] In invocation, says Barth, 'man in his whole humanity takes his proper place over against God. In it he does the central thing that precedes, accompanies, and follows all else he does'.[41] Invocation, properly understood, says Barth, is an action which includes within itself all other actions.[42] Commenting once again on the second petition of the Lord's Prayer, Barth says,

> When people turn bravely to God with this petition…their whole life and thought and word and deed are set in motion, oriented to the point to which they look with the petition….Praying bravely…they therewith take part…in the movement that characterises the being, thought, and action of the apostles and their communities….Praying the second petition bravely means following this movement and turning, having no other choice but to run [toward] the coming kingdom of God—to run toward this with all one's soul and all one's powers….The heart of the Christian ethos is that those who are freed and summoned to pray 'Thy kingdom come' are also freed and summoned to use their freedom to obey the command that is given therewith and to live for their part with a view to the coming kingdom.[43]

Nigel Biggar has remarked that this feature of Barth's ethics is 'one of its greatest virtues'. He continues:

> Prayer is the first and the last thing that we should do. It is basic to an ethic that takes God seriously as a living reality to whom human beings can and should

---

[38] Karl Barth, *Church Dogmatics II/2: The Doctrine of God* (ed. G. W. Bromiley & T. F. Torrance, trans. G. W. Bromiley; Edinburgh: T. & T. Clark, 1957), 180.

[39] Don E. Saliers, 'Prayer and Theology in Karl Barth,' in *Karl Barth, Prayer* (Louisville: Westminster John Knox, 1985), xiv

[40] Webster, *Barth's Ethics of Reconciliation*, 112, 114.

[41] Barth, *The Christian Life*, 43.

[42] Barth, *The Christian Life*, 212.

[43] Barth, *The Christian Life*, 262-263.

relate in a personal way. It is also basic to an ethic that recognizes that, before we turn to the business of deliberating about how we should conduct ourselves in the world, there is the prior task of contemplating what kind of being we are in the first place, and what is the context in which we are set. Prayer embodies and confirms a theological view of the agent's self and of her location.[44]

In sum, in this motif of waiting, hastening and prayer which Barth learnt from Blumhardt in the early days of his career, we find the nexus that binds together the various primary aspects of Barth's vision of Christian and ecclesial existence. The orientation of these practices which are initiated by the gracious action of the Holy Spirit is obviously eschatological, and thus highlights the eschatological nature of Barth's ethics. So too Barth's distinctive ordering of divine and human agency finds its most complete expression in the act of invocation, in which the human agent not only acts, but does so in dependence upon and submission to the greater will of God. Such prayer, of course, must issue in activity which Barth characterises as the doing of the 'little righteousness'. In this way, believers bear witness to the activity of God and his coming kingdom in their imperfect attempts to foreshadow the nature and life of God's kingdom. Finally, these activities are not the isolated activities of the individual, but rather as the *Paternoster* presupposes, they are the common activity of the gathered congregation as it seeks to hear and obey the command of God in its own particular time and locale.

Conclusion

This study has demonstrated that Barth had a definite vision of Christian and ecclesial existence in 1915-1922, and that he developed his theology with a specific intent to shape the way his listeners and readers actually lived. His vision portrays the church as an eschatological, moral community gathered by the proclamation of the gospel through the gracious activity of the Holy Spirit, watchfully waiting for the command of the moment by giving attention to Scripture, prayer and worship, in order faithfully to obey the command it receives and so live in accordance with the coming kingdom and the pattern of life perceived in Jesus, in solidarity with, and for the sake of the world as a sign of God's intention for all humanity. His eschatological ethics are an ethics of response to divine grace and initiative, which are necessarily ecclesial and thus a particular ethics, but which are also normative or universal in nature because they depict and bear witness to the true nature of reality and the manner of life which corresponds to the being and activity of God. The church is called to be 'God's vanguard', that people in the world who 'amidst the sham life of their

---

[44] Nigel Biggar, 'Karl Barth's Ethics Revisited' in *Commanding Grace: Studies in Karl Barth's Ethics* (ed. Daniel L. Migliore; Grand Rapids: Eerdmans, 2010), 26.

fellowmen, and for their benefit...are living the true life that men ought to live'.[45] They are to live in their own time and place as a community of 'fellowship and freedom' becoming 'for others what God has become for us: a cleansing, healing, life-giving presence'.[46] Is such a vision viable? Can a real church emerge based on the kind of moral vision Barth has set forth in his early works? Richard Hays directs our attention to Barth's own role in the church's opposition to the Hitler regime:

> The Barmen declaration stands as an emblem of the practical consequences of a community formed by a Barthian hermeneutic, witnessing prophetically in the name of Jesus Christ against all earthly pretensions to authority....In a time when the church is enervated by lukewarm indifference and conformity to the surrounding culture, Barth's theology offers it a potent shot of courage....By adopting Barth's hermeneutical perspective, the church can affirm its identity as a people whose vocation is above all obedience to the Word of God.[47]

---

[45] Barth, 'The Individual,' 243-244.

[46] Daniel J. Price, *Karl Barth's Anthropology in Light of Modern Thought* (Grand Rapids: Eerdmans, 2002), 308.

[47] Richard B. Hays, *The Moral Vision of the New Testament: Community, Cross, New Creation; A Contemporary Introduction to New Testament Ethics* (San Francisco: Harper Collins, 1996), 239.

Bibliography

Abrams, Lynn, *Bismarck and the German Empire, 1871-1918* (London: Routledge, 1995).

Albrecht, G., 'In Good Company: The Church as Polis.' *Scottish Journal of Theology* 50.2 (1997): 219-227.

Alexis-Baker, Andy, 'Theology is Ethics: How Karl Barth Sees the Good Life.' *Scottish Journal of Theology* 64.4 (2011), 425-438.

Anderson, Ray S., *The Shape of Practical Theology: Empowering Ministry with Theological Praxis* (Downers Grove: Inter-Varsity Press, 2001).

Armstrong, A.H., 'Karl Barth, the Fathers of the Church, and "Natural Theology".' *Journal of Theological Studies* 46.1 (1995): 191-195.

Bachmann, Philipp, Der Römerbrief verdeutscht und vergegenwärtigt: Ein Wort zu K. Barths Römerbrief. *Neue kirchliche Zeitschrift*, no. 32 (1921): 517-547.

von Balthasar, Hans Urs, *The Theology of Karl Barth* (trans. Edward T. Oakes; San Francisco: Ignatius, 1992).

Barrett, Lois Y., ed., *Treasure in Clay Jars: Patterns in Missional Faithfulness* (Grand Rapids: Eerdmans, 2004).

Barrigar, Chris, '"The Imperative Inherent in the Gift of Freedom": Karl Barth and Amartya Sen on Human Freedom.' *Asia Journal of Theology* 18.1 (2004): 110-137.

Barth, Karl, Die Hilfe 1913. *Christliche Welt*, August 14, 1914.

_____ *Zur inneren Lage des Christentums* (München: Christian Kaiser, 1920).

_____ *The Epistle to the Romans* (trans. E.C. Hoskyns; 6th ed.; Oxford: Oxford University Press, 1933).

_____ *The Resurrection of the Dead* (trans. H.J. Stenning; Eugene, OR: Wipf & Stock, 1933, reprint 2003).

_____ *Theological Existence Today: A Plea for Theological Freedom* (trans. R.B. Hoyle & C. Heath; London: Hodder & Stoughton, 1933).

_____ *The Knowledge of God and the Service of God According to the Teaching of the Reformation* (trans. J.L.M. Haire & I. Henderson; London: Hodder and Stoughton, 1938).

_____ *The Church and the Political Problem of our Day* (London: Hodder and Stoughton, 1939).

_____ *Der Römerbrief (Zweite Fassung) 1922* (Zürich: Theologischer Verlag Zürich, 1940; 17th Abdruck, 2011).

_____ *A Letter to Great Britain from Switzerland* (trans. E.H. Gordon & George Hill; London: Sheldon, 1941).

_____ *The Church and the War* (trans. A.H. Froendt; New York: Macmillan, 1944).

_____ *The Teaching of the Church Regarding Baptism* (trans. E.A. Payne; London: SCM Press, 1948).

_____ *Dogmatics in Outline* (trans. G.T. Thompson; London: SCM Press, 1949).

_____ 'The Real Church.' *Scottish Journal of Theology* 3 (1950): 337-351.

_____ *Christ and Adam: Man and Humanity in Romans 5* (trans. T.A. Smail; New York: Harper, 1956).

_____ *Church Dogmatics I/2: The Doctrine of the Word of God* (trans. G.T. Thompson & H. Knight; ed. G.W. Bromiley & T.F. Torrance; Edinburgh: T. & T. Clark, 1956).

_____ *Church Dogmatics IV/1: The Doctrine of Reconciliation* (trans. G.W. Bromiley; ed. G.W. Bromiley & T.F. Torrance; Edinburgh: T. & T. Clark, 1956).

_____ *The Word of God and the Word of Man* (trans. D. Horton; New York: Harper & Brothers, 1956).

_____ *Church Dogmatics II/1: The Doctrine of God* (trans. W.B. Johnston, T.H.L. Parker, H. Knight & J.L.M. Haire; ed. G.W. Bromiley & T.F. Torrance; Edinburgh: T. & T. Clark, 1957).

_____ *Church Dogmatics II/2: The Doctrine of God* (trans. G.W. Bromiley; ed. G.W. Bromiley & T.F. Torrance; Edinburgh: T. & T. Clark, 1957).

_____ *Church Dogmatics III/1: The Doctrine of Creation* (trans. O. Bussey, J.W. Edwards & H. Knight; ed. G.W. Bromiley & T.F. Torrance; Edinburgh: T. & T. Clark, 1958).

_____ *Church Dogmatics IV/2: The Doctrine of Reconciliation* (trans. G.W. Bromiley; ed. G.W. Bromiley & T.F. Torrance; Edinburgh: T. & T. Clark, 1958).

_____ 'Gospel and Law.' In *God, Grace and Gospel* (ed. J.S. McNab; Edinburgh: T. & T. Clark, 1959), 1-27.

_____ *The Humanity of God* (trans. J.N. Thomas & T.Weiser; St. Louis: John Knox, 1960).

_____ *Anselm: Fides Quaerens Intellectum: Anselm's Proof of the Existence of God in the Context of his Theological Scheme* (trans. I.W. Robertson; London: SCM Press, 1960).

_____ *Church Dogmatics III/2: The Doctrine of Creation* (trans. G.W. Bromiley, H. Knight, J.K.S. Reid & R.H. Fuller; ed. G.W. Bromiley & T.F. Torrance; Edinburgh: T. & T. Clark, 1960).

_____ *Church Dogmatics III/3: The Doctrine of Creation* (trans. R.J. Ehrlich & G.W. Bromiley; ed. G.W. Bromiley & T.F. Torrance; Edinburgh: T. & T. Clark, 1960).

_____ 'Foreword.' In *Predestination and Other Papers* (ed. P. Maury; London: SCM Press, 1960), 15-17.

_____ *A Shorter Commentary on Romans* (2nd ed; Richmond: John Knox, 1960).

_____ *Church Dogmatics III/4: The Doctrine of Creation* (trans. A.T. Mackay, T.H.L. Parker, H. Knight, H.A. Kennedy & J. Marks; ed. G.W. Bromiley & T.F. Torrance; Edinburgh: T. & T. Clark, 1961).

_____ *Church Dogmatics IV/3.1: The Doctrine of Reconciliation* (trans. G.W. Bromiley; ed G.W. Bromiley & T.F. Torrance; Edinburgh: T. & T. Clark, 1961).

_____ *Church Dogmatics IV/3.2: The Doctrine of Reconciliation* (trans. G.W. Bromiley; ed. by G.W. Bromiley & T.F. Torrance (Edinburgh: T. & T. Clark, 1962).

_____ *Theology and Church: Shorter Writings 1920-1928* (trans. L.P. Smith; New York: Harper & Row, 1962).

_____ *Evangelical Theology: An Introduction* (trans. G. Foley; Grand Rapids: Eerdmans, 1963).

_____ *The Great Promise: Luke 1* (trans. E. Hans Freund; Eugene, OR: Wipf and Stock, 1963).

_____ *God Here and Now* (trans. Paul M. van Buren; 2003 *Classics* ed; London: Routledge, 1964).

_____ *Prayer and Preaching* (trans. B.E. Hooke & S.F. Terrien; London: SCM Press, 1964).

_____ *Selected Prayers* (trans. K.R. Crim; London: Epworth, 1965).

_____ 'Past and Future: Friedrich Naumann and Christoph Blumhardt.' In *The Beginnings of Dialectic Theology* (ed. James M. Robinson; Richmond: John Knox Press, 1968), 35-45.

_____ 'Action in Waiting for the Kingdom of God.' In *Action in Waiting* (ed. Society of Brothers; Rifton, NY: Plough, 1969), 19-45.

_____ *Church Dogmatics IV/4: The Doctrine of Reconciliation (Fragment)* (trans. G.W. Bromiley; ed. G.W. Bromiley & T.F. Torrance; Edinburgh: T. & T. Clark, 1969).

_____ *Fragments Grave and Gay* (trans. Eric Mosbacher; London: Fontana, 1971).

_____ *Church Dogmatics I/1: The Doctrine of the Word of God* (trans. G.W. Bromiley; 2nd ed; Edinburgh: T. & T. Clark, 1975).

_____ 'Jesus Christ and the Movement for Social Justice.' In *Karl Barth and Radical Politics* (ed. G. Hunsinger; Philadelphia: Westminster, 1976), 19-45.

_____ *Final Testimonies* (trans. G.W. Bromiley; Grand Rapids: Eerdmans, 1977).

_____ *The Christian Life: Church Dogmatics IV/4 (Lecture Fragments)* (trans. G.W. Bromiley; Edinburgh: T. & T. Clark, 1981).

_____ *Ethics* (trans. G.W. Bromiley; Edinburgh: T. & T. Clark, 1981).

_____ *Letters 1961-1968* (trans. G.W. Bromiley; Grand Rapids: Eerdmans, 1981).

_____ *The Theology of Schleiermacher: Lectures at Göttingen Winter Semester of 1923/24* (trans. G.W. Bromiley; Edinburgh: T. & T. Clark, 1982).

_____ *Der Römerbrief (Erste Fassung) 1919* (ed. Herrmann Schmidt; Zürich: Theologischer-Verlag, 1985).

_____. *Church and State* (trans. G.R. Howe; Greenville, SC: Smith & Helwys, 1991).

_____ *The Göttingen Dogmatics: Instruction in the Christian Religion* (trans. G.W. Bromiley; Vol. 1; Grand Raids: Eerdmans, 1991).

_____ *The Holy Spirit and the Christian Life: The Theological Basis of Ethics* (trans. R.B. Hoyle; Louisville: Westminster John Knox, 1993).

_____ *The Theology of John Calvin* (trans. G.W. Bromiley; Grand Rapids: Eerdmans, 1995).

_____ *Protestant Theology in the Nineteenth Century: Its Background & History* (trans. B. Cozens; 2nd ed; London: SCM Press, 2001).

_____ *Epistle to the Philippians* (trans. J.W. Leitch; 40th Anniversary ed; Louisville: Westminster John Knox, 2002).

_____ *Prayer* (trans. S.F. Terrien; 50th Anniversary ed; Louisville: Westminster John Knox, 2002).

_____ *The Theology of the Reformed Confessions* (trans. D.L. & J.J. Guder; Louisville: Westminster John Knox, 2002).

_____ *The Church and the Churches* (Grand Rapids: Eerdmans, 2005).

_____ *The Word of God and Theology* (trans. Amy Marga; London: T. & T. Clark, 2011).

Barth, Karl & Eduard Thurneysen, *Come Holy Spirit* (trans. E.G. Homrighausen, K.J. Ernst & G.W. Richards; Edinburgh: T. & T. Clark, 1934).

Barth, Karl & William H. Willimon, *The Early Preaching of Karl Barth: Fourteen Sermons with Commentary by William H. Willimon* (Louisville: Westminster John Knox, 2009).

Bayer, Oswald, *Living By Faith: Justification and Sanctification* (trans. Geoffrey W. Bromiley; ed. Paul Rorem; Grand Rapids: Eerdmans, 2003).

Beintker, Michael, *Die Dialektik in der 'dialektischen Theologie' Karl Barths* (Munich: Chr. Kaiser Verlag, 1987).

Bender, Kimlyn J., *Karl Barth's Christological Ecclesiology* (Aldershot: Ashgate, 2005).

Berkhof, Hendrikus, *Two Hundred Years of Theology: Report of a Personal Journey* (trans. J. Vriend; Grand Rapids: Eerdmans, 1989).

Berkouwer, G.C., *The Triumph of Grace in the Theology of Karl Barth* (trans. H.R. Boer; Grand Rapids: Eerdmans, 1956).

_____ *A Half Century of Theology: Movements and Motives* (trans. L.B. Smedes; Grand Rapids: Eerdmans, 1977).

Bettis, Joseph D., 'Is Karl Barth a Universalist?' *Scottish Journal of Theology* 20.4 (1967): 423-436.

_____ 'Political Theology and Social Ethics: The Socialist Humanism of Karl Barth.' *Scottish Journal of Theology* 27.3 (1974): 287-305.

Biggar, Nigel, 'Hearing God's Command and Thinking About What's Right: With and Beyond Barth.' In *Reckoning With Barth: Essays in Commemoration of the Centenary of Karl Barth's Birth* (ed. Nigel Biggar; London: Mowbray, 1988), 101-118.

_____ *The Hastening That Waits: Karl Barth's Ethics* (revised ed; Oxford: Clarendon, 1993).

_____ 'Barth's Trinitarian Ethic.' In *The Cambridge Companion to Karl Barth* (ed. J. Webster; Cambridge: Cambridge University Press, 2000), 212-227.

_____ 'Karl Barth's Ethics Revisited' in Daniel L. Migliore, ed., *Commanding Grace: Studies in Karl Barth's Ethics* (Grand Rapids: Eerdmans, 2010), 26-49.

Bingham, J., *Courage to Change: An Introduction to the Life and Thought of Reinhold Niebuhr* (New York: Charles Scribner's Sons, 1972).

Bloesch, Donald G,. *A Theology of Word and Spirit: Authority and Method in Theology* (Downers Grove: Inter-Varsity Press, 1991).

Blumhardt, Christoph, 'Joy in the Lord.' In *Action in Waiting* (ed. Society of Brothers; Rifton, NY: Plough, 1969), 49-69.

Boulton, Matthew, '"We Pray By His Mouth": Karl Barth, Erving Goffmann, and a Theology of Invocation.' *Modern Theology* 17.1 (2001): 66-83.

Brazier, Paul, 'Barth's First Commentary on Romans (1919): An Exercise in Apophatic Theology?' *International Journal of Systematic Theology* 6.4 (2004): 387-403.

Bromiley, Geoffrey W., *Introduction to the Theology of Karl Barth* (Edinburgh: T. & T. Clark, 1979).

Brown, Colin, *Karl Barth and the Christian Message* (London: Tyndale, 1967).

Brown, William P., ed., *Character and Scripture: Moral Formation, Community and Biblical Interpretation* (Grand Rapids: Eerdmans, 2002).

Brunner, Emil, *The Christian Doctrine of God: Dogmatics Vol.1* (trans. O. Wyon; London: Lutterworth, 1949).

_____ 'The Epistle to the Romans by Karl Barth: An Up-to-Date, Unmodern Paraphrase.' In *The Beginnings of Dialectical Theology* (ed. James M. Robinson; Richmond: John Knox, 1968), 63-71.

Buckley, James J., 'A Field of Living Fire: Karl Barth on the Spirit and the Church.' *Modern Theology* 10.1 (1994): 81-102.

_____ 'Christian Community, Baptism and Lord's Supper.' In *The Cambridge Companion to Karl Barth* (ed. J. Webster; Cambridge: Cambridge University Press, 2000), 195-211.

Bultmann, Rudolph, 'Karl Barth's *Epistle to the Romans* in its Second Edition.' In *The Beginnings of Dialectic Theology* (ed. James M. Robinson; Richmond: John Knox, 1968), 100-120.

Burnett, Richard E., *Karl Barth's Theological Exegesis: The Hermeneutical Principles of the Römerbrief Period* (Tübingen: Mohr Siebeck, 2001).

Busch, Eberhard, *Karl Barth: His Life from Letters and Autobiographical Texts* (trans. J. Bowden; Philadelphia: Fortress, 1976).

_____ *Karl Barth and the Pietists: The Young Karl Barth's Critique of Pietism and Its Response* (trans. Daniel W. Bloesch; Downers Grove: Inter-Varsity Press, 2004).

_____ *The Great Passion: An Introduction to Karl Barth's Theology* (Grand Rapids: Eerdmans, 2004).

_____ *The Barmen Theses Then and Now* (trans. D. & J. Guder; Grand Rapids: Eerdmans, 2010).

Cahill, Lisa Sowle, 'Christian Character, Biblical Community, and Human Values.' In *Character and Scripture: Moral Formation, Community and Biblical Interpretation* (ed. William P. Brown; Grand Rapids: Eerdmans, 2002), 3-17.

Calvin, John, *Institutes of the Christian Religion* (trans. F.L. Battles, 2 vols; Philadelphia: Westminster, 1960).

Chalamet, Christophe, *Dialectical Theologians: Wilhelm Herrmann, Karl Barth and Rudolph Bultmann* (Zürich: Theologischer Verlag Zürich, 2005).

Chul-La, Han, 'A Comparison Between Calvin and Barth on Prayer.' *ATA Journal* 1.1 (1993): 65-76.

Chung, Sung Wook, *Admiration & Challenge: Karl Barth's Theological Relationship with John Calvin* (New York: Peter Lang, 2002).

Clough, David, *Ethics in Crisis: Interpreting Barth's Ethics* (Aldershot: Ashgate, 2005).

Cochrane, A.C., 'Karl Barth's Doctrine of the Covenant.' In *Major Themes in the Reformed Tradition* (ed. Donald K. McKim; Grand Rapids: Eerdmans, 1992), 108-116.

Coker, J., 'Peace and the Apocalypse: Stanley Hauerwas and Miroslav Volf on the Eschatological Basis for Christian Nonviolence.' *Evangelical Quarterly* 71.3 (1999): 261-268.

Collins Winn, Christian T., *'Jesus is Victor!' The Significance of the Blumhardts for the Theology of Karl Barth*, (Princeton Theological Monograph Series; Eugene, OR: Pickwick Publications, 2009).

Colwell, John E, *Actuality and Provisionality: Eternity and Election in the Theology of Karl Barth* (Edinburgh: Rutherford House, 1989).

_____ 'The Contemporaneity of the Divine Decision: Reflections on Barth's Denial of "Universalism".' In *Universalism and the Doctrine of Hell* (ed. N.M. de S. Cameron; Carlisle: Paternoster, 1992), 139-160.

_____ *Living the Christian Story: The Distinctiveness of Christian Ethics* (Edinburgh: T. & T. Clark, 2001).

Couenhoven, J., 'Grace as Pardon and Power: Pictures of the Christian Life in Luther, Calvin and Barth.' *Journal of Religious Ethics* 28.1 (2000): 63-88.

_____ 'Law and Gospel, or the Law of the Gospel? Karl Barth's Political Theology Compared with Luther and Calvin.' *Journal of Religious Ethics* 30.2 (2002): 181-205.

Cross, Terry L., *Dialectic in Karl Barth's Doctrine of God* (New York: Peter Lang, 2001).

Davies, W.D., 'Dr. Karl Barth's Interpretation of Romans 1.2 (Appendix A).' In *Paul and Rabbinic Judaism: Some Rabbinic Elements in Pauline Theology* (Mifflintown, PA: Sigler, 1998), 325-328.

Deegan, D.L., 'The Ritschlian School, The Essence of Christianity, and Karl Barth.' *Scottish Journal of Theology* 16.4 (1963): 390-414.

Demson, David E., *Hans Frei and Karl Barth: Different Ways of Reading Scripture* (Grand Rapids: Eerdmans, 1997).

Diem, Hermann, 'Karl Barth as Socialist: Controversy over a New Attempt to Understand Him.' In *Karl Barth and Radical Politics* (ed. George Hunsinger; Philadelphia: Westminster, 1976), 121-138.

Dulles, Avery, *Models of the Church* (New York: Doubleday, 1974).

Durkin, K., *Reinhold Niebuhr* (ed. B. Davies; London: Geoffrey Chapman, 1989).

Evans, C. Stephen, 'Empiricism, Rationalism and the Possibility of Historical Religious Knowledge.' In *Christian Perspectives on Religious Knowledge* (ed. C.S. Evans & M. Westphal; Grand Rapids: Eerdmans, 1993), 134-160.

Fergusson, David, 'Another Way of Reading Stanley Hauerwas?' *Scottish Journal of Theology* 50.2 (1997): 242-249.

_____ *Community, Liberalism and Christian Ethics* (Cambridge: Cambridge University Press, 1998).

Fiorenza, F.C. & J.C. Livingstone, *Modern Christian Thought Vol. II: The Twentieth Century* (Upper Saddle River, NJ: Prentice Hall, 2000).

Fletcher, W.C., *The Moderns: Makers of Contemporary Theology* (Grand Rapids: Zondervan, 1962).

Ford, David F., 'Barth's Interpretation of the Bible.' In *Karl Barth: Studies of His Theological Method* (ed. S.W. Sykes; Oxford: Clarendon, 1979), 55-87.

Fraenkel, P., ed., *Natural Theology: Comprising 'Nature and Grace' by Emil Brunner and the Reply 'No!' by Dr. Karl Barth* (London: Geoffrey Bles, 1944).

Franke, John R., *Barth for Armchair Theologians* (Louisville: Westminster John Knox, 2006).

Frei, Hans W., 'Revelation and Theological Method in the Theology of Karl Barth.' In *Faith and Ethics: The Theology of H. Richard Niebuhr* (ed. P. Ramsey; New York: Harper & Row, 1957), 40-53.

Gerber, L.E., 'The Virtuous Terrorist: Stanley Hauerwas and *The Crying Game*.' *Cross Currents* 43.2 (1993): 230-234.

Godsey, John D., ed., *Karl Barth's Table Talk*. Vol. 10, (*Scottish Journal of Theology Occasional Papers*; Edinburgh: Oliver and Boyd, 1963).

Gogarten, Friedrich, 'The Holy Egotism of the Christian: An Answer to Jülicher's Essay: "A Modern Interpreter of Paul".' In *The Beginnings of Dialectic Theology* (ed. James M. Robinson; Richmond: John Knox, 1968), 82-87.

Gollwitzer, Helmut, 'Kingdom of God and Socialism in the Theology of Karl Barth.' In *Karl Barth and Radical Politics* (ed. G. Hunsinger; Philadelphia: Westminster, 1976), 77-120.

Gorringe, Timothy J., 'Eschatology and Political Radicalism: The Example of Karl Barth and Jürgen Moltmann.' In *God Will Be All in All: The Eschatology of Jürgen Moltmann* (ed. Richard Bauckham; Edinburgh: T. & T. Clark, 1999), 87-114.

_____ Timothy J., *Karl Barth: Against Hegemony* (Oxford: Oxford University Press, 1999).

Gregory, Eric 'The Spirit and the Letter: Protestant Thomism and Nigel Biggar's "Karl Barth's Ethics Revisited"' in *Commanding Grace: Studies in Karl Barth's Ethics* (ed. Daniel L. Migliore; Grand Rapids: Eerdmans, 2010), 50-59.

Grenz, Stanley J., *Theology for the Community of God* (Grand Rapids: Eerdmans, 1994).

_____ *The Moral Quest: Foundations of Christian Ethics* (Leicester: Apollos, 1997).

_____ *Renewing the Center: Evangelical Theology in a Post-Theological Era* (Grand Rapids: Baker, 2000).

Grenz, S.J. & R.E. Olson, *Twentieth Century Theology: God & the World in a Transitional Age* (Downers Grove: Inter-Varsity Press, 1992).

Griffiths, Paul J., 'How Epistemology Matters to Theology.' *Journal of Religion* 79.1 (1999): 1-18.

_____ 'Witness and Conviction in *With the Grain of the Universe*.' *Modern Theology* 19.1 (2003): 67-75.

Guder, Darrell L., ed., *Missional Church: A Vision for the Sending of the Church in North America* (Grand Rapids: Eerdmans, 1998).

_____ *The Continuing Conversion of the Church* (Grand Rapids: Eerdmans, 2000).

_____ 'The Church as Missional Community.' In *The Community of the Word: Toward an Evangelical Ecclesiology* (ed. Mark Husbands & Daniel J. Treier; Leicester: Apollos, 2005), 114-128.

Gunton, Colin E., 'Karl Barth's Doctrine of Election as Part of His Doctrine of God.' *Journal of Theological Studies* 25.2 (1974): 381-392.

_____ 'The Triune God and the Freedom of the Creature.' In *Karl Barth: Centenary Essays* (ed. S. W. Sykes; Cambridge: Cambridge University Press, 1989), 46-68.

_____ *Theology through the Theologians* (Edinburgh: T. & T. Clark, 1996).

_____ 'Election and Ecclesiology in the Post-Constantinian Church.' *Scottish Journal of Theology* 53.2 (2000): 212-227.

_____ 'Salvation.' In *The Cambridge Companion to Karl Barth* (ed. J. Webster; Cambridge: Cambridge University Press, 2000), 143-158.

_____ *The Barth Lectures* (ed. P.H. Brazier; London: T. & T. Clark, 2007).

Gunton, Colin E., ed., *The Cambridge Companion to Christian Doctrine* (Cambridge: Cambridge University Press, 1997).

Gustafson, James M., *Ethics from a Theocentric Perspective Volume One: Theology and Ethics* (Chicago: University of Chicago, 1981).

_____ *Ethics from a Theocentric Perspective Volume Two: Ethics and Theology* (Chicago: University of Chicago, 1984).

Haddorff, David W. 'The Postmodern Realism of Barth's Ethics.' *Scottish Journal of Theology* 57.3 (2004): 269-286.

_____ *Christian Ethics as Witness: Barth's Ethics for a World at Risk* (Eugene: Wipf and Stock, 2011).

von Harnack, Adolph, *What is Christianity?* (trans. T.B. Saunders; New York: Harper & Brothers, 1957).

Hart, D.G., 'Machen on Barth: Introduction to a Recently Uncovered Paper.' *Westminster Theological Journal* 53 (1991): 189-196.

Hart, John W., *Karl Barth Vs. Emil Brunner: The Formation and Dissolution of a Theological Alliance, 1916-1936* (New York: Peter Lang, 2001).

Hart, Trevor, *Regarding Karl Barth: Essays Towards a Reading of his Theology* (Carlisle: Paternoster, 1999).

_____ 'Revelation.' In *The Cambridge Companion to Karl Barth* (ed. J. Webster;

Cambridge: Cambridge University Press, 2000), 37-56.

Hauerwas, Stanley, *Character and the Christian Life: A Study in Theological Ethics* (2nd ed; San Antonio: Trinity University, 1975).

_____ *A Community of Character: Towards a Constructive Christian Social Ethic* (Notre Dame: University of Notre Dame, 1981).

_____ *The Peaceable Kingdom: A Primer in Christian Ethics* (Notre Dame: University of Notre Dame, 1983).

_____ 'The Gesture of a Truthful Story.' *Theology Today* 42.2 (1985): 181-187.

_____. 'The Church as God's New Language.' In *Scriptural Authority and Narrative Interpretation* (ed. G. Green; Philadelphia: Fortress, 1987), 179-198.

_____ 'On Honour: By Way of a Comparison of Barth and Trollope.' In *Reckoning With Barth: Essays in Commemoration of the Centenary of Karl Barth's Birth* (ed. N. Biggar; London: Mowbray, 1988), 145-169.

_____ 'Discipleship as a Craft, Church as a Disciplined Community.' *Christian Century*, October 2, 1991: 881-884.

_____ 'On Learning Simplicity in an Ambiguous Age: A Response To Hunsinger.' In *Barth, Barmen and the Confessing Church Today: Katallagete* (ed. J.Y. Holloway; Lewiston: Edwin Mellen, 1992), 131-138.

_____ 'On Keeping Theological Ethics Theological.' In *From Christ to the World: Introductory Readings in Christian Ethics* (ed. T.D. Kennedy, A. Verhey & W.G. Boulton; Grand Rapids: Eerdmans, 1994), 130-144.

_____ 'What could it mean for the Church to be Christ's Body?' *Scottish Journal of Theology* 48.1 (1995): 1-21.

_____ 'On Doctrine and Ethics.' In *The Cambridge Companion to Christian Doctrine* (ed. C. E. Gunton; Cambridge: Cambridge University Press, 1997).

_____ *Sanctify Them in the Truth: Holiness Exemplified* (Edinburgh: T. & T. Clark, 1998).

_____ *With the Grain of the Universe: The Church's Witness and Natural Theology* (Grand Rapids: Brazos, 2001).

_____ 'Hooks: Random Thoughts By Way of a Response to Griffiths and Ochs.' *Modern Theology* 19.1 (2003): 89-101.

_____ *Matthew* (Grand Rapids: Brazos, 2006).

Hays, Richard B., 'Ecclesiology and Ethics in 1 Corinthians.' *Ex Auditu* 10 (1994):31-43.

_____ *The Moral Vision of the New Testament: Community, Cross, New Creation; A Contemporary Introduction to New Testament Ethics* (San Francisco: Harper Collins, 1996).

Healy, Nicholas M. 'The Logic of Karl Barth's Ecclesiology: Analysis, Assessment and Proposed Modifications.' *Modern Theology* 10.3 (1994): 253-270.

_____ *Church, World and the Christian Life: Practical-Prophetic Ecclesiology* (Cambridge: Cambridge University Press, 2000).

_____ 'Practices and the New Ecclesiology: Misplaced Concreteness?' *International Journal of Systematic Theology* 5.3 (2003): 287-308.

_____ 'Karl Barth's Ecclesiology Reconsidered.' *Scottish Journal of Theology* 57.3 (2004): 287-299.

Henry, David P., *The Early Development of the Hermeneutic of Karl Barth as Evidenced by His Appropriation of Romans 5:12-21* (Macon, GA: Mercer University Press, 1985).

Hesselink, I. John, 'Karl Barth on Prayer.' In Barth, Karl. *Prayer* (Louisville: Westminster John Knox, 2002), 74-94.

Hick, John, *Disputed Questions in Theology and the Philosophy of Religion* (London: Macmillan, 1993).

Holland, Scott, 'The Problems and Prospects of a "Sectarian Ethic": A Critique of the Hauerwas Reading of the Jesus Story.' *The Conrad Grebel Review* 10.2 (1992): 157-168.

Holloway, James Y., ed., *Barth, Barmen and the Confessing Church Today* (*Symposium Series* 28; Lewiston, NY: Edwin Mellen, 1992).

Horton, Michael S., 'A Stony Jar: The Legacy of Karl Barth for Evangelical Theology' in David Gibson & Daniel Strange, eds., *Engaging with Barth: Contemporary Evangelical Critiques* (Nottingham: Apollos, 2008), 346-381.

Hunsinger, George, 'Conclusion: Toward A Radical Barth.' In *Karl Barth and Radical Politics* (ed. G. Hunsinger; Philadelphia: Westminster, 1976), 181-233.

_____ 'A Response To William Werpehowski.' *Theology Today* 63.3 (1986): 354-360.

_____ *How to Read Karl Barth: The Shape of his Theology* (Oxford: Oxford University Press, 1991).

_____ 'Hellfire and Damnation: Four Ancient and Modern Views.' *Scottish Journal of Theology* 51.4 (1998): 406-434.

_____ 'Baptism and the Soteriology of Forgiveness.' *International Journal of Systematic Theology* 2.3 (2000): 247-269.

_____ *Disruptive Grace: Studies in the Theology of Karl Barth* (Grand Rapids: Eerdmans, 2000).

_____ 'The Church as Witness.' In, *Center for Barth Studies*, <http//www.ptsem.edu/grow/barth> (Accessed December 21, 2001).

Hunsinger, George, ed., *Karl Barth and Radical Politics* (Philadelphia: Westminster, 1976).

Hütter, Reinhard., *Suffering Divine Things: Theology as Church Practice* (trans. Doug Stott; Grand Rapids: Eerdmans, 1999).

_____ 'Karl Barth's Dialectical Catholicity: Sic et Non.' *Modern Theology* 16.2 (2000): 137-157.

Jaspert, Bernd, ed., *Karl Barth~Rudolph Bultmann Letters 1922-1966* (Grand Rapids: Eerdmans, 1981).

Jehle, Frank, *Ever Against the Stream: The Politics of Karl Barth, 1906-1968* (trans. R. & M. Burnett; Grand Rapids: Eerdmans, 2002).

Jenson, Robert W., 'The Hauerwas Project.' *Modern Theology* 8.3 (1992): 285-295.

_____ 'You Wonder Where the Spirit Went.' *Pro Ecclesia* 2.3 (1993): 296-304.

_____ 'An Ontology of Freedom in the *De Servo Arbitrio* of Luther.' *Modern Theology* 10.3 (1994): 247-252.

Johanson, Kurt I., ed., *The Word in this World: Two Sermons by Karl Barth* (Vancouver: Regent College Publishing, 2007).

Johnson, William S., *The Mystery of God: Karl Barth and the Postmodern Foundations of Theology* (Louisville: Westminster John Knox, 1997).

John Templeton Foundation, *The Gifford Lectures*. In, John Templeton Foundation, http://www.giffordlectures.org/ (Accessed November 13, 2007).

Jones, L. Gregory, 'Formed and Transformed By Scripture: Character, Community, and Authority in Biblical Interpretation.' In *Character and Scripture: Moral Formation,*

Community and Biblical Interpretation (ed. William P. Brown; Grand Rapids: Eerdmans, 2002), 18-33.

Jonsen, A.R., *Responsibility in Modern Religious Ethics* (Washington: Corpus, 1968).

Jülicher, Adolf, 'A Modern Interpreter of Paul.' In *The Beginnings of Dialectic Theology* (ed. James M. Robinson; Richmond: John Knox, 1968), 72-81.

Jüngel, Eberhard, *Karl Barth: A Theological Legacy* (trans. G.E. Paul; Philadelphia: Westminster, 1986).

_____ 'Invocation of God as the Ethical Ground of Christian Action: Introductory Remarks on the Posthumous fragments of Karl Barth's Ethics of the Doctrine of Reconciliation.' In *Eberhard Jüngel: Theological Essays* (ed. J. Webster; Edinburgh: T. & T. Clark, 1989), 154-172.

Kelsay, John, 'Prayer and Ethics: Reflections on Calvin and Barth.' *Harvard Theological Review* 82.2 (1989): 153-184.

Koontz, G.G. 'Meeting in the Power of the Spirit: Ecclesiology, Ethics and the Practice of Discernment.' In *The Wisdom of the Cross: Essays in Honor of John Howard Yoder* (eds. C. Huebner, S. Hauerwas, H. Huebner & M. Nation; Grand Rapids: Eerdmans, 1999), 327-348.

Krötke, Wolf, 'The Humanity of the Human Person in Karl Barth's Anthropology.' In *The Cambridge Companion to Karl Barth* (ed. J. Webster; Cambridge: Cambridge University Press, 2000), 159-176.

Lehmann, Paul, *Ethics in a Christian Context* (London: SCM Press, 1963).

Lejeune, R, *Christoph Blumhardt and His Message* (trans. H. Ehrlich & N. Maas (Rifton, NY: Plough, 1963).

Lindsay, Mark R, *Covenanted Solidarity: The Theological Basis of Karl Barth's Opposition to Nazi Antisemitism and the Holocaust* (New York: Peter Lang, 2001).

Lovin, Robin W, *Christian Faith and Public Choices: The Social Ethics of Barth, Brunner and Bonhoeffer* (Philadelphia: Fortress, 1984).

Lull, Timothy F., ed., *Martin Luther's Basic Theological Writings* (Minneapolis: Fortress, 1989).

Luther, Martin, 'Heidelberg Disputation (1518).' In *Luther's Works Volume 31: The Career of the Reformer 1* (ed. H.J. Grimm; Philadelphia: Muhlenberg, 1957), 35-70.

MacDonald, Neil B., *Karl Barth and the Strange New World Within the Bible: Barth, Wittgenstein and the Metadilemmas of the Enlightenment* (Carlisle: Paternoster, 2000).

Machen, J.G., 'Karl Barth and "The Theology of Crisis."' *Westminster Theological Journal* 53 (1991): 197-207.

Mangina, Joseph L., 'Bearing the Marks of Jesus: The Church in the Economy of Salvation in Barth and Hauerwas.' *Scottish Journal of Theology* 52.3 (1999): 269-305.

_____ 'The Stranger as Sacrament: Karl Barth and the Ethics of Ecclesial Practice.' *International Journal of Systematic Theology* 1.3 (1999): 322-339.

_____ 'After Dogma: Reinhard Hütter's Challenge to Contemporary Theology: A Review Essay.' *International Journal of Systematic Theology* 2.3 (2000): 330-346.

_____ *Karl Barth on the Christian Life: The Practical Knowledge of God* (New York: Peter Lang, 2001).

_____ *Karl Barth: Theologian of Christian Witness* (Louisville: Westminster John Knox, 2004).

Markham, Ian S., *Plurality and Christian Ethics* (Cambridge: Cambridge University Press, 1994).

Marquardt, Friedrich-Wilhelm, *Theologie und Sozialismus: Das Beispiel Karl Barths* (München: Chr. Kaiser Verlag, 1972).

_____ 'Socialism in the Theology of Karl Barth.' In *Karl Barth and Radical Politics* (ed. G. Hunsinger; Philadelphia: Westminster, 1976), 47-76.

_____ *Der Christ in der Gesellschaft, 1919-1979: Geschichte, Analyse und Bedeutung von Karl Barths Tambacher Vortrag* (Munich: Kaiser Verlag, 1980).

McAfee Brown, Robert, 'Scripture and Tradition in the Theology of Karl Barth' in *Thy Word is Truth: Barth on Scripture* (ed. G. Hunsinger; Grand Rapids: Eerdmans, 2012), 3-19.

McCarthy, David Matzko, *The Good Life: Genuine Christianity for the Middle Class* (Grand Rapids: Brazos, 2004).

McCormack, Bruce L., *Karl Barth's Critically Realistic Dialectical Theology: Its Genesis and Development 1909-1936* (Oxford: Oxford University Press, 1995).

_____ 'Barth in Context: A Response to Professor Gunton.' *Scottish Journal of Theology* 49.4 (1996): 491-498.

_____ 'The Sum of the Gospel: The Doctrine of Election in the Theologies of Alexander Schweizer and Karl Barth.' In *Toward the Future of Reformed Theology: Tasks, Topics, Traditions* (ed. D. Willis & M. Welker; Grand Rapids: Eerdmans, 1999), 470-493.

_____. 'Grace and Being: The Role of God's Gracious Election in Karl Barth's Theological Ontology.' In *The Cambridge Companion to Karl Barth* (ed. J. Webster; Cambridge: Cambridge University Press, 2000), 92-110.

_____ 'The Significance of Karl Barth's Theological Exegesis of Philippians.' In *Epistle to the Philippians: 40th Anniversary Edition* (Louisville: Westminster John Knox, 2002), v-xxv.

_____. 'The Being of Holy Scripture is in Becoming: Karl Barth in Conversation with American Evangelical Criticism.' In *Evangelicals & Scripture: Tradition, Authority and Hermeneutics* (ed. Laura C. Miguelez, Vincent Bacote, & Dennis L. Okholm; Downers Grove: Inter-Varsity Press, 2004), 55-75.

McDonald, Suzanne, 'Barth's "Other" Doctrine of Election in the *Church Dogmatics*.' *International Journal of Systematic Theology* 9.2 (2007): 134-147.

McDowell, John C., *Hope in Barth's Eschatology: Interrogations and Transformations Beyond Tragedy* (Aldershot: Ashgate, 2000).

_____ 'Learning Where to Place One's Hope: The Eschatological Significance of Election in Barth.' *Scottish Journal of Theology* 53.3 (2000): 316-338.

McFarland, Ian A., 'The Body of Christ: Rethinking a Classic Ecclesiological Model.' *International Journal of Systematic Theology* 7.3 (2005): 225-245.

McGrath, Alister E., *The Making of Modern German Christology* (Oxford: Basil Blackwell, 1986).

_____ *Christian Theology: An Introduction* (4th ed; Oxford: Blackwell, 2007).

McIntyre, J., *The Shape of Pneumatology: Studies in the Doctrine of the Holy Spirit* (Edinburgh: T. & T. Clark, 1997).

McKenny, Gerald P., 'Heterogeneity and Ethical Deliberation: Casuistry, Narrative, and Event in the Ethics of Karl Barth.' *Annual of the Society of Christian Ethics* 20 (2000), 205-224.

McKenny, Gerald P., *The Analogy of Grace: Karl Barth's Moral Theology* (Oxford: Oxford University Press, 2010).

McKim, Donald K., 'Karl Barth on the Lord's Prayer.' In K. Barth, *Prayer* (Louisville: Westminster John Knox, 2002), 114-134.

Migliore, Daniel L., 'Freedom to Pray: Karl Barth's Theology of Prayer.' In K. Barth, *Prayer* (Louisville: Westminster John Knox, 2002), 95-113.

Migliore, Daniel L., ed., *Commanding Grace: Studies in Karl Barth's Ethics* (Grand Rapids: Eerdmans, 2010).

Mueller, David L,. *Karl Barth* (Waco: Word, 1972).

Neill, Stephen., *The Interpretation of the New Testament, 1861-1961* (London: Oxford University Press, 1964).

Newell, Roger, 'Blumhardt, Johann Christoph (1805-80) and Christoph Friedrich (1842-1919).' In *The Dictionary of Historical Theology* (ed. T.A. Hart; Grand Rapids: Eerdmans, 2000), 76-77.

Niebuhr, Reinhold, *Moral Man and Immoral Society: A Study in Ethics and Politics* (New York: Charles Scribner's Sons, 1960).

_____ *The Nature and Destiny of Man: A Christian Interpretation Volume 1* (New York: Charles Scribner's Sons, 1941).

_____ *Essays in Applied Christianity* (New York: Meridian, 1959).

Niebuhr, Ursula M., ed., *Remembering Reinhold Niebuhr: Letters of Reinhold & Ursula M. Niebuhr* (San Francisco: Harper, 1991).

Nimmo, Paul T., *Being in Action: The Theological Shape of Barth's Ethical Vision* (Edinburgh: T. & T. Clark, 2007).

_____ Paul T., 'The Orders of Creation in the Theological Ethics of Karl Barth.' *Scottish Journal of Theology* 60.1 (2007), 24-35.

_____ 'Barth and the Christian as Ethical Agent: An Ontological Study of the Shape of Christian Ethics' in *Commanding Grace: Studies in Karl Barth's Ethics* (ed. Daniel L. Migliore; Grand Rapids: Eerdmans, 2010), 216-238.

Oakes, Kenneth, *Reading Karl Barth: A Companion to Karl Barth's Epistle to the Romans* (Eugene: Cascade Books, 2011).

Ochs, P., 'On Hauerwas' *With the Grain of the Universe.' Modern Theology* 19.1 (2003): 77-88.

Oden, Thomas C., *The Promise of Barth: The Ethics of Freedom* (Philadelphia: J.B. Lippincott, 1969).

O'Grady, Colm, *The Church in the Theology of Karl Barth* (London: Geoffrey Chapman, 1968).

_____ *The Church in Catholic Theology: Dialogue with Karl Barth* (London: Geoffrey Chapman, 1969).

Olson, Roger, *The Story of Christian Theology: Twenty Centuries of Tradition and Reform* (Leicester: Apollos, 1999).

O'Neil, Michael D. 'The Mission of the Spirit in the Election of God.' Unpublished Dissertation for the Master of Theology (Honours), Murdoch University, Western Australia, 2001.

_____ 'Karl Barth's Doctrine of Election.' *The Evangelical Quarterly* 76.4 (2004): 311-326.

_____ 'Communities of Witness: The Concept of Election in the Old Testament and in the Theology of Karl Barth.' In *Text and Task: Scripture and Mission* (ed. Michael

Parsons; Carlisle: Paternoster, 2005), 172-186.

_____ 'Ethics and Epistemology: Ecclesial Existence in a Postmodern Era.' *Journal of Religious Ethics* 34.1 (2006): 21-40.

_____ 'In the Power of the Lamb – And of the Lion: Power and Weakness in the Early Theology of Karl Barth.' In, *On Eagles' Wings. An Exploration of Strength in the Midst of Weakness* (ed. Michael Parsons and David J. Cohen; Eugene, OR: Wipf and Stock, 2008), 121-138.

Overbeck, Franz, *Christentum und Kultur. Gedanken und Anmerkungen zur modernen Theologie* (Basel: Benno Schwabe & Co, 1919).

Overbeck, Franz, *How Christian Is Our Present-Day Theology?* (trans. Martin Henry; Edinburgh: T. & T. Clark/Continuum, 2005).

Owen, John M., 'Why Church Dogmatics?' *Reformed Theological Review* 29.2 (1970): 46-55.

Pannenberg, Wolfhart, *Systematic Theology Vol. 1* (trans. G.W. Bromiley; Grand Rapids: Eerdmans, 1988).

Parker, T.H.L., *Karl Barth* (Grand Rapids: Eerdmans, 1970).

Parsons, Michael, 'Man Encountered by the Command of God: The Ethics of Karl Barth.' *Vox Evangelica* 17 (1987): 49-65.

Patterson, Sue, *Realist Christian Theology in a Postmodern Age* (Cambridge: Cambridge University Press, 1999).

Price, Daniel J., *Karl Barth's Anthropology in Light of Modern Thought* (Grand Rapids: Eerdmans, 2002).

Rae, Simon H., 'Gospel, Law and Freedom in the Theological Ethics of Karl Barth.' *Scottish Journal of Theology* 25.4 (1972): 412-422.

Rees, Frank D., 'The Word in Question: Barth and Divine Conversation.' *Pacifica* 12.3 (1999): 313-332.

Richardson, Kurt Anders, *Reading Karl Barth: New Directions for North American Theology* (Grand Rapids: Baker, 2004).

Roberts, J., *German Philosophy: An Introduction* (Cambridge: Polity, 1988).

Roberts, J. Deotis, *A Philosophical Introduction to Theology* (Eugene, OR: Wipf and Stock, 1991).

Roberts, Richard H., 'Barth's Doctrine of Time: Its Nature and Implications.' In *Karl Barth: Studies of His Theological Method* (ed. S. W. Sykes; Oxford: Clarendon, 1979), 88-146.

Robinson, James. M., ed., *The Beginnings of Dialectic Theology* (trans. M.E. Bratcher; Richmond: John Knox Press, 1968).

Robinson, James M., 'Introduction.' In *The Beginnings of Dialectic Theology* (ed. James M. Robinson; Richmond: John Knox, 1968), 9-30.

Rogers, Eugene F., 'Supplementing Barth on Jews and Gender: Identifying God by Anagogy and the Spirit.' *Modern Theology* 14.1 (1998): 43-81.

Rosato, Philip J., *The Spirit as Lord: Karl Barth's Pneumatology* (Edinburgh: T. & T. Clark, 1981).

Rose, Matthew, *Ethics with Barth: God, Metaphysics and Morals*, (Barth Studies; Farnham: Ashgate, 2010), 13.

Saliers, Don E., 'Prayer and Theology in Karl Barth.' In K. Barth, *Prayer* (Louisville: Westminster John Knox, 1985), ix-xx.

Sauter, Gerhard, 'Shifts in Karl Barth's Thought: The Current Debate between Right- and Left-Wing Barthians.' In *Eschatological Rationality: Theological Issues in*

288 *The Church as Moral Community*

Focus (Grand Rapids: Baker, 1996), 111-135.

Schellong, Dieter, 'On Reading Karl Barth from the Left.' In *Karl Barth and Radical Politics* (ed. George Hunsinger; Philadelphia: Westminster, 1976), 139-157.

Schlatter, Adolf, 'Karl Barth's *Epistle to the Romans*.' In *The Beginnings of Dialectic Theology* (ed. James M. Robinson; Richmond: John Knox, 1968), 121-125.

Schweiker, William, 'Radical Interpretation and Moral Responsibility: A Proposal for Theological Ethics.' *Journal of Religion* 73.4 (1993): 613-637.

_____ *Responsibility and Christian Ethics* (Cambridge: Cambridge University Press, 1995).

_____ *Power, Value and Conviction: Theological Ethics in the Postmodern Age* (Cleveland, Ohio: Pilgrim, 1998).

Scott, Waldron, *Karl Barth's Theology of Mission* (Downers Grove: Inter-Varsity Press, 1978).

Sherman, Robert J, 2003. Karl Barth, Sermon on Luke 1:5-23, December 16, 1917. In <*http://pages.unibas.ch/karlbarth/dok_letter2.html#barth*> (Accessed March 2, 2004).

_____ Karl Barth's Sermon for the Fourth Sunday in Advent, December 21, 1919. In <*http://pages.unibas.ch/karlbarth/dok_letter2.html#barth*> (Accessed March 2, 2004).

Smart, James D., ed., *Revolutionary Theology in the Making: Barth-Thurneysen Correspondence, 1914-1925* (London: Epworth, 1964).

Smart, James D. *The Divided Mind of Modern Theology: Karl Barth and Rudolph Bultmann, 1908-1933* (Philadelphia: Westminster, 1967).

Smit, Dirk, '"The Doing of the Little Righteousness": On Justice in Barth's View of the Christian Life' in *Loving God with our Minds: The Pastor as Theologian* (eds. Michael Welker & Cynthia A. Jarvis; Grand Rapids: Eerdmans, 2004), 120-145.

Sonderegger, Katherine. 'Barth and Feminism.' In *The Cambridge Companion to Karl Barth* (ed. John Webster; Cambridge: Cambridge University Press, 2000), 258-273.

Soskice, Janet Martin, 'Theological Realism.' In *The Rationality of Religious Belief* (ed. W.J. Abraham & S.W. Holtzer; Oxford: Clarendon, 1987), 105-119.

Spencer, Archibald James, *Clearing a Space for Human Action: Ethical Ontology in the Theology of Karl Barth* (New York: Peter Lang, 2003).

Spohn, W.C., *What are they Saying About Scripture and Ethics?* (rev ed; New York: Paulist, 1995).

Stassen, Glen H. & David P. Gushee, *Kingdom Ethics: Following Jesus in Contemporary Context* (Downers Grove: Inter-Varsity Press, 2003).

Stout, Tracey M., *A Fellowship of Baptism: Karl Barth's Ecclesiology in Light of His Understanding of Baptism* (Princeton Theological Monograph Series 139; Eugene: Pickwick, 2010).

Thielicke, Helmut, *Theological Ethics Volume 1: Foundations* (Grand Rapids: Eerdmans, 1966).

Thompson, Geoff, 'Our Lines and Concepts Continually Break Apart: Language, Mystery and God in Barth.' In *Barth: A Future for Postmodern Theology?* (ed. G. Thompson & C. Mostert; Adelaide: Australian Theological Forum, 2000), 191-209.

Thompson, Geoff & Christian Mostert, eds., *Karl Barth: A Future for Postmodern Theology?* (Adelaide: Australian Theological Forum, 2000).

Thompson, John, 'The Humanity of God in the Theology of Karl Barth.' *Scottish Journal of Theology* 29.3 (1976): 249-269.

_____ *The Holy Spirit in the Theology of Karl Barth* (Allison Park, Penn.: Pickwick, 1991).

Thurneysen, Eduard, 'Introduction.' In *Revolutionary Theology in the Making: Barth-Thurneysen Correspondence, 1914-1925* (ed. J.D. Smart; London: Epworth, 1964).

Torrance, Thomas F., *Karl Barth: An Introduction to His Early Theology 1910-1931* (Edinburgh: T. & T. Clark, 1962).

Vanhoozer, Kevin J., 'The World Well Staged? Theology, Culture and Hermeneutics.' In *God and Culture* (ed. D.A. Carson & J.D. Woodbridge; Carlisle: Paternoster, 1993), 1-30.

_____ 'Human Being, Individual and Social.' In *The Cambridge Companion to Christian Doctrine* (ed. C.E. Gunton; Cambridge: Cambridge University Press, 1997), 158-188.

Verhey, Allen, 'Able to Instruct One Another: The Church as a Community of Moral Discourse.' In *The Community of the Word: Toward an Evangelical Ecclesiology* (ed. Mark Husbands & Daniel J. Treier; Leicester: Apollos, 2005), 146-170.

Victorin-Vangerud, Nancy, 'The Counterpart of Others: Some Questions for Barth's Doctrine of Reconciliation.' In *Barth: A Future for Postmodern Theology?* (ed. G. Thompson & C. Mostert; Adelaide: Australian Theological Forum, 2000), 171-190.

Villa-Vicencio, Charles, 'Karl Barth's "Revolution of God": Quietism or Anarchy?' In *On Reading Karl Barth in South Africa* (ed. Charles Villa-Vicencio; Grand Rapids: Eerdmans, 1988), 45-58.

Volf, Miroslav, 'Theology for a Way of Life.' *Ex Auditu* 17 (2001): 125-141.

Wallace, M.I., 'Karl Barth and Deconstruction.' *Religious Studies Review* 25.4 (1999): 349-354.

Wannenwetsch, Bernd., 'Luther's Moral Theology.' In *The Cambridge Companion to Martin Luther* (ed. Donald K. McKim; Cambridge: Cambridge University Press, 2003), 120-135.

Watkin, Julia, *Kierkegaard* (Outstanding Christian Thinkers; London: Continuum, 1997).

Webb, Stephen H., *Re-Figuring Theology: The Rhetoric of Karl Barth* (New York: State University of New York, 1991).

Webster, John, *Barth's Ethics of Reconciliation* (Cambridge: Cambridge University Press, 1995).

_____ *Barth's Moral Theology: Human Action in Barth's Thought* (Grand Rapids: Eerdmans, 1998).

_____ 'Barth, Modernity and Postmodernity.' In *Karl Barth: A Future for Postmodern Theology?* (ed. G. Thompson & C. Mostert; (Adelaide: Australian Theological Forum, 2000), 1-28.

_____ 'The Grand Narrative of Jesus Christ: Barth's Christology.' In *Karl Barth: A Future for Postmodern Theology?* (ed. G. Thompson & C. Mostert; Adelaide: Australian Theological Forum, 2000), 29-48.

_____ 'Rescuing the Subject: Barth and Postmodern Anthropology.' In *Karl Barth: A Future for Postmodern Theology?* (ed. G. Thompson & C. Mostert; Adelaide: Australian Theological Forum, 2000), 49-69.

_____ 'Introducing Barth.' In *The Cambridge Companion to Karl Barth* (ed. J. Webster; Cambridge: Cambridge University Press, 2000), 1-16.

_____ *Karl Barth* (Outstanding Christian Thinkers; New York: Continuum, 2000).

_____ *Holiness* (Grand Rapids: Eerdmans, 2003).

_____ 'Karl Barth.' In *Reading Romans through the Centuries: From the Early Church to Karl Barth* (ed. Jeffrey P. Greenman & Timothy Larsen; Grand Rapids: Brazos, 2005), 205-223.

Webster, John, ed., *The Cambridge Companion to Karl Barth* (Cambridge: Cambridge University Press, 2000).

Wells, Samuel, *Transforming Fate into Destiny: the Theological Ethics of Stanley Hauerwas* (Carlisle: Paternoster, 1998).

Werpehowski, William, 'Command and History in the Ethics of Karl Barth.' *Journal of Religious Ethics* 9.2 (1981): 298-320.

_____ 'Narrative and Ethics in Barth.' *Theology Today* 18.3 (1986): 334-353.

Whitehouse, W.A., 'Review of *The Ethics of Karl Barth* by R.E. Willis.' *Scottish Journal of Theology* 29.2 (1976): 177-182.

Willimon, William H. & Stanley Hauerwas, *Resident Aliens: Life in the Christian Colony* (Nashville: Abingdon, 1989).

Willis, Robert E., *The Ethics of Karl Barth* (Leiden: Brill, 1971).

Wiser, Arthur, 'Introduction.' In *Action in Waiting* (ed. Society of Brothers; Rifton, NY: Plough, 1969), 1-15.

Wolf, E., C. von Kirschbaum & R. Frey, eds., *Antwort: Karl Barth zum Siebzigsten Geburtstag am 10. Mai 1956* (Zürich: Evangelischer Verlag AG, 1956).

Wood, Donald, '"Ich Sah mit Staunen": Reflections on the Theological Substance of Barth's Early Hermeneutics' *Scottish Journal of Theology* 58.2 (2005): 184-198.

Wright, Nicholas T., *The New Testament and the People of God* (Minneapolis: Fortress, 1992).

Wright, Terry J., 'Witnessing Christians from Karl Barth's Perspective.' *The Evangelical Quarterly* 75.3 (2003): 239-255.

Yeago, David S. & James J. Buckley, eds., *Knowing the Triune God: The Work of the Spirit in the Practices of the Church* (Grand Rapids: Eerdmans, 2001).

Yocum, John, *Ecclesial Mediation in Barth* (Barth Studies; Aldershot: Ashgate, 2004).

Yu, A.C., 'Karl Barth's Doctrine of Election: A Critical Study.' *Foundations* 13.3 (1970): 248-261.

Index

McKenny, G. P., 22, 285, 286
Migliore, D. L., 22, 271, 273, 278, 286
Militarism, 63, 124, 131, 260
Morality, 25, 32, 43, 54, 60, 61, 62, 63,
    78, 88, 105, 108, 109, 110, 112,
    118, 121, 122, 131, 153, 221
Nationalism, 83, 131, 153, 156
Natural Theology, 2, 16, 28, 30, 247
Naumann, F., 65, 130, 131, 132, 133,
    134, 135, 136, 145, 147, 277
Neill, S., 189, 286
Niebuhr, R., 2, 8, 9, 11, 12, 14, 17, 24,
    28, 278, 280, 286
Nimmo, P. T., 15, 22, 125, 286
Normative Ethics, 5, 16, 17, 21, 35, 36,
    147, 232, 240, 242, 257, 273
O'Grady, C., 88, 100, 204, 206, 286
O'Neil, M. D., 13, 17, 160, 212, 267,
    286
Oakes, K., 183, 286
Obedience, 10, 19, 21, 24, 31, 41, 79,
    82, 84, 86, 96, 97, 102, 103, 111,
    114, 123, 127, 161, 162, 163, 180,
    181, 203, 209, 211, 217, 218, 219,
    235, 243, 244, 252, 253, 262, 263,
    265, 267, 269, 271, 274
Oden, T. C., 8, 11, 12, 21, 242, 286
Ontology, 13, 14, 15, 16, 17, 19, 21,
    79, 88, 99, 100, 116, 221, 223, 243,
    247, 264, 265, 272
Overbeck, F., 130, 149, 150, 151, 152,
    153, 154, 155, 156, 157, 158, 162,
    165, 167, 222, 223, 287
Paternoster, 20, 150, 160, 172, 223,
    273
Personal Encounter, 173, 198
Pietism, 43, 52, 87, 89, 91, 99, 106,
    107, 108, 119, 127, 150, 157, 163,
    190, 201
Piety, 54, 70, 77, 115, 116, 130, 131,
    161, 162, 163, 201, 207
Pneumatology, 30, 31, 34, 36, 39, 41,
    212
Politics, 1, 31, 55, 63, 65, 66, 81, 82,
    83, 114, 131, 132, 147, 173, 180,
    231, 252
Praxis, 16, 43, 52, 53, 54, 55, 58, 71,
    83, 127, 132, 134, 135, 156, 167,
    182, 183, 221, 243, 244, 245, 246,
    247, 261
Prayer, 32, 36, 64, 68, 74, 84, 144,

148, 166, 167, 173, 174, 181, 213,
    225, 229, 243, 245, 255, 258, 262,
    263, 264, 268, 270, 271, 272, 273
Predestination, 12, 188
Price, D. J., 15, 24, 274, 287
Proclamation, 30, 36, 37, 40, 47, 74,
    84, 104, 138, 144, 154, 172, 173,
    174, 194, 220, 234, 262, 273
Rade, M., 47, 48, 49, 66
Ragaz, L., 56, 57, 64, 71, 79, 83, 87,
    89, 111, 112, 113, 126, 136, 254
Rationality, 18, 19, 267
Realism, Theological, 15, 16, 17, 78,
    85, 92, 127, 135, 146, 230, 247
Religion, 16, 46, 48, 50, 51, 52, 53, 54,
    56, 57, 58, 60, 61, 62, 63, 77, 78,
    82, 88, 91, 105, 106, 107, 108, 109,
    110, 127, 132, 133, 134, 135, 138,
    153, 156, 161, 162, 163, 165, 189,
    190, 195, 199, 200, 201, 202, 203,
    204, 208, 221, 230, 252, 259, 261
Repentance, 134, 166, 178, 179, 208,
    209, 219, 224, 225, 229, 231, 234,
    242, 243, 253, 262
Responsibility, 7, 11, 12, 15, 23, 53,
    75, 85, 111, 127, 143, 177, 215,
    219, 234, 239, 242, 249, 255, 269,
    270
Revelation, 6, 13, 16, 17, 20, 25, 32,
    38, 41, 46, 49, 68, 69, 76, 77, 129,
    132, 140, 147, 154, 158, 161, 164,
    184, 191, 192, 194, 195, 196, 197,
    198, 199, 200, 202, 204, 205, 206,
    207, 208, 209, 210, 211, 212, 213,
    214, 216, 218, 220, 239, 240, 254,
    262, 265, 268
Revolution, 55, 89, 111, 112, 113, 114,
    125, 126, 129, 142, 144, 145, 149,
    230, 231, 235, 236, 237, 245, 261
Righteousness, 14, 59, 60, 61, 62, 63,
    81, 82, 84, 86, 88, 93, 94, 95, 97,
    104, 110, 113, 118, 120, 121, 126,
    137, 141, 163, 181, 192, 194, 195,
    196, 198, 199, 201, 206, 207, 209,
    215, 216, 220, 230, 245, 252, 253,
    258, 263, 265, 270, 273
Ritschl, A., 46, 89, 106, 157, 248, 280
Robinson, J. M., 65, 131, 185, 186,
    187, 277, 278, 279, 280, 284, 287,
    288
Romanticism, 43, 220, 234

ND - #0068 - 090625 - C0 - 229/152/17 - PB - 9781842277829 - Gloss Lamination